SPEAKING TO YOU: CONTEMPORARY POETRY AND PUBLIC ADDRESS

Speaking to You: Contemporary Poetry and Public Address

NATALIE POLLARD

OXFORD
UNIVERSITY PRESS

Great Clarendon Street, Oxford, OX2 6DP,
United Kingdom

Oxford University Press is a department of the University of Oxford.
It furthers the University's objective of excellence in research, scholarship,
and education by publishing worldwide. Oxford is a registered trade mark of
Oxford University Press in the UK and in certain other countries

© Natalie Pollard 2012

British Library Cataloguing in Publication Data
Data available

Library of Congress Cataloging in Publication Data
Data available

ISBN 978–0–19–965700–1

Printed in Great Britain by
MPG Books Group, Bodmin and King's Lynn

Contents

Acknowledgements

First, thanks should go to Hugh Haughton, whose intellectual generosity and engagement kept me on track during my doctoral thesis on British poetry at the University of York.

I am indebted to Gareth Reeves who set me on the right road to contemporary poetry, Chris Long for teaching me how to do things with words, and to Richard Rowland, whose grasp of the literature of the early modern period, and of much else besides, has preserved me from some, if not all, error.

I must also thank the Arts and Humanities Research Council for funding my doctoral thesis, the Institute for the Advanced Study of the Humanities at the University of Edinburgh for the space and time which enabled me to work on earlier drafts of this book, and the University of Cape Town for the Research Fellowship which has allowed me to complete the final manuscript. I am indebted to Faber for permissions to quote from Don Paterson's poetry collections, and to Michael Schmidt at Carcanet for granting permission to quote from C. H. Sisson's *Collected Poems*. Warm thanks also to Terri Broll for her permission to use her artwork on the cover of this book.

More recently, thanks to Derek Attridge for reading my work with inspiring literary and philosophical insight, and to Peter Robinson, whose work and thought have helped me refine key aspects of my writing. Thank you to Andrew McNeillie for our excellent discussions about the lay of the land of contemporary poetry during my time in Cornwall. A big thank you to Carrol Clarkson at the University of Cape Town whose spirited conversations about contemporary art, writing, and photography, I am lucky to have enjoyed. Several people have read my essays, reviews, and earlier versions of chapters. I've gained a good deal, in quite different ways, from Clara Dawson, Peter Fifield, Matthew Bevis, Benjamin Madden, Alec Finlay, and Dorothy Butchard. Thanks especially to Wilf Wilson who has been a sustained source of encouragement throughout the work.

Part I, on W. S. Graham, had its beginnings in an article: 'The Pages are Bugged: The Politics of Listening in the Poetry of W. S. Graham', *The Cambridge Quarterly* 39:1 (Spring 2010) 1–22.

An earlier version of Chapter 10 appears as an article entitled 'Civil Voices: On Reading Geoffrey Hill Reading', *PEER English* 3 (2008) 74–83. Some aspects of Chapter 10 also appear as a chapter entitled 'The Tongue's Atrocities: Civil Violence, Lyricism and Geoffrey Hill', in *The Culture Mangle: Conflict and Violence in Language and Culture*, ed. Eilidh Macdonald and James R. Simpson, Tous Azimuts 4 (Glasgow: University of Glasgow French and German Publications, 2010) 97–116.

List of Abbreviations

ACP	W. H. Auden, *Collected Poems*
AM	Geoffrey Hill, *Alienated Majesty*
Avoidance	C. H. Sisson, *The Avoidance of Literature*
'Bond'	Geoffrey Hill, 'Our Word is Our Bond'
Cantos	Ezra Pound, *The Cantos of Ezra Pound*
CCW	Geoffrey Hill, *Collected Critical Writings*
Comus	Geoffrey Hill, *Scenes From Comus*
CP	C. H. Sisson, *Collected Poems*
CWG	W. S. Graham, *Cage Without Grievance*
DSP	Douglas Dunn, *Selected Poems 1964–1983*
EC	Geoffrey Hill, *The Enemy's Country*
ECP	T. S. Eliot, *Collected Poems: 1909–1962*
EP	C. H. Sisson, *English Poetry: An Assessment*
Essays	Ezra Pound, *The Literary Essays*
Eyes	Don Paterson, *The Eyes*
Gift	Don Paterson, *God's Gift to Women*
HCP	Geoffrey Hill, *Collected Poems*
HSP	Tony Harrison, *Selected Poems*
Implements	W. S. Graham, *Implements in Their Places*
LCP	Philip Larkin, *Collected Poems*
Letters	Ezra Pound, *The Letters of Ezra Pound 1907–1941*
Light	Don Paterson, *Landing Light*
LL	Geoffrey Hill, *The Lords of Limit*
Malcolm	W. S. Graham, *Malcolm Mooney's Land*
Marx	C. H. Sisson, *God Bless Karl Marx!*
MCP	Louis MacNeice, *Collected Poems*
'Menace'	Geoffrey Hill, 'Poetry as "Menace" and "Atonement"'
NBP	Don Paterson and Charles Simic, eds., *New British Poetry*
NCP	W. S. Graham, *New Collected Poems*
Nightfisherman	W. S. Graham, *The Nightfisherman: Selected Letters of W. S. Graham*
Nightfishing	W. S. Graham, *The Nightfishing*

'Notes'	W. S. Graham, 'Notes on a Poetry of Release'
OPP	T. S. Eliot, *On Poetry and Poets*
Orchards	Geoffrey Hill, *The Orchards of Syon*
Personae	Ezra Pound, *Personae: The Collected Shorter Poems*
'Postscript'	Geoffrey Hill, 'A Postscript on Modernist Poetics'
Prose	T. S. Eliot, *Selected Prose of T. S. Eliot*
RW	Philip Larkin, *Required Writing*
SCP	Wallace Stevens, *Collected Poems*
'Sevenoaks'	C. H. Sisson, 'Sevenoaks Essays'
SS	Geoffrey Hill, *Speech! Speech!*
SW	T. S. Eliot, *The Sacred Wood*
Treatise	Geoffrey Hill, *A Treatise of Civil Power*
Triumph	Geoffrey Hill, *The Triumph of Love*
WT	Geoffrey Hill, *Without Title*
WW	C. H. Sisson, *What and Who*

[handwritten annotation:] To say it's not I but you not Saussure but Austin—Searle not Derrida but Cavell

Smells of disturbance — the "goes ufo,," saying issue

Introduction

In his poem 'Dear Bryan Wynter', the contemporary Scottish poet W. S. Graham speaks to his now dead, and ever difficult friend, the St Ives school painter of the title. His address highlights the perplexities of a verbal experience often encountered in lyric texts:

> Speaking to you and not
> Knowing if you are there
> Is not too difficult.
> My words are used to that.[1]

Graham's addressee operates as a tantalizing figure, simultaneously present in and absent from the page. *You* is a conversational truant, continually evading the speaker's attempts at closer contact, refusing to confirm that the author is in dialogue with another at all. As Graham's poem points out, that elusiveness is also something we 'are used to' in lyric texts. Addressees often get away, mishear, misinterpret, elude the speaker's calls to listen or make themselves known. Hence W. H. Auden speculates what would happen 'If I Could Tell You' (he cannot), Robert Graves, that, 'You were by my side, though I could not see you', and Carol Ann Duffy that 'you are not here', 'I hold you closer, miles away'.[2] These addresses explore physical and linguistic distance: they at once summon a *you* and hold it at bay.

Yet addressing *you* directly also allows an author to have things both ways: 'speaking to you and not', 'knowing and not / Knowing'. One speaks to *you*, and misses *you*, at the same time. Graham's poem—an elegy to Wynter—addresses his particular *you* not as an embodied individual but as memory. His recently deceased friend is no longer coherent, locatable matter, but enigmatic, intangible, an absent presence configured through the poem's words. But that is also a feature of lyric addressees in

---

[1] W. S. Graham, 'Dear Bryan Wynter', in *Implements in Their Places* (London: Faber, 1977), quoted from *New Collected Poems* (London: Faber, 2004) 258. This volume is referred to as *NCP*. All references to Graham's poetry are quoted from *NCP*. Throughout the book, I will use the word 'lyric' interchangeably with 'poetry'. Unless otherwise stated, I do not mean to imply a special kind of poetic use is taking place in 'lyric' texts.

[2] W. H. Auden, *Collected Poems*, ed. Edward Mendelson (New York: Random House, 1976) 244, referred to hereafter as *ACP*; Robert Graves, 'The Prohibition', *Collected Poems* (London: Cassell, 1975) 462; Carol Ann Duffy, 'Miles Away' (1987), in *Selected Poems* (London: Penguin, 1994) 62.

general, as Graham well knows: it is only in language, in a poem's own articulations, that it can call interlocutors into being. Graham's lyric points out that poetic addresses cannot help but shape *you*, even when referring to an already-existing entity.

At once personal and public, Graham's poem speaks to two different *yous*—his explicitly named friend, and his (implicitly listening) audience. Through these doubled voicings, the lyric participates in a world of over-lapping social relations. If as readers, we feel we eavesdrop on a private conversation directed to a particular other, we are also aware that Graham cannily *invites* that sense of trespass, by deliberately adopting the exclu-sive-sounding address of the letter writing form: 'Dear Bryan Wynter'. Evidently, Graham's poem is not a letter intended for a single pair of read-ing eyes. To speak to Wynter over the printed pages of *Implements in Their Places* is to know these words will be received by more than one kind of slippery *you*. Friend and readership, private interlocutor and public body: these *yous* meet and mingle, at the line of text. Graham nudges us towards the recognition that poems—however exclusively they speak to particular recipients—are also addressed to readers. *I*'s speech takes shape in dia-logue with whoever may be listening: elegized friend; desired audience; companionable ghost; stern critic; ideal reader. Graham conducts a mov-ingly intimate address to Wynter, even as he negotiates a vast public world of voicing and reception.

This book explores in detail the work and thought of four key figures in contemporary British poetry, each of whom showcases lyric address's capacity for staging different kinds of publicly intimate contact with *you*. We attend first to Graham (1918–86), who, in his twenties, relocated from his native Greenock to live in Madron, Cornwall, where he kept close company with the community of St Ives school of painters that in-cluded Peter Lanyon, Bryan Wynter, and Roger Hilton. These artists are frequently Graham's addressees in his best-known, most recent collections *Malcolm Mooney's Land* (1970) and *Implements in Their Places* (1977).[3] We turn next to the Monarchist English poet, essayist, and life-long civil servant, C. H. Sisson (1914–2003), whose best-known work includes the modernist-inflected poetry collections, *In the Trojan Ditch* (1974) and *Anchises* (1976).[4] Next we attend to the highly acclaimed work of the English poet-scholar Geoffrey Hill (1932–), especially to his later, con-tentiously 'difficult' poetic works, *The Triumph of Love* (1998), *Speech! Speech!* (2000), and *A Treatise of Civil Power* (2007). We turn too, to Hill's

---

[3] See Graham's *NCP* 153–97 and 199–261.
[4] See C. H. Sisson, *Collected Poems* (Manchester: Carcanet, 1998) 135–86 and 189–237, referred to as *CP*.

much-celebrated early work—in particular *King Log* (1968)—bringing
the poetry into contact with Hill's prose statements in his dense and an-
gular public lectures, now gathered in *Collected Critical Writings* (2008).[5]
Finally, we consider the Dundee-born poet and publisher, Don Paterson
(1963–), who has produced six collections of poetry since his first, *Nil
Nil*, came out in 1991. Since then, Paterson has published *God's Gift to
Women* (1997) and *The Eyes* (1999), his versions of the early twentieth-
century Spanish poet, Antonio Machado, *Landing Light* (2003) and *Or-
pheus* (2006)—lyric versions of Rilke's *Sonnets to Orpheus*—and *Rain*
(2009).[6] Paterson is also a prolific editor and literary critic, and has pub-
lished a number of essays, anthologies, and critical works in recent
years.[7]

The work of each of these writers provides a lens onto the wider cur-
rents and trends in post-1960s English and Scottish poetry (the period
that *Speaking to You* treats as 'contemporary'). I should point out that
I am not concerned with whether or not these four represent 'the best'
of contemporary British lyricism. What I want to show is how, taken
together, they provide four key angles onto a range of influential post-
1960s poetry—and test out the ways lyricism today makes use of ad-
dress in public. In this poetic quartet, the shaping forces of history and
fast-paced modernity, intimate and civic speech, nation and region,
commercial and aesthetic demands, inspiration and literary reception,
are registered and scrutinized, through saying *you*. One might expect
lyric speech to be immediate, solitary voicing, but each of these writers
probes—and insists *you* recognize—the close links between contempor-
ary poetry and the forms and aesthetic strategies of earlier historical
periods. In particular, they listen back on, and find their addresses in
dialogue with, the Babel of Modernist and Movement writers (we will
focus especially on their relationships with T. S. Eliot, Ezra Pound, and

---

[5] See Geoffrey Hill, *The Triumph of Love* (1998; New York: First Mariner, 2000),
referred to as *Triumph*; *Speech! Speech!* (London: Penguin, 2001), referred to as *SS*; *A Trea-
tise of Civil Power* (London: Penguin, 2007), referred to as *Treatise*; see also Hill's *Collected
Poems* (Harmondsworth: Penguin, 1985) 61–103, referred to as *HCP*; and *Collected Criti-
cal Writings*, ed. Kenneth Haynes (London: Penguin, 2008), referred to as *CCW*.

[6] See Don Paterson, *Nil Nil* (London: Faber, 1993); *God's Gift to Women* (London:
Faber, 1997), referred to as *Gift*; *The Eyes* (London: Faber, 1999), referred to as *Eyes*; *Land-
ing Light* (London: Faber 2003) referred to as *Light*; *Orpheus* (London: Faber, 2006); *Rain*
(London: Faber, 2009).

[7] See Don Paterson, *Reading Shakespeare's Sonnets: A New Commentary* (London: Faber,
2010); 'The Lyric Principle: The Sense of Sound', *Poetry Review* 97:2 (Summer 2007)
56–72 and 'The Lyric Principle: The Sound of Sense', *Poetry Review* 97:3 (Autumn 2007)
54–70; *New British Poetry*, ed. with Charles Simic (Minnesota: Graywolf, 2004); *Don't Ask
Me What I Mean: Poets in Their Own Words*, ed. with Clare Brown (London: Faber,
2001).

Philip Larkin). Movingly implementing address's historical and etymo-
logical intimacies, these poets flag up different respects in which speaking
poetically to *you* is a shared, public act—not single-handed voicing. Each
differently underlines how address takes place through linguistic co-
operation and interchange in the *polis*; in the historically weighted civic
tongue.

'The poetry of a people takes its life from the people's speech and in
turn gives life to it', Eliot wrote, pointing out at least one respect in which
poems insist that we explore language—colloquial and academic, histor-
ical and poetic—as a powerful political and cultural force.[8] Even the most
intimate lyric addresses are more than private asides from 'the people's
speech'. Address, both when directed specifically to *you*, and when angled
towards an auditor obliquely, is intricately involved in, and subtly (or not
so subtly) manoeuvring, a public. Address is not a unique exception to
what we normally do with words. It flags up an aspect of what happens
continually in language: we speak to others (real, imagined, and some-
where between) and take shape with them, in speech. To read poetic ad-
dress is to be caught and held by a changing succession of public and
personal interlocutors. Such work issues a reminder that whether we are
in lyric or everyday speech situations, whether speaking to a *you* specific-
ally or speaking to many *you*s, and whether or not we use *you* with any
recipient in mind, we are continually thrown, in language, into the public
frameworks of address.

Late twentieth-century criticism about address often focuses on the
poet's *I*, concentrating on lyricism's subjectivism and separation from a
social world: 'a trope of detachment, of unworldliness', James D. Fernán-
dez writes of address: it is 'essentially antihistorical'.[9] For J. Mark Smith,
'no poem actually does address a reader, at least not in any ordinary sense
of the word "address" [...] I would like to insist upon what an unusual
sort of communication it amounts to'.[10] By these lights, address is an ex-
ceptional—and exceptionally asocial—act: saying *you* turns *I* aside from
whatever real occurrence is taking place, to a primarily verbal world, of
subjectivity, of imagination. In Barbara Johnson's view, for instance, saying
you is 'a digression in discourse' that 'brings the whole surrounding world
into the speech event'.[11] Such criticism tends to read address—whether to

---

[8] T. S. Eliot, 'Introduction' (1932), in *The Use of Poetry and the Use of Criticism* (Cam-
bridge, MA: Harvard University Press, 1933) 5.

[9] James D. Fernández, *Apology to Apostrophe* (Durham, NC: Duke University Press,
1992) 7–8.

[10] J. Mark Smith, 'Apostrophe, or the Lyric Art of Turning Away', *Texas Studies in Lit-
erature and Language* 49:4 (Winter 2007) 411–37, 412–13.

[11] Barbara Johnson, *Persons and Things* (Cambridge, MA: Harvard University Press,
2008) 5–8.

readers or intimately known interlocutors—either as a means of attempting (and failing) to break from isolation, or as a display of aloneness that centres, delightedly, on solitary verbal play: '[n]either the judge nor the addressee is really the object of the poetic utterance', concludes Barbara Johnson: '[t]he speech situation [...] is about the poet' (9).

It is only recently in British literary history that lyric address is associated with subjectivity and 'turning away'. In the early modern period, poets' addresses to wealthy patrons and monarchs play an important civic role—their artworks structure and maintain (and challenge) the social system and its complex networks of power relations. Saying *you*—in John Donne, Andrew Marvell, Robert Herrick, John Milton, Ben Jonson—is inextricably linked with politics, patronage, reception, and public recognition.[12] It would be difficult to claim, of say, Jonson's *The Forest* or Herrick's *Hesperides*, that '[n]either the judge nor the addressee is really the object of the poetic utterance'.[13] These writers often knowingly play on their audience's recognition that poetry is in dialogue with the patrons who have commissioned it; on whose good favour future writing acts depend. (Conversely: the monarch/patron's status in the eyes of her public depends on court poets who will sing her praises, and bend the public mind to her favour.) This situation of address is evidently not 'really' or merely 'about the poet'.

As if acutely aware of—and dissatisfied by—our post-seventeenth-century lyric disinclination to recognize the public clout of speaking to *you*, a number of contemporary poets ground their intimate addresses in classical, medieval, and early modern public contexts. Hence Sisson writes a 'Letter to John Donne' and addresses to 'Catullus' and 'Marcus Aurelius', and Hill's *you* has listened back on Milton's *Comus* and on *A Treatise of Civil Power*, as well as using address to probe the relationship between the praise-poem and medieval patronage, during the reign of King Offa.[14]

---

[12] Heather Dubrow, in *The Challenges of Orpheus: Lyric Poetry and Early Modern England* (Baltimore, MD: Johns Hopkins University Press, 2007), stresses the political and social contexts in which lyric address occurred. See particularly 83–4. Terry Walker's *Thou and You in Early Modern English Dialogues* (Amsterdam: John Benjamins, 2007) places the use of 'THOU or YOU' in the context of 'extra-linguistic factors' including 'age, sex and rank [...] of speaker and addressee, the degree of social distance between them [...] their social role [...] the specific context' (2).

[13] Ben Jonson, *The Forrest* (1616): many of these epigraphs are addressed to Jonson's aristocratic supporters and potential patrons—though his *you* offers praise shot through with criticism and steely scrutiny. See the intricate mix of commendation and condemnation in 'Epigraphs' (1616) and *Underwood* (1640), in *The Complete Poems*, ed. George Parfitt (London: Penguin, 1996); Robert Herrick, *Hesperides* (1648), ed. S.W. Singer (Boston: Little, Brown, 1856); Johnson, *Persons and Things* (9).

[14] See Sisson, *CP* 50, 89, 199; Geoffrey Hill, *Scenes From Comus* (London: Penguin, 2005); Hill's *Treatise* (see 5); 'Mercian Hymns', in *HCP* 105–35.

Not dissimilarly, Paterson's *you* scrutinizes the patronage systems in an-
cient Greek and Roman cultural life, as well as the political pressures on
poetic speech at the medieval Arabic court.[15] There are also comparisons
to be made between these texts and the seventeenth-century-minded, ver-
nacular addresses of Tony Harrison and Douglas Dunn.

   A significant landmark for each of these contemporary writers is Eliot's
assertion of the post-seventeenth-century 'dissociation of sensibility'. His
essay 'The Metaphysical Poets' identifies a post-Metaphysical severance of
passion from intellect, private from public language.[16] A good deal of
contemporary poetry thinks through this historical alteration, using the
contexts of classical, medieval, and early modern interlocutions to reclaim
poetic language not as primarily set-apart private speech, but as a pre-
dominantly public act.

   '[T]he seventeenth-century English metaphysicals are the greatest ex-
ample' of grittily contemplative, publicly 'self-rectifying' address, com-
ments Hill.[17] When he adds that, 'taking a long, historical view, I can
understand why I was impressed by Eliot's contempt for the "inner voice
[…]"', Hill is keen to differentiate his work from 'the unsatisfactory
poetry of the age of Pope […] [and] bad poetry in the age of Tennyson'
(281). He presents a critique of Augustan and Victorian poetry, on the
grounds that their modes of public address tend not to include, within
their *social* judgement, an acknowledgement of the *poet's* culpability. For
Hill, post-seventeenth-century lyric speakers are less adept at registering
the 'inner voice's' complicity in the public critique meted out.[18]

   Eliot, before Hill, had pointed out that the distinctive seventeenth-
century view of poetry as powerfully civic language was not to endure. By
the Romantic period, poetry's public–private status was already being re-
worked, and the societal importance of marking out room in artworks
for solitary reflection and self-correspondence was underlined (Shelley's

---

[15] See Paterson, 'The Reading', in *Light* 23–5; '*from* 1001 Nights: The Early Years', and
'Candlebird', in *Gift* 8, 55.

[16] T. S. Eliot, 'The Metaphysical Poets' (1921), in *Selected Prose of T. S. Eliot*, ed. Frank
Kermode (London: Faber, 1975) 59–67, 64. Cited hereafter as *Prose*.

[17] See Interview with Carl Phillips, Geoffrey Hill, 'The Art of Poetry No. 80', *The Paris
Review* 154 (Spring 2000) 272–99, 281.

[18] Hill, Interview with Phillips, 281. Contemporary poets have also used address to
draw on, and make reference to, Augustan and Victorian poetry—two great eras of civic
lyricism. Fusing learned satire, politics, and vitriol with the energy of direct address, Har-
rison's address, in 'v', for instance, listens back on Thomas Gray's 'Elegy Written in a Coun-
try Churchyard' (1750). Sisson couples savagely satirical and gracefully learned
address-forms in a manner reminiscent of the Augustanism of Pope. Duffy's *The World's
Wife* (London: Picador, 1999) employs Browningesque dramatic monologue forms. And
yet, as we shall see, classical and early modern poets remain more predominant models for
today's civic voicing than Pope or Gray, Browning or Tennyson.

'Defence' is a key example, as we will see). At least since the nineteenth century, criticism of address has more commonly emphasized its private, subjective aspects than its public and political inflections. Writing in 1833, under the influence of the previous generation's impulse towards self-communion, John Stuart Mill famously made the distinction that 'Eloquence is *heard*, Poetry is *overheard*'.[19] The distinction profoundly shaped many subsequent and contemporary accounts of address.[20] For Mill, art ought to be created in physical and mental isolation, where it can achieve freedom from any interfering hankering after listeners or audience. Such poetry involves 'the poet's utter unconsciousness of a listener. Poetry is feeling confessing itself to itself, in moments of solitude.'[21]

For Romantic writers before Mill, particularly Shelley, seclusion was a path to true imaginative vision, by which the poet would make himself free from the disguises and distortions of performing to others. Shelley had insisted that pronouns—'the words *I, you, they*'—are not 'signs of any *actual* difference' but 'merely marks employed to denote the different modifications of the one mind', a view he re-emphasized in 'A Defence of Poetry' when he argued that the 'the mind of the creator [...] is itself the image of all other minds'.[22] In Mill, as in Shelley, isolation is not merely self-interested: it was by achieving self-enclosure that the poet would attain universality; he could tap into the truth that lay within each of his readers, making it communally realizable. Mill's poet, in speaking sincerely for himself, speaks for us all: the poet's *I*, at its best, is interchangeable with the reader's. But, one might object by asking how this accounts for the numerous lyric poems that contradict this notion of poetic solitude by directing themselves to a *you*, often a specific, named recipient. Mill's answer (like Barbara Johnson's) was that addressing others is 'really' a form of self-address. Saying *you* is another way of saying *I*, and poetry is a purging of the consideration of others, an intrinsically individualistic act.

Whether or not one finds Mill's account convincing, in the first half of the twentieth century his ideas about address—particularly those concerning overhearing—were developed by numerous critics and became

[19] John Stuart Mill, 'What is Poetry?', in 'Thoughts on Poetry and its Varieties' (1833) 1.3b, in *Autobiography and Literary Essays*, ed. John M. Robson and Jack Stillinger (Toronto: University of Toronto Press, 1981) 341–65, 348.
[20] See Alan Richardson, 'Apostrophe in Life and in Romantic Art: Everyday Discourse, Overhearing, and Poetic Address', *Style* 36:3 (Fall 2002) 363–85, 363.
[21] Mill, 'What is Poetry?' 350.
[22] Percy Bysshe Shelley, 'On Life' (composed c.1819), in *Essays, Letters from Abroad, Translation and Fragments*, ed. Mary Shelley, 2 vols., vol. 1 (Philadelphia: Lea and Blanchard, 1840) 176–81, 180; 'A Defence of Poetry' (composed 1821), published in *Essays*, 25–62, 32.

good distillation

highly influential. Amongst those who re-echo Mill's thesis are Northrop Frye and T. S. Eliot, and all three are frequently quoted in subsequent critical accounts.[23] Although both Frye and Eliot draw heavily upon Mill's original formulation, they also add significant distinctions and revisions of their own, and begin, albeit somewhat unsuccessfully, to counter his notion of address as spontaneously asocial and self-directed. Frye's notion of poetry as overhearing, and particularly his idea that the overhearing is to some degree calculated ('the poet [...] *turns his back* on his listeners')[24] at once approvingly echoes Mill's rhetoric, and begins to disrupt Mill's supposition of the poet's '*utter unconsciousness*' of listeners. For Frye, one can only turn one's back on listeners if one has already engaged with them, so that turning away is a *response* to the recognition of another individual's presence. Implicit in Frye's account is that to turn away is to *present* one's back to others: rejection is a form of social engagement. According to Frye, there is a significant amount of work to be done with listeners before one can begin to be 'utterly' unconscious of them. So too, his notion of poetry as an act of calculated self-deception—'the *concealment* of the poet's audience from the poet'—involves the poet performing the difficult (because contradictory) task of concealing his recognitions from himself. The motivation for deliberately performing an act of concealment paradoxically relies upon one's awareness of what must remain concealed.

Crucial questions arise here. To whom is the poet pretending? To whom is he performing? Is he really performing and pretending at all? Eliot's helpful demarcation of this territory in 'The Three Voices of Poetry' contextualizes the different elements of pretence and performance that arise from Mill's view of the poem as an act of social avoidance, and focuses largely upon the question of to whom, and as whom, poets can speak.[25] Mill's (and Frye's) apothegm that *all* poetry is self-dialogue corresponds closely with what Eliot sees only as poetry's first voice: 'the voice of the poet talking to himself—or to nobody' (89). Eliot adds two other categories which conceive of poetry as turned towards and actively

---

[23] See Ann Keniston, *Overheard Voices: Address and Subjectivity in Postmodern American Poetry* (New York: Routledge, 2006); William Waters, on Mill, Frye, and Culler, in *Poetry's Touch: On Lyric Address* (New York: Cornell University Press, 2003) 2–4; Virginia Walker Jackson's discussion of Mill and Frye in 'Dickinson's Figure of Address', *Dickinson's Misery: A Theory of Lyric Reading* (Princeton: Princeton University Press, 2005) 129–31; Anne Ferry on Mill, Frye, and Culler in 'Who "Hears" the Poem', *The Title to the Poem* (Stanford: Stanford University Press, 1999) 128–9.

[24] Northrop Frye, *Anatomy of Criticism* (Princeton: Princeton University Press, 1957) 249–50, emphasis added.

[25] T. S. Eliot, *The Three Voices of Poetry* (London: Cambridge University Press, 1953), in *On Poetry and Poets* (London: Faber, 1957) 89–102; cited hereafter as *OPP*.

negotiating with others. The second voice is 'the voice of the poet addressing an audience [...] the poet speaking to other people', and the third is the voice of poetic drama: 'not the ventriloquism which makes the character only a mouthpiece for the author's ideas', but 'the voice of each character—an individual voice [...] [that] could only have come from that character' (89–100). For Eliot, these voices are anything but mutually exclusive, and even in a poem apparently dominated by the first voice, elements of the second and third are at work: 'I think that in every poem, from the private meditation to the epic or the drama, there is more than one voice to be heard' (100). In a move reminiscent of Wittgenstein's private language argument,[26] Eliot dismisses the idea of poetry as pure self-dialogue:

> if the poem were exclusively for the author, it would be a poem in a private and unknown language [...] a poem which was a poem only for the author would not be a poem at all. (100)

Nevertheless, not all critics have considered the poem's performative aspect sufficient to prove its public orientation in the way Eliot suggests. In his highly influential essay on 'Apostrophe', Jonathan Culler—like Eliot—recognized that saying *you* was a performative act. Yet to the question of whether lyrics that hail *you* set out to probe shared social issues, Culler's essay answered a resounding no.[27] Culler was attending not to the frequently encountered category of public address that Eliot identified (and on which *Speaking to You* focuses). Rather, he homed in on the specific case of *apostrophic* voicing. It is this quite different focus that led Culler to draw his famous conclusion that saying *you* is a deeply self-involved staging of contact: a conclusion at some variance from Eliot's (and my own) argument that poetry is a civic act; a way of really 'speaking to other people':

> apostrophe [...] seems to establish relations between the self and the other [but] can in fact be read as an act of radical interiorization and solipsism. Either it parcels out the self to fill the world, peopling the universe with fragments of the self, as in Baudelaire's apostrophes to his pain, his mind, his soul, [...] or else it internalizes what might have been thought external (things, says Rilke, 'want us to change them entirely...into ourselves'). (146)

For Culler, the apostrophizing poet '*seems* to establish relations' with one singled-out addressee. But he is 'really' concerned to create a

---

[26] See Part 1 of Ludwig Wittgenstein, *Philosophical Investigations*, trans. G. E. M. Anscombe (Oxford: Basil Blackwell, 1953) esp. §256 onward. Referred to hereafter as *PI*.

[27] Jonathan Culler, *The Pursuit of Signs: Semiotics, Literature, Deconstruction* (Ithaca: Cornell University Press, 1981) 135–54. Referred to as *Pursuit*.

particular impression of himself before a wide audience. Similarly, the poet uses the apostrophic *you* to constitute versions of the *I*—'peopling the universe with fragments of the self'—rather than exploring *you* in your own right. For Culler, both vocative forms are *self*-dramatizing, rather than dialogic: 'the apostrophic postulation of addressees refers one to the transforming and animating activity of the poetic voice. The "you" is a projection of that voice' (148). Thus, in apostrophe, the very semblance of outward-directed focus is a means of becoming still more inward: 'radical interiorization', 'solipsism', 'apostrophe involves a drama of "the one mind's" modifications more than a relationship between an *I* and a *you*' (148).

Culler's essay was field-changing: it prompted critics to recognize speaking to *you* as a subtle lyric technique that demanded closer attention. 'Apostrophe' re-ignited literary-critical interest in lyric interlocution, which had long been ignored or underappreciated. And yet, one finds, in much subsequent scholarship, that Culler's close identification between apostrophe (a slippery term that Culler reads as the poet calling to an inanimate object, person, or concept, which cannot reply) and self-dramatization has prompted a number of critics—Barbara Johnson, and J. Mark Smith for example—to argue that the self is the 'real' subject matter of addresses in all poems that conduct address.[28] On this view, the addressee is relegated to a position of instrumental importance, and saying *you* comes to look as though it were, in every case, merely a means of redirecting attention, dramatically, to the poem's *I*. Culler had indeed observed that in the act of *apostrophe*, the speaker dominates his *you* to further himself—but this is not by any means true for all instances of address, as a number of subsequent theorists have implied.

'[T]he "du" of the poem, is present in the poem *only to delegate*, so to speak, its potential activity to the speaking voice', writes Paul de Man.[29] 'Art [...] posits man's physical and spiritual existence, but in none of its works is it concerned with his response', wrote Walter Benjamin, and added: 'No poem is intended for the reader, no picture for the beholder, no symphony for the listener.'[30] Echoes of the notion that the addressing writer refuses to negotiate with, or even to consider, another, are also present in Walter J. Ong's widely influential essay 'The Writer's Audience

[28] Smith's thesis effectively treats address and apostrophe as interchangeable: 'all instances of lyric address turn out to be apostrophe' (413).
[29] Paul de Man, *Allegories of Reading* (New Haven: Yale University Press, 1979) 29. Emphasis added.
[30] Walter Benjamin, 'The Task of the Translator' (1923), in *Illuminations: Essays and Reflections*, ed. and introd. Hannah Arendt, trans. Harry Zohn (New York: Schocken, 1969) 69–82, 69.

is Always a Fiction'.[31] So too, in Ann Keniston's *Overheard Voices: Address and Subjectivity in Postmodern American Poetry*, and Bonnie Costello's 'John Ashbery and the Idea of the Reader', one hears echoes of the doctrine that the writer's audience is 'always' a fiction.[32]

Such criticism is influenced by the notion that we live in a state of Cartesian isolation from others, and reads the vocative poem as an (unsuccessful) attempt to bring us back into contact with them. Treating address as synonymous with apostrophe, such criticism tends to read acts of speaking to *you* as doomed attempts to 'reconcile' alienated minds through a series of rhetorical strategies. That is to say, the apostrophic model is misleading, in so far as it has encouraged subjectivist interpretations of poetry, which are often accompanied by the charge that saying *you* is primarily navel-gazing, or solipsistic. It is time, I think, that this long-familiar notion that *I* calls to a *you*, but cannot confirm anything beyond its own unanswered and unanswerable speech, is met with an anti-subjectivist, anti-Cartesian account of address in response.

Although there are few investigations of British, Irish, and European addresses, amongst these, William Waters's *Poetry's Touch: On Lyric Address* stands out, as a helpful, lucidly argued study of the subject.[33] Waters concentrates largely on poetry in the post-Romantic lyric vein, predominantly on Rilke (as did Culler and de Man). He asserts that 'we as readers may feel in second-person poems [...] an intimation of why poetry is valuable, why it matters to us, and how we might come to feel answerable to it' (2). A similar questioning might fruitfully be carried into an analysis of the relationship between contemporary British addresses. More problematic, however, is Waters's sense that the question of address's function and value inevitably leads to a discussion of why 'at least since the Romantics and Hegel, the preponderance of attention has gone to the "lyric I" and lyric subjectivity'. Waters reads subjectivism as repeatedly present in twentieth-century approaches to lyrics that are 'calling upon things that do not hear—the west wind, a skylark, death, one's pen', and in which 'the word you in poetry is suspended from doing what it usually

---

[31] Walter J. Ong, *PMLA* 90:1 (January 1975) 9–21. Ong thinks the written audience is fictitious in two chief respects: 'First [...] the writer must construct in his imagination, clearly or vaguely, an audience cast in some sort of role—entertainment seekers, reflective sharers of experience [...] Second [...] the audience must correspondingly fictionalize itself. A reader has to play the role in which the author has cast him [...] They have to know how to play the game of being a member of an audience that "really" does not exist' (12). Ong thinks this is a condition of all writing-acts. In speech-acts, however, interlocutors are 'really present' (12)—not fictitious.

[32] Bonnie Costello, *Contemporary Literature* 23:4 (Fall, 1982) 493–514.

[33] See also Smith's 'Apostrophe, or the Lyric Art of Turning Away', which is at least in part another exception: Smith is attentive to Geoffrey Hill, Hopkins, Herbert, and Paul Celan, as well as Walt Whitman and Elizabeth Bishop (411–37).

Mandelstam — message in a bottle
— Hirsch

does' (2). But contemporary British lyric addresses repeatedly declare
themselves as moving upon a social world. In such addresses, *you* is often
'doing what it usually does', and in ways that insist upon the social, his-
torical, and political affiliations of our doing.

Is a lyric address delivered in the present, in the now of reading, or
does it speak from the past? Who is the *you* spoken to? Is *I* really the
poet? Who is really addressing whom? Because much contemporary
criticism of address selects examples from poems in which the difficulty
of determining who is addressing whom, and in what context, is stra-
tegic, Ezra Greenspan finds himself wondering 'if it is possible at all, to
identify the addressee of a poem', and Waters is prompted to speak of
lyric address's 'uprootedness from any specified communicative situ-
ation'.[34] But this is far from always the case: contemporary lyric addresses
repeatedly ground themselves in particular contexts, histories, narra-
tives, and 'communicative situations'. A topical example is Carol Ann
Duffy's 'Politics', a passionate address on the 2009 political expenses
scandal, published by the *Guardian* a month after Duffy's appointment
as Poet Laureate: 'How it makes of your right hand / a gauntlet, a glove-
puppet of the left', 'to your education education education; shouts
this— / Politics!—to your health and wealth; how it roars, to your /
conscience moral compass truth, POLITICS POLITICS POLITICS'.[35]
So too, is Tony Harrison's 2003 'Baghdad Lullaby', published in the
Guardian in response to Geoff Hoon's remark on Radio Four's *Today*
programme, a week earlier, about the merits of using cluster bombs.[36]
A generic example would be Derek Mahon's address to the deceased
Louis MacNeice in 'In Carrowdore Churchyard', or Seamus Heaney's
'Open Letter'.[37]

Contemporary British poetry proffers a plethora of different addresses.
Some hail specifically named, apparently stable figures. Some speak to a
succession of particular, but changeable, recipients. Others use the voca-
tive voice to unknown, unquantifiable, or elusive others. Others again
address readerships, editing bodies, and public audiences. There are those
that turn to smaller coteries or groups of acquaintances, who may seem to
be set apart from the political and public fray. And there are those that

[34] Ezra Greenspan, *Walt Whitman and the American Reader* (Cambridge: Cambridge
University Press, 1990) 229; Waters, *Poetry's Touch* 8.
[35] Carol Ann Duffy, *The Guardian*, Saturday 13 June 2009 <http://www.guardian.co.
uk/books/2009/jun/12/politics-carol-ann-duffy-poem>, accessed 27 December 2010.
[36] Tony Harrison, *The Guardian*, Wednesday 9 April 2003 <http://www.guardian.co.
uk/world/2003/apr/09/iraq.writersoniraq>, accessed 4 June 2008.
[37] Derek Mahon, *Collected Poems*, ed. Peter Fallon (1999; Oldcastle: Gallery Press,
2007) 17; Seamus Heaney, 'An Open Letter', in *Ireland's Field Day* (London: Hutchinson,
1985) 23–32.

bend the ear of past literary or musical masters. (A full list would continue well beyond these examples.) All these types of addresses tap a range of recognizable, public idioms, although they may not, or cannot, finally commit to any one of their addressees or contexts. One writes out of what we might call a *surplus* of '*specified* communicative situations', each jostling for attention. Such addresses are not *under*specified occasions, but bombarded by multiple specifications, ranging between public duties and figures. We find too many possible *you*s, each fitting the poem's address. The slippery facets of address that Waters so eloquently charts (changing speakers, a confusion between *I* and *you*, a faltering between talking about and talking to) are still very much present in the work of the poets we consider: but that slipperiness is bound to, and dependent on, the particulars of the public world, too.

One might, then, agree with Waters about subjectivity as the wrong model to interpret lyric address, if for rather different reasons. In this Babel of communicative voices and models, voicing the claim for address as 'really' the author's subjectivity is just another possibility, clamouring to be confirmed as truth, amongst many equally likely possibilities. As Mikhail Bakhtin has argued: 'language is not a neutral medium that passes freely and easily into the private property of the speaker's intentions; it is populated—overpopulated—with the intentions of others'.[38] Michael Steven Macovski writes that *I*s and *you*s, speakers and addressees, listeners, hearers, overhearers, and authors are not mutually exclusive positions, but 'representation[s] of dialogue: a synecdoche for the interactive voices that constitute a text'.[39] Macovski, like Bakhtin, is helpful to the reader wishing to counter the dominant monologic account of lyric. For him, one should read the 'internal auditor not as a reader-surrogate but as one among many reactions within a textual chorus [...] the addressee bespeaks a composite text, a polyphonic discourse [...] a field of mutually resonant utterances' (23).

To take Geoffrey Hill's *The Triumph of Love*, by way of example:

> *A Book of Golden Deeds, The Worst*
> *Journey in the World:* Finders. Keepers:
> *Dandy, Beano, Film Fun, Radio Fun,* mis-
> teachers of survival: Laurel and Hardy
> cutting, pacing, repacing, their
> flawless shambles [...][40]

[38] Mikhail Bakhtin, *The Dialogic Imagination*, ed. Michael Holquist (Austin: University of Texas Press, 1981) 294.
[39] Michael Steven Macovski, *Dialogue and Literature: Apostrophe, Auditors, and the Collapse of Romantic Discourse* (Oxford: Oxford University Press, 1994) 22.
[40] Hill, *Triumph* 110:57.

Hill's description of Laurel and Hardy's calculatedly shambolic acting teases out how the 'flawless' slapstick routine both masterfully weaves together, and finds itself haphazardly comprised through, a succession of 'cutting, pacing, repacing' acts and speeches. The contemporary poet's performance is not entirely dissimilar. One's identity in poems, in the auditorium, in everyday life, is emergent in ways of being in the world variously (conversationally, imaginatively, textually, bodily, digitally) that are embedded in shared rehearsals and performances; in 'composite texts' and in acts of utterance and re-utterance.

This sense of an identity that arises provisionally, through acting with others, is a notion that manifests also in the work of the contemporary Northern Irish poet, Paul Muldoon. In 'As Your Husband Looks Up to our Window', from *Horse Latitudes*:

> The man who's unwinding the red-and-white-striped awning
> of the *boucherie* across the street takes in not the wide-screen Sensurround
> on which it might be just now dawning
>
> but the letter box between ham and hock.

Whilst

> dawning
> in a home theatre near you is the sequel-spawning
> realisation that mont-de-piété signifies not "piety-mound"
> to the man who's unwinding the red-and-white striped awning
>
> but the methodical deboning and debrowning
> of a pig in a poke [...][41]

In Muldoon's lines, poetic speech to *you* emanates not from the inner life of a set-apart *I*, but from impinging social and media chatter (the 'the wide screen', 'the home theatre', 'the *boucherie*'), and from verbal connections stumbled upon *between I* and *you* ('pig in a poke'/'ham and hock'). The poem 'methodically' teases out a gradually 'dawning', 'unwinding' 'recognition' that these very words, in speaking to *you*, are 'just now' being drawn from a medley of haphazardly linked, 'sequel-spawning' everyday personal and public sayings and doings.

The deft multivocality of this kind of address can be heard in the work of a number of contemporary poets, and is exemplified at some length in the poetry of Graham and Hill. Such multivocality, to my ear, is a contemporary re-working of those carefully crafted etymological improvisations that were characteristic of Modernist polyphony. In Pound's Canto 38, for instance: 'An' that year Metevsky went over to America del Sud / (and the Pope's manners were so like Mr Joyce's, / got that way in the

[41] Paul Muldoon, *Horse Latitudes* (London: Faber, 2006) 30.

Vatican, weren't like that before) / Marconi knelt in the ancient manner / like Jimmie Walker sayin' his prayers'.[42] And in *The Pisan Cantos*:

> "This alone, leather and bones between you and τὸ πάν"
>
> $\qquad$ [*toh pan*, the all]
>
> (Chu Hsi's comment)
>
> $\qquad$ *Cantos* 80:511

In Pound, as in Eliot's *The Waste Land*, colloquialisms and dialect inter-locutions mix with Greek and Latin references and snippets of untranslated text. *Doubles entendres* are interspersed with lyric addresses, buffoonery with the savage humour of the music hall, and the comic patter sketch with quotations from Dante.[43] Such work is busy with transhistorical hearings, mishearing, and re-hearings. It is 'overpopulated' with the criss-crossing aural patterns established through the addresses of various *I*s and *you*s.

One hears that public chorus whether or not a poem speaks to others in the second person. The text does not have to say 'you' to sound a medley or speak publicly, since in words we do this continually: 'The new art is everywhere with its whiplash line / [...] / its biomorphic shapes, motifs of cat and moth; / base metals and industrial design', writes Derek Mahon in his allusively entitled poem, 'Rue des Beaux-Arts', itself an ad-dress to Auden: 'you are talked of even yet'.[44] ' "I am life a / thousands a walking millions nuances walking as / one" ', writes Alice Notley.[45] More recently, Anne Stevenson has spoken of 'a wordlife running from mind to mind', and observed that: '[t]he way you say the world is what you get / What's more, you haven't time to change or choose. / The words swim out to pin you in their net'.[46] The second person pronoun is *not* what makes address occur—though it does flag up local instances of address's contin-ual occurrence. As Thomas Reid (1710–96), the leading philosopher of the Scottish 'common sense' school, argued:

> The second person of verbs, the pronoun of the second person, and the vocative case in nouns, are appropriated to the expression of social oper-ations of mind, and could never have had place in language but for this

---

[42] Ezra Pound, Canto 38 (1937), in *The Cantos of Ezra Pound* (London: Faber, 1975) 38:187, referred to hereafter as *Cantos*.

[43] T. S. Eliot, *The Waste Land* (1922), in *Collected Poems 1909–1962* (1963; London: Faber, 1974) 61–86. Referred to as *ECP*.

[44] Mahon, 'The Yellow Book', in *Collected Poems*, 251 (XIV); Auden, 'Rue des Beaux-Arts' 172.

[45] Alice Notley (1981) in *Moving Borders: Three Decades of Innovative Writing by Women*, ed. Mary Margaret Sloan (Jersey, NJ: Talisman House, 1998) 193–4.

[46] Anne Stevenson, 'Making Poetry', *Collected Poems* (Northumberland: Bloodaxe, 2004) 17; Stevenson, 'Saying the World', *Collected Poems*, 18.

purpose: nor is it a good argument against this observation, that, by a rhet-
orical figure, we sometimes address persons that are absent, or even inani-
mated [sic] beings, in the second person. For it ought to be remembered,
that all figurative ways of using words or phrases, supposes [sic] a natural
and literal meaning of them.[47]

My position might be seen as analogous to that of linguists and philoso-
phers of language who, like Reid, place address in close proximity to or-
dinary linguistic practice.[48] Poetic address is not linguistically aberrant, or
highly 'unusual'. It exemplifies rather than contradicts everyday speech. It
demands that we are attentive to our quotidian verbal ingenuity. As Alan
Richardson points out, in his article on 'Everyday Discourse, Overhearing
and Poetic Address', rather than 'confound[ing] the transparent referenti-
ality that is quickly possible in ordinary discursive communication',[49]
many of the 'addresses to intimates found in conversation poems, [are] so
familiar from everyday discourse that they often fail to register as apostro-
phes at all'.[50]

   J. Mark Smith has been anxious that reading address as a part of our
ordinary everyday language-games causes one to 'lose sight of much of
what particularizes poems' (412). Waters not dissimilarly fears that it
opens one to the charge of making 'all a poem's hailings [...] equally void
of effect and therefore essentially interchangeable' (3). But poems that use
the second-person pronoun often do so precisely to draw attention to the
specific contexts of their polyphony, just as saying *you* in Hill (as in Pound,
Yeats, or Eliot) is a marker of particular histories, roles, relationships, con-
flicts, malapropisms, negotiations, and manipulations that the poem per-
forms in its historical moment. Lyrics that give voice to the slippery *you*
mark out a changeable place in which one may perform any (or many) of
a number of quite everyday acts: address oneself or another; speak to a
singular reader and a general audience; hail fellow poets and editors and
critics; address God, the age, the men and women of the time, and the
citizens of a nation. This slipperiness is not to be confused with the sug-
gestion that all these particular interlocutions are equivalent, collapsible
into one 'essentially interchangeable' position. When Duffy uses *you*

---

[47] Thomas Reid, *Essays on the Intellectual Powers of Man* (Cambridge, MA: MIT Press,
1969) 74.

[48] Reid's philosophy of common sense has been linked to J. L. Austin's *How to Do Things
With Words* (Oxford: Clarendon Press, 1962), and John Searle, *Speech Acts* (Cambridge:
Cambridge University Press, 1969). Each of these writers is attentive to the actual use of
language—the way words are applied, in real contexts and situations—as the primary
ground for working out theories of language.

[49] Smith, 'Apostrophe, or the Lyric Art of Turning Away' 413.

[50] Richardson, 'Apostrophe in Life and in Romantic Art: Everyday Discourse, Over-
hearing, and Poetic Address' 371.

heatedly to address the Labour government (and her imagined body of
assembled readers poring over the Saturday papers); when Hill uses *you* to
commemorate the philosopher Gillian Rose and the writer Elias Can-
etti;[51] and when Auden uses *you* in 'In Memory of W. B. Yeats' (1939,
197), that address is highly contextualized and specific, as well as part of
a recognizable poetic tradition, and inflected with the idiom of the every-
day discursive situation: 'You were silly like us', 'an afternoon of nurses
and rumours' (197–8). Using the quotidian, flexible *you* need not either
'confound' everyday speech, or collapse lyric particularities into that
much-feared 'essential interchangeablity'.

In this case, the deictic words *I* and *you*—which can be used to address
fellow poets, lovers, friends, readers, editors, politicians, England, the
Queen, Nature, God, oneself, beasts and monsters, the dead, or no one at
all—might better be thought of as positions one steps into provisionally,
rather than embodiments of real, permanent characteristics. In writing,
speaking, and reading, one often cannot help making personal contact with
others (this is what Waters aptly terms 'poetry's *touch*'), but this occurs not
because *you* is based upon, or formed from a real person outside of lan-
guage, but because of something real that occurs *in* words. Roles and rela-
tions, self and other, are fluid tenets of language, continually up for change
and reconstruction. This fluidity becomes clearest in poetic addresses when
deictic figures of speech are used: 'I' and 'you', as well as 'here', 'there', 'this',
'that', 'now'; for instance in Keats: 'This living hand, now warm and capable /
Of earnest grasping [...] / [...] / [...]—See here it is— / I hold it towards
you'.[52] Antony Easthope, drawing on the work of linguists such as Emile
Benveniste and Tzvetan Todorov, uses the helpful term 'marks of utterance'
for these self-declaring aspects of writing (demonstratives, second-person
pronouns, and deictics), combining what Benveniste calls 'signs of person'
with Todorov's idea of revealing 'the imprint of the process of enunciation
in the utterance'.[53] Easthope's terminology helps one to differentiate between
texts that flag up their performative aspect (vocative poems, for example,
that present an *I* speaking to a *you*), and texts that play down the impression
of themselves as speech-acts (often realist novels written in the third person);
as Benveniste puts it, commenting of Balzac: 'events seem to narrate them-
selves' (41).

Yet, in poems that address others as you, 'signs of person' are all too
often mistaken for signs of the immediately personal—'the poet himself'

[51] Geoffrey Hill, 'To the High Court of Parliament', *Canaan* (London: Penguin, 1996),
1; 'In Memoriam: Gillian Rose', 'On Reading *Crowds and Power*' in *Treatise* 35, 46.
[52] John Keats, 'This Living Hand', *The Complete Poems of John Keats* (Hertfordshire:
Wordsworth Press, 2001) 461.
[53] All quotations from Antony Easthope, *Poetry as Discourse* (London: Methuen, 1983) 41.

speaking immediately, directly to 'the reader', as though both were stable, embodied figures, occupying the same textual time and space. In contrast, *I* and *you* are less fixed and discrete entities than changeable linguistic potentials. Terms like 'author' and 'recipient', 'writer', and 'reader' are fluid and alterable, akin to pronominal categories. It is possible—and desirable—to move away from the doctrine that lyric address is the man-oeuvre of a monologic poetic self estranged from others, and to offer an alternative picture of lyric addresses. From this new vantage point, ad-dress emerges as a continually negotiated feature of language that estab-lishes changeable identities, that gives rise to *I*s and *you*s, speakers and listeners, authors and readers. This focus on contemporary address offers new openings onto the political today, and suggests the complexity of what repeatedly happens in lyric poems, and in everyday speech and writing.

Reed Way Dasenbrock has written: 'today most critics and theorists hold that the connection between poetry and politics is not limited just to situ-ations in which poets become politically involved in explicit ways, but instead all cultural expression is related to the social and political con-text—whether implicitly or explicitly—in which it is produced [. . .] even the choice to eschew explicit political involvement or references consti-tutes a form of political action'.[54] Address offers a key into the 'civil, per-sonal and political work' performed by and through twentieth-century poetic texts. Reflecting on, and often speaking back to, Modernist writ-ers, the addresses of many contemporary poets insist that artworks are, by turns, implicit and explicit 'political action'. This book is attentive to how they tap, in different ways, the politics of private speech and space. The first section, on W. S. Graham, focuses on the public nature of the appar-ently personal and private uses of addresses to known recipients. Graham, whose densely verbally playful early work was initially detrimentally as-sociated with Dylan Thomas and New Apocalypse writing, began to rise to critical acclaim in the 1950s, with the publication of his volume *The Nightfishing*, and the subsequent publication of his Modernist-inflected volumes, *Malcolm Mooney's Land* and *Implements in their Places*, which were largely favourably received.[55]

[54] Reed Way Dasenbrock, 'Poetry and Politics', in *A Companion to Twentieth-Century Poetry*, ed. Neil Roberts (Oxford: Wiley Blackwell) 51–63, 51.
[55] W. S. Graham, *The Nightfishing* (London: Faber, 1955); *Malcolm* (London: Faber, 1970); *Implements* (London: Faber, 1977).

v̌ațc   v̌ civil

The intimate lyric *you* has been employed rather differently—though again as a part of national and historical negotiation—in the work of C. H. Sisson, the subject of part two. This English poet, critic, and life-long civil servant is likely recalled for his collection *In the Trojan Ditch*, which propelled him to relative fame in the 1970s.[56] Sisson's essays have been influential too. He may be remembered for prompting the fierce debate on art, politics, and 'commitment', which raged in *Stand* magazine between 1977 and 1979 (particularly between Michael Schmidt, Donald Davie, and Jon Silkin), following the publication of his essay on the *Action Française* writer, Charles Maurras.[57]

Geoffrey Hill, the best known of this trio today, is still best appreciated for his early poetry (volumes from *For the Unfallen* to *The Mystery of the Charity of Charles Péguy*), rather than for his more 'difficult' later volumes: *Canaan*, *The Triumph of Love*, and *Speech! Speech!* have prompted complaints of inaccessibility and elitism.[58] Hill, like Sisson, is an influential critic as well as a poet: a good number of his lecturers and published essays have been gathered by Kenneth Haynes as the *Collected Critical Writings*.[59] Hill's lyric addresses, which are the focus of the third section, flag up the fraught role of the public intellectual who hails an audience, a body of critics and reviewers, and a book-buying public.

This tentatively traced trajectory from the 'implicitly' public-political address to the more 'explicit' ends with a fourth section on the highly successful mainstream poet, publisher, and academic, Don Paterson. Scrutinizing the commercial and aesthetic demands made on the twenty-first-century poet, Paterson's *you* brings institutional, academic, and media voices into intimate contact: his historically minded addresses depict poets provokingly compromised by their manoeuvres in the contemporary poetry industry. Both in his recent prize-winning collections (*Landing Light* and *Rain*), and in his critical prose (*New British Poetry* and *Reading Shakespeare's Sonnets*), Paterson's work demands audiences attend to literature's commercial production, circulation, and reception.[60]

All four poets draw on Modernist (particularly Eliotic and Poundian) polyvocality in their own characteristic ways. Each sets out to establish the relationship between address and politics, poetry and audience,

[56] C. H. Sisson, *In the Trojan Ditch* (Manchester: Carcanet, 1974).
[57] See 'The Symposium' on 'Commitment and Poetry' in *Stand* 20:2 (1978) 11–75, and *Stand* 20:3 (1978) 8–17, 20–7. See particularly Jon Silkin, 'The Rights of England'; Donald Davie, 'A Rejoinder to Jon Silkin'; Michael Schmidt, 'Stand: Symposium on "Commitment"'.
[58] Geoffrey Hill, *For the Unfallen* (London: André Deutsch, 1959); *The Mystery of the Charity of Charles Péguy* (London: André Deutsch, 1983); *Speech! Speech!*
[59] See note 5.
[60] See note 6; see also *NBP* xxv–xxviii; and *Shakespeare's Sonnets* 38.

Bulser

revising the notion that lyric address is only implicitly political. And each combines lyric hailing and personal voicings with entrenchedly public contacts and contexts. The later poets' styles of interlocution put into play, and depart from, high Modernism, looking back on and reassessing Eliot and Pound. They also explore the often hostile interpretations of Modernism by Movement writers, focusing predominantly on Philip Larkin—a figure whom Graham, Sisson, and Paterson especially (though often obliquely) respond to, and against. In this, there are points of similarity between these poets' work and other contemporary poets, notably Tony Harrison, Douglas Dunn, and Carol Ann Duffy.

All four of these poets combines a propensity for address, and gravitation towards the second-person pronoun, with a contemporary rethinking of lyric in the public, historical, and political spheres. Each opens the lyric mode onto the civic sphere in a different manner, and to different degrees. Graham, who addresses predominantly his St Ives community of artists, writers, lovers, and companions, uses his interlocutors to explore the issues of class, patronage, national allegiance, and identity as they emerge flexibly, often disturbingly, in language: 'Know me by the voice / That speaks outside my choice', 'Who crossed these words before me / Crossed my meaning out'.[61] This poet's choice of addressees may seem closest to the 'implicit' politics Dasenbrock describes, even if the poetry's 'references constitute a form of political action':

> The word unblemished by the tongue
> Of History has still to be got.
> You see, Huntly, it is the way
> You put it. Said Moray's Earl,
> You've spoilt a bonnier face than your ain.[62]

Graham's addresses often make a riddle of the apparent difference between self and other, *you* becoming me, and me, *you*. Yet this is historically located and politically inflected verbal riddling. In proffering the theory of language as a meeting place of alterable voices, Graham's addresses insist that it is unavoidably in language that *I* and *you* take shape and find meaning. His tapping of straight-talking idiom, colloquial speech, parodic use of cliché, as well as his use of national and regional registers and speech-rhythms locate and sharpen the implicit socio-political critique behind his philosophical and linguistic invocations, often coolly reorienting his audience to the worldly conditions that affect the production and reception of these poetic texts: 'this, my boy, is the

---

[61] Graham, 'Seven Letters', *NCP* 128; 'Baldy Bane', *NCP* 149.
[62] Graham, 'Implements in Their Places' 252.

Lyle ✗ — Coterie

poem / You paid me five pounds for'.[63] Through his lyric addresses, Graham's speakers assert changeable national and personal identities, employ literary, historical, and quotidian disguises, and show how our everyday language is continually at work in staging strategic roles and relations with others.

Hill and Sisson, in contrast, are more evidently 'explicit' about their work's political involvement. Hill's attention to the negotiations of the voice and page can be traced from early poems such as 'Poetry as History', up to his 2007 volume, *A Treatise of Civil Power*.[64] In the latter, one finds lyrics commemorating and criticizing significant cultural landmarks and literary, historical, musical, and political figures and works: 'To the Lord Protector Cromwell', 'Holbein', 'On Reading *Milton and the English Revolution*' (13; 7; 4). These addresses reformulate, and insert themselves into, the cultural history of the public artefacts they laud, even as they examine the ethics of art's function in offering this public praise, in re-envisaging memorials: 'Poetry's its own agon that *allows us / to recognize devastation* as the rift / between power and powerlessness' (*Treatise* 38). Hill's lines, from 'In Memoriam: Gillian Rose', incorporate the italicized words of Hill's addressee into his work's argumentation, entwining past and present, commemoration and critique, addressee and addressing poet. They re-enact Eliot's observation that: 'what happens when a new work of art is created is something that happens simultaneously to all the works of art which preceded it. The existing monuments [...] [are] modified by the introduction of the new (the really new) work of art among them.'[65]

Meanwhile, Sisson's royalist, nationally minded addresses are similarly attentive to the complex interplay between *I* and *you* in past and present artworks. For Sisson, poetry is a communal act that participates in the transhistorical forging of a nation and a people, as well as contributing to their intimate private understandings: 'A poem can have meaning only in terms of words other people use, and which we have from our ancestors. It is a part and not a whole.'[66] Repeatedly, Sisson's lyrics are addressed lyrically, to 'you', and also publicly: 'To the Queen', 'For the Primate of All England', and to the populace: 'Vigil and Ode for St George's Day'.[67] Such lyrics re-sound private and public speech styles, interweaving

---

[63] Graham, 'Private Poem to Norman Macleod' 227.

[64] Hill, 'Poetry as History' (1968), in *HCP* 84.

[65] T. S. Eliot, 'Tradition and the Individual Talent' (1919), in *The Sacred Wood: Essays on Poetry and Criticism* (1920; London: Methuen, 1972) 47–59, 50. *The Sacred Wood* referred to hereafter as *SW*.

[66] C. H. Sisson, 'Poetry and Myth' (1977), in *The Avoidance of Literature: Collected Essays*, ed. Michael Schmidt (Manchester: Carcanet, 1978) 514–18, 514; cited hereafter as *Avoidance*.

[67] Sisson, *CP*. See 83; 384; 349.

contemporary idioms with a culture's literary-historical civil voicings: 'Sweet rose of England, nothing can be true / Except so far as words and you agree', 'the saying is you / And what the words carry is history' (473). Sisson's work draws on the public epigrammatic tradition of the early modern period, pulling its contemporary addresses to *you* into the texture of literary voicings, explorations of patronage and power encountered in Donne, Marvell, Herrick, Vaughan, and Milton. Sisson, like his early modern forebears, uses the poem to test out the traditions that inform what should count as appropriate address, exposing propaganda and re-negotiating popular sentiment. If such art calls out to any *you* that will answer, it also demands *your* historical and theological tenacity. This is far from always an accommodating civic cry.

For each of these poets, poetry's public power, so evident in the early modern tradition, might still be claimed, and found live and fertile, in address today. In this respect, Sisson, Hill, Graham, and Paterson—like Eliot and Pound—set out to revive the public English lyric tradition, building links between poetic address and its roots in the fecund literary past. Drawing on ancient as well as contemporary hailings, addressing Greek and Roman, French, German, Chinese, American, Russian, and Irish writers, and alluding to historical, philosophical, and theological texts, such poets might be seen as what Pound called 'the antennae of the race'. They tune into the diverse, mutually antagonistic strands that comprise the cultural heritage; they sound competing addresses that jostle for *your* attention.[68] Their sharp-tongued emulations of oppositional voices, swapping of roles and positions, deliberate violations of grammar, and fragmentations of identifiable speakers, are reminiscent of the role-changing personas, mingling speech-styles, accents and registers of Pound's *Cantos* and Eliot's *The Waste Land*: ' "You! hypocrite lecteur!" '[69]

These poets also diverge from Eliot and Pound. Although they take part in a dialogue with past masters, our writers also question, and often criticize, the nature of that mastery, redressing contemporaries for over-valuing these historical interlocutors, as well as taking the latter to task for encouraging an audience's veneration. 'Cloven, we are incorporate', Hill reminds *you* in his address to the audience that negotiates the public image of the Nobel prize-winning author Elias Canetti: '*Names collect / their own crowds* [...] *hardly at all connected / with the real natures of the men who bear them*'.[70] Not dissimilarly, Sisson often uses address to insist that a poem is an artefact of literary-historical continuity. His lyrics speak

---

[68] Ezra Pound, 'Henry James' (1918), in *Literary Essays of Ezra Pound*, ed. T. S. Eliot (London: Faber, 1954) 295–338, 297. Referred to hereafter as *Essays*.
[69] See Pound, *Cantos* at 61–86; Eliot, *The Waste Land* in *ECP* 65:76.
[70] Hill, 'On Reading *Crowds and Power*', *Treatise* 46.

to, and make heard, Classical, Biblical, Shakespearean, and early modern sources. His addresses to 'Catullus', 'Saint Anthony', and 'Letter to John Donne' are by turns aggressive and satirical, as well as tender and nostalgic: 'I understand you well enough, John Donne', he writes, 'you were a man of ability / Eaten by lust and by the love of God' (89; 167; 50). Such interlocutions berate both their famed addressee, and those who might imagine that contact with renowned cultural figures is isolated activity, or exceptional, 'poetic' or transcendent. A similar tone is struck by Paterson, who uses *you* insistently to show the reader's hand (and ear) in acts of historical re-sounding. Tuning *you* in to the context of Ancient Greek patronage, 'The Reading' turns on its recipients: speaking as Simonides, Paterson bluntly confronts *you* with the demand for 'your coupons, O my rapt listeners, / I'll have nailed by the end of this poem'.[71] For Sisson, Hill, and Paterson, being historically comprised is a matter of fact; a common, and often a humbling recognition: 'what makes "man" is not the fact of "I," the individual, but the fact of the species'.[72] The art of contemporary British address is certainly no form of rescue from the fragmented present, nor a means of triumphantly soldering it together again.

Although poetic language is not exceptional—and nor are its interlocutions—an address in a published, circulating poem *is* an exceptionally public act. For unlike most casually made quotidian addresses, it speaks to a public body; it is witnessed by gathered spectators. It has the power to make resonant not only the artist's words, but also the words of the citizen, both of which perform different kinds of civil negotiations daily. Both retrieve present relationships and identities from past cultural deposits, in their dealings with ordinary *I*s and *you*s. Eliot's argument for *poetic* 'impersonality'—his suspicion of the idea of art as unique self-expression of the poet's interior, and his proposition that the poet is a conduit for the voices of the culture—is taken up by these contemporary poets as what Sisson termed 'the fact of the species'. It is not just the artist that speaks impersonally, but rather all *I*s and *you*s. Address, in being such a public act, comes with certain responsibilities. One of which is to expose the 'gentle reader' in an ungentle position. Each of our poets shows that apparently passive reading figure as having a hand in the process of composition, either economically, as the influential 'Still gentler purchaser!', or linguistically, as the speaker whose dialects, academicisms, political sentiments, lovers' whispers, are writing in the poem (often as well as, or instead of, the poet).[73]

Issue of universal

---

[71] Paterson, 'The Reading', *Light* 23.
[72] Sisson, 'Sevenoaks Essays' (1967), *Avoidance* 202–22, 208.
[73] Lord Byron, *Don Juan*, Canto 1, 221. See Jerome McGann on Byron's use of 'you' in accosting reception: 'Private Poetry, Public Deception', in *The Politics of Poetic Form: Poetry and Public Policy* (New York: Roof, 1990) 119–48.

These four writers exhibit chameleon role-changing, varied, and variant lexicons, and mimic altering speech-styles: the language of commerce is juxtaposed with the language of tragedy, farce with editorial annotation, nursery rhymes with historical narrative. In this, their texts are often highly reminiscent of the different voices of Eliot's *The Waste Land*: 'HURRY UP PLEASE ITS TIME', 'Son of man, / [...] you know only / A heap of broken images', 'O O O O that Shakespeherian Rag — / It's so elegant / So intelligent' (68:141; 63:20–1; 67:128–30). Yet the policing carried out by these contemporary voices feels more edgily fractious, often because it demands, much more strongly than Eliot and Pound, that interlocutors are brought to an uncomfortable consciousness of the patronage extended in their being addressed by art. 'Applaud, won't you, if only first time round', Hill enjoins his imagined contemporary audience, in *Orchards of Syon*.[74] In the addresses of the post-1990 work of Hill and Paterson, a readership is called upon to respond to the economic and institutional factors that govern which voices and imagined audiences are drafted into the texture of the poetic work: 'it ís a gift, one that you owe me', writes Hill. 'Welcome [...] / [...] / to those undecided shades in Waterstones, / trapped between the promise and the cost, / [...] bastard title, biog note / acknowledgements and prefatory quote', writes Paterson: 'a big hi! to those holders, old and new / of the critic's one-day travel-pass'.[75]

These are poems that often take charge of others, marking out auditors in their hailings. 'I address the musing mind', writes Sisson in 'The Garden of the Hesperides', whilst in 'A Visitor' he tells *you* to 'Put on your coat / And go home' (282; 260). Paterson's and Graham's speakers repeatedly summon hearers directly: 'Listen, for this I tell' (Graham, 26); 'you're not taking this seriously enough' (Paterson, *Light* 29). Hill's 'Integer Vitae' insists that we 'vivify what we catch from others' voices' (*Treatise* 24). In so doing, these poets often conceive of addressees as actively negotiating the poem. For Sisson, in 'The Model', 'the conversation / Is because you are', whilst Graham's 'Wynter and the Grammarsow' must ask *you* to 'Give me the password' and 'wince me your grip' (*CP* 473; *NCP* 187). Often, these poems are forced politely to host invading *you*s, and are made hostage to a range of public and private needling voices. For Graham, 'Ireland Scotland England expects. / He She They expect. My dear / Expects', whilst in Hill, the poem is a 'THEATRE OF VOICES, noble | if nót / ridiculous' ('Implements' 244; *SS* 104:52). Ghosting such

---

[74] Geoffrey Hill, *Orchards of Syon* (Washington: Counterpoint, 2002) 6–8, referred to hereafter as *Orchards*.
[75] Hill, *Orchards* 6–8; Paterson, 'A Talking Book', *Light* 26.

hailings is a recognition of the artwork's participation in that theatre of public words continually borrowed, turned upon, and returned, which is not dissimilar to that motivating Pound's impatient address in his first Canto: 'Lie quiet, Divus' (*Cantos* 1:5). His interlocutor, the Renaissance scholar Andreas Divus, whose Latin translations of Homer were used in many subsequent translations of the *Iliad* and *Odyssey*, was a figure to whom the *Cantos* owed much. Pound's hailing ('Lie quiet, Divus') is an address that apparently silences that *you* whilst simultaneously paying particular tribute to its historical auditor: 'I mean, that is Andreas Divus, / In officina Wecheli, 1538, out of Homer' (1:5). So too, in the work of these contemporary poets, saying *you* opens up how artworks participate in shaping our shared, civil world, and as such, arise from it, are compelled to be wedded to it.

All four poets implicitly move to contest the notion of lyric address as private and primarily self-directed. The work of Hill, in particular, uses address to examine poetry's fraught status as inescapably *public* verbal action: poems are 'ceremonies of speech' conducted 'to address / intrusive suffering'.[76] 'Our word is our bond', as Hill has insisted.[77] This sense of the self as communally realized—created *in* one's civil formulations—is present also in Graham's lyric emphasis that: 'Words make their world', Paterson's dictum that the poet '*meets the millions / at the line of speech*', and in Sisson's poetic concern about the duties created through past utterance: 'If I were accused of what I have said', 'If you had hopes once they have turned to reason / If you had reason it has turned to evidence: / The evidence is against you'.[78] In all four poets language 'bonds', and compels us; we are held by what we say. This differentiates the writers under study from a 'postmodernist' poetics, aligning them more closely with the thought of Eliot and Pound. Like the Modernists, Graham, Sisson, Hill, and Paterson resist the notion that words can be used to create a faithful exchange between thing and referent. But language's freedom from mimesis does not open up a verbal free-for-all, a pure *jouissance*. Rather, it suggests the poetry's opening onto political responsibility, and its concerns about the impact of the verbal present on the future. 'Be upstanding', commands Paterson, 'Now: let us raise the fucking *tone*'.[79] Art is, as it was for the Modernists, inured to social implications and consequences. Hill, in *Tenebrae*, poses the poet as a succession of role-changing verbal garbs and guises, presiding over the Feast of Fools: 'He is the Lord of

76 Hill, *Scenes from Comus* 57.
77 Hill, 'Our Word is Our Bond' (1983), in *CCW* 146–69, 168.
78 Graham, *NCP* 164; Paterson, *Light* 70; Sisson *CP* 470, *CP* 196.
79 Paterson, 'Prologue', *Gift* 1.

Misrule. / He is the Master of the Leaping Figures, / the motley factions' (*HCP* 174). Vincent Sherry comments on Hill: 'he engages variously [...] ambitions, responsibilities, and susceptibilities: the relation between public and private discourse, moral liability in speech, and the arrogance and limitations of poetic art'.[80] Hill himself writes that poetry should tap into that 'rhythm of social duties, rites, ties, and obligations from which an individual severs himself or herself at great cost and peril'; it should 'connote [...] the continuity of human responses in general'.[81]

Nevertheless, for these poets, 'social duties' and 'continuity' should manifest in one's lyric art not through toeing the party line and glibly pleasing one's audience. Poems should use address to *be* difficult, to answer back, sportively or deflatingly, impatiently or rudely. 'I could know you if I wanted to. / You make me not want to' Graham declares in 'Implements' (243). That lyric frankness is reminiscent of Philip Larkin's straight-talking naturalistic addresses: 'Ah, were I courageous enough / To shout *Stuff your pension!*'[82] It also moves with a motivation not entirely dissimilar to Movement anti-elitism, and a wish to poke fun at bourgeoisie respectability: 'It used to make me throw up, / [...] / O when will England grow up?'[83] 'Above / All, shut up', Graham commands, taking some pleasure in offending his imagined audience's social niceties in his poem 'The Beast in the Space': 'Am I too loud?' (158; 160). Comparably, Sisson's lyric, 'The Pattern', commands its auditor to 'Strip off the words that they are pleasant with', insisting that *you* join the speaker in questioning: 'And what is left?' (480). In so speaking, Graham and Sisson might be seen to align themselves with the combatively vernacular idiom that the Movement tapped in the 1950s and 1960s. Paterson and Hill perhaps go still further, bluntly stripping off verbal pleasantries in a finely crafted mixture of lyric and twenty-first-century demotic. 'Up yours / O'Shem', writes Hill; 'Some call you an angel. Some call you a cunt. / They are both on the money', Paterson writes, unsparingly detailing 'your shagging / and drinking and lapses in personal hygiene'.[84]

Such addresses simultaneously intersperse candid plain speaking with 'being difficult' in the Modernist sense. They show that speaking lyrically to *you* (in one sense an accessible address) is also a move invested with the weight of tradition, and cannot exempt itself from what Larkin called

---

[80] Vincent Sherry, *The Uncommon Tongue: The Poetry and Criticism of Geoffrey Hill* (Ann Arbor: University of Michigan Press, 1987) 4.

[81] Hill, 'Redeeming the Time' (1972–3), in *CCW* 88–108, 93.

[82] Philip Larkin, 'Toads', *Collected Poems* (London: Marvell and Faber, 2003) 62. Referred to as *LCP*.

[83] Larkin, 'Naturally the Foundation Will Bear Your Expenses', *LCP* 84.

[84] Paterson, 'The Book at Bedtime', *Light* 51.

disparagingly, 'the myth-kitty'.[85] Contemporary poetry, as the addresses of our writers show, is capable of a Larkinesque straight-talking anti-elitism in the very act of asserting that voice does not exist outside of a specific history, context, and time. However apparently unmediated, candid, or artless poetic address can seem, it is anchored by 'the weight of tradition'—not least of all the tradition of speaking plainly (here our contemporary quartet return upon, and offer a corrective to, their Movement forebear). In 'Our Word is our Bond', Hill writes with some admiration of Austin's coupling of his emphasis on 'ordinary language' with his acknowledgement of normalcy's 'treacherous' difficulty: 'the innumerable and unforeseeable demands of the world upon language'; the hard graft of speaking to *you* plainly, with the weight of history on one's tongue (*CCW* 147–56). As we have seen, Graham's lyric addresses, too, have some investment in the notion that 'speaking to you' is 'difficult', but should not be '*too* difficult'. Graham combines an exasperated sense that 'there must be some / Way to speak together straighter than this' with his indebtedness to the toil of speaking 'straighter', meaning both 'plainer' and 'more upstanding' (187). In such addresses, words themselves are put out to work.

The sense of address as sportive combat is especially strong in Hill, as becomes clear in the third section, but it manifests also in the work of Sisson, Graham, and Paterson. These four poets—each from working-class or lower middle-class backgrounds—use their work to critique those in thrall to prestige and privilege, academic and financial. They rail against those who privilege fine speech and elevated poetic diction, who try to use art to make, as Paterson once put it: 'something axiomatic on the nature / of articulacy and inheritance'.[86] Working against what Douglas Dunn has called 'your love of "haves", amusement at "have-nots"', these poets scrutinize the politics and economics of the awards ceremony, the institutional accolade, the thrill of advancement, fame, and finery.[87] 'I myself dress up in what I can / Afford', writes Graham in 'Approaches to How They Behave', looking askance at fashion, taste, and the modishness of poetry that presciently taps into 'the time's slang' (*NCP* 180). 'My parents / never owned a house', 'my people [...] / [...] bought no landmark / other than their graves' writes Hill (*Treatise* 44). For both, albeit in very different ways, a good measure of working-class bravura is put into play. Graham, particularly, exposes the poet-figure as far from sombre or elevated, often suggesting a slapstick element to the poetic act. His speakers

[85] Philip Larkin, 'Statement' (1955), in *Required Writing* (London: Faber, 1983) 79. Cited hereafter as *RW*.

[86] Paterson, 'An Elliptical Stylus', *Nil Nil* 21.

[87] Douglas Dunn, 'Green Breeks', *Selected Poems 1964–1983* (London: Faber, 1986) 179. Referred to hereafter as *DSP*.

may trip over themselves in amusingly inelegant 'stumble[s] / In the spiked bramble', and can be caught out by words: 'Language ah now you have me' (*NCP* 160; 207). Sisson, too, emphasizes that lyrics are not privileged sites, but places where speakers get their hands, and tongues, dirty. Often, his poems remind us that: 'Such a fool as I am you had better ignore / Tongue twist, malevolent, fat mouthed', 'I lie and babble with the rest'.[88]

As we will come to see, Graham, Sisson, Hill, and Paterson are each suspicious of, and keen to point out the shortcomings of, poets who readily affiliate themselves to institutions, disciplines, theories, and funding bodies, or who vociferously forge national allegiances. This can be seen in Graham's response to Hugh MacDiarmid's nationalist agenda; Sisson's response to the Movement poetic; Hill's keen criticisms of Eliot's status as broadcaster and public figure; Paterson's lyric upbraiding of *avant-garde* poets for their (alleged) valorization of anti-readerly inaccessibility.[89] Seeking not merely polite accommodation within the existing strictures, tastes, and values of the literary establishment, nor *acceptance* from the bourgeois (or the radical) critic, these poets' addresses are often used to offend those *you*s whose suburban tastes and values have assumed (and wish to preserve) a glib monovocality. Hill terms them 'the custodians of speech', 'the professionally opinionated'.[90] 'I speak not your Highnesses *en masse*', insists Paterson, demanding that *you* 'shake yourself awake' (*Light* 28–9). But can any contemporary writer entirely resist the smooth patter, false assurances, glib language of the polite literary occasion: the poetry reception, the academic conference, the tempered exchanges of men of letters? '*Is that right, Missus, or is that right?* I don't / care what I say, do I?', writes Hill, characteristically drawing the problem to the addressee's attention (*Triumph* 40:21). Each poet's differently dissenting poetic address exemplifies, in a fresh light, how late twentieth-century poetry makes considerable use of voices that reject, and explore the politics of being seen to reject, what Robert Crawford calls, in writing of Douglas Dunn, 'the apparently unshakeable dominance of metropolitan Englishness'.[91] Address often works as a literary takeover bid that tries on 'dominance' anew. It is not only attempting to 'shake' or entirely collapse it.

To what extent can such literary addresses move effectively in opposition to conservative immobility, staid linguistic convention, and assumed authority? On the one hand, Graham, Sisson, Hill, and Paterson, like

---

[88] Sisson, 'The Usk' 165; 'Fifteen Sonnets' 406.
[89] Paterson, see *New British Poetry*, Introduction xx–xxx.
[90] Hill, Hill conference, Keble College Oxford, 2008.
[91] Robert Crawford, *Devolving English Literature* (Edinburgh: Edinburgh University Press, 2000) 280.

mid-century Movement poets, are working to parody the closed values of the establishment, the stuffy idiom of the old boys' network. One might be put in mind of Larkin, who similarly pokes savage fun at the '*decent chap, a real good sort,* / [...] / *Head and shoulders above the rest*' (123), and the mannered politeness of middle-class sociability:

> *My wife and I have asked a crowd of craps*
> *To come and waste their time and ours: perhaps*
> *You'd care to join us?* In a pig's arse, friend.
>
> 'Vers de Société', *LCP* 147

Larkin's addresses, however, remain importantly different in character from those of these later poets, in that he regards his straight-talking companionability as working against unnecessary Modernist 'difficulty'. Larkin's *you*, like those addresses of many Movement lyrics, aims to hail friends, readers, and contemporaries casually, using everyday language, familiar idioms: 'Get out as early as you can, / And don't have any kids yourself', Larkin advises his interlocutor matter-of-factly in 'This Be The Verse' (142). 'I try to write lucidly / That even I can understand it', Enright discloses, as if in an aside to the common reader. 'I think you remember, George, / For your own reasons', Donald Davie writes, in an address to his companion: 'for George Dekker'.[92]

Perhaps surprisingly, Larkin himself rarely uses the second-person pronoun, preferring instead the inclusive 'we' or 'one', which holds a body of *you*s together, as if they stood as one, sharing the same perspective and position: 'And we are nudged from comfort, never knowing', 'What will survive of us is love'.[93] Still more frequently, Larkin makes use of a definite article which transforms the particular experience of *I* or *you* into a general perspective, but avoids the personal pronoun: 'The eye can hardly pick them out / From the cold shade they shelter in', 'The thousands of marriages / Lasting a little while longer', 'However we follow the printed directions of sex / However the family is photographed under the flag-staff— / Beyond all this, the wish to be alone'.[94] Such addresses tend to enact an evasion of *you* that, as Virginia Walker Jackson complains, 'converts the isolated "I" into the universal "we" by bypassing the mediation of any particular "you"' (129). It is an evasion of *your* 'mediation' that is motivated, as Jackson sees it, and I think rightly, by what Herbert F. Tucker calls 'the thirst for intersubjective confirmation of the self, which has

---

[92] D. J. Enright, 'Life and Letters' (1953), in *Collected Poems 1948–1998* (New York: Oxford University Press, 1998) 10; Donald Davie, 'Rutland', *Collected Poems 1971–1983* (Manchester: Carcanet, 1983) 35.

[93] Larkin, 'Arrivals, Departures' 74; 'An Arundel Tomb' 117.

[94] Larkin, 'At Grass' 75; 'MCMXIV' 99; 'Wants' 52.

made the overhearing of a persona our principle means of understanding a poem'.[95] Larkin's hailings move under the pressure of that Millean notion of 'overhearing' that emphasizes each individual as a fundamentally separate aloneness. For Larkin, like Mill, address offers not real interplay between *I*s and *you*s, but recognition of our essential estrangement: it is 'the lament of a prisoner in a solitary cell, ourselves listening, unseen, in the next'.[96]

Larkin's emphasis on common diction, and his gravitation towards everyday communicative situations and familiar phrasings and addresses was, at least on the surface, anti-elitist, and anti-authoritarian in nature. In that respect his work, and that of much Movement writing, is not dissimilar to much contemporary lyricism, as exemplified by the bluff middlebrow tone put on from time to time by our four poets. The chief difference lies in the Movement's allying 'normal', everyday speech with anti-Modernist styles and principles, as if they would not be persuaded to meet. Writing of contemporary poetry, Peter Howarth has commented: 'it would be nice to imagine the aspiring poet [...] resolving not to be co-opted by either side, and encouraging herself by the thought of half-a-dozen contemporary poets who don't fit into such either/or generalisations'.[97] But, motivated by the urge to democratize literature to a wider reading public—a community of like-minded, everyday *you*s—that anti-Modernist shift was, and continues to be, highly influential. It can be seen in much of the work of our more popular contemporary poets, including Carol Ann Duffy, Wendy Cope, Sean O'Brien, and Andrew Motion. To take the latter, by way of example:

> I took your news outdoors, and strolled a while
> In silence on my square of garden-ground
> Where I could dim the roar of arguments,
> Ignore the scandal-flywheel whirring round
>   'Spring Wedding', 2005

Motion's lyric address, here, avoids the linguistic convolutions of experimental and Modernist writing. Like Larkin, whose biographer he is, Motion's address steers away from the panoply of speaking voices and disorienting formal devices that one sees in the evidently experimental poetry of Eliot and Pound, Basil Bunting and David Jones, and later, in

[95] Herbert F. Tucker, 'Dramatic Monologue and the Overhearing of Lyric', in *Lyric Poetry: Beyond New Criticism*, ed. Chaviva Hôsek and Patricia Parker (Ithaca and London: Cornell University Press, 1985) 226–43, 242.

[96] Mill, 'What is Poetry?' 350.

[97] Peter Howarth, *British Poetry in the Age of Modernism* (Cambridge: Cambridge University Press, 2005) 1.

the work of Veronica Forrest-Thomson, J. H. Prynne, Geraldine Monk, and Denise Riley, and which is also present, in dialogue with realist speech styles, in the poetry of Douglas Dunn, Jo Shapcott, Sisson, Graham, Hill, Roy Fisher, Tony Harrison, and Selima Hill, amongst numerous others. In so doing, even as Motion's address marks out poetry's role in public ceremony—the lines were written in honour of the Prince of Wales's marriage to Camilla Parker Bowles[98]—his verse plays down, as Modernist poetry (and latter-day Modernists) did not, its performance of literary, cultural, and historical negotiations, and its speaker's and addressees' varied and variable identities.

Even though, as Howarth states, 'it is [...] certain that British poetry has been irrevocably changed by modernism [...] it follows according to the logic of "Tradition and the Individual Talent" that the arrival of free verse has, if ever so slightly, altered the whole tradition of poetry, including the poetry written expressly to ignore it', much contemporary poetry in the Movement vein proclaimed to be written precisely 'to ignore it' (3). Gravitating towards realist speech-styles, and stringently avoiding collage, myth, fragmentation, and free verse, Movement poetics effectively signposted its difference from Modernism. But it also elided signposting to its readers its significant similarities: its explorations of fraught cultural, national, and political agendas in an increasingly polysemous modern world. These are explorations that recurred over the contested and difficult figure of *you*.[99] Many of the Movement's seemingly transparent, nonchalant addresses tended to screen poetry's participation in the construction, or preservation, of social, political, and national narratives *with their readers*. Using reassuringly common idioms and habitual expressions, Larkin's poetry, for instance, often played up the everyday nature of the sentiments espoused: the second-person pronoun helps the speaker appear to be already on the reader's side, part of the *you* addressed:

> [...] that padlocked cube of light
> We neither define nor prove,
> Where you, we dream, obtain no right of entry.
> 'Dry Point' 49

[98] See the BBC website for the poem, and the context of Motion's address, Saturday 9 April 2005 <http://news.bbc.co.uk/1/hi/uk/4427239.stm>, accessed 6 August 2009.

[99] As Alex Davis and Lee M. Jenkins point out, such work: 'puts up barriers to understanding the diversity of poetic modernism [...] accepting too quickly and uncritically the commonplace that modernism is a transnational or even supranational entity', 'Locating Modernisms: An Overview', in *Locations of Literary Modernism: Region and Nation in British and American Modernist Poetry*, ed. Davis and Jenkins (Cambridge: Cambridge University Press, 2000) 3–29, 3–4.

Comparably, in 'Places, Loved Ones':

> You ask them to bear
> You off irrevocably,
> So that it's not your fault
> Should the town turn dreary,
> The girl a dolt.   (46)

In both poems, Larkin seems to speak to readers directly: his *you* is part of an implied 'us'. The audience is hailed as one of his kind, so that pronouns appear interchangeable: 'Where you, we dream', we are essentially the same. In speaking thus, *I* speaks for us all, in a shared verbal currency and a set of easily acknowledged, communal values: the poem brooks no dissent. Larkin's speaker addresses us as a persona he hopes we will recognize as an ordinary chap, a companionable everyman, slightly disgruntled, dreaming of the 'right of entry', the 'irrevocable' love, that one and all will share and desire.

It also helps that this accessible, frank speaker has, as quotidian addressees, real people that exist outside the poem. In 'Born Yesterday (for Sally Amis)':

> May you be ordinary;
> Have, like other women,
> An average of talents:
> Not ugly, not good-looking,
> Nothing uncustomary
> To pull you off your balance   (54)

Here, the speaker (Larkin) and interlocutor (Sally Amis) seem knowable and stable. One is allowed to assume the *I* is Larkin himself, speaking to a named recipient, to whom the poem is dedicated. But if Larkin's *you* can be located as an embodied and real individual—the daughter of the poet's friend, Kingsley Amis—any impression of easy companionship is troubled by the actual age of its addressee. At the time of writing, Sally Amis is a newborn baby. Larkin's apparently stable correspondence with his interlocutor is further troubled by the speaker issuing a plea to *you* to remain 'average', as if his addressee might well be threatened by the introduction of something 'uncustomary' which would 'pull you off your balance'. *I* has to persuade *you* to stay 'ordinary', as if this were rather a precarious, imperilled value—more difficult to achieve than beauty or talent. As David Gervais has commented, 'this process, manifestos apart, was never a simple triumph of the ordinary as Larkin seems to have liked to think. Rather it was the Movement's gift to *seem* ordinary, to be wolves who went dressed as sheep.'[100]

---

[100] David Gervais, *Literary Englands: Versions of 'Englishness' in Modern Writing* (Cambridge: Cambridge University Press, 1993) 212.

Gervais's comment puts one in mind of Tom Paulin's critique of Larkin in 'Into the Heart of Englishness'.[101] Reading the opening lines of Larkin's 'Afternoons' (115):

> Summer is fading;
> The leaves fall in ones and twos

Paulin argues that the poem uses an accessible lyricism, reminiscent of the rural simplicity of A. E. Housman's style, and the familiar theme of a personally observed landscape, to get away with positing as natural and unarguable a very specific, national agenda:

> The sad lyricism is rooted in a culture, but the poem's plaintive terseness encourages us to elevate the emotion into a universal value and to miss Larkin's real theme – national decline. [...] this is a metaphor for a sense of diminished purpose and fading imperial power. Incipient middle age is like a return to the middle ages, to the English people's faint, marginal, early history. The poem's lonely voice promises an exit from history into personal emotion, but that private space turns out to be social after all. This lyric poem is therefore a subtly disguised public poem, for it comments on a social experience.[102]   *Of course ; the personal is political*

To Paulin's mind, Movement lyrics forestall this recognition, harking back to an imperialist vision of past unity which appears to transcend conflict and political struggle. Whether or not one agrees with Paulin about Larkin, one might derive from his general observation that certain poems, often in the Movement vein, create a relationship with *you* that appears, for some reason, to free itself from the political. The everyday, unacademic speaker makes out to be 'one of us'; his address innocent of pretension or conceit, and of the concealed highbrow manipulations of 'difficult' writing.

In contrast, one might identify the often embattled language of address of, say, Douglas Dunn: 'Let me hear you admit / [...] / What likes of us did for the likes of you; / We did not raze this garden that we made, / Although we hanged you somewhere in its shade',[103] or Thomas Kinsella: 'You condescend to hear us speak / Only when we slap your cheek', 'We speak in wounds. Behold this mess. / My curse upon your politesse',[104] or Seamus Heaney: 'Still, for Jesus' sake / Do me a favour, would you, just

---

[101] Tom Paulin, 'Into the Heart of Englishness' (1990), in *Philip Larkin*, ed. Stephen Regan (Basingstoke: Palgrave Macmillan, 1997) 160–77. See also Keith Tuma, *Fishing By Obstinate Isles: Modern and Postmodern British Poetry and American Readers* (Illinois: Northwestern University Press, 1999) 194–5.
[102] Paulin, 'Into the Heart of Englishness' 160–1.
[103] Dunn, 'Gardeners' (1979), *DSP* 106.
[104] Thomas Kinsella, *Butcher's Dozen* (1972), in *Collected Poems* (Manchester: Carcanet, 1991) 135–6.

this once?',[105] as flagging up not mere personal grumbles with a private interlocutor, but social and political concerns. Certainly, for Dunn, Heaney, and Kinsella, as for Harrison: 'Larkin's invitation to consensus, his desire to transform the experience of what he often viewed as the decay of meaning attendant upon the passing of an older England into new and debased but nevertheless shared values and perspectives is replaced by "a recognition that the individual and acts of culture are defined by issues of access, ownership, property and rights"', as Keith Tuma has argued.[106]

Part of the problem with Larkin's rejection of 'difficulty' is that it paradoxically ends up distorting lived experience. Difficulty is also a part of the ordinary public world; a part of our daily verbal and social struggle with others. In barring this from the lyric space, a poem falsely suggests that quotidian language is 'really' straightforward and transparent. The poet cannot be straightforwardly at one with his addressee, as if art were a mere vehicle for sharing meanings with *you*. Rather, *I* and *you* engage in confused, confusing, and sometimes hostile relations. One could call to mind, for instance, the addresses of Dunn, Heaney, Kinsella, and Harrison, which show us the turbulence, and violence, of the verbal process. An essential component of the aesthetic act is that it offers a medium in which civic relations are negotiated and shaped, and roles, relations, and minds changed. If Modernist addresses made clear that poetry is not a neutral, friendly, or tidy space, the work of Graham, Sisson, Hill, and Paterson is important in bringing this recognition into the conflicted present. These writers are of particular interest in a study of contemporary poetic address, given their sense of language as historical, densely peopled. These poets offer us idiosyncratic perspectives onto a shared recognition about contemporary poetry: they remind us insistently that lyric language—far from private contact—is embedded in the *polis*. Poetic address is public action, engaging in, and taking shape from, a shared history of voicings resounding in everyday contemporary discourse: 'Politics, RAPMASTER, múst be a part / of óur conformable mystery, this / twinship of loathing and true commonweal' (*SS* 95:48).

*

This book's focus on mainstream contemporary British poetry does not set out to indicate a dominant geographical, cultural, and literary centre to address. Nor is addressing *you* in public in any way exclusive to Graham, Sisson, Hill, and Paterson. The close relationship between speaking to *you*

---

[105] Seamus Heaney, 'Weighing In', *The Spirit Level* (London: Faber, 1996) 18.
[106] See Tuma, *Fishing By Obstinate Isles* 195. Tuma quotes from David Kennedy's Bloodaxe anthology of New Generation poets, at 15.

and poetry's operations in the public sphere is evident in the work of a wide range of poets writing today. It's found elsewhere, for instance, in the *avant-garde* British poetry of J. H. Prynne, Geraldine Monk, and Lee Harwood; in the contemporary Irish work of, say, Muldoon, Heaney, and Kinsella (as we've touched on); as well as in much American lyricism: Robert Creeley, Denise Levertov, John Ashbery, Louise Glück.[107] For the sake of clarity and concision, I have chosen to focus on four comparable figures within post-1960s mainstream British lyricism, each of whom attempts accessibly to listen back on his Modernist and Movement forbears. I have not included any extensive focus on *avant-garde*, Irish, or American writing (where comparable social and literary-historical address are frequently played out, but manifest rather differently).

That said, experimental writers are not absent from the book's weave—they turn up as occasional points of reference; just as the addresses of Heaney and Muldoon, Wallace Stevens and Plath are touched on, from time to time, as orientating figures. I should add that, even within what might be called 'mainstream' British writing, other figures, besides our particular lyric quartet, could have been selected as major protagonists, and would have created a comparable narrative thrust. Tony Harrison, Douglas Dunn, and Carol Ann Duffy come to mind, as do Anne Stevenson, Tom Leonard, and Roy Fisher. Again, we'll find addresses by these poets entering the story at various points, as we journey through the book: for our four poets find themselves in dialogue with the wide range of twentieth- and twenty-first-century socio-political and aesthetic voices that are heard in British poetry's intimate interlocutions.

To my mind, it is the later volumes of these four poets that pull together the richest range of addresses and contexts. For this reason, this book predominantly explores the poets' mature works (from the late 1960s onward). These volumes most fluently move between hailing

---

[107] For *avant-garde* poets using address see J. H. Prynne, *For the Monogram* and *High Pink on Chrome* ('Please delete, don't sleep yet, not / too sure to get shot through upstream', 'you hadn't noticed that'), in *Poems* (Newcastle: Bloodaxe, 1982) 461, 216; Geraldine Monk, *Ghost & Other Sonnets*: 'Couched / Blusters of embarrassments. You! You!' (Cambridge: Salt, 2008) 8; Lee Harwood, '5 Rungs up Sassongher' ('I don't even know yet / Talking to you? to myself? to the "ether"?') in *Collected Poems* (Exeter: Shearsman, 2004) 472. For Irish poets using address, see notes 37, 41, 103, 104 above. For Creeley, see 'For W.C.W', ('There, you say, and/there'), in Robert Creeley, *Selected Poems, 1945–2005*, ed. Benjamin Friedlander (London: University of California Press, 2008) 87; Denise Levertov, 'The Rights' ('I want to give you / something I've made / some words on a page') in *Here and Now* (San Francisco: City Lights, 1957); John Ashbery, 'Not You Again', in *Your Name Here* (New York: Farrar, Straus & Giroux, 2001) 7; Louise Glück, 'Scilla' and 'End of Winter' ('not I, you idiot, not self, but we, we—') in *The Wild Iris* (New York: Ecco Press, 1993) 14. See John E. Vincent, *John Ashbery and You: His Later Books* (Athens and London: University of Georgia Press, 2007).

different kinds of *you*, as well as revealing these *particular* writers' most developed literary historical visions. (I am not articulating a generalizable sense of progress in poetic achievement to the present.) Additionally, the later works of these poets are especially articulate about their ties with, and in their criticisms of, Eliotic and Poundian Modernism. Graham's work, moving from his early New-Apocalypse leanings in the 1940s and 1950s, where the poems are characterized by much Thomasian word-play, becomes tighter, leaner, and more angular in the 1960s, 1970s, and 1980s, where we can hear more clearly the interplay between Eliotic, Joycean, and Poundian voices and the straight-talking, unabashedly heckling Larkinesque addresses. Hill's volumes from the 1990s onward are of particular interest in their sportively barbed relations with editors, critics, and audience-figures: in reassessing the politics of literary production in the earlier part of the century, Hill's poems also listen in to the civic negotiations in Ancient Greek and Roman culture, Anglo-Saxon panegyric, and the fraught lyric interlocutions of the early modern and Romantic periods. Not dissimilarly, Paterson's *Orpheus*, *Landing Light*, and *Rain* (as well as the earlier *Nil Nil*, *God's Gift to Women*, and *The Eyes*) are informed by the historical sense that the poem's language is indebted to a people's embattled representations of identity and locale: 'superimposed over absolute silence, / [...] / You have *Scottish Renaissance*, *Café Volatire* / and *Library*' (*Gift* 47); 'whispering *Are ye sure? Are ye sure?* / [...] / the bus will let us down in another country / with the wrong streets and streets that suddenly forget / their names at crossroads' (*Gift* 12). Amongst Paterson's sources for the literary and romantic discourses of the twenty-first century are the intimate demands of medieval Arabic courtly culture, and of classical patronage systems. Each of these writers can be seen negotiating, in his work from the 1970s onward, the shaping pressures of ancient and modern poetry upon contemporary address.

Sisson proves a slight exception: his addresses are most intertextually inflected, and pull together most tightly the threads of national, civic, and personal address, around the 1970s (around the same period as Graham's late poems). But these volumes are written and published in his mid-period: *In the Trojan Ditch* (1974), *Anchises* (1976), and *Exactions* (1980). These volumes owe a clear debt to Modernist syntax and form, as well as notions of history and language. The link is weakened, and I think to the work's detriment, towards the end of Sisson's career, in the volumes published after 1983, particularly in *Antidotes* (1991) and *What and Who* (1994), which have more in common, I find, with the nostalgic conservative address typical of some Movement verse. At this point in his career, Sisson is also less successful at handling the plain-speaking vernacular voice. These volumes, which predominantly address an unspecified *you*, or renounce *you* altogether for a generalized *them*, often lecture and hector their interlocutors, becoming increasingly dogmatic about communicating their imperilled sense of the historical, cultural, and national understandings of the present.

Through their addresses, these poets bring literary trends and fashions, dominant formal and political ideologies into contact with explorations of class and cultural antagonism, which often take place as they give voice to a *you*. Their interlocutions bend to accommodate but also answer back to the demands that shape the literary mainstream. There is some noisy retaliation against the 'pigheadedness of the editors and contributors [...] the noisy politics of the moment'.[108] These poets are by no means alone in issuing vituperative, socially minded addresses: a number of well-known British texts use the second-person pronoun alongside the heckling, argumentative, rude, and demotic vernacular: Tony Harrison's 'v' is a good example; so too, Douglas Dunn's *Barbarians*, Carol Ann Duffy's 'Poet for Our Times', and Tom Leonard's 'The 6 O'Clock News', come to mind— as do the often savagely counter-cultural addresses of Linton Kwesi Johnson and Benjamin Zephaniah.[109] Our four poets offer different angles into the social, public speech tapped by much British writing today. Hostile address becomes a fruitful tool in negotiating the tides of public taste: speaking to particular and general *you*s, literary texts comment on and participate in the economic, social, and political imperatives that govern poetry's dissemination and valuation. 'You áre / wantonly obscure, *man sagt*. ACCESSIBLE / traded as DEMOCRATIC, he answers' writes Hill, using address to a slippery *you* to scrutinize the debates and disagreements that surround art's role in public life (*SS* 118:59). To read such address is to encounter work that raises its eyebrow at the notion of speaking to others as 'obscure', or as *always* 'an act of radical interiorization and solipsism'. These four British poets provide us with fresh and accessible perspectives onto how lyric addresses operate as public acts today. In each, to speak to *you* is to talk intimately, immediately, and to insist on the political and social clout of that voicing. In each, address underlines the fraught role of language—both public and personal—in establishing shared senses of reality, identity, and nationhood.

[108] Sisson, Editorial from *PN Review* 5:2 (1977), see *Avoidance* 559.
[109] See Tony Harrison, *Selected Poems* (1984; London: Penguin, 1987) 235–49, cited hereafter as *HSP*; Dunn, *DSP*; Duffy, *Selected Poems*; Tom Leonard, *Intimate Voices: Selected Work, 1965–1983* (London: Vintage, 1995).

PART I

W. S. GRAHAM

Approaches To How You Behave

1
Speaking To You

[…] this dedication is for others to read:
These are private words addressed to you in public.
'A Dedication to My Wife', T. S. Eliot

Throughout his career, W. S. Graham wrote of his need to address 'the difficulty of speaking from a fluid identity'.[1] 'Difficulty' and 'fluidity' indicate a poetry racked by numberless alterations. But constant change also offered a paradoxical consistency: 'This / Is the place fastened still with movement', he wrote in 'The Nightfishing' in 1951: 'At this last word all words change', 'my place constantly anew'.[2] Graham's sense in 'The Nightfishing' that language organizes us—'Each word speaks its own speaker' (115)—is supported by his later lyric insistence that 'words make their world'.[3] For Graham, the mutability of being 'Between this word and the next' is not an isolating, but a shared condition.[4] *I* and *you* change, and change in, the alterable public world. Just as for the earlier generation of Modernist writers—one might name Eliot, Pound, and Stevens—reality is a fluid facet of language, up for negotiation, so it is for Graham, whose poems and letters portray being as fragmented, constituted through experience.

Linking language with inconsistency, flux—'in this poem I am / Whoever elsewhere I am', 'This is myself (who but ill resembles me)'[5]— Graham's most widely read volumes, *The Nightfishing*, *Malcolm Mooney's Land*, and *Implements in Their Places* form the chief focus of this chapter.[6] In each, Graham depicts a world in which words are not obediently

---

[1] James Vinson and D. L. Kirkpatrick, eds., *Contemporary Poets*, 2nd edn. (New York: St. Martin's Press, 1975) 575.
[2] 'The Nightfishing' (1951), in *NCP* 116–17. All references to Graham's poetry will be quoted from this volume.
[3] 'The Thermal Stair' (1970), *NCP* 164.
[4] 'The Dark Dialogues' (1959), *NCP* 174.
[5] 'Dialogues' 169; 'Nightfishing' 117.
[6] *The Nightfishing; Malcolm Mooney's Land* (London: Faber, 1970); *Implements in Their Places*, all in *NCP*.

representative, and language neither serves as a vehicle for self-expression, nor lends itself to autobiography. In this, as I will argue, Graham's lyrics differentiate themselves from the mid-century realist poetics of Philip Larkin, D. J. Enright, and Donald Davie, in so far as these writers attempted faithfully to represent an amenable, agreed-upon world. For Graham, any appeal to a 'true' self or experience before language is unreliable, suspect, since even 'myself [...] ill resembles me'. Semblance and dissemblance play through his writing, for each 'I' cannot remain coincident with itself, and may be exposed as a forgery.

Graham's critics have often complained that his oeuvre is repetitively subjectivist, 'essentially private'.[7] Many consider him solipsistic, obsessed with isolation, or vainly struggling for connection. Others regard his verse as intellectually abstracted, trapped in 'its own intoxication with language', 'excessively literary', exhibiting 'a tenuous, mistrustful dependence on the word'.[8] Such comments are not unlike those grumbles levelled against Modernist poetics.[9] Graham, like his Modernist forebears, often writes of estrangement and verbal misunderstandings. But he, like them, emphasizes the constitutive *social* role that language plays, both in the poems, where language is 'a shape arising from all men', and in the letters, where he observes: 'A way of speaking, if it is any good [...] creates its understanders.'[10] Words are a means of mutual sense-making; they establish the roles of speakers, recipients, 'understanders'. Words alter and create, giving birth to selves and relations.

No longer simply reflective or representational, Graham's language '*makes* a world of ideas enriching to enter'.[11] This illuminating comment is taken from Graham's complimentary letter to the English poet

---

[7] See Alan Bold, *Modern Scottish Literature* (London and New York: Longmans, 1983) 71–5. Also Damien Grant, who writes of Graham's 'obsession with identity, consciousness and articulation', in 'Walls of Glass: The Poetry of W. S. Graham', *British Poetry Since 1970: A Critical Survey*, ed. Peter Jones and Michael Schmidt (Manchester: Carcanet, 1980) 22–38, 28.

[8] John Kinsella, 'Under the Surface', Rev. of *New Collected Poems*, *Observer*, Sunday, 29 February 2004, 17; Kenneth Allott, *The Penguin Book of Contemporary Verse* (Harmondsworth: Penguin, 1962) 309; Michael Schmidt, *An Introduction to Fifty Modern British Poets* (London: Pan, 1979) 302.

[9] See J. C. C. Mays, 'Early Poems from "Prufrock" to "Gerontion"', in *The Cambridge Companion to T. S. Eliot*, ed. Anthony David Moody (Cambridge: Cambridge University Press, 1994) 108–21, 115; Leonard Diepeveen, *The Difficulties of Modernism* (London: Routledge, 2003); and Jonathan Culler and Kevin Lamb, eds., *Just Being Difficult? Academic Writing in the Public Arena* (Stanford: Stanford University Press, 2003).

[10] Letter to Ruth Hilton, 21 March 1967, published in *The Nightfisherman: Selected Letters of W. S. Graham* (Manchester: Carcanet, 1999) 210. Unless stated otherwise, all references to Graham's letters will be quoted from *Selected Letters*, hereafter referred to as *Nightfisherman*.

[11] Letter to C. H. Sisson, 31 December 1967, 212, my emphasis.

C. H. Sisson; a letter that paved the way for what became a series of literary exchanges between the two writers. Language's 'making', in this case, is clearly not mere abstraction; for Graham's way of speaking makes out of Sisson a new 'understander', a real poetic co-respondent and ally. Writing, for Graham, is not, as many of his critics have argued, an entry point into a private verbal realm, 'a bounded, protected place [...] [where] the author can play freely without interference from anybody else'.[12] Rather, writing is an opening onto the flexible public sphere, an assertion of one's place in the world of writers, readers, artists, critics, reviewers, and publishers. In Graham's letters, this is a world in which such figures as Edwin Morgan, Sven Berlin, David Wright, Harold Pinter, and J. F. Hendry are addressed. In the poems, too, Graham speaks to a host of artists and writers, including the poet and critic Robin Skelton, the St Ives painters Bryan Wynter, Roger Hilton and Peter Lanyon, and the American poet and editor Norman Macleod.

Retaining his position within these communities, however, demands a good measure of worldly savvy from the impoverished Scottish writer. 'I am well aware I write to you for my own furtherance', Graham confesses wryly, in a 1969 letter to Edwin Morgan.[13] His need to beg furtherance forms a familiar refrain in the letters, which often find themselves shamefacedly requesting favours (usually financial) from colleagues and fellow writers. As if in exchange for money, goods, or poetic recommendation, Graham repeatedly proffers a conspicuous display of verbal ingenuity: 'EMBARRASSING LETTER [...] I would like you to lend me £5 [...] I enclose a stamped, addressed envelope and hope we shall have the favour of your business in the future [...] Yours truly, chairman of the bored, W S Graham. THE MILK OF HUMAN KINDNESS IS CONDENSED.'[14] Graham's daily realities turn out to be dependent upon clever verbal contact: language is his means of securing simple, domestic necessities: 'The £5 is necessary to pay milk and existing grocery bill and get some coal against the season's blast', 'first let me get this over with [...] The Electricity Bill and a bill for the glazier have come in [...] Now would it be best for you to post to us two cheques for those amounts.'[15] On the one hand, poetry-writing is viewed by such lean, economic lights. Writing is Graham's primary means of paying his way,

---

[12] Matthew Francis believes that poems are unavoidable forms of social engagement, but that Graham works under the illusion that poems offer him 'bounded, protected places'. In so doing, Graham's words leave his speakers and recipients feeling isolated from one another (24–5).

[13] 14 October 1969, 234.

[14] Letter to Roger Hilton, 8 November 1968, 222–3.

[15] *Nightfisherman* 223; Letter to Bryan Wynter, 11 May 1968, 213–14.

not just some elitist luxury: 'This is against POETRY (Chicago), paying me in June the amount of £26 10 0. Remember this is not a funny half-blackmail-lone. [sic] I'll send POETRY'S cheque and you please will cash it' (214), 'the Scottish Arts Council have awarded me £300. That is an inside WC on to our house [...] a wee bit recognition'.[16] On the other hand, luxuries are not necessarily private matters, and singing for his supper does not prevent Graham from luxuriating in that song. If Graham's words operate as currency, the process of barter remains laced with mischief and delight, as well as prosaic frugality. It is, after all, precisely because Graham is being paid for it that he can afford a private joke, on the Scottish Arts Council's expenses: '£300. That is an inside WC [...] a wee bit recognition'.

For Graham, lyricism is not separate from the workaday world, from proletarian concerns, or from the economic drive for money and success. His poems and letters are public spaces, desirous to circulate and, in certain respects, to co-opt addressees. Graham is not afraid of starkly pointing up the politics of poetic patronage, even in apparently personal addresses to friends in 'private poems':

> Remember the title. A PRIVATE
> POEM TO NORMAN MACLEOD.
> But this, my boy, is the poem
> You paid me five pounds for.[17]

Such writing enables Graham to poke fun at the idea of writing as an ideal realm of exclusive privacy and pure personal contact. He leads us on, of course: the title, and the style of the poem itself, are set up to lure readers into thinking of the lyric as autobiographical, with readers listening in on Graham's personal correspondence. Direct address between the named author (Graham) and the really existing, named recipient (Graham's friend, the painter Norman Macleod) creates the impression of immediate dialogue, as if the poem were conversing in front of us, unmindful of its readers. The poem is written in the second-person, the pronominal form commonly associated with personal contact, one-to-one conversation: 'you', 'my boy'. Notational and casual idiom—'Remember the title'—similarly conspire to create the impression of direct contact between Graham and Macleod, a correspondence that seems so caught up in speaking with its addressee that it forgets its audience. But the poem, it turns out, is highly attentive to audience reception, to being scoured more generally, by 'the vast bat of unseen eyes'. Concerned to put on a

---

[16] Letter to Robin Skelton, 7 May 1970, 241.
[17] 'Private Poem to Norman Macleod' (1974), in *NCP* 227.

fine performance, Graham dons the guise of privation in order to enter-tain and intrigue his unknown readership. He writes at least as much to conjure, through address, this book-buying audience, as his named inter-locutor. Continually alert to its future published, public status, and to the appeal of tapping into the form of poem-as-letter, the poem uses the notion of lyricism as private correspondence to attract future readers. They will want most of all, Graham predicts, to listen in on words not intended for them to hear. This writing pulls the concepts of reader and writer, speaker and addressee, *I* and *you* into a complex network of rela-tions and contacts. Such addressees are at least as much Graham's readers, as his explicit, known recipients. This slippery *you* calls out for further investigation.

Graham's lyric focus on saying *you*, then, takes shape as he performs complex negotiations in the political-cultural fray. His address oscillates between resistance to and fascination with the shaping forces of social and national identity. Born in Greenock in 1918, and growing up during the second generation Scottish Renaissance (1920–45), Graham could not fail to be aware of the significance that many of his poetic contemporar-ies, in particular Hugh MacDiarmid, placed upon constructing a specifically Scottish literary language. Graham was a contemporary and occasional correspondent of MacDiarmid's, but he was not a follower of the Scottish Renaissance, and he did not regard his own poetry as a plat-form for the assertion of national identity or cultural independence: 'I do recognise a Scots timbre in my "voice" although I can't see myself, in any way, as characteristic of Scots poetry.'[18] Graham is also strongly critical of Hugh MacDiarmid's insistence upon using, and upon making others use, poetic language as a nationalist statement. In a characteristic parody of MacDiarmid's eager reconstitution of Lowland Scottish or 'Synthetic Scots' dialects, Graham writes: 'the Scottish Lit Scene [...] I don't hold with and seems to get more embarrassing with its playing bards glumerin lufts keekin wi sna.'[19]

Although Graham regarded many of the aims of the Scottish literary scene as prescriptive and artificial, the poems do not reject his Greenock background. Until the end of his career, Graham is still frequently draw-ing on memory, place, and the past, as the titles of poems such as 'A Page About My Country' (281), 'Loch Thom' (220), 'Sgurr Na Gillean Ma-cleod' (223), 'To Alexander Graham' (222) make clear. The lyrics also frequently incorporate early experiences of Clydeside speech and life, and 'Baldy Bane', 'The Broad Close', and 'The Greenock Dialogues' are

---

[18] Vinson and Kirkpatrick, *Contemporary Poets* 575.
[19] Letter to Moncrieff Williamson, undated, *c.*January 1949, 80.

interspersed with dialect words and specifically Scottish ballad rhythms.[20] Anthologists of the 1940s and 1950s, however, repeatedly turned a blind eye to Graham: his exclusion from *An Anthology of the Scottish Renaissance 1920–1945*[21] caused him anger at the time ('the smug insensitive cheek of it'), and wounded pride subsequently.[22] As late as 1970 he writes: 'I have always been a wee bit hurt (JOKE OR NOT JOKE?) that Scotland have never said anything about their exiled boy here, me.'[23]

'Exile' is an interesting choice of word, indicating banishment by others, rather than a choice willingly made, whilst the grammatically in-correct 'Scotland have' sets up the language of a victimizing group of others ('them') against the final, isolated 'me'. That 'me'—thrust towards Graham's reader, friend, and fellow-poet, Robin Skelton—comes close to a performed address, in which Graham is able to stage a version of himself as a sufferer of years of cultural and financial estrangement (even as he invites his interlocutor to share his energetic delight in having 'just had word that the Scottish Arts Council have awarded me £300'). If Graham felt estranged from Scotland as a result of his relocation to St Ives in 1954, those feelings were, of course, partly a result of his own self-exile—not merely inflicted upon him, as the syntax of his address to Skelton rather misleadingly implies. Graham's phrasing ('their [...] boy') indicates both his persisting sense of belonging, and his ability loudly to insist upon it, in spite of his stated intellectual and geographical banishment. As Ralph Pite and Hester Jones comment: '[h]is writing arises out of a sense of non-affiliation, partly chosen and partly imposed upon him'.[24]

In the poems too, relationships with others are a mixture of choice and imposition, taking their shape as much from accident as from inten-tion, and as much from willed exile as affinity. Alignment with others, particularly with established movements or schools of thought, is beset with difficulties: perpetual alteration and reworking make alignments precarious, changeable, unstable. Meanwhile, the desire for alignment often involves, Graham would argue, a mistaken belief that changeless stability is preferable to flux. In his essay 'Notes on A Poetry of Release' Graham writes that he *wishes* to be 'a man who searches continually

[20] 'Baldy Bane' (1954), *NCP* 145–50; 'The Broad Close' (1954), *NCP* 141–5. Both draw upon Scottish place, dialects, and rhythms in their ballad form. 'The Greenock Dia-logues' (1993) incorporates dialect words, whilst many sections of the poem 'Implements in Their Places' vividly evoke Scotland.
[21] Maurice Lindsay, ed., *Modern Scottish Poetry: An Anthology of the Scottish Renaissance, 1920–1945* (London: Faber, 1946).
[22] Letter to William Montgomerie, undated [Autumn 1946] 68.
[23] Letter to Robin Skelton, 7 May 1970, 241.
[24] 'Introduction: Contacting Graham', in *W. S. Graham: Speaking Towards You*, ed. Ralph Pite and Hester Jones (Liverpool: Liverpool University Press, 2004) 1–9, 3.

[who] is a new searcher with his direction changing at every step'; a man flexible enough to continue negotiating his sense of to what, and to whom, he belongs.[25] To Graham's mind, flexibility depends on resisting the urge to follow in others' footsteps. A writer who longs for a greater fixity of direction will search for more well-trodden ground, affiliating himself to institutions, disciplines, and funding bodies, or vociferously forging national allegiances. Or he may court favour, attention, and popular recognition. Graham, in contrast, is uneasy about setting too much store by others' veneration: 'Everybody seems to love me. But That is Not The Point.'[26]

In a letter to Moncrieff Williamson in 1950, Graham writes of his indebtedness to Eliot, who had supported him in his early work, and had shown a good deal of enthusiasm about his long poem 'The Night-fishing': 'A nice letter from Tommy E. saying the N.F. is a whizz for sticking together and being a long poem.'[27] Graham's phrasing is casual ('Tommy E.', 'a whizz'), and his tone lightly self-ironizing. The thrill of approbation is to be played down. Even on occasions of fairly unambiguous literary success, Graham remains suspicious that recognition, flattery, and fame might anchor him, rather too rigidly, to the designs of others. Gleeful at being awarded a Civil Pension in 1974 he writes: 'Christ, what a responsibility. Dammit does this mean I will no longer be able to excuse my laziness and drunkenness by pleading money-worry?'[28] Similarly, after a trip to Canada, full of heady excitement at the success of his poetry readings, Graham is keen to deflate his ego with a reminder of the institutional character of that praise. He has some fun at the faculty's expense: 'every reading went well. I have never read better. When I came back Nessie had had a pile of postcards from various deans, administers, fuckulty members, and plain wild students, saying how great the poetry and the readings were.'[29] If aligning himself too thoroughly with their approval would risk sliding into staid, faculty acceptability, an iconoclastic description of his admirers goes some way towards distancing him from the praise they offer. Their compliments, Graham feels, remained positioned, political, for the 'members' are keen to reward only what they already believe a poet ought to offer. In spite of their praise, 'I could feel impatience in me at their constant effort to make a Canadian culture.'[30]

[25] 'Notes on a Poetry of Release' (1946), in *Nightfisherman* 379–83.
[26] Letter to Nessie Graham, 21 November 1973, 269.
[27] Quoted in Peter Kravitz, ed., 'The Life and Work of W. S. Graham', *Edinburgh Review* 75 (1987) 6–109, 10; not included in *Nightfisherman*.
[28] Letter to Robin Skelton, 31 January 1974, 274.
[29] Letter to Bill and Gail Featherstone, 4 December 1973, 270.
[30] Letter to Charles Monteith, 29 March 1974, 277.

Emerging clearly from Graham's work is the sense that a poet is inadequately defined though his exclusive relation with cultural or national identity. One has to avoid confining poetry's significance to how well, or ill, it fits with literary movements, with, say, The Movement, or Modernism, or the New Apocalypse poets. But exiling oneself from trends is not the same as being 'inward-directed' or 'obsessed with the self'. Had he lived to hear it, Graham would have been likely to have had much sympathy with a comment made by Geoffrey Hill: 'What we call the writer's "distinctive voice" is a registering of different voices.'[31] 'Distinctive' speaks of distinction, of being perceived as unique, and distinguishable. What work, then, does this 'registering of different voices' perform upon a writer's distinguished individual voicing? Hill's remark questions the notion of uniqueness as individual and unrepeatable, by implying a writer's unique tone is, at least in part, derivative. Distinctive voices are not pure and original, but always informed by the interlocutions of other writers and writings, manoeuvring the common circumstances of language spoken to, and with, other *yous*. Secondly, Hill disturbs the notion of authority and praise implicit in being distinguished. The gravity and poise associated with honoured poetic distinction arrives only after the messy creative event, for *I*'s 'distinctive voice' is a result of differences that have been knit together precariously; the influence of past literary masters, the tastes of the poet's present readership, the current political climate. 'A registering of different voices' does not necessarily indicate elevated self-possession, or harmony with the varying voices one registers as present. One could orchestrate a cacophony.

This voicing, then, however distinctive, is not solipsistic. 'He do the police in different voices' Eliot wrote, and used as his working title for *The Waste Land*.[32] That is a registering of the different, and authoritative, voice of Eliot that polices Hill's own comment from *The Enemy's Country: Words, Contextures and Other Circumstances of Language*. Eliot's words are a circumstance of language that contextualize Hill's more recent noticing. Uniqueness of voice leads us back to other users, and uses, of the language. Uniqueness, in that sense, is social, negotiated with other *yous*. Those writers who receive praise for distinctiveness are likely to tell us as much about their audience, and its current preoccupations and established

[31] 'Dryden's Prize Song', originally a 1986 Clark Lecture at Trinity College, Cambridge. Published in Geoffrey Hill, *The Enemy's Country: Words, Contextures and Other Circumstances of Language* (Stanford: Stanford University Press, 1991) 63–82, 80, hereafter referred to as *EC*. See *CCW* 241.

[32] That sentence, found at the top of some of the typed pages of the manuscript of *WL*, is from chapter 16 of Charles Dickens's *Our Mutual Friend*: the boy Sloppy is described as a 'beautiful reader of a newspaper. He do the Police in different voices'.

modes of thought, as about their radically singular departure from it. Distinctiveness, for Graham too, is inevitably measured against recognizable (read social and worldly) circumstances of language.

Viewing the poems in this public light involves reading Graham against the grain of much contemporary criticism. Graham is often portrayed as a distanced, private lyricist, rather than as social, or sociable. Tony Lopez has written of Graham's poems as 'largely isolated from an extended social world [...] The social presences it implies are more often drawn out of memory than from any sense of current community.'[33] Community is again sounded in the title of Matthew Francis's more recent monograph, *Where the People Are: Language and Community in the Poetry of W. S. Graham*, so that one might think Francis's book will gesture towards the existence of wider social influences at play in Graham's poems.[34] But for Francis, the community of Graham's poems is merely an *imagined* verbal gathering; and the addressees are not contact with others, but an 'extension of his [Graham's] own mind' (26). Francis, like Lopez, speaks repeatedly of Graham's *'failure* to escape [...] from self-reference'. Not dissimilarly, the chapter on 'Dependence' in Peter Robinson's 2005 *Twentieth Century Poetry: Selves and Situations*, though it speaks at length of Graham's 'primary need for relationship', writes of 'this aloneness and isolation of the self [...] [as] an irreducible condition' that is 'only temporarily relieved' by Graham's lyric addresses to loved ones.[35]

On reading Graham, it is easy to see why the idea that his work is a private, set-apart activity, has been dominant. The poems repeatedly conduct intimate addresses to lovers, family members, and close friends. The *I* of a Graham poem speaks 'To My Brother' (98), 'To Alexander Graham' (222), to 'Dear Bryan Wynter' (258), 'To My Wife at Midnight' (166). Graham's addresses to *you* flag up their status as personal correspondence, as imagined dialogues between the poet and those closest to him. Graham's address to his sleeping fiancée, 'I Leave This At Your Ear', offers a good example of what appears to be such lyric privacy at work:

> I LEAVE THIS AT YOUR EAR
> *For Nessie Dunsmuir*
>
> I leave this at your ear for when you wake,
> A creature in its abstract cage asleep.
> Your dreams blindfold you by the light they make.

---

[33] Tony Lopez, *The Poetry of W. S. Graham* (Edinburgh: Edinburgh University Press, 1989) 127.

[34] (Cambridge: Salt, 2004).

[35] Peter Robinson, *Twentieth Century Poetry: Selves and Situations* (Oxford: Oxford University Press, 2005) 74, 70.

[handwritten note: question — are you working from practical facts of audience or implicit + insured]

> The owl called from the naked-woman tree
> As I came down by the Kyle farm to hear
> Your house silent by the speaking sea.
>
> I have come late but I have come before
> Later with slaked steps from stone to stone
> To hope to find you listening for the door.
>
> I stand in the ticking room. My dear, I take
> A moth kiss from your breath. The shore gulls cry.
> I leave this at your ear for when you wake.   (166)

Such lines are not only addressed personally to Graham's loved one, they also catch her at a moment of unconsciousness, of unexpected vulnerability. It's easy for the reader to feel like a trespasser on a private scene between author and recipient. One is made to witness an intimacy that is seemingly not intended for one's own eyes and ears—this intimate exchange between Graham and his personally known, privately hailed auditor. The poem's dedication to a *named* recipient—'*For Nessie Dunsmuir*'—heightens one's temptation to think of the lyric as recounting an actual occurrence from Graham's life: a real encounter with the woman, Nessie. So too, the accessibility of the writing contributes to the impression of mimesis: the poem/cage may be 'abstract', but this lyric, unlike Graham's more 'difficult' writing, presents an instantly recognizable domestic scene, in clear, familiar language: 'I leave this at your ear for when you wake'. Graham, it seems, is directly identifiable as this *I*; an *I* speaking directly, exclusively to Nessie. Readers listen in, observers of the poet's estrangement, but distanced from him, too.

Is Francis right, then, when he points out that, in Graham's poems, 'text [. . .] substitutes for the real-time, personal, meaningful encounter between living human beings' (24)? Like Francis, we might read such lyrics as examples of Graham's tendency to draw real individuals, and instances, into an elaborately constructed private poetry world. Here, only imagined, verbal contact can be made. Since Nessie embodies both the position of addressee *and* intended future reader, we might think we are encouraged to see 'you' as Graham's exclusive, privately hailed double-recipient. There is no room here for other auditors to participate in the dialogue, to interrupt Graham's aloneness. On this view, the poem creates a sphere of private contacts and contexts, shielding its speakers and recipients from the public sphere, but also locking them in lyric solitude.

Yet these are, in several respects, illusory impressions. The lyric will not, and cannot, confine Graham and Nessie, or *I* and *you*, to passivity and textual isolation. The act of naming Nessie gives her a curiously active verbal presence. 'Nessie Dunsmuir' cannot also occupy the position of 'reader' without effecting a series of curious and illogical reversals. How could Nessie give voice to the poem's first line, for instance: 'I leave this at your ear for when you wake'? Were Nessie herself to read/speak this line, Graham's *you* would become her *I*; she would become the waiting addresser, addressing only herself. Logically, Nessie must occupy the position of sleeping listener in relation to the poem's speaker. The poem knowingly threatens mischief: if Graham's *I* becomes Nessie's own, if *you* turns into the poem's real reader and takes command of words addressed to her, the poem's sense is imperilled. The poem is not gravely, isolatedly '*For* Nessie Dunsmuir', but a playful exploration of what it might mean for poems to encounter and address others. More accurately still, the poem is questioning the conditions required in being *for you*, and it brings that privately wielded pronoun into the resonant space of the published address (like Eliot's 'private words addressed to you in public', in the epigraph to this chapter). Graham, like Eliot, is teasing about the extent to which an intimate lyric of address must be spoken *by* its poet, *to* other recipients: 'Remember the title. A PRIVATE / POEM TO NORMAN MACLEOD. / But this, my boy, is the poem / you paid me five pounds for' (227). As poetic *you*, Nessie must occupy the position of sleeping listener, enabling the lyric to be 'left at her ear' for Graham's readers publicly to witness. Francis writes that Graham 'dreams of speech, and of the intimacy that can take place between people who are physically present to each other' (25). But the poem is not merely waiting about for the waking of its addressee; it is already in the fullest moment of being when she is sleeping. In that sense, the poem enjoys its state of anticipation, a state of play that neither poet nor reader is desirous to end.

This might look as if it opens Graham to another common critical charge, of 'hiding in the safety of the text'; of a navel-gazing reluctance to make contact with his addressee. But on that reading it is difficult to account for the relationship between Graham's *I* and *you*, which is curiously mutual, oddly dialogic. Since the poem is written '*for* when you wake', both the lyric, and the woman, remain 'abstract', caged, and 'asleep', corresponding counterparts, mirroring each other. The poem, in one sense, is immediate, for it is spoken almost entirely in the speaker's present tense: *I* 'leave', 'wake', 'make', 'stand', 'take'. But the poet-figure's speech and all of his present-tense actions are motivated by an event which he hopes will take place in a shared future: '*when* you wake', '*for* [. . .] you'. The phrasing implies that the lyric's own awakening will correspond with receiving *your* attention: in the meantime, the poem, like its recipient, metaphorically slumbers. Unable to prevent himself imagining that his lines require the 'ear' of Nessie to come into being fully, he imagines his poem as passive, mere potential: 'abstract [. . .] asleep'. Are 'these words', then, as

Francis thinks they are, 'a poor substitute for hugs and kisses'; a lament at the loneliness of the textual condition? Graham's poem tests out this view: it implies that saying *you* is an impotent act until the address is really received by another's (Nessie's) ears. It suggests that to speak to another, in the fullest sense, one needs to be heard. Full of potential sounds, then, Graham's lines remain in a state of stilled anticipation, longing to be received by another. Yet the poem will not endorse a view of language as verbal isolation, for it turns silence itself into a form of intense provocation. Silence is often envisaged as full of response and reception in Graham's work.

> And yet I say
> This silence here for in it I might hear you.
> I say this silence or, better, construct this space
> So that somehow something may move across
> The caught habits of language to you and me.[36]

Silence, in these lines, is used to make the addressee's sounds more apparent. It is what enables the speaker to 'hear you'. In matters of address, then, silence offers help not hindrance; a vehicle for more intense focusing upon its opposite state: '*for* in it I might hear you'. Meanwhile, such lines reveal the impossibility of conceiving of silence as a permanent, or absolute, condition. The poem doubly reinforces its transitory nature: '*this*' silence '*here*', where 'here' is at once *this* particular place, and also *now* (a particular time). It is no accident that Graham draws the temporal and spatial particularity of 'here' into relation with the homophone 'hear', offering a paradoxically *auditory* affinity between sound and silence, between *your* absence and presence. His playful phonetic punning is also a summons; a rage to conjure *you*, in spite of *your* absence. Through such paradoxes, Graham's work draws attention to the complexity of regulating addresses. It is precisely because speaking and listening will not be brought under absolute control (one cannot confine address to a single *you*, nor offer an address fixed to a single moment) that the poet can engage in displays of linguistic creativity and improvisatory skill.

Clearly, this is neither a straightforwardly autobiographical, nor an isolated, address: Graham's work sets out to explore the effects of saying *you* to many others, designating a series of changeable listeners, hearers, and addressees. In both 'The Constructed Space', and in the lyric 'For Nessie Dunsmuir', the impression of the poet's isolation is a carefully staged effect. Paradoxically, in creating the appearance of solitude the poet must pay close attention to really being received in the public fray, to the

---

[36] 'The Constructed Space' (1958), in *NCP* 162.

presence of a readership's watchful eyes. Such a lyric neatly comes full
circle, closing as it begins, in a state of unrelieved anticipation of its en-
counter with *you*; a *you* that is both a public and a private recipient, a real
readership as well as its named fiancée.

Pite and Jones have observed, correctly I think, that 'Graham's poetry
often arises out of and refers to [...] friendships with other writers and
artists'; predominantly his St Ives contemporaries: the community of
poets and painters that included Bryan Wynter, Norman MacLeod, Brian
Higgins, and Roger Hilton.[37] However, it is also important to remember
that Graham's apparently exclusive addresses to friends and lovers are
often only in part to those named figures; his ear is closely attuned to
'speaking to you in public', and fascinated by what responses that un-
familiar public world will give. In repeatedly hailing private recipients
that cannot, or will not, respond, Graham's poems make room for un-
known voices and strangers to enter. 'I Leave this At Your Ear' addresses
Graham's wife as a sleeping interlocutor; 'Dear Bryan Wynter' and 'Lines
on Roger Hilton's Watch' (235) are elegies to his recently deceased friends.
'To my Mother' and 'To Alexander Graham' are addressed to deceased
family members, whilst in 'Private Poem to Norman Macleod' Graham's
address attempts to span vast geographical distances after a much-
lamented gap in correspondence. Such poems, as we will see, turn from
their declared recipients, to whomever else may be listening, opening
themselves to an unknown, unquantifiable *you*. These addresses are inher-
ently double: a plural, public *you* exists behind or beyond the specifically
denominated known, familiar 'you'.

One way in which Graham's poems issue this flexible invitation is by
complicating the roles of speaker and addressee, often by poking fun at
the notion of a stable specificity of address. Other Graham titles seek out
deliberately underspecified auditors: 'A Note to the Difficult One', 'Dear
Who I Mean' (206; 160). These poems might seem esoteric and asocial:
their evasion of particular contexts and persons seem to produce ab-
stracted addresses, unanchored pronominal play. But Graham's poems,
even as they flirt with the beyondness of address, are very much inured to
the speech-forms and conversational habits from the quotidian world.
They can speak as plainly, and as directly as, say, a Larkin poem. 'I hardly
see you nowadays / Being down here on the jetty / Out of town', Graham
writes 'For John Heath-Stubbs'; 'Don't fool me. Is it you?', he writes in
'Implements in Their Places'.[38] Meanwhile, a title such as 'Dear Who
I Mean' hardly demonstrates profound estrangement from the daily

---

[37] Pite and Jones, 'Introduction: Contacting Graham' 6.
[38] 'For JHS' 274; 'Implements' (1972) 240.

world. Rather, it indicates the text's reliance upon the everyday social sphere in which commonplace letter-writing addresses are exchanged, and from which this poem's own address takes shape. What is witty and disconcerting about Graham's lyric is that its realist details knowingly exploit the conventions of addressing speech or writing to a known other, questioning the limits of familiar correspondence:

> Dear who I mean but more
> Than because of the lonely stumble
> In the spiked bramble after
> The wrecked dragon caught
> In the five high singing wires
> Its tail twisting the wind
> Into visibility, I turn
> To where it is you lodge
> Now at the other end
> Of this letter let out
> On the end of its fine string
> Across your silent airts   (160)

Toying with the interlocutor's expectation that letter-writing will be specific, private contact, the poem uses a conventional, personal address-form as the first word of the poem: 'Dear'. Yet in refusing to confirm that the words are directed at any one *you*, 'who I mean' tests out the privacy of the letter's address upon many, or any, *yous*. 'Dear who I mean' is the poem's shrug of the shoulders at the notion of any one personal addressee (implying '*whoever*'), and it turns aside the very notions of personal address that it taps in using the letter form. The line that pulls 'who I mean' into question immediately slips out of that mode of questioning: 'who I mean but *more*...'. More of what? More recipients? More meaning, specifically more meaning than the speaker can procure alone?

One might expect the lyric to invite 'you' to answer, but *I* dissolves the possibility of response, collapsing the question in detail: '*in* the spiked bramble', '*after* / The wrecked dragon', '*to* where it is', '*Across* your silent airts'. Perhaps Graham refuses to contact whoever might be addressed by such lines, speaking at, not with, *you*. Yet if the poem's verbal evasiveness closes down the possibility of receiving a letter back, in another sense, Graham's repeated deferrals set the stage for *your* impatient rebuke. This increasingly meandering address seems increasingly unlikely to supply the answers its speaker strains for: his audience might well be provoked to retort, or interrupt. The speaker's evasiveness works as a form of provocation to *you*, precisely to the extent that *I* appears to vex the possibility of hearing *your* response. Graham's lines here are, as they so often are in the late work, both 'speaking to you and not', both avoiding and maintaining particular contacts.

One might also view Graham's poems as 'speaking to you and not' in a rather different sense; which again invites responses from the wide public world of interlocutions. Even Graham's named *yous*, his specified addresses arising from what Pite and Jones called his 'friendships with other artists and writers', slip out of their designated contexts, and beckon to an inscrutable audience. This readership is figured not as companionably comprised in Graham's image, 'one like me', but as amorphous crowd, or disconcerting stranger: 'I seem to know your face from some / One else I was'.[39] This *I* speaks to *you*, but also past *you*, to unspecified, unimaginable others: 'you, whoever you are, / That I am other to', 'that step / That seems to fall after / My own step in the dark' ('Dialogues' 168; 173). In a poem to his friend Bryan Wynter, for instance, Graham combines both the familiar and discomforting rhythms of address:

> Maybe we could have a word before I go,
> As I usually say. I mean there must be some
> Way to speak together straighter than this,
> As I usually say. There is not a long time
> To go between the banks of rubbish and nature
> Down to the old beginning of the real sea.
>   'Wynter and the Grammarsow' 187

This is a moment of easy companionability with a close friend. 'Maybe we could have a word before I go' is a way of quickly securing attention, with the unelevated and idiomatic 'have a word'. It is a great example of 'speaking straighter' than one might expect a poem to be able to. The conversation with Wynter is not conducted on a higher plane than ordinary talk, nor is it inaccessible to readers.

Yet the lines are simultaneously a comment on the complexity of such directness, and the use of the accessible and the everyday in art. Any belief in the existence of a 'way to speak [. . .] straighter than this' is undermined by the addition, 'As I usually say', which places straightness in the straitjacket of unvarying routine. The generative possibilities syntactically established at the beginning of both sentences—'we could', 'there must be'—settle down twice over into the too-easy familiarity of 'As I usually say'. The inclusion of 'As I usually say' might be regarded as comfortingly commonplace, a further example of the speaker's enjoyment of the rhythms of 'straighter' speech. However, its repetition produces a slide from potentiality into inertia. The rising possibilities set up at the

<hr>

[39] 'Clusters Travelling Out' 192.

beginning of both sentences collapse into ungratified wistfulness, banality: something repeatedly unattained, perhaps unattainable. Although the lines declare that it 'must be' possible to attain a straighter style of speech, to iron out asymmetries, they are reluctant to do so.

After all, Graham's attempt to shape his words clearly, and accessibly for Wynter's comprehension are also a way of buttonholing Wynter (and the reader). 'A word before I go' spells out the imminent departure of the speaker: *you* need to listen up, and listen carefully. The lines are in one sense speaking plainly, but they are also motivated by a desire to secure a listener's attention by creating an ingeniously crafted, familiar sound effect. Accessible phrases are part of its arsenal. They enable *I* to secure *your* assent to its interpretation of art's role, by speaking winningly, exploiting familiar diction. Such lines are as much outward-directed commentary on the difficulty of clear speech, of straight talking in art and poetry, as a private correspondence with a single interlocutor. Hailing anyone who will listen, Wynter and Graham are embarked on a shared project of mutual address: 'we', and their addressees are as much the readers and viewers of artistic works, as each other.

If, however, speaking plainly is more complex than it first appears, the apparent benefits of straight speech may themselves also be called into question. It is precisely when Graham attempts to speak 'straighter than this' that his address sounds most rehearsed and comically affected: 'As I usually say'. Beckett's wittily woeful line, 'No one that ever lived ever thought so crooked as we' ghosts Graham's address, here, running that isolated, exceptional 'No one' alongside much more commonplace misalignment.[40] Graham's amusingly crooked syntactical re-modifications underline the provisional quality of the descriptive mode, hinting that language, like thought, will not stay still politely. There is a sense that any single literal, or naturalistic, description cannot be trusted; that multiple perspectives, speeches, *hearings*, are needed. For Graham, as for Eliot, Joyce, and Beckett, words and thoughts are continually on the move, and will not settle down to obey an artist's, or an addressee's, demands for straightforward representation. Words reverse the expected polarity of obedience, and start organizing the poet's world for him:

1

> What does it matter if the words
> I choose, in the order I choose them in,
> Go out into a silence I know
> Nothing about, there to be let

---

[40] *Endgame* (1958), in *Samuel Beckett: The Complete Dramatic Works* (London: Faber, 1986), 97.

In and entertained and charmed
Out of their master's orders? And yet
I would like to see where they go
And how without me they behave.

2

Speaking is difficult and one tries
To be exact and yet not to
Exact the prime intention to death.[41]

The close repetition of '*I* choose' draws attention to the speaker's exacting and priming impulses, his pride in deliberately selecting his language, and organizing it into a well-structured sentence. But the very lines that demonstrate his single-handed precision simultaneously reveal that his meticulousness has failed to produce a regulated effect. Who is it that has charmed 'the words / I choose' from him? And to whom are the poem's current words addressed? If Graham's words have been 'charmed / Out of their [...] orders', are there other speakers and listeners shadowing the lines, giving orders, taking control? The poem may offer a hint in this direction when it details the 'ins' and 'outs' of its syntactical ordering. It creates a liminal spatial zone which is neither quite in nor out, but repeatedly turning between: '*in* the order I choose them *in*', '*in*to a silence', 'let *in*', 'go *out in*to', 'ab*out*', 'charmed / O*ut*'.

Eliot, too, included that motif of 'turning' in his vignette-laden poem, 'Geronion'—'Who turned in the hall, one hand on the door'—held between deliberate stalling and active transit.[42] 'Geronion's ins and outs might be allied with the 'time to turn back' in 'The Love Song of J. Alfred Prufrock', which fluctuates between fear of *you*, and desire to secure *you* as auditor; engagement with, and escape from, an interlocutor.[43] Betweenness can also be traced in 'the key' that is made to 'Turn in the door once and turn once only', in *The Waste Land* (*ECP* 79:61–86). Here too, turning is poised perpetually between imprisonment and release, desired solitude and a demand for correspondence. Graham's work, like Eliot's, is fascinated by language's comings and goings, contacts and avoidances. In 'Approaches', 'in' occurs four times, wrestles with 'out' (which occurs twice), and the tussle between them even breaks apart and exploits individual words for their capacity to carry semantic possibilities: 'ab*out*', '*in*to', '*en*tertained'.

For both poets, 'turning' flirts with a turn away from contact, as well as turning between possibilities. But Eliot's turns and returns,

---

[41] 'Approaches to How They Behave' (1970), *NCP* 178–84, 178.
[42] 'Geronion' (1920), in Eliot, *ECP* 40.
[43] In *Prufrock and Other Observations* (Bloomsbury: The Egoist, 1917), quoted from *ECP* 13–17.

hesitations and delays, often speak of the frozen indecisiveness felt
when poised before fearful choices: 'a thousand small deliberations /
Protract the profit of their chilled delirium', 'And time yet for a hun-
dred indecisions, / And for a hundred visions and revisions, / Before
the taking of a toast and tea' ('Gerontion' 38; 'Prufrock' 14). Such
'turning' and 'returning', 'indecisions [...] visions and revisions' are
far from bereft of aural and semantic pleasure, the lines enjoy the
repetition of rhyme on 'indecision', 'revision', getting a kick out of the
very 'deliberations' they say they find chilling. Eliot's verbal ingenuity,
then, holds at bay the fear of descending into the routine drudgery of
'the taking of a toast and tea', the series of mechanically repetitive ac-
tions that leave agents caught between futile alternatives; 'delaying',
'coming and going', 'one hand on the door'. Graham's verbal turns, in
comparison, feel less discomfited by 'indecisions' and revisions: the
playfulness of the rhythms and rhymes are less an attempt to stave off
a sense of sterility or futility about making linguistic choices, than a
celebration of the irregularity of returns, revisions. For Graham, even
repetitions are manifested differently each time, susceptible to muta-
tion: the poems do not appeal to a fixed original act or object, from
which copies can be made, assessed, or corrected. This leaves a poet's
words at risk of being unregulated, wayward. But Graham finds 'en-
tertainment' and 'charm' in this change and disruption, where another
poet might identify merely a failure of verbal mastery ('out of [...]
order'), a loss of aesthetic transcendence.

Revealing one's susceptibility to the disruption of 'what I thought was
worth saying' indicates a positive adaptability for Graham, a delight in ad-
dress's capacity to exhibit change, and to produce a certain degree of dis-
order. But Graham is less anarchically opening the work to disorganization,
than exploring alternative forms of organization. It is an exploration that is
often envisaged as cooperation with those it addresses: 'I [...] / [...] put my
ear to you / To hear Botallack tick', Graham writes in his elegy to Roger
Hilton, which imagines addressing the fiery, often raging drunk, Hilton
'through' the deceased's watch.[44] In 'Lines on Roger Hilton's Watch':

> Which I was given because
> I loved him and we had
> Terrible times together.
> [...]

---

[44] 'Lines on Roger Hilton's Watch' (1976), in *NCP* 235–7.

I lift you up from the mantel
Piece here in my house
Wearing your verdigris.
At least I keep you wound
And put my ear to you
To hear Botallack tick.

You realise your master
Has relinquished you
And gone to lie under
The ground at St Just.

Tell me the time. The time
Is Botallack o'clock.
This is the dead of night.

[...]

Watch, it is time I wound
You up again. I am
Very much not your dear
Last master but we had
Terrible times together.

Graham's address is keeping time with *you* (in both senses), and also making 'you / [...] tick'. But even when the speaker is able to keep his relationship with *you* going like clockwork, this consensual co-operation is simultaneously a fraught collaboration. The address, as so often in Graham, is simultaneously a plea to be co-opted by its recipient, a demand for verbal tussles: '*it is time I wound / You up again*', he puns, brilliantly, extending the play on enraging *you*, on making you 'tick' as the very means of ordered poetic and temporal progression (237). Is the poem a well-wrought object if what opens and closes the text is the foregrounding of struggle, disorder, angularity in its relations: 'I loved him and we had / Terrible times together' (235)? Graham moves at once to create the semblance of a circular, balanced poetic order out of the disruptive and destructive 'terrible' relations between *I* and *you*, and indicates that any poetic order it achieves is still comprised from what is 'terrible' and unruly. The poem's end may be neatly in its beginning, but in the poem, as in the clock, what keeps such verbal tidiness in orbit is the unstable drive for being 'wound up' by another, by a circular, clockwise motion that, like time's own 'tarnished ticking [...] / [...] with your bent hand' has no destination, end point, or beginning (235).

MAKE IT RENEWED: CANONICAL
COLLABORATIONS

> To be new in the right way is difficult.
>
> W. S. Graham, Letter to Roger Hilton

As critics have often pointed out, Graham resembles his Modernist fore-
bears in numerous respects: one encounters in his address a pastiche of
traditions and styles of interlocution, attentiveness to silences and *aporias*,
a tendency to expose the constructed linguistic relations between, and the
identities of, *I* and *you*.[45] Graham's attention to 'newness' involves a re-
sounding of past voices, in which speaking to *you*—with all its attendant
gaps, dislocations, frustrations—demands both a readership's and a poet's
engagement with past speech-forms and lexicons. 'Feeding the dead is
necessary', as Section 63 of 'Implements' insists, using that single line to
issue an instructive injunction, and a self-reminder (255). Section 66 di-
rects itself, and its audience, to another literary interlocutor—Kipling
'scribbling on his cuff'—whilst Section 70 commands, 'Heraklion, listen',
and Section 50 finds 'a mixed company' in Kandinsky, Shelley, Crane,
Melville, Eliot, and David Jones (251–6).

If, in gravitating towards sources of order and authority, Graham's work
is won over by canonical interlocutors, ancient and modern, his words,
like Eliot's, are glad to speak with, as well as to disrupt, the tradition. For
Graham, the literary-historical voices of the Modernist inheritance are
amongst the masterful *yous* charming the language from a poet's single-
handed control. They are also those masters upon whom Graham's lan-
guage, entertainingly works its own charm. In his 1946 essay 'Notes on a
Poetry of Release', he writes:

> The shape of all of us is in this language. Our riches and poverties have af-
> fected every word. For the language is a changing creature continually being
> killed-off, added-to and changed like a river over its changing speakers [...]
> Each word is touched by and filled with the activity of every speaker. Each
> word changes every time it is brought to life. (*Nightfisherman* 380)

Even whilst readjusting that literary master (his colloquial 'killed-off'
plays down the dead more than the Modernist poet would, and might be

---

[45] 'A technically accomplished writer of free and rhythmical verse in the Modernist
tradition' (Adam Piette, 'W. S. Graham and the White Threshold of Line-Breaks', in *W. S.
Graham: Speaking Towards You*, ed. Pite and Jones, 44–62, 45). Angela Leighton reads
Graham's literary relationships with the St Ives painters as a route back to the Modernist
aesthetic. See *On Form: Poetry, Aestheticism, and the Legacy of a Word* (Oxford: Oxford
University Press, 2007) 209; 216.

seen to privilege instead what is 'brought to life'), Graham's pronounce-
ment puts into play a view of language as a principle of change, as historical
alteration and regeneration, that he would have been familiar with from
Eliot:

> No poet, no artist of any art, has his complete meaning alone. His signifi-
> cance, his appreciation is the appreciation of his relation to the dead
> poets and artists. You cannot value him alone; you must set him, for
> contrast and comparison, among the dead [...] The necessity that he
> shall conform, that he shall cohere, is not one-sided; what happens when
> a new work of art is created is something that happens simultaneously to
> all the works of art which preceded it. The existing monuments form an
> ideal order among themselves, which is modified by the introduction of
> the new (the really new) work of art among them. The existing order is
> complete before the new work arrives; for order to persist after the super-
> vention of novelty, the *whole* existing order must be, if ever so slightly,
> altered [...]⁴⁶

For both writers, language is a populated, highly participatory
medium: 'the shape of all of us', 'not one-sided', 'no poet [...] has his
complete meaning alone'. It is a medium busy with the voicings of
many *I*s and *you*s, both living and dead. Emphasizing his reliance
upon literary history, upon past voicings, Eliot writes of the necessity
of attending to the 'existing monuments', the 'relation to the dead
poets and artists', in order to make sense of contemporary artworks;
whilst, for Graham: 'History continually arrives as differently as our
most recent minute on earth. The labourer going home in the dusk
shouts his goodnight across the road and History has a new score on
its track. The shape has changed a little' ('Notes' 379). For both, art
has a discernible social structure, 'shape', 'track', 'score', and to par-
ticipate in it is both to mould oneself on history, and to change it. In
Eliot, 'modification' is a tentative, occasional process—'*if ever so
slightly* altered'—and the existing 'ideal order' is particular about what
it is changed by: it can only be transformed by 'the new (the*really*
new) work of art'.

   In Graham, alteration is more widespread and vigorous: 'the language is
a changing creature *continually* being killed-off, added-to and changed'.
Change is not an occasional achievement, confined to high art, or a sign of
having one's work marked out for special treatment. Rather change is a
continual principle, part of a Heraclitean flux. This manifests in Graham
somewhat differently from how it appears in, say, the poet Louis Mac-
Neice, who, in 1934, found himself more ghosted by fears about poetic

---

⁴⁶ Eliot, 'Tradition and the Individual Talent' (1919), in *SW* 47–59, 49–50.

passivity in the face of ebb and flow, loss and change: 'The tide comes in and goes out again I do not want / To be always stressing either its flux or its permanence […] / But to keep my eye only on the nearer future / And after that let the sea flow over us'.[47] MacNeice's lines have to pull themselves back from the resignation that plays around their acknowledgement of flux and finitude, and his addresses do not always manage this successfully: 'Exiles all as we are in a foreign city, / Can't we ever, my love, speak in the same language?', 'In endless orbit and in lieu of a flag / The orator hangs himself from the flagpost'.[48] In Graham, in contrast, that Heraclitean emphasis on continual alteration and instability is determinedly active; the flipside of Prufrock's fear of, and flight from, those 'human voices [that] wake us, and we drown' (17). If the massing tide of words threatens death by drowning, it also has the re-animating capacity to resurrect, with renewed energy: language is 'changed like a river over its changing speakers […] Each word changes every time it is brought to life' ('Notes' 380).

For Graham, as for Eliot, to 'conform, to cohere' is both to show one's command of past accents—by conversing cooperatively with cultured addressees and past masters—and to change the form of that mastery, to handle the past on present terms. But literary charm, by these lights, is not only elegant and graceful, but also potentially strenuous, conflicted. It speaks of struggle in the act of graceful triumph, where to address one's masters is to challenge, not merely to adulate, them. Mastery is not a stable concept, for if it contains the concepts of victory, authority, skilfulness, and proficiency, these continually need to reassert themselves against change and fall. A poem's display of verbal ingenuity remains highly precarious. Graham's poems are not viewed as achieved objects, but as a continued process of alteration and struggle:

> Speaking is difficult and one tries
> To be exact and yet not to
> Exact the prime intention to death.
> […]
>   […] The inadequacy
> Of the living, animal language drives
> Us all to metaphor and an *attempt*
> To organize the spaces we *think*
> We have made occur between the words.
>   'Approaches' 178, emphasis added

'Speaking is difficult', 'one tries', 'and yet', 'inadequacy'. Graham's poem is less a vaunted aesthetic object, than a humbled 'attempt' and process. His poem struggles to be at home with its awareness of being an 'ap-

---

[47] 'Wolves', in Louis MacNeice, *Collected Poems*, ed. Peter McDonald (London: Faber, 2007) 26. *Collected Poems* referred to hereafter as *MCP*.
[48] 'Babel', *MCP* 228; 'In Lieu' 583.

proach', or set of 'Approaches', not a finished artefact. 'An attempt / To organise' makes organization refutable: one might never get round to *being* organized, if one merely *attempts* it. The infinitive form, emphasized by the enjambment, underlines the continually intended nature of that ordering. 'Organization' could well remain a potential future act for such a speaker; it might never be brought to fruition. In these lines, even what 'we think' is not coincident with what 'we have made occur'. Is language, then, a distorting medium, unable to do justice to our meanings?

Distortion, verbal slippage, and lost meaning were also pertinent to Modernist poetics, though their expression took a different form. 'It is impossible to say just what I mean!', railed Eliot's Prufrock: ' "That is not it at all, / That is not what I meant, at all" '. (16). Pound's *Hugh Selwyn Mauberley* found itself undergoing similar verbal agonies: 'Wrong from the start', 'Bent resolutely on wringing lilies from the acorn'.[49] In *Mauberley*, a determined physicality characterizes the poet-figure's misplaced and 'bent' verbal resolve: lilies cannot be wrought from acorns, in spite of how much energy is invested. Not dissimilarly, hand-wringing irritability plays around Prufrock's frustrated repetitions: 'not it', 'not what I meant', 'It is impossible' (16). Eliot's addressees mishear, misunderstand, get him wrong. Although Eliot's *you*s do seem to go to the trouble of listening (which Graham's speakers can rarely be sure of), and of interpreting Prufrock's words, they nevertheless perceive him incorrectly.

Graham's work, too, draws attention to the difficulty of bringing words under control, particularly for his interlocutors. But he is often rather more casual about saying so: 'Whoever / Speaks to you will not be me' he informs *you* matter-of-factly, then muses: 'I wonder what I will say' ('Clusters' 191). Holding on to 'what I meant' is not at issue for a speaker who, at any moment, 'will not be me'. Conversely, it will not matter if an *addressee* later misses, or changes, the meaning, since meaning, for such a speaker, can only be a present-tense activity—that is, present in the act of utterance. Meanwhile, in Graham, misinterpretations occur on both sides of the reading/writing process, and involve both 'you' and 'me': 'we two go down / Roaring between the lines / To drown. Who hears? Who listens?' ('Nightfishing' 132). Is there, again, an echo here of Prufrock's own ending: 'Till human voices wake us and we drown'? (17). And of Eliot's final pronominal shift, in that poem, from *I* to *we*, which seemed to hint that companionship was possible, even, or especially, in the act of dissolution? Drowning, for both poets, is something we can do together, even if we can't tell who is there: 'Who hears? Who listens?' (*NCP* 132).

---

[49] Ezra Pound, *Hugh Selwyn Mauberley* (1920), in *Personae: The Collected Shorter Poems* (New York: New Directions, 1971) 185–204, 187. Referred to hereafter as *Personae*.

Graham's touch, I think, is lighter than Pound's and Eliot's when it comes to 'Communication's / Mistakes in the magic medium' (*NCP* 200). His poetry is teasing about language's 'impossibility'; its instabilities of meaning. The lyrics take pleasure in showing the comic side of words' ability to expose speakers as wrong-headed, and often deliberately, humorously, work to wrong-foot them:

> It is how one two three each word
> Chose itself in its position
> Pretending at the same time
> They were working for me. Here
> They are. Should I have sacked them?
> 'Implements' 245

On the one hand, such lines place agency in words, not in speakers. Again, they indicate language's alarming ability to 'choose itself', and the poet's incapacity to control it. Literary success, it appears, is not consciously controlled, and is only haphazardly achieved: 'each word / Chose itself in its position'. Graham's speaker, like Eliot's and Pound's is 'wrong from the start', operating under the misguidedly literal-minded belief that he is 'employing' language to serve his own purposes. And yet this apparently literal 'working for me' will not stay so for long, taking on a lightly self-mocking metaphorical application when the speaker adds, as if with a wink: 'Should I have sacked them?' To whom is this question addressed? Asking his unspecified addressee to get the joke, Graham teasingly presents *you* with the offending words, as if putting them, in the poem's present, before an addressed jury: 'Here / They are', he writes, hauling the words into the 'now' of reading, turning their misdeeds into a shared verbal problem. The poem asks: 'what shall we do with this, with *our*, recalcitrant language?' It's difficult to know who or what is guilty of pretence here, since the speaker delights in pretending to us that he believes his words are disobedient workers, while even in these lines they are very much 'working for me'. The poem adeptly puts out those words to do good comic toil for his addressees.

In such teasing addresses Graham shows a certain degree of ease with the *betweenness* of ordinary language. Graham's poems are beguiled by their thwarted attempts to summon, hail, and address *you*. Finding oneself 'Speaking to you and not / Knowing if you are there', is a common experience in a Graham poem; so much so that the poet-figure has grown accustomed to the lack of reciprocation: 'My words are used to that'.[50] Graham's *I* can never be sure whether its address has been received, if *you*

---

[50] 'Dear Bryan Wynter' (1977), in *NCP* 258.

is really present, or is capable of hearing at all: 'A Letter More Likely to Myself', 'The Lost Other', 'Are You Still There?' (42; 71; 207). Yet the poet-figure far from always laments that uncertainty, that silence:

> Do not think you have to say
> Anything back. But you do
> Say something back which I
> Hear by the way I speak to you.
>
> 'Implements' 247

Apparently, this addressee's verbal reciprocation is not demanded, for the speaker alleviates *you* from the obligatory pressure of 'have to'. One might contrast this with Eliot's relentlessly obligatory addresses in *Little Gidding*: 'You are not here to verify, / Instruct yourself, or inform curiosity', 'You are here to kneel / Where prayer has been valid'.[51]

But struggling to free *you* from his demand for reciprocation does not free Graham's speaker from his longing for *you* to respond: his lines turn yearning into the only form of companionable presence they can find. That brave-faced statement of self-sufficiency 'Do not think you have to say / Anything back' is undercut by the beginning of the next sentence: 'But you do'. Similarly, the beginning of the following line 'Say something back', severed from the earlier part of the sentence by the enjambment, operates as a renewed plea for contact, as well as an assertive statement: 'you do / Say something back'. The stanza's parting shot: 'I / Hear by the way I speak to you' ingeniously turns the silent listener into the crucial agent who stimulates the speaker's 'saying' and 'hearing'. It is an extraordinarily tenuously achieved companionship. Does the last word of the section, 'you', indicate the speaker's triumphant turn outward, to a finally heard addressee? Does the neat end rhyme, 'Do' / 'you', underline a shift towards aural unification between Graham's *I* and *you*? The section may conclude on a note of affirmative reaching towards the figure of the other: 'I speak to you', but Graham's lines ensure that *I* never receives *your* longed-for answer. Similarly, in 'Dear Bryan Wynter':

> Speaking to you and not
> Knowing if you are there
> Is not too difficult.
> My words are used to that. (258)

This puts into play a great deal more than a simple expression of self-absorbed resignation at *your* absence. The enjambment ingeniously carries on the play of words on contradictory levels, allowing the poet-figure to

---

[51] *Little Gidding* (1940), in *ECP* 215.

have his actions and addresses both ways: he is at once 'speaking' and not-speaking, 'knowing' and not-knowing. The affirmative-sounding 'Knowing if you are there' is severed by a line break from the lack of knowledge ('not / Knowing') described by the passage, so that the individual line sustains a local affirmation of knowledge that the full sentence denies. By placing 'knowing' at the beginning of the line, Graham allows heavy stress to fall on the word, further emphasizing the other at which speech is *directed*: 'you are there', whilst refusing to confirm that other's presence. Meanwhile, 'speaking to you and not' seems to catch and hold the poet-figure in two contradictory positions at once. 'My words are used to that' is applicable equally to the uncertain experiencing of 'you' and to the linguistic strategies brought in to negotiate the uncertainty.

The lines are reminiscent of Thomas Hardy's lyric 'The Voice', where the presence of 'you' is powerfully asserted even in the act of articulating the woman's absence: 'Can it be you that I hear' the speaker wonders, before answering his own question, 'yes, as I knew you then'.[52] The very line that depicts the joyousness of the speaker's certainty ('yes [...] I knew') draws attention to the merely transitory value of such affirmation. The stress falls heavily on 'knew', underlining the sense of irrevocable pastness: it is only inadequate memory and conjecture that confirm the vision of the silent and intangible other. The lines, like Graham's, are at once 'speaking to you and not', for the affirmation is generated by the poem answering its own questioning. In Graham's work too, even the lines which claim it 'is not too difficult' to accept the uncertain presence of 'you' attempt to affirm the existence of that intangible other: 'knowing [...] you are there'.

I began this section by testing out the critical view that Graham uses poetry as 'a bounded, protected place'; a place where 'the writer can play freely [...] without interference from anybody else' and that 'the price he pays for this is loneliness'.[53] If this view is correct—if Graham's work longs to create a verbal safe haven, a place of escape free from the threatening demands of others—then the poems lock themselves into a highly unsuccessful struggle to achieve verbal isolation from others. For Graham's work repeatedly shows that it is fantasy for any speaker or listener to imagine he can 'play freely', safely alone in words, delightedly isolated. His words do not offer an unfettered space, but a place busy with *yous*. Speakers

---

[52] 'The Voice', in *Thomas Hardy*, ed. Samuel Hynes (Oxford: Oxford University Press, 1984) 161–3.

[53] Francis, *Where the People Are* 25. Calvin Bedient makes a similar point in 'Absentist Poetry: Kinsella, Hill, Graham, Hughes', *PN Review* 4:1 (1977) 18–24: 'in part he [Graham] writes poetry simply to shelter in its "constructed space" from the unconstructed space of both language and the world' (23).

repeatedly entangle themselves with addressees, interlocutors, invading figures, readers, recipients.

Rather than seeking to remove himself from such contacts, I think, Graham takes gratification from poetry's hard work in negotiating routes through this succession of verbal engagements, inviting, rebuffing, teasing, avoiding, dallying with, and propositioning *you*s. A series of imagined auditors listen in, and demandingly interfere with, such language, with Graham often imagining them literally breathing down his neck; a terrifying, but erotic presence: 'What form stood watching behind me / Reading us over my shoulder', 'She / Monster muse old bag or. Something / Dreamed is yes you're welcome always / Desired', 'you have come to stand / There rank-breathed at my elbow'.[54] Like Yeats's 'foul slut who keeps the till', Graham's 'rank-breathed' *you* is exciting, provokingly vile.[55] In a later poem, 'Her rank breath of poet's bones' is a stimulating source: the invading addressee is a muse figure that Graham's lines half-summon, and are half-invaded by: 'I half-expected you', 'you're welcome always'.[56] Graham is fascinated by being productively disgusted, provoked, invaded, enticed, by others in verse, and by setting up scenarios where he can be taken over by the figures, both from the past and the present, that he speaks to. He will accommodate himself to whichever figures 'entered and breathed beside me' (241).

Such poetry is clearly neither a free for all, nor a free from all. Francis quotes Graham's lines from 'The Dark Dialogues' as evidence of our author's desire for asocial, unrestricted play (Francis 24–5):

> A place I can think in
> And think anything in,   (168)

But this reading assumes that Graham's lines are simply expressing his own, 'real' longing to 'think anything', to have an unbounded textual experience. Francis interprets such lines as indicative of an isolationist poetics, of Graham's longing for a verbal play that can finally be unfettered and alone, free from the interfering, or alarming, demands of others. Yet it is neither clear to me that Graham is necessarily the *I* that speaks, nor that these lines champion verbal release. The poem carefully avoids advocating a position of estrangement, or a fantasy of linguistic escape.

---

[54] 'Five Visitors to Madron' (1967), in *NCP* 188–9. Similarly, compare Robert Graves's 'The Reader Over My Shoulder': 'You, reading over my shoulder, peering beneath / My writing arm—I suddenly feel your breath / Hot on my hand or on my nape', in *Collected Poems* 58.

[55] Yeats's 'The Circus Animals' Desertion' (1939), in *W. B. Yeats: The Major Works*, ed. Edward Larrissy (Oxford: Oxford University Press, 1997) 180.

[56] Graham's 'Implements' 241; 'Five Visitors' 188.

Rather, Graham's rhetoric is continually pulling us back to the shared backdrop of speech that allows individual voicings to take shape. The full stanza reads:

> I speak across the vast
> Dialogues in which we go
> To clench my words against
> Time or the lack of time
> Hoping that for a moment
> They will become for me
> A place I can think in
> And think anything in,
> An aside from the monstrous.   (167–8)

This 'I' speaks neither in actual, nor for desired, isolation. Its hinterland is 'the vast / Dialogues in which we go'; an entrenchedly communal verbal landscape. Vastness speaks of immensity, of fearfully unthinkable unbounded space and time, so that the poem might well be afraid of getting lost in 'monstrous' plenitude. But it also steels itself to depict precisely this terrifying expanse of different 'dialogues', of differing speakers and listeners. This is very different from closing down a plentifully diverse store of perceptions in order to champion the vantage point of a single solitary consciousness. In inviting readers to contemplate fearful expanses—the very expanses spread out before us, in these lines—Graham is not 'hiding in the safety of the text', but clenching that text to speak of what is most fearful, even scarcely thinkable, in our common language, and to set listeners on the trail. If this is Graham's attempt to 'think anything', it is an invitation and a challenge to readers to do so, in turn. 'Anything' may well be less frightening when conceived of with others, with *you*.

> So too, in the previous stanza:
> And who are you and by
> What right do I waylay
> You where you go there
> Happy enough striking
> Your hobnail in the dark?
> Believe me I would ask
> Forgiveness but who
> Would I ask forgiveness from?

Graham's speaker begs answers from a 'you' that seems to incite, rather than merely distract, his poetic impulse: 'who are you', 'by / What right do I waylay / You', 'I would ask / Forgiveness but who / Would I ask forgiveness from?' (167). Such speech may be prompted by the belief that *you* will provide answers, mapping out fearfully unknown aspects of the *I*. Yet *I* is also lured on by the act of questioning another, by its need for a *you* to speak towards. *You* orients thought and being, just as in the final stanza of the section, the changeable *I*, 'turning between / This word and the next' (174), takes some comfort in defining itself in relation to *you*: 'And you, whoever you are, / That I am other to'. Being 'waylaid' may be exactly what *I* longs for most: 'always language / Is where the people are' (168). Francis's 'place I can think [...] anything in', anchored in this world of contacts and contexts, shows up as an occasional 'aside', a 'momentary' stay against the 'vastness' of speeches and listenings. It opens up another way of encountering the verbal world. Even Graham's pronominal play ('we go') indicates that 'I' is encountered against a shared experience of thought, against which that place 'I can think in' is temporarily attempted. The perspective of the 'I' is a possible variation on a common way of perceiving (together), not a longed-for permanent condition of estrangement: 'Hoping that *for a moment* / They will become for me / A place'. Here, as in the 1949 poem, 'Three Letters', Graham is alert to the perils of craving 'my ease', of being 'Stopped for a second dead / Out of the speaking flood', even as he desires to test out how an experience only 'for me', however temporary, might take shape (101).

Not only do such addresses to *you* give structure, *bounds*, to the hazy notion of being able to think 'anything' (itself a highly familiar, unoriginal fantasy of verbal independence), they also highlight the limitations of apparent linguistic freedom. Graham's poems and letters repeatedly question the limits of independence, pulling us back to meanings made with, and against, others: if 'the shape of all of us is in this language' that is a changeable shape in which 'we' continually alter ('Notes' 380). Lyric addresses may be sites of play, but also of labour, battle, strategic camouflage, literary and historical struggle: the poet both collaborates with, and upbraids, 'past masters', readers, publishers, book-buying audiences, friends, fellowpoets, patrons. We will see more of this in subsequent chapters, as we consider addresses in which Graham's propensity for combative relations with *you*—relations in which national identity and literary tradition are played out—is bound up with questions about fashion-following, emulation, affectation, and disguise.

2

Occupied Territory

The consciousness of what one really is [...] is 'knowing thyself' as a product of the historical process to date which has deposited in you an infinity of traces, without leaving an inventory.

Antonio Gramsci, *Selections from the Prison Notebooks*

FASHIONABLE ENOUGH: ADDRESS AS EMULATION, AFFECTATION, DISGUISE

Graham's plain-speaking addresses often warn *you* to stay alert to what is 'fashionable *enough*', insisting both upon one's need to be in touch with the age's tastes, and to resist being merely, glibly, 'in fashion':

> Language is expensive if
> We want to strut, busked out
> Showing our best on silence.
> [...]
> You wear your dress like a prince but
> A country's prince beyond my ken.
> Through the chinks in your lyric coat
> My ear catches a royal glimpse
> Of fuzzed flesh, unworded body.
> Was there something you wanted to say?
> I myself dress up in what I can
> Afford on the broadway. Underneath
> My overcoat of the time's slang
> I am fashionable enough wearing
> The grave-clothes of my generous masters.
> 'Approaches'   179–80

The artist of a Graham poem should not allow his language to be passively swayed by others, either by contemporary ('the time's slang') or traditional ('my generous masters') tastes. In Graham's metaphor of verbal clothing, words might have to be worn, but should not be donned vainly: mere 'slang' is 'my overcoat', and the tattered cast-offs of the figures of the literary past clothe the poet.

There is little truck with posing modishly for an audience here. Or at least so Graham would have his audience believe. Graham's lines do also *affirm* the persistent vitality of dead masters, beyond fashion, taste, and 'the time's slang'. The lines imply, seriously, that Graham follows his literary forebears in highly respected poetic traditions, and also ensure that influence and style are worn lightly. Dress, like speech, is made to seem less a matter of abstract calculation than hand-to-mouth pragmatism: 'what I can', 'fashionable enough'. One has better things to do than clothe oneself to conform to contemporary tastes. 'I [...] dress up', Graham writes, as if like a child, he experimented with words improvised from an odd assortment of garments pulled out of a dressing-up box. 'Grave-clothes' pokes fun at poetry's serious attempt to put on the intellectual garb of venerable traditions, so that the lyric remains closely attentive to the pretensions at work in address's capacity ceremonially to venerate names: 'And for your applause [...?]', 'May I also thank [...]' (*NCP* 218).' The lyric underlines the ease with which a poet can slip into intellectual posturing. But whilst W. S. Graham hardly looks dignified or 'fashionable' robed in the grave-robbed hand-me-downs of 'my generous masters', the poem also gravely dons the garb of its Modernist masters, in particular the verbal apparel of W. B. Yeats. The section is highly reminiscent of 'A Coat':

> I made my song a coat
> Covered with embroideries
> Out of old mythologies
> From heel to throat;
> But the fools caught it,
> Wore it in the world's eyes
> As though they'd wrought it.
> Song, let them take it,
> For there's more enterprise
> In walking naked.[1]

In putting on the metaphor of being clothed in words, Graham knowingly fashions himself in Yeats's high modern style, letting Modernist voices be sounded through the fabric of his contemporary poem. Yeats, too, envisaged poetry's 'song' or 'lyric coat' as a highly wrought garment, woven carefully from 'old mythologies', uninterested in affectation, so there is a degree of trend-following at play in Graham's literary re-donning of this lyric garb. Graham's poem, like Yeats's, plays the 'old' off against the new, for in both texts, the idea of language as crafted fashion*ing* is pulled into relation with the idea of words as followers of fashion.

---

[1] 'A Coat' (1914), in *Major Works* 59.

But is Graham, then, following 'foolishly', or enterprisingly reworking his generous master? Precisely because Yeats, like many of the Modernists, had already successfully stressed the need to innovate freshly with the past, Graham's poem could be accused of tapping into that achieved popular consensus 'worn for the world's eyes'. Is he exploiting a Yeatsian style, in claiming his poem will not settle for mere modishness? One could answer that Graham's writing deflates the idea of neatly tailoring one's words for social occasions: it rudely refuses either to follow dress codes or to fit in with the suitable vocabularies and idioms of an age: 'I am fashionable *enough*', 'I dress myself up in *what I can*', he writes curtly. Yet that too, is a recollection of Yeats: 'For there's more enterprise / In walking naked' his poem declares roundly. Yeats may be suggesting that one should renounce language altogether, if one's song is 'caught' by fools. The poem implies that it is advisable to withdraw into bare silence: one should nakedly refuse to cooperate with those who wear words in the wrong, foolishly venerating, way. Yet it is also keen to go on singing its song, deliberately creating a verse that fashion-following figures are unlikely to want to be heard reciting, since it is highly critical of that following itself. What, then, is Graham doing, when he 'catches' hold of Yeats? To catch Yeats against his will may also be to catch him in the right way; the way that allows Yeats to be sounded again, and against, Graham. This combative re-sounding is more than passive, recapitulating veneration of the master: it alters, whilst harking back to, Yeatsian mastery. Though Graham wears Yeats's lyric coat in the world's eyes, he has also really 'wrought' it. Proclaiming, in any case, to be happy to be seen in unfashionable, old-fashioned garb, Graham would not be put off by Yeats's stern rebuke to literary fashion-followers: the rebuke may even be viewed as an incentive by the younger poet to do the job better than these mere 'fools'.

Both poets, then, remain fascinated by the fashions they claim to resist. For words that have 'dressed *up*' seem to have gone to some effort to look good: Graham's 'fashionable enough' continues to judge, and to justify his appearance in accordance with, just how fashionable or unfashionable he can get away with being. Similarly, Yeats's refusal to participate in the world of fashion-following makes use of those it rejects: Yeats continues to define his word-wearing style against these literary emulators, precisely to the extent that his own 'song' dons an unornamented, plain-speaking garb, which he hopes fashion-followers will not think new enough to pass off as their own. But in doing so, Yeats's lyric must tune itself closely to the event of its reception; and it throws down a challenge to subsequent literary acts that work, not dissimilarly to Graham's poem, as incitement to future writers.

Using words as materials for dressing-up entertains word and dress as forms of serious role-playing: language is guise and disguise, self-exploration, formation and protection. Words, like clothes, may be social encumbrances, but they are also necessary to function within society, with others. They are also a means of exploring the literary community's social norms and expectations, aspirations and pretensions. Like Yeats's 'song', Graham's verse works against what might be seen as poetical affectation: the poems can be seen common-sensically making-do, improvising, 'busking'. Occasionally, however, the work indicates its desire for something grander; the 'expensive' word, the word which 'glamours me', a 'royal glimpse' (178–80). This fantasized *richesse* runs through the addresses of 'Approaches', which imagine they can 'strut', 'showing our best', in a display that is no longer dependent upon the 'generosity' of old masters, or the consideration of what one can 'afford'. Here the fantasies are played out in terms of a glamorous addressee:

> You wear your dress like a prince but
> A country's prince beyond my ken.　(180)

The fantasy doesn't last long. Graham has scarcely conceived of this royal state before we find him raising an objection: even before the enjambment one runs up against that limiting '*but*'. Meanwhile, the unprincely dialect construction 'beyond my ken' further emphasizes the speaker's removal from the word-wearing glamour of the addressee. The lines hark back to questionings of national identity and allegiance, testing language's power to operate in the historical fray. The lines glance towards the politics of the Jacobite cause, the strategic negotiations between England and Scotland over the Union, and especially the figure of Bonnie Prince Charlie, in whom the tropes of literal and figurative disguise culminate. Defeated at Culloden after an abortive attempt to lead a rebellion, the Prince went into hiding, donning numerous disguises to avoid capture until his escape to France. Graham's allusive disguise is neither child's dress-up, nor mere frivolous posturing, but a matter of life and death, necessary camouflage and nationalist loyalty.

It is also, however, disguise brought into contact with its more negative associations: fraudulence, ideological manipulation, exposure and betrayal. Graham's *you* ensures that self-fashioning word-wearing is associated with the cultural and artistic political negotiations employed in the process of creating, and sustaining, royal mythologies, particularly the ingenious political self-inventions and dissimulations of the exiled Stuarts. The mythological construct of the 'patriot' Prince was carefully connected with the belief that Scotland had declined from classical purity, and designed to encourage the people's nostalgia for a Scotland uncorrupt and free from imperial responsibilities. Artistic representations of Charles put forward a view of Scotland as a nation weakened by English bondage; a nation that required the restorative genius of a bold, heroic Stuart king who represented the true, ancient spirit of the Scottish nation. Such idolization of 'Bonnie Prince Charlie' carried on despite (or because of) his Culloden defeat: his army continued to be perceived by many as a valiant campaign of failed liberation, motivated by bold, Highlander patriotism. This was a disguised view of the facts. Charles Edward's army was far from exclusively comprised of Highlanders: it contained both Lowland and Highland men, as well as English, French, and Irish men. But Culloden was, and still occasionally is, recalled as a Highland battle; a heroic last attempt of an old culture to throw off the mastery of the new.[2]

As Graham's lines continue, they too become increasingly attentive to the calculated misrepresentations at play in royal self-fashioning, and to the falsely 'worded body' of powerful mythologization that surrounds it. Potential exposure is rife. 'Your lyric coat', and even the body beneath, threaten to unravel, to be seen through. The lines focus more on 'the *chinks* in your lyric coat', than on any impressive acts of verbal and iconographic self-fashioning, whilst flaws, cracks, and imperfections haunt the princely disguise:

> Through the chinks in your lyric coat
> My ear catches a royal glimpse
> Of fuzzed flesh, unworded body.
> Was there something you wanted to say?   (180)

Graham's eyes home in on precisely what this princely *you* would conceal: 'fuzzed flesh', 'unworded body'. His invasive gaze is drawn to the fleshy, bodily, the not-quite-decent: 'fuzzed', 'unworded', as if the prince's being bereft of words were akin to naked disclosure, his being improperly exposed. 'Was there something you wanted to say?' the speaker demands, his invitation to dialogue emphasizing the addressee's red-faced muteness still further. This *you* seems to be half-undressed by Graham's lines, as if, word by word, his poem were stripping the 'country's prince' of clothing and decency, as well as verbal power. Keen to expose the unelevated and bodily behind the royal trappings, the unformulated stammerings underneath the apparently eloquent 'lyric coat', it is Graham's penetrating 'glimpse' that is commandingly 'royal' in such

---

[2] For historical commentary on Culloden and analysis of the mythologization of Charles and the Jacobite cause see: Robin Nicholson, *Bonnie Prince Charlie and the Making of a Myth: A Study in Portraiture 1720–1892* (Cranbury, NJ: Bucknell University Press, 2002); Paul Kleber Monod, *Jacobitism and the English People, 1688–1788* (Cambridge: Cambridge University Press, 1993).

lines. Is Graham's *you* a fake, merely wearing his dress 'like a prince'? Do Graham's lines allude to Charles's status as 'Young Pretender'; a title his enemies used to cast doubt on his claim to royal ascent, to his rightful place as this 'country's prince'? Or to Graham's own temptation to dress up in royal garb and perform an allusive literary 'strut'? What kind of pretender would Graham's poet be?

'Approaches' is highly alert to, and deftly presents its readership with, a densely woven network of lyric addresses that are used to probe the cultural power of art and patronage. It raises questions that we can see in the politico-historical addresses of a range of contemporary Scottish writers, including Douglas Dunn, Tom Leonard, Kathleen Jamie, Ian Hamilton Finlay, and Edwin Morgan. These poets use address to probe how the interactions between language and culture, place, people, history, and politics take place. Jamie's 'The Queen of Sheba', for instance, scrutinizes just poetic-public conduct and royal continuity, and probes the literary rendering of cultural heritage and contemporary politics.[3] So too, Dunn's *Barbarians* ranges through history, questioning '[a]ll the dead Imperia' and the literary language of cultural authority, while *St Kilda's Parliament* offers a range of grittily historical addresses, from the mock-serious 'Address on the Destitution of Scotland' to the critical handling of Walter Scott's 'Green Breeks'.[4] Not entirely dissimilarly, Finlay's concrete poetry—especially his garden-poem, *Little Sparta*—accosts *you* with the historicity of words at every turn and path; through language etched into stones, plaques, benches, headstones, and bridges. *Little Sparta* confronts visitors with the living power of ancient language and object, reminding *you* that the past is alive in our understandings of the contemporary world, and that history instructively scripts political and personal words and deeds in the present.[5] Each of these poets flags up the power of contemporary language that stands in honour of particular historical *you*s; and which depends upon shared art-forms to promote, and engender, national, regional, geographical, political, and royal self-fashioning. Emphasizing the importance of auditors remaining highly visually and verbally aware when being addressed by historical, aesthetic, and national narratives, Graham's poems (like those of his peers) are highly alert to an audience's and poet's need to resist—or at least remain suspicious of—the lure of self-congratulation that plays around the power that comes with

---

[3] Kathleen Jamie, 'The Queen of Sheba', *Waterlight* (Northumberland: Bloodaxe, 1994) 85–8.

[4] Dunn, see *DSP* 149 and 177–81.

[5] See Jessie Sheeler and Andrew Lawson, *Little Sparta: The Garden of Ian Hamilton Finlay* (London: Frances Lincoln, 2003); Yves Abrioux and Stephen Bann, *Ian Hamilton Finlay: A Visual Primer* (London: Reaktion Books, 2007).

popular attention, and the present power of art-forms that were wielded as propaganda through history.

Hugh MacDiarmid once complained that Graham's work was 'purely aesthetic', irresponsibly 'playing with the materials of great poetry': 'this work would seem to have no root in its native soil [...] I cannot regard Graham's work as in any way answering to the crucial needs and possibilities of our time.'[6] Graham did not regard his own poetry as a platform for the assertion of national identity or cultural independence: 'I do recognise a Scots timbre in my "voice" although I can't see myself, in any way, as characteristic of Scots poetry.'[7] But Graham's work, as we have seen, is hardly inattentive to being read in the Scottish tradition, nor insistent upon being entirely exiled from it (see also 'Baldy Bane', 'To Alexander Graham', 'A Page About My Country', 'Sgurr na Gillean Macleod').[8] What Graham *is* highly resistant to is the idea that nationalist 'answering' is the only, or primary, form of cultural responsiveness by which 'the crucial needs and possibilities of our time' should be judged. His comments on Scotland in the letters reinforce his distaste for (what he sees as) the Scottish literary scene's insistence that literary-political responsiveness should follow this staunchly nationalist agenda:

> Have I given up Scotland? Not that I know. I certainly couldn't write the poems I do without being Scots [...] But the selfconsciousness of what the Scottish art scene seems to be today embarrasses me tae hell.[9]

This is a writer that sees himself as answering, and facetiously answering back to, the apparent need for 'selfconscious' national and literary categorization, as asserted by figures including MacDiarmid and Edwin Morgan. Graham's work is not an 'irresponsible' retreat from the call to explore poetry's historico-political involvement in the public fray, but (like MacDiarmid's own controversial, critical poetic) a principled, and equally self-conscious refusal to fashion itself in accordance with the age's style of political poetics: he will not work as a champion of the cause of the Scottish literary scene by writing a 'characteristic' Scots poetry.

For Graham (as for MacDiarmid), it is the artist's refusal to adapt his work to please his audience, or to placate dissenting critics, which is amongst the 'crucial needs of our time'. Graham's criticism of the need to win praise is hedged about with concern for the right way of wearing literary and political garb, of appropriately drawing on, and drawing itself

---

[6] Hugh MacDiarmid, Rev. of *CWG*, in *The Free Man*, c.1942; quoted by Lopez, *The Poetry of W. S. Graham* 11.

[7] Vinson and Kirkpatrick, *Contemporary Poets* 575.

[8] Graham, *NCP* 145; 222; 281; 223.

[9] Letter to William Montgomerie, 24 September 1969, 229.

into, historical accounts and venerated literary traditions. Graham's poetic structures do not renounce Scottish, or European, or Anglo-American models. But in Graham's work, literary alignments remain decidedly performative; characterized by a self-scrutinizing trying-on of a style rather than a straightforward or unselfconscious wearing of it.

MEN MADE OUT OF WORDS: RULING VOICES

'Literature belongs to no one man', wrote Ezra Pound: 'all values ultimately come from our judicial sentences'.[10] For the American poet, Wallace Stevens, too, 'it is a world of words to the end of it, in which words, far from isolating us, compel communality'.[11] Graham's poems, like Stevens's, listen back on and reform the Modernist consideration that understandings, meanings, and selves are shaped in a common language, speaking with, and answering back to, particular Modernist interlocutors, in so doing. 'I need ideogram',[12] wrote Pound of the Cantos; a text in which 'I' is itself the unstable nexus of invading languages, genres, cultures, texts, aliases, and persons (Ulysses, Odysseus, Elias, Elijah, Otis, Ytis, Io), and in which cross-cultural polyvocality punctures the notion that the poetry is being directed from 'inside'. In Pound, as in Graham, the text is talked over and across by conflicting contemporary and historical voices competing for the reader's ear. 'Lie quiet Divus. I mean that is Andreas Divus', Pound addresses the Renaissance scholar and his translating predecessor, interrupting the invoked oral tradition with the invasion of this lyric 'I' (*Cantos* 1:5). Such tactics emphasize that oral and written traditions are communal creations, changing with speakers, listeners, writers, readers, translators, and re-translators: 'This is not a work of fiction / nor yet of one man' (*Cantos* 99:708).

Communal verbal compulsion was not always viewed positively by Modernist poets. 'A world of words to the end of it' brooks no dissent, and hardly offers flexibility. For Stevens, a central, vexed problematic of Modernism is the relationship between language and being; the extent to which what one says dictates what one is. A speaker may shape his language, but he is likewise frighteningly shaped by it. In Stevens's tellingly entitled poem, 'Men Made Out of Words', and in his pronouncement

---

[10] Pound, 'Hell' (1934) in *Essays*, 201–13, 207; Letter to Felix E. Schelling (190), 8 July 1922, in *The Letters of Ezra Pound 1907–1941*, ed. D. D. Paige (London: Faber, 1951) 245–9, 249. Referred to hereafter as *Letters*.

[11] Wallace Stevens, 'Description Without Place' (1947), in *Collected Poems* (London: Faber, 1984) 302. Referred to hereafter as *SCP*.

[12] Letter to Katue Kitasono (382), 15 November 1940, *Letters*, 447.

'men make themselves their speech', Stevens emphasizes both men's power
to shape the language for themselves, and language's exertion of itself over
its speakers (*SCP* 310; 302). These lyrics question whether men can be
anything more than the sum total of their speech, and sees them reduced
to a disempowered, nameless collective: 'men', with no differentiating
characteristics or individuality. *I*s and *you*s become a mouthpiece for that
linguistic will, part of an indistinct verbal mass.

Cohabitation in 'a world of words' is seen more generatively, on the
other hand, by Graham, as well as by mid-century philosophers of lan-
guage, whom Graham had exposure to during his course in philosophy
and literature at Newbattle Abbey in the 1930s. Tenets of Graham's poetry
reflect arguments made by ordinary language philosophers, particularly
Wittgenstein, Austin, Searle, and Cavell. When Graham writes in 'The
Thermal Stair' that 'words make their world', his poem reminds one of
Stevens's lyric statement ('It is a world of words to the end of it'), and
re-envisages that world-making in more approbatory, Wittgensteinian
terms.[13] If, in Graham's poem, words constitute reality, they do so change-
ably: 'surprise us', 'seeing new'. Language enables meaning, rather than
flatly 'defining' it. This is not dissimilar to the thesis in *Philosophical Inves-*
tigations that what words mean depends upon their use; a use that emerges
in shared language-games with adaptable rules: 'is there not also a case
where we play and—make up the rules as we go along? And there is even
one where we alter them—as we go along?'[14] One might remember that
Pound, too, in relation to language's rhythm, had been moved to com-
ment, not altogether approvingly: 'There aren't any rules.'[15]

When Graham, in a letter to Ruth Hilton in 1967, writes that, 'Not
knowing the rules, most of the game I, spectator, see, hear and suffer', he
at once emphasizes the Wittgensteinian rule-bound verbal play of self-
fashioning, and implies, like Stevens (and Pound), that 'not knowing the
rules, most of the game' may be a verbal recipe for a confusion of sights
and sounds, for 'suffering'.[16] Yet in so doing, Graham's letter points out
that the very possibility of expressing suffering in this way relies on making
moves within the game that he and others understand. These are moves
that he evidently enjoys making, in writing to *you*:

---

[13] 'The Thermal Stair' (1970), in *NCP* 164. Stevens, *HCP* 302.

[14] Wittgenstein, *PI* §83, 39.

[15] Letter to Mary Barnard (275), 23 February 1934, *Letters* 339. See also Geoffrey Hill's
Canaan 74: 'The strident high / civic trumpeting / of misrule'. See *Tenebrae* (*HCP* 174):
the poet is a succession of role changing guises: 'the Lord of Misrule. / [...] Master of the
Leaping Figures, / the motley factions'. Even as it parades the threat of a non-rational verbal
order overruling the laws of reason, the poetry gravitates towards recognizable, patterned
verbal discourse.

[16] 21 March, 209–10.

I'll buy that [...] Make me twig No. 99995 on the greatest oak in a forest
of terrible thousands. But save me from life as a dressing-table leg [...]
Make me forget to stir the lentil pot of my moral broth. Make me make.
Make me make me (*Nightfisherman* 210).

Such addresses demand that others come out to play: they invite their
addressee to join in with, and to help fashion, the speaker ('Make me
make me'). Ruth is to participate in Graham's rule-bending meaning-
making. For Graham, like Wittgenstein, words take on meanings with
others in the culture: meanings are flexible, shared, verbal processes.[17] In
writing to Ruth that 'The thing is to find or create (in this case the same
thing) a language, a timbre of thought or voice, which I will live in', he is
scripting her participation into this 'timbre', not envisaging a lonely habi-
tation. For Graham, if '[w]e say ourselves in syllables',[18] we engage in
consensual language practices that take place within interpretative human
communities, a kind of *sensus communis*. Rather than fearing that the acts
of understanding and interpretation take place only 'in syllables', Graham
reads words as the stuff that enables the human community to function
meaningfully: the capacity to 'say ourselves' is tied to the practical inter-
ests of ordinary, imaginative people.[19]

In Graham, it is not negative that artists open themselves to language's
shaping force. If words speak their speakers, this enables productive
change: language, like 'the painter's / Mark surprises him / Into seeing
new' ('Thermal Stair' 164). 'Seeing new', here, offers an opening up of
poetic perception. Lyric insight depends upon the poet's responsiveness to
suddenness and chance, not his reliance upon calculated attainment. Sim-
ilarly, the language of invitation, dialogue, and response plays through
Graham's lines. In addressing this *you* (his recently deceased colleague),
Graham's work counterposes the urge for single-handed mastery over lan-
guage, and the Stevensian fear of men being reduced by words to a face-
less collective 'we':

> You said once in the Engine
> House below Morvah
> That words make their world

---

[17] *PI* §83, 39. See also Austin's *How to Do Things With Words* 5. '[T]o utter [...] sen-
tences is not just to "say" something, but rather to perform a certain kind of action.'

[18] Stevens, 'The Creations of Sound' 271.

[19] See Kant: 'we must take *sensus communis* to mean the idea of a sense shared [by us all],
i.e., a power to judge that in reflecting takes account (a priori), in our thought, of everyone
else's way of presenting [something], in order as it were to compare our own judgement
with human reason in general [...] Now we do this as follows: we compare our judgement
not so much with the actual as rather with the merely possible judgements of others, and
[thus] put ourselves in the position of everyone else.' Immanuel Kant, *The Critique of
Judgement*, trans. Werner Pluhar (Indianapolis: Hackett, 1987) 160.

> In the same way as the painter's
> Mark surprises him
> Into seeing new.
> Sit here on the sparstone
> In this ruin where
> Once the early beam
> Engine pounded and broke
> The air with industry.   (164)

In contrast to Stevens, Graham's address here opens itself to—and to being altered by—whatever answering responses it receives from *you*. One of those responses occurred in Lanyon's and Graham's shared past, and did change the poet: 'you said once [...] / That words make their world'. Deferring to *you*, the poem acknowledges that authorship of its insight belongs to another. If, for Graham and Lanyon, 'words make their world' this is not evidence of words' imprisoning treachery. Rather words are part of friendly dialogue, conversation between companions. In elegizing the recently deceased Lanyon, Graham's recalled conversation offers what is now empirically unavailable: words give him continued access to this lost *you*. This is quite different from his addressing the absent *you* to confirm his abject isolation (as Francis et al. have argued). Lanyon's words, both in the poem's present and its remembered past, enable Graham to work with his addressee, in a language that is ours, not mine or yours.

'You said...', 'Sit here on the sparstone', 'I called and you were away', 'Give me your hand [...] / To steady me': such addresses strive to make contact, not just with their known addressee, but all those who read the lines (164). Both 'the painter's mark' and 'what you said' have currency through circulation in a speaking community where they are manoeuvred, and altered by, *your* collective soundings and resoundings. This is to tap the elegiac, Romantic urge 'to speak and soar to you' in terms of communal speech. The lines treat address as part of general public intelligibility, a huge common vocabulary; what Stanley Cavell called 'agreement in valuing'.[20] Again, the desire to be united with 'you', to transcend death and distance, manifests differently from Stevens's Modernist-Romantic encounters with another. Address, for Graham, collects a critical community around it, a community generatively driven to write, speak, paint, and elegize, in the face of loss, fear, isolation, and change. In Stevens's 'The World as Meditation', a greater privation is envisioned:

> She has composed, so long, a self with which to welcome him,
> Companion to his self for her, which she imagined,
> Two in a deep-founded sheltering, friend and dear friend.   (455)

---

[20] Stanley Cavell, *The Claim of Reason* (Oxford: Oxford University Press, 1979) 94.

The Romantic urge to fuse with an estranged loved one, Penelope with Ulysses, enters Stevens's twentieth-century lyric alongside ontological linguistic anxieties. Will absolute identification with another cause the loss of one's sense of self? Direct dealings with another imperil *I*'s stability, as the epigraph warns: '*Je vis un rêve permanent, qui ne s'arrête ni nuit ni jour.*' Is it better to live in a world of (solitary) meditation, only contemplating others from a distance? Or is this out-of-touch '*rêve permanent*' the worrying product of self-isolation? For Stevens, Penelope may be both true and constant to her longed-for lover: 'Never forgetting him that kept coming constantly so near'. But her constancy also depends upon Ulysses's deferred non-arrival, a deferral which paradoxically enables her to maintain her state of faithful anticipation. It is not 'one, in a deep-founded sheltering' that she yearns for, but 'two': 'friend and dear friend'; a conservation of separatenesses. The poem implies that Penelope is able to remain 'composed' despite the fervour of her longing for Ulysses's presence, precisely because he never appears to alter or shake her composure: he does not enter into or dream her dream. Ulysses remains a manipulable product of Penelope's thought. He is unthreateningly what 'she imagined', just as her 'self with which to welcome him' is safely, single-handedly constructed—so long as he never turns up to receive that offered welcome.

When, three poems later in *The Rock*, Stevens dares to envisage 'the intensest rendezvous' actually taking place, the experience is oddly abstract, coolly 'composed':

> Here, now, we forget each other and ourselves.
> We feel the obscurity of an order, a whole,
> [...]
>
> [...] being there together is enough.
>   'Final Soliloquy of the Interior Paramour', *SCP* 458

'Here, now', 'We feel': the lines narrate the moment of fusion in the present tense, emphasizing the transformation that should have occurred. Yet this moment of forgetting remains mere potential. 'Here, now, we forget' undermines the very forgetfulness it claims to achieve. If we really had forgotten how to distinguish between 'each other and ourselves', we would not be able to make the observation. The lines might be interpreted as: 'at this very moment [...] we are scheduled to forget, but we have not'. Similarly, 'being there together' figures 'there' as elsewhere, a place beyond the reach of separate individuals. 'Enough' smacks of limit and limitation: fusion not as overwhelming, but as just sufficient, and hence still under the speaker's control. Such poetry remains distanced from its own avowed attempts to envisage unity. As if holding back from full identification with the *you*s they include in voicing *we*, the speakers of such poetry remain self-protectingly '[s]upremely true each to its separate self'.[21]

Graham's addresses (like Pound's and Eliot's) insist that both in 'being there together' and in being 'true' to my 'separate self', *I* is constituted from a network of relationships between original and translation, reader, writer, and subject: 'As I hear so I speak so I am so I think / You must be', 'Here where all dialogues write'.[22] In those dialogues, the sounds of past traditions—Romantic and Modernist, philosophical and quotidian, Scots and English—jostle with the lyric present: 'I tie my verse in a true reef / Fast for the purposes of joining' (247). Yet, since Graham's lyrics often take verbal pleasure in showing that they emanate not from a consistent and discrete single author, but from 'all' changeable idioms, registers, and persons, the poems might seem to renounce order, protection, unity, excusing themselves from the Modernist striving to 'make it cohere'. In Graham, poetic calling often enables those called, and the language itself, to respond invasively: 'These words as I uttered them / Spoke back at me' (246). Addressees interrupt the poem, as if desirous to speak in the author's place. Similar impressions of literary hijacking are generated in the early poem: 'Remarkable Report By Some Poetic Agents', where the poet shrugs his shoulders at the attempt to retain authority and certainty: 'Chiefly by accident (which I myself prefer) / Freedom is reached', 'There was from March 3rd to April 3rd the appearance of reality'.[23] Creative work is performed 'by' the poetic agents, not the author: the phrasing 'Some Poetic Agents' can hardly muster the energy to try and pin them down. We are merely told: 'A man shouted out, involved in outcry'. Likewise, in 'The Nightfishing' Graham writes, 'Men shout. Words break. I am', as if he were composed from a plethora of articulations, from the voices of a powerfully unspecific, interchangeable body of 'men'.[24]

Yet Graham's role-play and role-swapping take place more in the manner of a principled, latter-day Modernist rule-testing than a postmodern jouissance, even if Graham also seeks to test out the appropriateness of the latter as a means of handling the age's transhistorical fragments. Writing as if part of his artistic duty were to let 'mingling' voices be sounded through him, Graham envisages the poet as an instrument through which the sounds of, and across, time are registered, organized,

---

[21] Stevens, 'Re-Statement of Romance' (1936), in *SCP* 125.

[22] Graham, 'Implements' 248; 'Seven Letters' 123.

[23] Graham, 'Remarkable Report by Some Poetic Agents' (1943) 53.

[24] Graham, 'Nightfishing', 116. See Coleridge's definition of primary imagination in the *Biographia Literaria*: 'The primary IMAGINATION I hold to be the living Power and prime Agent of all human Perception, and as a repetition in the finite mind of the eternal act of creation in the infinite I AM' (New York: Leavitt; Boston: Croker, 1834) 172, ch. 3.

made recognizable: 'I am the shell held / To Time's ear and you / May hear' ('Dialogues' 172). Graham's poet is by turns a broadcaster, making Time's sounds audible to *you*, and an aural mirror, enabling time to perceive its own, previously unheard, sounds. As recently exited instrument (a 'shell'), Graham's poet is in part an echoing space, passively awaiting others' sounds ('I am held'), and also an active object, demanding independent song ('you hear'). The delicate, once-living instrument requires sensitive aural and physical handling ('held / To [...] you'), rather as MacNeice's cradled brandy-glass enabled the cherished sounds of 'time' to be heard: 'Only let it form within his hands once more— / The moment, cradled like a brandy-glass'.[25] Graham's recapturing of poetic voices is at once precarious, like MacNeice's 'cradled [...] glass', and boldly resonant, like Shelley's vision of the poet-figure as 'lyre', in 'Ode to the West Wind':

> Scatter, as from an unextinguished hearth
> Ashes and sparks, my words among mankind!
> Be through my lips to unawakened earth
> The trumpet of a prophecy! [...][26]

Commanding as they are, both Graham's and Shelley's lyrics assert that they need to be moved by external forces. These poems emanate neither merely from the core of the self, nor entirely from the culture: the poet's address provides a meeting-place for both individual and collective voices. Particularly, both Shelley's and Graham's *I*s appeal to *you* to be occupied, sounded, used. 'Make me thy lyre', 'Be thou me', Shelley's speaker begs, and commands, its auditor: 'Scatter', 'Be through my lips'. Graham's poem, too, is half necessary instrument ('The trumpet of a prophecy!'), and half instrumental; an empty vessel (trumpet, lyre, shell) passively awaiting another. That poem needs *you* to fill it, to let it be voiced and received: 'held to time's ear', 'you may hear'.

The speaker of a Graham poem, then, is not a single consistent figure, but a changing point of spatial or aural focus, asking to be occupied by, and in relation to, others. *I* swerves between the literary styles, accents and demands of:

> [...] A mixed company.
> Kandinsky's luminous worms,
> Shelley, Crane and Melville and all
> The rest. Who knows? Maybe even Eliot.
>   'Implements' 251

---

[25] MacNeice, 'The Brandy Glass' (1937), in *MCP* 92.
[26] Percy Bysshe Shelley, 'Ode to the West Wind' (1820), in *Shelley: Poetical Works*, ed. Thomas Hutchinson (London: Oxford University Press, 1970) 579.

Graham's *I* manifests quite differently from Shelley's. Repeatedly invaded by a succession of changing *you*s, and by the continually altering common registers of quotidian and of literary language, 'I go / Floating across the frozen tundra / Of the lexicon and the dictionary' (246). 'Implements' floats across the tundra of phrasings, clichés, domestic idiom, as well as political, literary, and aesthetic registers. Such verse is highly attentive to its Modernist, postmodern, Romantic, and post-Romantic heritage, as well as drawing on Anglo-American, Scottish, and European aesthetic contexts. If language is a 'frozen' structure, at least temporarily solid, the diction of such poetics rests upon that structure for its movement and motion, but it also relies upon its potential to achieve a certain liquidity. Sometimes precarious, sometimes graceful, these poets' words may fall down upon, or through, the thawing surface at any moment: as in Graham's inelegant verbal 'stumble in a bramble'.[27] In Graham, lyrics are not spaces of secure interlocution but of bungling and tongue-twisting addresses calling to be deciphered by *you*. Such poetic language repeatedly draws attention to ineptness, slapstick, and fierce provisionality; determined not to portray lyricism as unambivalently impressive, verbally masterful, Graham speaks of 'communication's mistakes in the magic medium'.[28]

But what kind of investment might this Modernist-inspired poet have in depicting late twentieth-century poetry as a perilous crossing over, criss-crossing, and double-crossing of common idioms? Does his investment in address hope to explore poetry's capacity for responsible speech? If so, Graham's sense of poetical responsibility might be comparable to Pound's exploration of the force of poetry's satirical addresses; the punch of their social corrective: 'O generation of the thoroughly smug and thoroughly uncomfortable'.[29] As we will see in the next section, Graham's sense of appropriate redress to his audience is often coupled with his fluid adoption of changeable poetic roles: in 'Malcolm Mooney's Land' the author-figure steps between the positions of critic and creator, reader and writer, audience and actor, speaker and spoken-to, and spoken-through, to issue its corrective.[30]

In *English Poetry Since 1940*, Neil Corcoran writes that, for Graham, 'solipsism is mitigated by the sense that consciousness becomes most alive in these written exchanges between writer and reader, that the most alert self-consciousness may be created and shared within the poem's language: so that the poem is always dialogue, community,

[27] 'Dear Who I Mean', *NCP* 160.
[28] Graham, *NCP* 200.
[29] 'Salutation' (1916), in *Personae* 85.
[30] 'Malcolm Mooney's Land' (1970), in *NCP* 153.

invitation and intertext'.[31] I would agree that dialogue, community, and intertext are central to Graham's work, but, as we have seen, these are not dependent upon Graham's occasionally 'mitigating' solipsism through snatched moments of verbal 'sharing' or 'invitation'. Rather, Graham's work pulls the rug out from under the solipsist's feet: in language, pure privation and self-imprisonment are not possible. Put this recognition alongside the pronouncement that words make our world, and you can see how, for Graham, isolation becomes a fallacy (just as, for Wittgenstein, a purely 'private language' would not hold water).[32] Graham's poems and letters point out that they cannot help but negotiate the discourses of a culture. The poet's distinctive voice is a dialogue busy with that 'mixed company' of differing, mingling voices.

[31] Neil Corcoran, *English Poetry since 1940* (London: Longman, 1993) 50.

[32] *PI* §§244–71 shows that a language in principle unintelligible to anyone but its originating user is impossible. Such 'language' would necessarily be unintelligible even to its originator, for she would be unable to establish meanings for its signs. Further, if each individual had her own private definitions for all words, communication would be impossible: that language works at all is proof of commonality of experience.

3

Read Me if You Dare: Address and Misbehaviour

ENTER THE POEM: ADDRESSING READERS

Addressed words often slip, slide, and behave badly in Graham, vexing their author as they move between changing dialogues, speakers, readers, addressees, and contexts. A speaker must 'approach how they behave' gingerly, taking care not to upset them further through a clumsily worded introduction. But Graham's address to his readers often looks more friendly and personal. It tries to get on good terms with its audience, pulling us into its social world:

> Let us get through the suburbs and drive
> Out further just for fun to see
> What he will do. Reader, it does
> Not matter. He is only going to be
>
> Myself and for you slightly you
> Wanting to be another [...]¹

Such address is not altogether dissimilar from Prufrock's direct and inviting summons: 'Let us go then, you and I' (13). Graham's 'Let us get through the suburbs and drive' feels almost as if the author were engaging us in a private aside, 'just between you and me'. In the guise of speaking to us directly, Graham's speaker slips casually into an easy, familiar idiom: 'Let us [...] drive', 'just for fun', trying to put his reader at ease: 'Reader, it does / Not matter'. Yet this voice, like Eliot's, sets out to unsettle, bewitch, and disturb, dismissing the expected cautions and customs we use to handle a poem. What may well 'matter' to the audience, simply 'does / Not matter' to the author, or so he claims. Here, as so often in his work, Graham's lyric performs strategic attacks upon the idea of reading as disengaged, safe observation, and moves to implicate his audience in the action occurring—whatever 'it' may be.

---

¹ 'What is the Language Using Us For?' (1974), in *NCP* 199.

However, one learns not to trust Graham's winsome, amiable address, any more than his nettling, demanding address: a similar challenge to recipients lies behind both. Whether kindly, or combative towards *you*, Graham is out to pull his audience into the poetic weave, to make them listen back on their own poetic footfalls. 'No, listen', Graham writes in an early poem, buttonholing his reader: 'Listen, for this I tell' (26). Writer and reader are often posed eye-to-eye, as well as ear-to-ear, for the later poems, too, produce unsettlingly confrontational, even physical, encounters: 'Language and light begin to go / To leave us looking at each other'.[2] Here, in 'Ten Shots of Mister Simpson', contact is made threatening, even mortally dangerous: 'touch your face / And look through into my face and into / The gentle reader's deadly face' (213). Are we readers deadly despite being 'gentle', or deadly because we want to think ourselves gentle? And how could readers look into the speaker's *face*, in a poem? Disturbingly, this face-to-face poetic encounter enables a reader to see his own face, through or in the text, as if the text were a mirror, reflecting each reader's scrutinizing visage back to him. One feels caught in the act, reading these lines. In looking for, and at, another (Graham), one is confronted by the image of oneself, wrinkling one's brow with the intensity of looking. Address is a form of such verbal capture, for the reader finds himself appearing in the poem's action, or complicit in its making. If, in 'Ten Shots', 'You shall / Emerge here within different / Encirclements in a different time', then in 'Private Poem' (both in *Implements*) one finds, 'The spaces in the poem are yours' (213: 228). In the poem that gives this 1977 volume its title, *you* is even commanded to compose part of the text itself:

> I leave you this space
> To use as your own.
> I think you will find
> That using it is more
> Impossible than making it.
> Here is the space now.
> Write an Implement in it.
> YOU ....
> YOU ....
> YOU ....
> YOU ....
> Do it with your pen.
> I will return in a moment
> To see what you have done.   249–50

---

[2] 'Ten Shots of Mister Simpson' (1974), in *NCP* 214.

In a similar way, 'What is the Language Using Us For?' pokes fun at the notion that a safe, passive audience perspective is available. This poem's action takes place between 'us', between Graham and ourselves. 'Malcolm Mooney', though a named figure, is not written of as a real person, nor even as a real character. In this he resembles Pound's 'Hugh Selwyn Mauberley', and Eliot's 'J. Alfred Prufrock', figures used by these writers to parody the notion of the poet speaking directly as 'real person' as well as the idea of speaking omnisciently about an invented 'character'. Such figures as 'E.P.', and, in *The Pisan Cantos*, Odysseus' 'ΟΥ ΤΙΣ' ('No Man'), also toyed with the distinction between fact and fiction: in creating aliases for the author-figure, these poems treated the lyric *I* as a construction, a 'Pound' or an 'Eliot'.[3] In such works, the poet cannot be relied upon to determine the distinction between self and persona. Graham's 'Malcolm Mooney', on the other hand, is not just an ironized author-figure, but an ironized personification of the act of poetic invention itself: 'Slowly over the white language / Comes Malcolm Mooney', 'Where am I going said Malcolm Mooney' (199–200). Since the latter question is one both writer and reader have a hand in asking and answering, Graham hints that *you* might find yourself in the curious position of creating Mooney (and the poem), as well as putting questioning, self-reflexive words about lyric art in poetry's mouth: 'Where am I going?' (i.e. 'where is this poetry going?', 'Are *you* altering its direction?'). Mooney is treated as a space into which the writer and reader project themselves, and tussle for authority. If Mooney 'is myself', he is also *you*: 'He is […] // […] you / Wanting to be another' (199). Graham's audience finds itself suddenly in ontological competition with this author.

But just as unexpectedly, Graham lays down his authorial hand in an enticing invitation. Stepping out of his role as textual master, he collaboratively steps into the role of spectator, seemingly re-aligning himself with his addressees: 'let *us* […] / […] see / What he will do', 'Let us observe' (199). For one textual moment, author and reader stand side by side, craning their necks to witness the unpredictable actions of the fictitious Malcolm Mooney. Now, pronouns contribute to the impression of the text as shared no-man's-land. 'Let us' oscillates between an imperious authorial command that disregards the wish of the reader, and the author's less-than-assertive plea for our permission. The reader is not merely watching the actions of Graham and Mooney, but actually engaged in complex negotiations with Graham over the territory of the poem.

---

[3] 'E.P. Ode Pour L'Eection de Son Sepulchre', *Personae* 187; *The Pisan Cantos LXXIV–LXXXIV* (1948), in *Cantos* 74:425.

Meanwhile, the typography indicates that the nature of the poem's contact with this 'you' is always, at least in one sense, public. The poem taps the Victorian vocabulary of audience; its capitalized 'Reader' figure flags up the historicity of literary address's engagement with its interlocutors.[4] Graham's text harks back, with gentle irony, to the 'gentle Reader' of Victorian fiction, a figure that was often politely appealed to for guidance, for moral (and financial) approval.[5] His own reader, no longer a private, ahistorical *you*, now becomes part of a body of 'Readers'. One finds oneself strangely cast as a member of a vast Victorian public that must be won over; that Graham imagines deferring to in order to secure future success and a source of income. The use of this 'Reader' is, in such instants, an acknowledgement of Graham's keen awareness of his own readership. Graham's 'Reader' lacks the intimacy of 'you' because it reinforces the roles available in print, roles that are enforced by that public, published medium.

We find a similar effect in his 1975 poem 'Enter a Cloud':

> Thank you. And for your applause.
> It has been a pleasure. I
> Have never enjoyed speaking more.
> May I also thank the real ones
> Who have made this possible.
> First, the cloud itself. And now
> Gurnard's Head and Zennor
> Head. Also recognise
> How I have been helped
> By Jean and Madron's Albert
> Strick (He is a real man.)
> And good words like brambles,
> Bower, spiked, fox, anvil, teeling.[6]

Though these lines again address the reader as part of an amassed body of spectators (in this case, an applauding public), they also approach that public very differently from 'What is the Language Using Us For?'. Graham's rhetoric here is that of an actor making a speech after an award-

---

[4] See Dorothy Mermin, *The Audience in the Poem: Five Victorian Poets* (New Brunswick, NJ: Rutgers University Press, 1983); also Emily Allen, *Theatre Figures: The Production of the Nineteenth-Century British Novel* (Columbus: Ohio State University Press, 2003) 14: 'For every image of "the" reading public as a unified community of respectable, like-minded readers, there is a corresponding one of monstrous dispersal [...] this massing of unknown readers [...] the intimacy of authorial address in the Victorian novel is [...] individuated over and against the ungentle, clamouring masses'.

[5] See Garrett Stewart, *Dear Reader: The Conscripted Audience in Nineteenth-Century British Fiction* (Baltimore: Johns Hopkins University Press, 1996).

[6] 'Enter A Cloud', *NCP* 218.

winning performance: 'May I also thank the real ones / Who have made this possible'.[7] Juxtaposing his public writerly voice with his spectators' imagined responses, Graham anticipates his work's future criticism, exploring the politics of reception by addressing us: '*And now . . .* for your applause . . . ?' The address attempts to anticipate the moves of his critic-readers, and to arrange the stage for their arrival, in the hope of out-manoeuvring them. Using the lyric space to negotiate *your* poetic and critical responses, Graham's lines envisage reaching into the space that will exist after the poem ceases; the space *you* occupy as *you* thumb his pages.[8]

This gracious public tone evidently has designs on those it speaks towards. By offering thanks to his addressees in advance, Graham places the onus on his audience to correct him, to withdraw their applause only if it is undeserved. Of course, partly through the appealing directness of the speech, 'Thank you [. . .] for your applause', 'recognise / How I have been helped', and partly through the ironized formality of the occasion, the poem makes it difficult, awkward, for any member of the audience to object. By turning the poem into a parody of a polite social gathering, a public ceremony, Graham knows that the conventions of such occasions will appear to apply: the assumed pleasantness and ceremonial public-spiritedness associated with such events will most likely allow him to pull off these crowd-pleasing tactics with good face, and win audience assent. The poet knows it is politic to assume applause, rather than waiting to receive it: he is more likely to secure favourable responses if he speaks as though favour has already been bestowed.

If Graham employs the formal idiom of the awards ceremony to secure 'applause', it is precisely such formality that his poem gleefully takes advantage of, and mocks. Parodying the obsequiousness common to these occasions, Graham inverts the expected call of named patrons and supporters that thanks are traditionally offered to, putting in their place simple scene, word, and thing: 'May I also thank [. . .] / [. . .] / First, the cloud itself. And now / Gurnard's Head and Zennor / Head', 'And good words like brambles, / Bower, spiked, fox, anvil, teeling' (218–19). Thanks will not be extended to esteemed literary patrons here, not even humorously, to 'Tommy E'. Rather, the poem is addressing the (unesteemed) 'community' of listeners, Graham's friends and colleagues who have really

---

[7] 218. Compare this with Patrick Kavanagh's heavily ironized turn to address an imagined reading audience in section XIV of *The Great Hunger* (1942): 'The curtain falls / Applause, applause'. *Collected Poems* (London: Penguin, 2005).

[8] One might think also of Sylvia Plath's unsettling addresses to an imagined assembled audience in 'Lady Lazarus': 'The peanut-crunching crowd', voyeuristic and violent: 'Shoves in to see / [. . .] / The big strip tease. / Gentlemen, ladies / These are my hands / My knees'. 'For the eyeing of my scars, there is a charge'. *Ariel* (1962), in *Collected Poems*, ed. and introd. Ted Hughes (London: Faber, 1981) 245–6.

'helped to make this happen', including 'Albert / Strick (He is a real man)', as well as 'words' themselves: 'Bower, spiked, fox, anvil' (219). Graham's poem is closely attentive to the pretensions at work in ceremonially venerating names, especially already venerated names, and the work carefully treads a line between humorousness and gravity, iconoclasm and traditionalism, underlining the ease with which the applause-seeking, readership-pleasing poet can slip into intellectual posturing. The readerly *you* is as much a figure to be sparred with, discomfited, tricked, as to be flattered, thanked, indulged.

CHALLENGING SPEECHES: DISORIENTING FAMILIARITY

In Graham, speaking to *you* often involves a wittily incendiary, plain-speaking address. The letters do not mince their words, even with their closest addressees: 'Dear you know well who answer me this if you dare', writes Graham in his playfully sparring correspondence with Bryan Wynter.[9] 'Damn you anyhow. I am sick of it', he writes to Roger Hilton: 'how can you waste your time just saying any old drivel (old school word) that comes into your head [...] TRY TO BE BETTER'.[10] Though the tone of the poems is somewhat less stern, sharp rebukes are meted out to a series of personal, but unspecified, *yous*: 'I could know you if I wanted to. / You make me not want to', 'Shut up. There's nobody here'.[11] Meanwhile, one finds Graham by turns ticking off, implicitly rebuking, and highlighting the more dubious qualities of his colleagues and loved ones: 'Doubtful ringmaster of / The successful circus of your despairs', 'uneasy, lovable man'.[12]

Frequently, the second-person pronoun is used to emphasize, by making personal, Graham's attack upon class pretensions, and upon the impudent social expectations engrained in language: 'England expects, Ireland expects'—just as Scotland, in the form of MacDiarmid et al., also 'expects' ('Implements' 244). Graham's address is often a way of turning a general social grumble into a provoking incitement to 'you'; the slender pronoun putting up its fists for a fight: 'I'm speaking to you'. It is an invitation to do verbal battle. Although the invitation is written in a straight-talking,

---

[9] Letter to Bryan Wynter, 19 November 1958, 162.

[10] Letter to Roger Hilton, 7 November 1966, 204; Letter to Roger Hilton, 24 September 1969; Extracts from 'Reply to a discourse by Roger Hilton which he calls ART IS A CRIME', undated, Extract 138, *Nightfisherman* 230–3, 233.

[11] 'Implements' 243; 'The Beast in the Space' (1967), in *NCP* 157.

[12] 'Wynter and the Grammarsow' 186; 'Thermal Stair' 166.

unadorned hand, its machinations are far from crude or simple. With elegant truculence, Graham's battle-call combines workaday, off-the-cuff colloquialism with a highly socially attuned lyricism, closely attentive to the politics of 'speaking to you'. The poems oscillate between unsettlingly direct addresses that seem to hail readers combatively—'I speak to you' (247), 'I am ready if you are' (207), 'Don't fool me' (240)—and specific addresses to named artists and literary figures, where address is used more formally, as a means of forming, and reformulating a literary-linguistic community: 'How Are the Children Robin' (For Robin Skelton) (234), 'For John Heath-Stubbs' (274), 'To Leonard Clark' (275), 'An Entertainment for David Wright On His Being Sixty' (284). Graham's addresses round on the traditional expectations one may harbour about one's role as distanced reader, challenging real and imagined interlocutors.

Graham may be repeatedly on the lookout for new forms of verbal misbehaviour, but he does not banish all traces of common politeness, small-talk, and cliché from his poems: his disruptions of habitual speech rely upon its presence. Ceremony remains, albeit half-spoofed and improvised. The poems particularly target glib phrasings and well-meaning, timeworn axioms. Lines like 'How are the children [...]', 'An entertainment [...] on being sixty' tap into appropriate codes of conduct before quickly displaying their irreverence towards them. These poems play games with the conventions of address expected between colleagues and literary figures on social occasions. The poem to David Wright testily asserts: 'You being sixty / Is not my concern', and then goes on to offer a nuanced objection to the formalities: 'I like you fine but this / Writing before people / To a man because he's sixty / Escapes me' (284; 285). Similarly, the poem politely entitled 'How are the children Robin' impatiently begins, '[i]t does not matter how', seemingly rejecting the demand to ask the courteous question. Such work is keen to show up the flimsiness of social niceties (234).

As in addresses to his friends, so in the more abstracted interlocutions of 'Implements', Graham attacks the protective 'barrier of propped words' of middle-class sociability, and the contemporary patter that passes for intimacy, in which only expected platitudes can be exchanged: 'He cocked his snoot, settled his cock, / Said goodbye darling to his darling, / [...] / [...] It was the wrong night', 'Moving in her perfumed aura, / [...] / She greets her hostess with a cheek-kiss / And dagger', 'I am a darling but what will they think / When *NCP* I arrive without my darling' (241–2). In satirizing the clichés of address, Graham's poems still need to address. But they also point out that relationships with *you* can withstand a little verbal rough weather: indeed, Graham's speakers demand it: 'Bite me your presence', 'A Note to the Difficult One' ('*NCP*' 154; 206).

Rude banter, heckling, and sporting literary attacks play through such addresses, testing the limits of the stable and socially acceptable. Simultaneously, Graham's desire to question acceptability makes him curiously dependent upon its existence. It is both by necessity and by design that Graham's attacks organize themselves around recognized articulations and social roles: his poems find themselves stepping into and flexing themselves against existing social and artistic positions. In this respect, the poems can feel extremely, even reassuringly, everyday, despite their disorienting verbal experimentations. As often as not, Graham uses recognizably commonplace surroundings, and utterly quotidian, realist details, such as might be found in the work of Larkin, Enright, and Davie: 'He switches the light on / To find a cigarette / And pours himself a Teachers', 'This is the house I married / Into, a room and kitchen / In a grey tenement', 'Cheerio' (236; 169; 288).

On the other hand, it is precisely such reassuringly normal scenarios that Graham's addresses revisit with an ear for the abnormal and disordered. Banal realist paraphernalia: 'utensils', 'a colander', are invested with an uncanny sense of threat or violence, whilst 'gazed out of all composure' by *your* probing eyes, the performing *I* is 'forced to wear a mask / Of a held-up colander', 'Terror-spots itch on my face now' ('Five Visitors' 190). Moments of suppressed violence and social dislocation play up the weird and menacing, as if threatening uncertainties lurked on the reverse side of perfectly ordinary objects, actions, and relations. Identities seem to battle out with other *you*s savagely, beneath an only apparently reassuring, familiar surface.

In Graham, familiar expressions are prime locations both for expectations to be uncannily reversed, and for our fiercely polite negotiations of *I* and *you* to be poked fun at, humoured. Dependable phrases are often played with in ways that cause public exposure—of incompetence, or misbehaviour—and subsequent embarrassment. During an imagined conversation in 'Implements' one speaker's 'good nicely chosen verb' is spoiled by a noun that takes 'the huff' (246). Graham imagines the speaker forced to keep face in company, in this tight spot: 'I was embarrassed but I said something / Else and kept the [...] verb'. Venting his discomfiture under his breath in a classically restrained aside, the speaker can't quite manage lowering himself to the demotic: 'Nouns are the very devil' (246). Since this is hardly characteristic of Graham's own, far less restrained, expletive idiom, one feels he may be somewhat mocking the speaker's moderation, his reliance upon the conventional formulations of frustration.[13]

---

[13] 'How shall I behave? What shall I wear? I'm coming anyhow and I'll have to make the best of it fuckthem...' [sic] (Letter to Bill Featherstone, 19 July 1973, from Lopez, *The Poetry of W. S. Graham* 7), 'As usual I am worried about my fucking poetry' (Letter to Roger Hilton, 26 September 1968, 218).

Graham makes clear that a speaker who relies too heavily on ready-made stock phrases will not be ingenious enough to withstand the ensnaring verbal medium of 'graft and treachery'.

Perhaps an acceptance of bad linguistic behaviour, rather than an attempt to conceal it with good grace and etiquette, is required? If words are devils, it may be better to be of the devil's party, and know it. 'Language ah now you have me', Graham imagines himself confessing in his poem of the same name:

> Language ah now you have me. Night-time tongue,
> Please speak for me between the social beasts
> Which quick assail me. Here I am hiding in
> The jungle of mistakes of communication.
>
> I know about jungles. I know about unkempt places
> Flying toward me when I am getting ready
> To pull myself together and plot the place
> To speak from. I am at the jungle face[14]

The poem puts to work that familiar 'now you *have* me'; a phrase that is normally used jocularly, to admit having being discovered committing some small social wrong. But politely admitting one's *faux pas* puts one, quite unwittingly, into language's possession: 'you have me'. The Pinter-esque threat of 'being had' pulls in various directions, like the word-play in *The Homecoming* on Ruth's 'being taken'.[15] Both imply physical, psychological, and sexual coercion, 'had' against one's will, as well as containing the force of a lie: 'taken for a ride', 'being had'. Graham's poem ends: 'Too much. I died. I forgot who I was', 'It is my home / Where [...] the pleasure / Monkey is plucked from the tree' (209).

Does Graham's 'ah' reassuringly work against this effect of feared loss of control? The non-articulate sound also offers some verbal resistance: it is a moment of hesitation in the midst of plucking '[to]o much', which might insure the speaker from indulging in the excess of monkey-ish 'pleasure'. From one direction, to say 'ah' is to try out a teasingly knowing tone, like that used by a jolly, but wicked, uncle. The 'ah' of a firmly self-possessed, serial social offender defuses the tension of exposure: by simply shrugging his shoulders at public reproach, and making a display of his minimal adherence to social norms, the speaker could actually get away with it. Simultaneously, that short syllable indicates the dissolution of smooth social patter: 'ah' is a slide into inarticulacy caused by the exposed

---

[14] Graham, 'Language Ah Now You Have Me' (1976), in *NCP* 207–8.
[15] Harold Pinter, *The Homecoming* (London: Faber, 1991), at 50. RUTH: 'If you take the glass [...] I'll take you'. LENNY: 'How about me taking the glass without you taking me?'

blunder, the stammering embarrassment of being caught out. Since the 'beasts' that 'assail' the speaker are verbal, and Graham played into their hands in line one, these linguistic predators are now able to run off with the poem's meaning: 'Night-time tongue, / Please speak for me between the social beasts / Which quick assail me' (207). Apparently it is a matter of time before language is assailed; before one is disgraced by one's disobedient, badly behaved words. Behind the feared loss of verbal control lie various threats, amongst them social humiliation, loss of prestige or authority, removal from one's ordained position, psychological or sexual victimization.

Yet of course, Graham is really asking for it ('Please'), and being given what he wants. The words that express his abandonment to language simultaneously sustain control over it: if words 'speak for me', and assail him, they have also most obediently complied with his behest. Such verbal misbehaviour is half by instruction. To Graham, the menace behind 'the bad word', or the language of 'spite [...] graft and treachery' is exciting, seductive, for it is precisely when words are 'charmed / Out of their master's orders' that dialogue and response take place ('Approaches' 178; 'Implements' 246–7; 'Approaches' 178). If language rudely 'has me', Graham's poem is happening *to*, as well as *through*, him. The world answers back, is full of bold and ungracious, as well as civilized and considerate, addresses. The words that 'Spoke back at me out of spite' are, for Graham, points of reciprocal contact ('Implements' 246). They contact the public world, busy with common uses and devilish abuses of language.

TO TELL YOU THE TRUTH

Graham's contemporary, Philip Larkin, also had in mind the abuses of language, when, in his 'Statement' in 1955 he defined his post-war project in opposition to the Modernists, rejecting 'casual allusions in poems to other poems or poets, which [...] I find unpleasantly like the talk of literary understrappers letting you see they know the right people'.[16] Larkin was unlike Graham in resisting Modernist form and technique, but he was like Graham in keenly, and often rudely, assailing social and literary expectations. Both poets use their art to rally against a poetics of privilege, class, and status, rounding on preserved hierarchy and deference. Both are conscious of the *social* dimension of speech and poetry. In particular, these writers heatedly denounce a rhetoric that is allied with attention to 'the right people', where 'right' smacks of a class-based coterie, or gracious

---

[16] Larkin, *RW* 79.

addresses to the appropriate audience, in a fitting tone (though in practice this resistance is not entirely consistent). Parodying the social duties of the bored middle-class host—*'My wife and I have asked a crowd of craps / To come and waste their time and ours: perhaps / You'd care to join us?*—Larkin's work parades itself as an incendiary fingers-up to polite, accepted social niceties.[17] Hostile also to the pretensions of the academic world, and the elevated claims of high art, a number of Larkin's poems mockingly imitate the complacent hypocrisies of academic idiom: 'Naturally the Foundation will Bear Your Expenses' (84). For Larkin, poetry is not a space of especially dignified behaviour: 'Jan turns back and farts, / Gobs at the grate, and hits the queen of hearts', and he refuses to avert his eyes and ears from irreverent and demotic language: 'They fuck you up, your mum and dad', 'Get stewed: / Books are a load of crap'.[18]

Although Graham similarly refuses to elevate art to the status of a specially erudite, elite activity, he would not endorse the view that 'books are a load of crap'. (Neither, one might point out, would Larkin, especially in his role as Hull librarian, despite enjoying the anti-highbrow mischief of making the pronouncement.) Graham is certainly not reluctant to be read in a high literary vein, nor to be associated with the authority of venerated writers. Making a performance out of his work's affinities with the poetics of Eliot, Pound, and Stevens as well as with Joyce, Graham had written, early in his career, with approbation of the language that 'goes on speaking again and again beyond behind its speaking words, a space of continual messages behind the words like behind Joyce's words'.[19]

Yet despite—or perhaps because of—his ancestral investments, Graham's work is suspicious of holding too eager an esteem for literary movements, institutions, artworks, and venerated names. He excludes these from his poems in general, unlike, say, Auden, who addressed and dedicated poems to such renowned artists as Yeats, Eliot, Henry James, E. M. Forster, A. E. Housman, and Sigmund Freud, and composed ceremonial addresses to public figures of authority and status: *'Lines addressed to Dr Claude Jenkins, Canon of Christ Church, Oxford, on the occasion of his Eightieth Birthday. (26th May 1957)'*.[20] Graham, in contrast, shuns the idea of addressing 'the right people', particularly coterie audiences, or select crowds of well-known academic and critical readers. Rather: 'I am a simple / Boy from Greenock', beckoning often to nameless, unspecified addressees, and to particular close friends (Norman Macleod, Peter Lanyon) to 'help me / In my impure, too-human purpose' (276; 183).

[17] 'Vers de Société', *LCP* 147. All Larkin quotes are from *LCP*.
[18] 'The Card-Players' 135; 'This Be the Verse' 142; 'A Study of Reading Habits' 102.
[19] 'Notes', *Nightfisherman* 382.
[20] Auden, *ACP* 197; 440; 242; 157; 148; 215; 443.

Graham's poems of dedication, likewise, are made not to Eliot, or Yeats, or Freud, or well-known literary, historical, or political figures, but to his colleagues, loved ones, and more surprisingly, can come addressed to often-overlooked objects and ideas: 'Dear Who I Mean' (160).

Graham may sometimes turn up clad as the inspired creator, even the vaunted god of the text, but for him, poetry is an only occasionally transcendent realm, marked by 'too-human purpose', and by the poet's having 'maim[ed] // Himself somehow for the job'.[21] Graham is not dissimilar to Larkin in underlining both art's, and the artist's, ordinariness, but neither is he more than a hair's breadth from that observation as it enters the twentieth century via the linguistically and philosophically attuned energies of Modernist poetics. When Graham writes that 'The poet does not write what he knows but what he doesn't know',[22] he is echoing Eliot's *East Coker* (1940): 'And what you do not know is the only thing you know' (3:201). Graham and Eliot remind their readers that language is constitutive of reality, fundamentally implicated in the way the world is constructed as meaningful. Poetic meanings are susceptible to the slippages and instabilities of the very language used to produce them: 'Words strain, / Crack and sometimes break, under the burden, / Under the tension, slip, slide, perish'.[23] For both, the poem is vulnerable, perishable, all-too-human.

Graham's writer-figure, then, is drawing on both traditions when he exposes his susceptibility, presenting readers with verbal slip-ups and uncertainties. Rather than feeling compelled consistently to produce masterful images of satisfying clarity, Graham intersperses moments of delight in the capacity for aesthetic manipulation with moments of bewilderment, absurdity, lack of surety, luck, or bungling ineptness: 'I saw myself wearing / A clumping taliped / Disguise', 'I / Was tripped and caught into the whole / Formal scheme which Art is'.[24] When he proclaims, however, that 'Speaking is difficult', or muses, 'surely there must be something to say', he also taps into a matter-of-fact plainness of style that we might well expect to find in Donald Davie or D. J. Enright (178; 161). Graham's 1970s volumes in particular, make clear his unelevated status by executing an ill-tempered, deliberately ungracious address: one is assailed by a pugilistic speaker that forces us to witness the writer-figure's rude, argumentative, and drunken behaviour: 'Above / All, shut up', 'Am I too loud?' ('The Beast in the Space' 158; 'Yours Truly' 160). Just as we encounter a

---

[21] 'Thermal Stair' 164. The maiming, as Peter Robinson points out, is far from entirely negative. *Selves and Situations* 90.

[22] Letter to Edwin Morgan, 22 September 1943, 14.

[23] *Burnt Norton* (1935), in *ECP* 194.

[24] 'Yours Truly' 160; 'Approaches' 182.

shameless admission of routine drunkenness in the work of those other verbal combatants of the 1970s and 1980s, Kingsley Amis—who published such spirited manifestos as *On Drink, Every Day Drinking*, and *How's Your Glass?*[25]—and Larkin: 'I work all day, and get half-drunk at night',[26] so we find Graham inciting his interlocutor to intoxication: 'we'll sit and drink / And go in the sea's roar' ('Thermal Stair' 165).

This is to say that Modernist experimentations with language do not necessarily go hand in hand with a rejection of plain speaking, or a desire to flee from ordinary comprehensibility, or to neglect art's public-political engagements. Graham's work brings together both the socially attuned aspects of neo-realism, *and* the stylistic challenges and linguistic-epistemological questionings laid down by Modernist writing. His work has in common with neo-realist writers the urge to deflate pretensions by speaking in ordinary language, 'With a thought or two up my sleeve', 'to tell you the truth' (182; 264). It shares also a pleasure in rudely rebuffing the highbrow and intellectual, in poking fun at the self-congratulating literary societies and the elite circles of poetry circulation, the 'fuckulty'; a desire coolly to mock the sterility of conformity with the demands of venerable institutions, literary and academic figures: 'He has been given a chair in that / Timeless University. / The chair of Professor of Silence' (241). Nevertheless it is attentive to the places where poetry's carefully constructed rhetorical effects begin to break down, and alert to the poet's faltering attempts to preserve the impression of organized normality, and impressions of coherence. The everyday ordered 'real' world that can be relied upon in a Larkin or Enright poem, is a performed impression in Graham's work: the real is an ingenious verbal effect, even if it is a generally agreed-upon, reassuring, and communal one.

[25] Kingsley Amis, *On Drink* (New York: Harcourt, 1972); *Every Day Drinking* (London: Hutchinson, 1983); *How's Your Glass?* (London: Weidenfeld, 1984).
[26] Larkin, 'Aubade' (1977), in *LCP* 190.

PART II

C. H. SISSON

To the Public: National Orientations

4

The Words of a Myriad: Orientation and Avoidance

'It is in part due to the direction he took from Eliot that Sisson has always been a writer with an orientation, defining himself through positive relations with his country and its institutions, rather than adopting the alienated stance', wrote Michael Schmidt, in his Introduction to C. H. Sisson's collected prose, *The Avoidance of Literature*.[1] At first glance, the poems and essays of this conservative civil servant—who wrote most of his best poetry in the 1960s and 1970s, and rose to short-lived prominence when his verse was collected and published in *In the Trojan Ditch*—seem to confirm Schmidt's view that the work is oriented, politically minded, and peopled.[2] The prose makes evident Sisson's interest in art's involvement in the public fray. As if directly addressing themselves to, and demanding dialogue with, a range of contentious literary-political figures across the ages, Sisson's essay titles form a litany of transhistorical names: 'Charles Péguy', 'Charles Maurras', 'William Barnes', 'W. B. Yeats', 'T. S. Eliot', 'Ezra Pound', 'The Case of Walter Bagehot', 'The Politics of Andrew Marvell', 'Geoffrey Hill', 'Martin Seymour-Smith', 'Coleridge Revisited'.[3]

Such public orientations are not confined to the prose. Sisson's *Collected Poems* too is scattered with lyrics that engage relations with particular civic figures, national agendas, and theological disputes: 'An Essay on God and Man', 'Thinking of Politics', 'Vigil and Ode for St George's Day', 'The Mind of Man'.[4] One finds poems that specifically address public bodies and figures: 'To the Queen', 'The State of the Arts (Dedicated to The Lord Goodman)', 'To His Grace the Archbishop of York', 'For the Primate of all England', 'For The Queen's Jubilee'.[5] Sisson's lyrics have spoken to a succession of changeable historical *you*s, from classical interlocutors (Catullus, Marcus Aurelius, The Queen of Lydia, Ovid),[6] medieval

---

[1] Sisson, *Avoidance* 10. All references to Sisson's essays are quoted from this volume.
[2] Sisson, *In the Trojan Ditch*.
[3] Sisson, *Avoidance* 44, 96, 192, 255, 275, 295, 349, 30, 467, 496, 549.
[4] All references to Sisson's poetry are quoted from *CP*. See *CP* 129, 456, 349, 436.
[5] *CP* 83, 154, 361, 384, 288.
[6] *CP* 89, 199, 90, 153.

and early modern addressees ('A Variation on Eustache Deschamps', 'A Dialogue with Maurice Scève', 'Three Sonnets from the French of Jean-Baptiste Chassignet', 'Letter to John Donne')[7], and on to nineteenth- and twentieth-century auditors: one encounters a number of poems obliquely addressing Charles Maurras as *you* (including 'In Arles', 'Martigues', 'Saint-Rémy'),[8] as well as poems 'For my Brother', and for the Irish painter Patrick Swift (345; 152). Acting out the Modernist recognition that words continually direct us to our shared history, Sisson, like Pound and Eliot, has insisted throughout his career that history is carried in, as well as changed by, the common language: 'Words are not ours but the words of a myriad, having point only because of their history', he writes in 'Sevenoaks Essays'.[9] His words often play up our *logopoeic* bond to others: 'We speak as historical persons [...] we do not speak as ourselves. If we are selves, it is by virtue of other selves that we are so' ('Sevenoaks' 204). Picking up on this sensitivity to language's historical sense, Donald Davie wrote that Sisson was 'one in the line of the great modernists (Eliot, Pound, Yeats, yes indeed Wyndham Lewis), [...] like every one of them, even as his mind reaches forward through time that is to come, at the same time and by that very token reaches improbably far back through time that has been'.[10]

However, Sisson's decision to entitle his collected criticism *The Avoidance of Literature* sits somewhat uneasily alongside Schmidt's eagerness to find his work 'positively' socially and historically inflected, and also modifies Davie's sense that Sisson is readily following 'in the line of the great modernists', 'like every one of them'. Are there respects in which Sisson's poems and prose attempt to complicate such relations; to evade historical and literary figures, even those they address? If Sisson's title, *The Avoidance of Literature*, is a recommendation of literary avoidance, then who or what does Sisson think should be avoided? Or, if Sisson's title is an argument *against those* who propose poetry should avoid contact with (and allusion to) literary figures, then whom does he imagine himself contradicting?

Sisson's addresses mingle their (often Modernist) attentiveness to the 'positive relations' of historical and cultural understandings with interlocutions that do adopt a variety of alienated stances: 'you have receded', 'you could be lost before daybreak'.[11] But if, in certain respects, Sisson's addresses succeed at breathing new life into Eliotic and Poundian forms

---

[7] *CP* 436, 413, 445, 50.   [8] *CP* 182, 183, 189.

[9] 'Sevenoaks Essays' (1967), in *Avoidance* 204. Referred to as 'Sevenoaks'.

[10] Donald Davie, 'The Politics of an English Poet', *Poetry Nation* 6 (1976) 86–91, 86.

[11] Sisson, 'Antres' 205; 'The Corridor' 204. Also in *Anchises* (Manchester: Carcanet, 1976).

and styles, in others (as we will see) they fall considerably short. The degree of Sisson's adeptness in revisiting what Eliot had seen as the fruitful combination of passion and intellect in early modern address-forms can be measured alongside those publicly minded addresses conducted by contemporary poets—notably Douglas Dunn and Tony Harrison. These poets also probe the politics of the seventeenth-century epigrammatic tradition, and assess address's link with nationhood and propaganda in the present. Reading Sisson alongside this range of twentieth-century addresses helps to shed light on what is at stake in the interplay between Modernist and Movement impulses, and also illustrates a few problems both with Sisson's handling of public address forms, and with his credentials as a poet 'in the line of the great modernists'.

In a poem entitled 'No Address', Sisson defies his title's apparent negation of dialogue, turning to hail a succession of historical addressees directly:

> In my leprosy I have lost speech
> Which before I had with several.
> Now no voices, not even my own.
>
> Pliny, Horace, Cicero, talk to me;
> I am a dead language also.
> The poetry owners cannot make me out
>
> Nor I them. And the big mouths of learning
> Open and close over my thoughts without biting.
> Under the shadow of politics I have no teeth.
>
> I am no man, Caesar, to stand by you,
> Nor have the whimsical humour of pre-war Oxford
> But my unrecognised style was made by sorrow.
>
> Inching towards death, let me go there quickly.
> Silently, in the night or in the day-time,
> Equally, I would take it like a Roman.[12]

This is no avoidance of history, dialogue, or reciprocity. Sisson's address not only names names ('Pliny, Horace, Cicero') and speaks in the second person to Caesar ('I am no man, Caesar, to stand by you'), but demands that these particular deceased auditors 'talk to me'. Of course, that ambivalent phrase 'talk to me' works more humbly, too, so that Sisson's lines may be read as a plea to these absent classical authors to respond to his address: 'please talk...'. It is also worth bearing in mind that Sisson's address might not be only directed transhistorically to Pliny, Horace, and Cicero, but also to Sisson's present-day readership: 'Pliny, Horace, and

---

[12] 'No Address' (1974), in *CP* 152.

Cirero are the writers that talk to me'. Sisson's lines, then, imply that it may be *only* these past masters that are willing to engage in dialogue with, and inform the work of, the poet: '*they* are talking to me...even if you won't', as is reinforced by his adding: 'The poetry owners cannot make me out / Nor I them'.

On the one hand, Sisson's addresses here deliberately contradict the verbal failure implied by his title—'No address'—and the alienation of the first lines: 'In my leprosy I have lost speech', 'Now no voices, not even my own'. The poem assertively offers its speech to specific historical auditors, and makes them listen. On the other hand, these addresses rely upon an irrevocable sense of pastness and alienation from the present, in order to connect with their historical interlocutors; hence the logic of the lines: 'talk to me; / *I* am a dead language *also*'. As in Sisson's title, *The Avoidance of Literature*, so too in the address to Caesar, both remoteness from and involvement with historical and literary figures are in play. The poem directly hails and anchors itself to a specific, contextualized *you* (Caesar), and also evades the consequences of that verbal relation: '*I am no man*, Caesar, to stand by you'. Sisson's is an address that speaks face-to-face with its interlocutor precisely to assert that he cannot support *you*.

'I am no man', this speaker informs his classical auditor. That address sounds like a confession of poetic failure of nerve, words, and action. Lyric address, it seems, is not capable of standing up for what, and who, it should support. It runs the risk of exposing the speaker as weak and unmanned. But Sisson is also calculatedly probing the politics of speaking, writing, and remaining silent, not dissimilarly to Geoffrey Hill, who raised the question: 'Must men stand by what they write'? Hill's later line, from 'The Mystery of the Charity of Charles Péguy', is delivered on the heels of a poetic snapshot of the same Roman dictator: 'Caesar's ghost, his wounds of air and ink / painlessly spouting'.[13] Such work questions whether lyrics are merely 'painlessly spouting' words, or whether they are prepared to get their hands dirty; to involve themselves in the painstaking etymological and archival labour necessary for accurate literary-historical revisitation.

On one level, Sisson's poem holds up for question a lyric's power to re-think, and meaningfully to contribute to, historical accounts. If Sisson's present-day casting of Caesar as *you* poetically rehashes a well-worn historical account, 'ghost[ing] Caesar's ghost'—as well as doubling it, as Andrew Marvell did in his 'Horatian Ode'—it also confesses to falling short of the determined allegiance required to bring that ghost to life:

---

[13] Hill (1983), in *HCP* 183. This poem is subsequently referred to as 'Péguy'.

'I am no man [...] to stand by you'.[14] Both Hill and Sisson are alike in portraying poetry's potential failure of allegiance as a restaging of that failure in Caesar's former colleague Brutus ('In Brutus' name martyr and mountebank / ghost Caesar's ghost') whom the dictator had spotted among the crowd of assassins that was to stab him twenty-three times ('Péguy', 183). Caesar's contested last words were an address to Brutus, which have been reported variously as: 'You too, child?', 'And you, Brutus?', 'You too, Brutus?', as well as being sounded in Shakespeare's *Julius Caesar*: '*Et tu, Brutè? Then fall, Caesar'.*[15] Others have insisted that Caesar remained silent, calling into question the historical validity of this alleged address.[16] Though each of these historians stands by what he wrote, only one can be correct. Like Sisson, Hill writes '[i]n Brutus' name' to call attention to the interlacing of historical and literary accounts, both of which concede the painstaking labour involved in poetry's 'painless' spouting of 'wounds of ink and air' in naming historical names and ghosting familiar ghosts.

Evidently, Sisson's is no frivolous, nor merely private, address. His lyric voicing of *you* (like Marvell's) is bound up in questioning the language in which affairs of state are conducted, continued, and disrupted, and in probing poetry's capacity to achieve a measure of verity in forging links between history and art, past and present voicings. In its delving into remote episodes in history, its attention to the language in which myth, literature, and history are written, and its opening of allusive intertextual webs, Sisson's address might be seen as moving in sympathy with Eliotic and Poundian notions of the poem not as a process of self-expression, but a place in which 'the dead poets, his ancestors, assert their immortality most vigorously'.[17] Since Caesar's assassination precipitated the end of the Roman republic, Sisson's final pronouncement ('I would take it like a Roman') may work as an assertion of Sisson's determined, but thwarted, wish to follow in, and to breathe new life into, the classical vein. The poem's addresses argue against the temptation to avoid or relinquish past forms, as one would give in to easeful death: merely 'taking it', too readily, passively, or silently, even as they concede the impossibility of full resuscitation.

'[T]he historical sense compels a man to write not merely with his own generation in his bones, but with a feeling that the whole of the literature of Europe from Homer and within it the whole of the literature of his

---

[14] In Marvell's 'An Horatian Ode Upon Cromwell's Return From Ireland' (written *c.*1650, published 1681) 'Caesar' is not just one. He symbolizes the recently assassinated Charles I, *and* mutates into the victorious Cromwell. In Andrew Marvell, *The Complete Poems*, ed. Elizabeth Story Donno (London: Penguin, 1996) 55–8.

[15] William Shakespeare, *Julius Caesar* (London: Penguin, 2000) 3:1:78.

[16] See Suetonius, in *Lives of the Caesars*, trans. J. C. Rolfe, ed. Catharine Edwards (Oxford and New York: Oxford University Press, 2000) 3–42.

[17] Eliot, 'Tradition' (1919) *SW* 48.

own country has a simultaneous existence and composes a simultaneous order' Eliot wrote, in 'Tradition and the Individual Talent' (*SW* 49). Many of Sisson's poems demonstrate a comparable disavowal of the notion of poetic language as inward-directed 'originality', and heatedly rebuff twentieth-century individualism: '"I am" may read "We are." / So damn the individual touch / Of which the critics make so much', Sisson insists, in 'My Life and Times', an early poem, from the 1965 collection *Numbers* (45). 'Land of my fathers, you escape me now / And yet I will in no wise let you go', he writes near the end of his career, in the 1994 poem, 'Thinking of Politics', putting that assertion into the form of direct historical address (456). Sisson often reiterates, in the second person, that: 'you will not be taken in: // The complication is in me. / The history riddled in my brain' (88). Throughout his poetic career, then, Sisson uses address not to step away from the social and historical space, but to rail against any perspective that would enable the poet to see himself as asocial, unique, exceptional. Many of his poems pronounce that we take shape from each other verbally and conceptually, and nowhere more clearly than in moments where Sisson appeals to the dialogue and address taking place through the textual fabric: 'I turn to you', 'the conversation / Is because you are' ('The Model' 473).

This sense of language as historically inflected and peopled is also strongly evident in Sisson's prose. 'A poem can have meaning only in terms of words other people use, and which we have from our ancestors. It is a part and not a whole', he asserts in 'Poetry and Myth'.[18] Six years earlier, writing of Pound, and tracing his allegiance with that Modernist master, Sisson commented:

> he holds that until you know certain master-works you will not be able to see clearly what you are reading. The original and the derivative sort themselves out as one's knowledge expands. It could be argued—though Pound does not explicitly argue it—that an age which believes that self-expression is a simple matter is ill placed to grasp this truth. People think that there is something sacred about an individual opinion, however ill-informed. A young man anxious to persuade will imagine he is emitting 'his own ideas' when it is evident to any instructed bystander that those ideas have a history going back for two hundred or some other number of years. It is the same with poetry. The simple soul pouring out his heart is almost certain to be pouring out literary methodologies of traceable recent ancestry.[19]

---

[18] (1977), in *Avoidance* 514.
[19] 'Ezra Pound' (1971) (referred to in the text as 'Pound') in C. H. Sisson, *English Poetry: An Assessment 1900–1950*, ed. Rupert Hart-Davis (Manchester: Carcanet, 1971) 305 (referred to hereafter as *EP*).

Sisson's essay on Pound insists that *you* must actively seek ways to reconnect with the rich, and highly complex, veins of tradition that continue to shape present-day language: from classical, medieval, early modern, and Romantic influences: 'the attempt to render the world without a sense of its past is an illusion as well as an impiety' (*Avoidance* 315). Like Pound and Eliot, Sisson argues that poets should maintain sensitivity to the affiliations that are carried through their verbal style, since to Sisson, a poet's language is crafted from the language 'going back for two hundred or some other number of years'. He writes admiringly of Pound's 'testing to see what holds good of the extinct rhythm of the rather more muscular language that preceded our own'—a testing that 're-established, for his successors as well as for himself, connections which had long been severed' (309).

Although these views align Sisson with central tenets of Modernist thought, they also place him at some remove from the mid-century Movement poetry, prevalent and highly influential at the start of his poetic career. Larkin's 1955 'Statement' against Modernist complexity argued that modern poetry should avoid inaccessible and highbrow 'allusions' to 'a common myth-kitty', and unnecessarily difficult writing about the presentness of the past: 'As a guiding principle I believe that every poem must be its own sole freshly created universe', Larkin wrote. 'A poet's only guide is his own judgement.'[20] In this sense, Sisson's comments in the 1971 essay on Pound implicitly work against the arguments conducted in the 1950s and 1960s by Larkin. Particularly, he moves against that assertion that poetry should reject Modernist principles in favour of a style organized around the individual *I*'s experiences. Sisson argues against a Larkinesque privileging of self-expression and individual opinion: 'until you know certain master-works you will not be able to see clearly what you are reading'. Like the Modernists, Sisson views personal expression not as the hallmark of independent thought, but of an extremely derivative notion of originality: 'they have struck a not very rich vein of tradition. Their ideas [...] come from where other people's ideas come from', 'those ideas have a history going back for two hundred or some other number of years' ('Sevenoaks' 5:212; 'Pound' 305). Significantly, however, as we will come to see later, Sisson's essay only *implicitly* criticizes, and does not name Larkin, nor does it mention Larkin's 'Statement' directly.

There are important contrasts between the frank, conversational style of Movement address, and Sisson's more abstracted and philosophical hailing. Sisson's poems repeatedly express a keenness for 'conversation' ('We call to each other, we are many', 'I move towards you', 'So I ad-

dress the musing mind'), but that conversation is much more often con-
ducted with disembodied, theoretical recipients, than with specific
historical or artistic figures in particular contexts.[21] 'What is a person /
But a metaphysical assertion?', he writes in 'The Question': 'Can who be
what or what be who? / The question is resolved in you, / Though not
by you'.[22] Unlike a good deal of Movement address, which often spoke
to familiar, stable, and embodied *yous*, Sisson's interlocutions, some
decades later, move to discomfit us; using *you* to underline the precar-
ious, changeable nature of relations, and to confront readers with a suc-
cession of unsettlingly underspecified, and formally experimental,
addresses: 'Do you ask? // I do not ask / I am not the man who asks',
'Under the uneasy eye of Dulcimer / I betray you? I, I, I?'[23] Sisson's *you*,
in such lines, is a long way from the address of, say, the 1954 Larkin
poem, 'Born Yesterday', in which the speaker is able to identify his 'you'
as a known, real figure (Sally Amis), or that of 'Lines on a Young Lady's
Photograph Album': 'Not quite your class, I'd say, dear, on the whole'
(*LCP* 54; 43). Sisson's interlocutions are not geared towards making us
feel like comfortable insiders ('your class, dear'), but toward splicings of
meaning, questionings of identity, philosophical probings, as well as
radical fragmentations of form.

   In many of the addresses penned by Sisson at the mid-point of his
career (around the time *In the Trojan Ditch* is published), language itself
is made to feel at risk of breakdown, erasure, dissolution. For instance, in
the traditionally entitled 'Dialogue of the Soul and God', a new poem
from that 1974 volume:

> Lord Wind
> I am your patience so I am not I
>
> If you were you
> I would dissolve
> So not in peace
>
> I, I
> The entropy of every beast
> Sigh out your wind
>
> Dissolve
> Be less than nothing now
>   *CP* 180

The address of such as lines as, 'If you were you / I would dissolve', does
not draw attention to its recipient as a reassuringly companionable figure.

---

[21] *CP* 390; 464; 282.   [22] (1994), in *CP* 464.
[23] 'The Corridor' (1975), see *CP* 206; 'In the Trojan Ditch' (1974), see *CP* 159.

Rather, it figures *you* as a lithe, and inconstant verbal relation being created, changed, cast off, ritualized, demythologized as it moves between audience and speaker: 'dissolve', '[b]e less than nothing now'. Not dissimilarly, in 'Antres', a poem published two years later, in *Anchises*, Sisson's *you* is addressed as, at best, a perilously mobile recipient, and at worst, a non-presence:

Shade, shadow less than nothing within my dream,
Less than myself in that you have receded
Within this shell, yet more
In that you have gone further and fared worse and also because
I pursue you still, and am unpursued
While it is I who am open to every persuasion

Yet within myself
There is no such thing as you are, I miss you
There are caverns you go through like an echoing voice
I am not even an echo
Yet all this is me, for it is not you

I cannot catch at my antres, or you wandering
Nothing therefore
And it is no use representing that as blackness,
Placing sentries, touching upon the walls
Though they drip moistly, suggesting downfall.

Nothing is not pepper or salt, or any taste
Cinnamon, ginger
It does not water the palate nor arrose the smell
Can it imagine, holding within itself
The recession of anybody?

CP 202

This paradoxical *you*—a 'nothing' that has 'shape' and 'shadow', that 'recede[s]' and 'echo[es]'—is both physically and conceptually elusive: 'There is no such thing as you are, I miss you', 'Shape, shadow less than nothing', 'The recession of anybody'. Lured on by this evasive creature, the poem both attempts to apply logic to make intimate contact with what it knows has 'receded', and longs to renounce the other: 'yet more', 'therefore', 'and also because'. The speaker's determination to 'pursue you still', to 'catch [...] at you', to 'place [...] sentries' is coupled with his recognition that his lyric words inadequately, and unstably, take their bearing from the *you* that remains silent: 'all this is me for it is not you', 'it is no use representing that as blackness'. If *you* is a hunted creature, escaping the lyricist's conceptual probing ('within this shell', 'you have fared words'), it is also (peculiarly) a worthy conversational partner, faring the verbal struggle, teasing the speaker out of, but also *into*, thought: 'suggesting', 'imagine', 'I am open to every persuasion'. In such poems, Sisson, like Graham, is highly alert to the relations between *I* and *you* that are altered and manoeuvred as one speaks and writes. *I*, however unanswered, is not alone in his language. Like Graham's, Sisson's verse formally and ideologically moves in support of that Eliotic assertion that:

> When a poet's mind is perfectly equipped for its work, it is constantly amalgamating disparate experience; the ordinary man's experience is chaotic, irregular, fragmentary [...] Our civilization comprehends great variety and complexity, and this variety and complexity, playing upon a refined sensibility, must produce various and complex results. The poet must become more and more comprehensive, more allusive, more indirect, in order to force, to dislocate if necessary, language into his meaning.[24]

Admiringly quoting Donald Davie's statement that 'For poetry to be great, it must reek of the human', Sisson's prose, too, has aligned him with this Eliotic recognition, as it enters Davie's own thought.[25] For Sisson too, messy human feeling is best captured through what Davie termed 'variety and complexity', 'various and complex results'. Sisson writes: 'disorder has its merits. Human variety [is] not smoothed out by common professional habits [...] Literature lives by it.'[26] Sisson's comments echo Eliot in 'The Metaphysical Poets' at just that point in his essay that Eliot observed: 'it appears likely that poets in our civilization, as it exists at present, must be *difficult*' (*Prose* 65).

Reading Sisson is certainly not as difficult as reading Eliot or Pound, nor is his work as uncompromisingly erudite. As we have seen, unlike these poets, Sisson does not conduct addresses in a manner that is *bafflingly* complex or painstakingly intertextual in nature. Nor do Sisson's poems speak to *you* in several languages, unlike Eliot's *The Waste Land* ('*Mein Irisch Kind / Wo weilest du?*') or Pound's *Pisan Cantos* ('Your eyen two wol sleye me sodenly / I may the beauté of hem nat susteyene').[27] In Modernist and contemporary poems, it is often precisely at the moment of being intimately hailed as *you* that the addressee is made to feel the limitations of his verbal proficiency. *You* is often prompted to recognize its need for the help of a translator. Lyric address's propensity to seem immediate—a direct conversation between *I* and *you*—is inverted, so that

[24] Eliot, 'The Metaphysical Poets' (1921), in *Prose* 64–5.
[25] Donald Davie, 'The Reek of the Human', *Articulate Energy: An Inquiry into the Syntax of English Poetry* (1955; London: Routledge, 1976) 161–5, 165.
[26] (1977). In *Avoidance* 554–62, 557.
[27] Eliot, *ECP* 64 I.33–4. Pound, *Cantos*, Canto 81:520. Pound quotes Chaucer's 'Merciles Beaute', composed *c.*1389, published 1886. See also *The Complete Works of Geoffrey Chaucer*, ed. F. N. Robinson (Boston and New York: Houghton Mifflin, 1933), 638, 1–3.

the addressee must acknowledge, in the moment of being spoken to, his need for another, who will aid in deciphering the text. These teasingly allusive addresses mediate textual relations, flagging up the untranslatability of the poem's play of languages, the alterity at the heart of one's own interlocutions.

In spite of such differences, many of Sisson's addresses during the 1970s and 1980s work more in support of experimental Modernism, than in service of Movement transparency and accessibility. Sisson's address in 'Ulysses', for instance:

> Ulysses in your boat
> In the curved waters where the eddies are
> As the stream turns
> > an old dressing-gown
> Swirling in the water
> > round and round
> Where is Sackcloth?
> > drowned drowned drowned.

CP 223

Combining the use of traditional Greek mythology with a savagely ragged free verse form reminiscent of *The Waste Land*, such poetry liberates itself from regular metre and rhyme. The poem, like many others during this period, opens up a Babel of communicative voices, and a sense of ruptured chronological understanding that is evidently more reminiscent of Modernist than Movement poetics. Formally, 'Ulysses' shares much in common with Sisson's long poem, 'The Corridor', and both bear resemblance to Graham's numbered verse-paragraph poem, 'The Dark Dialogues' (see *NCP* 167). A number of the shorter poems in Sisson's next volume, *Exactions*—'Sequelae', 'The Desert', and 'Au Clair de la Lune'— also move in this vein.[28] Other poems from this period—working in what might be dubbed the latter-day-Modernist style—contain syntactical disjunctions and repetitions and refrains reminiscent of, say, Eliot's *Ash Wednesday* and 'The Hollow Men'—see 'Burrington Combe', and 'Nobody Hears What We Say', both in *Exactions*.[29]

For Sisson, a poet's style is not an innocent expression of his 'inner mind'. It is, rather, a declaration of allegiance with, or of dissent from, literary others. His stylistic complexity, his renegotiation of the subjective, and his transgression of the boundaries between poetical and

---

[28] C. H. Sisson, *Exactions* (Manchester: Carcanet, 1980), in *CP* 292; 239; 241.

[29] T. S. Eliot, *Ash Wednesday* (1930), *ECP* 93–106; 'The Hollow Men' (1925), in *ECP* 87–92; Sisson, *CP* 281; 286.

historical, art and interpretation, act out a declaration of alliance with Eliotic and Poundian principles. Because this alliance deliberately disturbs the circulation of the more mimetic, self-expressive Movement poetics at its height near the beginning of Sisson's poetic career, Sisson is far from recommending an 'avoidance' of literature in the Larkinesque sense that would banish referentiality and allusiveness from the poem's texture. Instead, his addresses indicate an avoidance of certain strains of literary thought prevalent in the mid-century, and a closer orientation with lyricism in the public fray as it manifests in Eliotic and Poundian Modernism. Sisson's allegiances, however, are not all of one kind: there are numerous respects in which his work is—for better or worse—far from signed up to the Modernist project. In such work, as we will come to see, what Schmidt sees as Sisson's 'positive' 'orientation' to the country and its institutions paradoxically comes to depend rather strongly on 'the alienated stance' so often deployed by Larkin and Movement nostalgic, conservative poetics.

5

Sweet Rose of England: Public Bodies

Sweet rose of England, nothing can be true
Except so far as words and you agree.

Sisson, 'The Rose'

Address in Sisson often tests out how far a poet can create 'agreement' between the poem of the present and 'words' from other ages. Speaking to *you* through and across chronological time, Sisson's lyricism puts itself into intimate conversation with a range of long-deceased auditors. Sisson's *you* is more often a historical than a contemporary figure. As in Eliot and Pound, whose allusive invocations demanded that the reader return to particular episodes in history and mythology, so in Sisson one is directed to contemplate the personal histories of political and literary persons, and to consider the fruitfulness of a dialogue with them in the present. Sisson's poems say *you* not only to unspecified, theoretical interlocutors, but also to historical auditors, including John Donne, Catullus, Thomas à Kempis, and Marcus Aurelius. These poems hail their addressees almost conversationally, as if they established personal contact with them. 'Catullus my friend across twenty centuries', writes Sisson in 'Catullus', whilst in 'Marcus Aurelius', he commandingly informs his Stoic forebear that 'I will be an emperor and think like you'.[1]

To what extent do Sisson's public addresses make contact with a *you* that is also a historical recipient? Those addresses directed towards named figures are key to Sisson's exploration of the relationship of the body and passions with the mind and reason, but how successfully do they test out Eliot's earlier concept of the 'dissociation of sensibility'? One might also question whether Sisson is attentive to his public *you*s equally, and consider in what respects, and why, he might be more concerned with some (largely historical, usually early modern) rather than others (largely contemporary). It helps to examine Sisson's *you*s alongside a handful of other contemporary poets' intertextual, historical hailings. The interlocutions

---

[1] 'Catullus' (1968), in *CP* 89; 'Marcus Aurelius', *CP* 199.

of Dunn and Harrison are pertinent points of comparison in tracing the links between contemporary addresses to the nation, and the early modern tradition of patriotic, propagandist, public hailing. Such address forms can be seen, for instance, in Donne, Herbert, Milton, and Jonson, as well as in Marvell's poem 'Upon Appleton House: To my Lord Fairfax',[2] and in Robert Herrick's 1648 *Hesperides* book, and Sisson has made use of Donne and Herrick in particular, in the poems.

A good example is Sisson's address in his poem, 'A Letter to John Donne', in which the first line wields a second-person pronoun towards this early modern interlocutor. *I*'s direct voicing of *you* creates the impression that immediate dialogue is taking place between Sisson, at this moment in the 1960s, and his absent seventeenth-century addressee. Moving between present and past, Sisson writes:

> I understand you well enough, John Donne
> First, that you were a man of ability
> Eaten by lust and by the love of God
> Then, that you crossed the Sevenoaks High Street
> As rector of Saint Nicholas:
> I am of that parish.
>
> To be a man of ability is not much
> You may see them on the Sevenoaks platform any day
> Eager men with despatch cases
> Whom ambition drives as they drive the machine
> Whom the certainty of meticulous operation
> Pleasures as a morbid sex a heart of stone.
>
> That you should have spent your time in the corruption of courts
> As these in that of cities, gives you no place among us:
> Ability is not even the game of a fool
> But the click of a computer operating in a waste
> Your cleverness is dismissed from the suit
> Bring out your genitals and your theology.
>
> What makes you familiar is this dual obsession;
> Lust is not what the rutting stag knows
> It is to take Eve's apple and to lose
> The stag's paradisal look:
> The love of God comes readily
> To those who have most need.
>
> You brought body and soul to this church
> Walking there through the park alive with deer
> But now what animal has climbed into your pulpit?

[2] Composed *c.*1651, published posthumously (1681), in *The Complete Poems* 75–99.

> One whose pretention is that the fear
> Of God has heated him into a spirit
> An evaporated man no physical ill can hurt.
>
> Well might you hesitate at the Latin gate
> Seeing such apes denying the church of God:
> I am grateful particularly that you were not a saint
> But extravagant whether in bed or in your shroud.
> You would understand that in the presence of folly
> I am not sanctified but angry.
>
> Come down and speak to the men of ability
> On the Sevenoaks platform and tell them
> That at your Saint Nicholas the faith
> Is not exclusive in the fools it chooses
> That the vain, the ambitious and the highly sexed
> Are the natural prey of the incarnate Christ.   (50–1)

Sisson's use of the first person ('I understand', 'I am of that parish'), his intimate register ('Eaten by lust', 'love'), his casually noticed daily activities ('you crossed the Sevenoaks High Street'), and his direct address ('I understand you', 'you were a man of ability'), put our poet and his forebear into seemingly intimate communion, and these historical periods into dialogue. The poem not only creates the impression of parity between its addressee and its speaker—*you* 'crossed the Sevenoaks High Street' as *I* does today; whilst *you* were 'rector of Saint Nicholas', now 'I am of that parish'—but also takes command of address's power to produce the sense of time's simultaneity. It is an impression that becomes still stronger towards the poem's end, when the speaker writes an urgent second-person exhortation to his imagined auditor, as if 'through' time:

> Come down and speak to the men of ability
> On the Sevenoaks platform and tell them
> That at your Saint Nicholas the faith
> Is not exclusive in the fools it chooses   (51)

'The finest of Sisson's poems remind me a little of John Donne, in that in them a passionate nature examines the nature of its passion', writes Robert Nye: 'The relationship of the flesh and the spirit is never ignored in Sisson's best verse.'[3] But is Sisson's address at risk of collapsing the specificities of these different eras with that passionate discursive gesture of alignment with his auditor? One might imagine that Sisson's poem conducts a dialogue with *you* that attempts to exist outside of, or to transcend, time. Even as Sisson's elaborate poem of public address commands

---

[3] Robert Nye, 'Letter from England: Jones and Sisson', *Hudson Review* 28:3 (1975) 468–77, 476–7.

Donne to step down from the pulpit to deliver a cracking redress, the poem plays on the notion that Donne's speech can occur across time: all those who have misjudged the balance of the passions, all 'men of ability' from past and present, will be upbraided. Sisson's deliberate, and well-judged, temporal unspecificity in 'You may see them on the Sevenoaks platform *any day*' allows foolishness to be viewed both as a characteristic of men of all eras, as well as a common 'daily' propensity. But this risks appearing to privilege the fundamental similarity of 'men' (of all ages) in their passionate natures. The poem relies upon the idea that we share (and will acknowledge) this common fleshly failing. It is because we, like Nye, accept this, that Sisson's transhistorical address can take place—and that the address Sisson demands of Donne can be sounded meaningfully, and equally, in his own and in the present age.

From another perspective, however, the poem balances its close verbal liaison with the particularities of Donne's own historical situatedness. Although Sisson implies his forebear's speech is to be conducted in and across history, the poem makes clear that it is the present age which is to benefit from, and which *requires*, Donne's words: 'But *now* what animal has climbed into your pulpit?' (emphasis added), 'the game of a fool, / [...] the click of a computer', 'they drive the machine'. Sisson's poem must hit upon the right form of hailing his seventeenth-century auditor: he must bring back from this literary encounter something instructive for his present listeners. Sisson's poem is an address to his contemporaries (as well as to Donne) that is mediated on at least two levels through the specificities of Donne's historical voice. Firstly, the poem calls on its forebear to issue a public address to these contemporary fools. Secondly, Sisson's own lyric address to Donne brings the style and form of early modern critique to bear, not only letting Donne's voice be heard, but sounding it himself, through his 'Letter'.

It is Eliot's famous pronouncements on the 'dissociation of sensibility [...] from which we have never recovered' that are, I think, motivating Sisson's sense of the rupture between present 'inward-directed' poetics and the negotiative addresses of the seventeenth century, and prompting his urgent plea to his interlocutor.[4] In his 1921 essay on 'The Metaphysical Poets', Eliot lamented that the 'direct sensuous apprehension of thought' (*Prose* 63) common in sixteenth- and seventeenth-century literature is largely lost to contemporary poetics:

> something [...] happened to the mind of England between the time of Donne or Lord Herbert of Cherbury and the time of Tennyson and Browning; it is the difference between the intellectual poet and the reflective poet.

---

[4] Eliot, 'The Metaphysical Poets', in *Prose* 64.

Tennyson and Browning are poets, and they think; but they do not feel their thought as immediately as the odour of a rose. A thought to Donne was an experience; it modified his sensibility. When a poet's mind is perfectly equipped for its work, it is constantly amalgamating disparate experience; the ordinary man's experience is chaotic, irregular, fragmentary. (64)

Following in the Eliotic vein, Sisson's 'Letter to John Donne' strategically issues a historical address to a writer who placed emphasis upon both inner and outer experience, linking our linguistic and our fleshly natures. Finding bodily passion and spiritual virtue combined in his recipient, Sisson calls upon Donne to issue a corrective to the congregation precisely because he is visited by, not innocent of, bodily sins: 'I understand you well enough, John Donne / First, that you were a man of ability / Eaten by lust and by the love of God', 'extravagant whether in bed or in your shroud'. The coolly assessing tone of 'I understand you well enough' is softened by the much gentler reciprocity of the later address: 'You would understand'. Similarly, 'I am grateful' is weighed carefully against the recognition of Donne's human imperfection: 'I am grateful particularly that you were not a saint / But extravagant', 'You brought body and soul to this church'. Again, it is as much the natural outer world as the spiritual which performs crucial work here. Images of physical vitality stand alongside the more abstract concept of 'soul', emphasizing the importance of the animal in the human; of pain and suffering as well as elevated understanding; of the 'body' as well as mind. Sisson's request, then, that a judgement is issued upon 'men of ability' is begged from a canonical poet, preacher, Member of Parliament, Doctor of Divinity, and Royal Chaplain, who is also envisaged as one of fallible flesh and bodily instinct. The literary master Sisson's poem calls upon to issue an address of condemnation upon the public congregation is himself susceptible and all-too-human, not idealized as omnipotently immune from sin.

'"[T]he beautiful in art is the result of an unmistaken working of man in accordance with the beautiful in nature"', Sisson wrote in an essay on William Barnes, published in *Art and Action* in 1965; the same year the 'Letter' to Donne was published.[5] Sisson quotes the nineteenth-century English minister and poet: 'for man, beauty is "fitness for the good continuance of the animal as such"' (*Avoidance* 198). His essay praises not only Barnes's keen poetic attentiveness to the idioms, dialects, and registers used in his native Dorset, but also his attention to the intelligently verbal aspects of our physicality: 'the study of language took him back to physical apprehensions, and an esthetic idea of the

---

[5] 'William Barnes', *Avoidance* 192–201, 198.

physical man and woman was never far from the mind of this majestic parson with long bead and flossing cassock' (198). When Sisson's 'Letter' writes of Donne that 'You brought body and soul to this church', it seems to me by way of similar praise (*CP* 50). Sisson aligns himself with the version of the bodily he finds in Donne and Barnes (and which Eliot protests the loss of), and against the merely mechanical physicality of the men he would have Donne redress: 'apes denying the Church of God', 'they drive the machine'. When Sisson issues his plea that Donne: 'Bring out your genitals and your theology / What makes you familiar is this dual obsession', he is commending the man's refusal to sever the corporeal from the religious, the body from the mind: 'Lust is not what the rutting stag knows / It is to take Eve's apple and to lose / The stag's paradisal look'.

Is Sisson's prose commentary on, as well as his poetical dialogue with, particular seventeenth-century poets (Donne, Marvell, Vaughan) an attempt to recreate the close connection between politics and poetry, public and private addresses, that was characteristic of the early modern period? Exerting pressure over Sisson's address-poem, and motivating our poet's sense of how the seventeenth century should 'speak to the men of ability' in the present, are what he sees, following Eliot, as two post-seventeenth-century fissures: the severance of thought from feeling, and the severance of inner life from public-political life. In a 1972 essay on the Metaphysical poet Henry Vaughan, Sisson praises the appropriateness of Vaughan's 're-vulsion' from those exhibiting 'abstracted spirituality and [...] contempt of the physical world—precisely, their putting of their own conceptions before the evidence of the senses'.[6] To Sisson's mind, like Eliot's, the unweaving of intellect from passion, mental from bodily phenomena—and the *loss* of the use of these in a politically informed poetry—manifested not just as a change in the poetic landscape, but a problematic transformation of the people's ability to engage fully, imaginatively, with history, nation, and with each other.

Writing of Andrew Marvell's 'An Horatian Ode Upon Cromwell's Return From Ireland', Sisson comments: 'It is rarely that a crucial event in our national history is adequately celebrated in verse. When this does happen, the national consciousness is enriched by something more than the mere event and something more than the mere poem.'[7] Enriching though the 'Horatian Ode' turned out to be to later readers, one might point out that Marvell's poem was more than a little belat-

---

[6] 'Songs in the Night: The Work of Henry Vaughan the Silurist' (1972–3), in *Avoidance* 343–4.
[7] 'Reflections on Marvell's Ode' (1951), in *Avoidance* 110.

edly received by 'the national consciousness' of its own day.[8] This does not necessarily jeopardize Sisson's argument that Marvell's poem has in mind 'something more than the mere poem', given that the 'Ode' offers a publicly minded address that responds to—even if it cannot (yet) operate in—those fraught political climes.[9] Sisson's sense of lyric enrichment as lying somewhere between real 'event' and 'mere poem' is perhaps what is motivating his own civic poems of address to heads of state, on occasions of national celebration: 'For the Queen's Jubilee', 'Vigil & Ode for St George's Day'.[10] It is also behind his patriotic poems addressed to the 'Land of my fathers', the 'Sweet rose of England', and 'For the Primate of all England', yet with a similar, and uneasy, dividedness.[11] As one might note, Sisson himself does not write a poetry that 'adequately celebrates' any 'crucial event in our national history'. And nor does he concern himself with adequately celebrating crucial events or persons in *literary* history—unlike, say, Graham, whose energetic addresses 'dive to knock on the rusted, tight / Haspt locker' of the past, and invite back to the surface 'Shelley, Crane and Melville and all / The rest [...]'.[12] It is not at all clear whether this is an oversight or an inability, or whether Sisson thinks, perhaps mistakenly, that 'adequate celebration' is no longer a possibility, at least not in contemporary verse.

This somewhat anti-social strain in Sisson's work can present certain problems, particularly with his address. Reading the 'Letter', one might well form the misleading impression that Sisson's historically minded interlocution is an anomalous, isolated case; that other twentieth-century and post-war poets are not attentive to early modern sources. The very directness and intimacy of this *I*'s address to Donne feels exclusive, as if others were not seen as part of this poem's *you*, just as in a number of Sisson's historically minded addresses, the dialogue is rendered privately, even possessively: '*my* friend across twenty centuries' ('Catullus'), '*my* friend on the verandah' ('In Memoriam Cecil De Vall').[13] The audience is not implicated in or invited to share such hailings: the work rather assumes

---

[8] The poem was composed in 1650, after Cromwell's return, but was not published in Marvell's lifetime. It was first published in *Miscellaneous Poems* (1681), though the sheets containing it were removed—almost certainly because of their pro-Cromwellian bent—and only remain in two known copies. It is unknown whether Cromwell ever saw it. Even after 1681, the publication and dissemination were highly problematic.

[9] See Thomas Healy's chapter, 'Andrew Marvell, "An Horatian Ode Upon Cromwell's Return from Ireland"', in *A Companion to Literature from Milton to Blake*, ed. David Womersley (Oxford: Blackwell, 2008) 165–70, 166.

[10] *CP* 288; 349.

[11] 'Thinking of Politics' 456, 'The Rose' 473, *CP* 384.

[12] Graham, 'Implements in Their Places', *NCP* 251.

[13] *Numbers*, *CP* 65.

that its readership is not comprised of even a handful of other speakers, readers, and writers who engage in like-minded literary dialogues with historical figures. Sisson's conversations with literary masters are not adept at showing how it is in both producing and *receiving* artworks written to others that address takes place. The conversation is envisaged as exclusive, even though Sisson's readers will, in his place, give voice to the poem's *I*, and Donne will be hailed as their *you*. In addressing Donne in the second person, the 'Letter' cannot avoid making him into a meeting point for numberless reading *I*s and *you*s, though it certainly does not feel this way, reading Sisson's poem.[14] His 'Letter' rather misses a trick, then: much more national, and 'eventful', ground might have been trodden had this *I* alluded to subsequent poetical and critical renegotiations of Donne's legacy, imagining its own address speaking as part of, and updating, a community of live voicings.[15] A similar effect could be created in making clear Donne's status as a *publicly* memorialized figure, commemorated as a priest in the calendar of the Church of England, as well as by a memorial housed at his place of burial, in St Paul's Cathedral, and viewed every year by scores of visitors confirming the Metaphysical poet's status as civic and literary landmark.

In order to restore Sisson's poetics of address to its literary context, one must bear in mind that he is far from alone in contemporary poetry in finding the early modern period a fertile literary source. In addition to Sisson, Thom Gunn, for instance, employs a fictive Elizabethan-Jacobean context—and Ted Hughes's work has looked back on and forged reconnections with the sixteenth century. Something comparable is seen also in the thought of Hill: 'If I'm asked how you get bodily gesture into the rhythm and syntax of poetic speech, I answer that we can hear and see it in poets as diverse as Wyatt, Donne, Dryden and Hopkins. The physical is important to me [...] The irruption of spoken questions and demands breaks into my thinking self like a physical blow.'[16] So too, Tony Harrison's

---

[14] He may be actually (even unwittingly) echoing Donne, whose use of direct address ('Come madam') is somewhat misleading, in that it is not received by, or designed for, the *you* it purports to speak to, but by, and for, the audience of the socially restricted confines of manuscript circulation. The question of how 'public' such address is remains highly complex.

[15] Consider Tony Harrison's relation with Donne, particularly in 'Durham': 'we, / alone two hours, can ever be / love's antibodies in the sick, / sick body politic'. Quoted from Tony Harrison, *Selected Poems* (1984; London: Penguin, 1987) 70. The Northern Irish poet James Simmons (1933–2001) has also written a scathing address to, and attack upon, Donne, entitled 'John Donne'. See *Judy Garland and the Cold War* (Belfast: Blackstaff, 1976). Wordsworth's and Coleridge's contributions to the conditions for the 1839 publication of *The Works* (London: Parker) might also be of interest.

[16] 'A Matter of Timing', *Guardian*, Saturday 21 September 2002, 'Features and Reviews', 31.

addresses, like Sisson's, repeatedly return to early modern contacts and contexts—to Milton, Wyatt, Donne, Marvell.[17] Such work demands *you* attend to the negotiations that art makes in its efforts to live, and intervene, in a world of politics that remains steeped in the neoclassical pastoral of the early modern period (in our age often unwittingly). Like these writers, Sisson's is a poetry of locale rooted in the politico-theological language of an earlier communal order.

Amongst those who have often powerfully given voice to, as well as acknowledged and wrangled with, their debt to seventeenth-century writers, are also contemporary poets with markedly different political agendas from the writer under study. Perhaps one would not expect to hear mentioned in the same breath as Sisson's name the poets Tony Harrison and Douglas Dunn. Nevertheless, the addresses of the Scottish republican, Dunn—whose poems have often portrayed the perplexities of regionalist identity in terms of seventeenth- and eighteenth-century revolutionary politics, and envisioned alternative English histories—are especially pertinent points of comparison. In particular, Dunn's 1979 volume *Barbarians*, a series of country-house poems drawing on Jonson and Marvell, puts to work the poetic forms consecrated to an allegedly 'disinterested tradition', asserting the revolutionary impulse, but making it answerable to countering voices.[18] Meanwhile, Harrison's work has made considerable use of Milton, Donne, and Marvell. 'Newcastle is Peru' (1969) echoes Donne's 'To his Mistress Going to Bed',[19] particularly in its last lines that chime with Donne's 'O my America! my new-found land' (*HSP* 65). Also Harrison's 1981 work, *A Kumquat for John Keats*, works in Marvellian mode, as critics have often noted: 'much of the imagery echoes directly or ironically "The Garden" [...] Marvell describes the "happy Garden-state" of man in Paradise alone, Harrison provides his Eden with an Eve.'[20] In addition, as Rick Rylance comments of Harrison's 1978 poem, 'On Not

---

[17] See 'On Not Being Milton', a title which is teasingly self-contradictory, immediately going on to take a sixteen-line epigraph from Milton's 'Ad Patrem'; see also 'The White Queen'—which riffs off Wyatt's 'They Flee From Me'—and 'Newcastle is Peru' and 'Durham'.

[18] *Barbarians* (1979), in *DSP*.

[19] Composed around 1590–1600, the poem circulated only in manuscript in Donne's lifetime (it survives in over 70 manuscript copies, though none in Donne's hand). Refused a licence for publishing in Donne's posthumous collection, *Poems* (1663), it was first published in the anthology *The Harmony of the Muses* (1654). Only in 1669 was it finally included in Donne's *Works*. See John Donne, *The Complete English Poems*, ed. A. J. Smith (London: Penguin, 1986) 124.

[20] See Harrison *HSP* 192. All critical quotes from Sandie Byrne, 'On Not Being Milton, Marvell or Gray', in *Tony Harrison: Loiner*, ed. Sandie Byrne (Oxford: Clarendon Press, 1997) 57–84, at 64–5.

Being Milton', 'ambivalence about Milton is part of a wider ambivalence in Harrison's work which celebrates the literary as it criticises it'.[21]

Despite the obvious disparity in the political affiliations of Dunn and Harrison, and Sisson, these poets have in common an urge to bring seventeenth-century public lyric address-forms into contact with the embattled nationalist politics of the present. In Sisson, one vein of this can be traced in those allusive addresses that insert themselves into, and comment upon, the political context in which seventeenth-century epigrammatic poetry circulated (a good example is the 1980 poem 'The Garden of the Hesperides' (255), which will be considered in some detail below). Another vein is his attentiveness to how one might view and use poetic language in a manner akin to that of early modern literature, not merely as decoration but as a force in state affairs. As is clear in the arguments of many critical texts on the poetry of the early modern period, including James Turner's *The Politics of Landscape*,[22] David Gervais's aforementioned chapter on 'Pastoral Versions of England' in *Literary Englands*,[23] Stanley Stewart's *The Enclosed Garden*,[24] Hugh Jenkins's *Feigned Commonwealths: The Country-House Poem and the Fashioning of the Ideal Community*,[25] gardens and natural landscapes were strategic sites upon which monarchic power was constructed, and republican challenges to such power were conducted.

This understanding is often strongly present in Sisson's pastoral addresses. Poems including 'The Garden', 'The Herb-garden', 'The Garden of Hesperides', 'No Garden', 'To a Garden Asleep', 'The Garden of Epicurus', 'Et in Arcadia Ego', like Dunn's own pastoral addresses, connect contemporary British poetic conceptions of nation, language, and identity with the fraught aesthetics and politics of nationhood in the sixteenth and seventeenth centuries.[26] Using the iconography of England as a glorious garden of perfect forms (Eden, Blessed Isle, and Hesperidian Garden), 'The Rose', published late in Sisson's career, in *What and Who* (1994), combines the poet's address to the loved nation-garden as *you* with the notion of lyric gardens as ideological battlefields:

[21] 'On Not Being Milton', *HSP* 112; Rick Rylance, 'Tony Harrison's Languages', in *Contemporary Poetry Meets Modern Theory*, ed. Anthony Easthope and John O. Thompson (Hemel Hempstead: Harvester Wheatsheaf, 1991) 56–67, 56.
[22] James Turner, *The Politics of Landscape: Rural Scenery and Society in English Poetry, 1630–1660* (Cambridge, MA: Harvard University Press, 1979).
[23] Gervais, *Literary Englands* 1–27.
[24] Stanley Stewart, *The Enclosed Garden: The Tradition and the Image in Seventeenth-Century Poetry* (Madison, Milwaukee, and London: University of Wisconsin Press, 1966).
[25] Hugh Jenkins, *Feigned Commonwealths: The Country-House Poem and the Fashioning of the Ideal Community* (Pittsburgh: Duquesne University Press, 1998).
[26] Sisson, *CP* 202, 258, 255, 296, 455, 94, 442.

What the words carry and the things you say
Must be related, but the saying is you
And what the words carry is history
To which you add your infinitesimal day.
Sweet rose of England, nothing can be true
Except so far as words and you agree.

And how is that possible? My dear,
The tongue you speak must so become your tongue
That it becomes like kisses on your lips,
Given and received at once. Then, without fear,
Your diction answers to the clear line sung
By lutenists, which dips as the voice dips.

So, when words had the colour of the flesh,
And passed from mouth to mouth, and were not laid
Like corpses on a script or on a tape,
The fields rang with laughter, or the fresh
Cry of misfortune. Now speech is a trade,
The word congealed and all meanings escape.   (473)

Sisson's lines address an entrenchedly public concept, '*England*' in the second person, articulating national concerns in the intimate register of private relations: 'my dear', 'kisses on your lips'. It is an address that has analogies with Dunn's use of *you* in the mock-dated, mock-located poem 'Gardeners' ('England, Loamshire, 1789').[27] Both poets fashion interlocutions that weave together political enterprise and the language of direct, personal requirement. Their writing flirts with the tone of exclusive address to an intimately beheld *you* in order to detail the ambivalences and contradictions that arise when social demands are brought into the contemporary lyric space:

Townsmen will wonder, when your house was burned,
We did not burn your gardens and undo
What likes of us did for the likes of you [...]   (106)

Dunn's address, like Sisson's, uses the intimate second-person pronoun to draw to an interlocutor's attention how poetry is bound up publicly in representations of the age's national, economic, and political realities, what he calls in 'In the Grounds', 'England's art of house and leaf' (*Barbarians*, *DSP* 101). Drawing upon early modern pastoral modes of address, so often associated with courtly might, monarchist support, patriotism, and patronage, many of the poems from Dunn's *Barbarians* foreground the

---

[27] (1979), in *DSP* 105–6.

violent impulses that haunt artistic depictions of nation, landscape, and power, both in contemporary language and in early modern lyric art: 'the craftsmanship we fashion / To please your topographical possession' ('Gardeners' 105), 'you do not know, how, unkempt // And coarse, we hurt a truth with truth, still true / To who we are: barbarians, whose chins / Drool with ale-stinking hair, whose horses chew / Turf owned by watching, frightened mandarins' ('In the Grounds' 101), 'One day we will leap down, into the garden, / And open the gate—*wide, wide*' ('The Come-On' 100).

If Dunn's 'Gardeners' uses *you* to flag up the violence of the urge to fight for, and to dignify, alternative versions of a national order, Sisson's national *you* in 'The Rose' is conceived of not as a process of physical violation, but of continual linguistic co-option, persuasion, and struggle: '*must* be related', '*nothing* can be true / Except so far as words and you agree', 'the tongue you speak *must* so become your tongue' (473). For Sisson, it seems that violence is only just held at bay through verbal negotiation; through a poetical power-play that involves close attention to the loved national tongue. For Sisson, as for Dunn, England is defined less through being a concrete geographical location and a country, than through its being a *way of saying*, a collective idea dependent upon language: 'the saying *is* you'. One is put in mind of Benedict Anderson's definition of nations as 'imagined communities': a nation 'is *imagined* because the members of even the smallest nation will never know most of their fellow-members, meet them, or even hear of them, yet in the minds of each lives the image of their communion'.[28] This view of England as a succession of ideas, and *you*s, rather than a fixed whole, is one which many contemporary critics have found persuasive. 'Every idea of England predicates a slightly different England [...] England is not something that is simply there but something we have to construct for ourselves' writes David Gervais, in *Literary Englands* (1–2). If Gervais's insistent phrasing 'we have to construct', indicates his belief that some England should be constructed, imagined, asserted (a belief I suspect Sisson shares), for both writers the 'England' that is asserted remains, like a personally known addressee, a slippery concept. As a changeable idea, nationhood requires contact through ordinary face-to-face lived encounters with others. England is a collective *you*, that is by turns fought over, honoured, rebuffed, adored, and repeatedly reconfigured through citizens' and poets' language.

Like Anderson and Gervais, Sisson marks out an England that is a product of common thought, myth, history, belief. This national *you* cannot be sustained by an exclusive elite, for it takes shape and meaning through the numberless observances of local and national rituals, artistic acts, performances, private and public ceremonies, greetings between

---

[28] Benedict Anderson, *Imagined Communities: Reflections on the Origin and Spread of Nationalism*, 9th edn. (London: Verso, 1999) 6.

ordinary citizens: 'It is by answering one another / That we exist', 'We call to one another, we are many', 'An ocean of voices' ('Conversation' 162; 'Words' 390–1). This England can only become real in being tangible to its citizens; in being felt upon the pulses and sounded by the tongues of the people who comprise her.

In these respects, Sisson's public addresses bear more than passing resemblance to those conducted by Harrison and Dunn, at least in 'The Rose'. Each writes a poetry in which speaking to *you* is not an aside from the communal or national. The interlocutions of each are heavily invested with a sense of the tongue as an instrument of power; with a view of address as a form of action and public consequence, as it was in the early modern period, where lyric addresses were treated as the means of shaping and reshaping allegiances. In saying *you* to particular historical others, and to public institutions and concepts, these writers make evident that a poem's address is capable of violently deciphering and re-envisioning the idea of a nation and the national tongue.

I promised a moment ago to detail another species of allusive address in Sisson: the address that dwells upon, thinks itself into, and imagines itself responding to, the particular social and political contexts in which early modern epigrammatic poetry was disseminated. A poem that works well in this framework is 'The Garden of the Hesperides', a historically situated, self-consciously patriotic poem, in which Sisson's address to *you* plays off and re-sounds particular critical, pastoral, and panegyric voices (*Anchises*, *CP* 255–7). The reader has to do her own literary historical foraging to locate those addresses, however. Sisson does not spell it out. Although his 'Hesperides' subtly reads its own lyric contribution as part of a live address in a chorus of literary, critical and editorial, historical and twentieth-century speakers, at first reading, the subtlety is so great that it is likely to be lost upon its reader: [29]

> If I knew what to say, I would say it;
> But as I do not, I send it,
> This:
> When there was time and place, I lost it;
> Now there is not, I regret it;
> That.
>
> (255)

---

[29] That chorus has hardly been willing to mete out praise for Herrick's poem. The poem was criticized in its own day, and in the twentieth century. Eliot attacked what he saw as the inconsistency and failed continuity of the epigram book, regarding it as a perfect example of 'minor' verse, and Leavis argued it was 'trivially charming'. See Eliot's 'What is Minor Poetry?' (1944), in *OPP* 46–7, and F. R. Leavis, *Revaluation: Tradition and Development in English Poetry* (London: Chatto & Windus, 1936) 36.

[…] you are the writing on the wall

Or I am the wall and you are the writing;
Would I understand, if I knew my letters?
Will you teach me? What if I am ignorant?
Beyond teaching, savage? […]

(255)

My object is to say, there may be you,
Equal in nothingness, as in all else:
Therefore the water shines, therefore the dew
Hangs on the grass as big as melons.

(257)

The immediacy of these intimate interlocutions is balanced against the public, historical, and political resonance of Sisson's address. 'The Garden of the Hesperides' draws on the strongly monarchist poetics of the seventeenth-century epigrammatist Robert Herrick, whose Caroline epigram book was also entitled *Hesperides*.[30] Herrick's *Hesperides* is often seen as having portrayed England in line with Charles I's propagandist wishes, as an ordered, paradisiacal realm, a mythic land of prosperity and eternal spring.[31] Since Herrick's poem depicts a contentment that the King's rule was a long way from establishing in reality, his verse has sometimes been viewed as mere glib panegyric, attempting to retreat from serious political problems into a realm of idyllic misrepresentation and illusion. Graham Parry comments, 'the strong royalist sympathies of the verse were hardly in accord with the time, and the evocation of a world of ceremony and ritual was inappropriate to the present mood of Puritan victory'.[32]

Sisson's address in his own Hesperidean idyllic garden, his fragrant apples, shining water, his 'dew […] as big as melons', might also look 'inappropriate to the present mood' of its time. Sisson's 'Hesperides' was published in *Exactions* in 1980, just over a year after the Winter of Discontent, and during a period of severe recession, soaring unemployment, public and industrial unrest, and a widespread strike movement. Sisson, then, chooses a rather uncomfortable moment to tap into that early modern royalist dream of England as a safely enclosed garden of wealth, health, and eternal pleasure. But like Herrick's, Sisson's lyric address of longing, his repeated calls to *you*, are hardly a mere refuge from hard political times. Nor are they innocent of political intent. Rather, Sisson's apparently private lyric hailing deliberately associates itself with

---

[30] Herrick, *Hesperides: Or the Works Both Humane and Divine.*
[31] See Turner, *Politics of Landscape* 92.
[32] See Graham Parry, *Seventeenth Century Poetry: The Social Context* (London: Hutchinson, 1985) 154; Jonathan F. S. Post, 'Caroline Amusements', in *English Lyric Poetry: The Early Seventeenth Century* (London and New York: Routledge, 1999) 111–23.

seventeenth-century propagandist poetics, in which embattled address-poems by royalist and republican writers often presented to their audiences and patrons conflicting versions of, and hopes for, a conflicted England that it tactically presented as idyllic:

> Where ev'ry tree a wealthy issue beares
> Of fragrant Apples, blushing plums, or peares,
> And all the shrubs, with sparkling spangles, shew
> Like morning sun-shine tinsilling the dew.
> Here in green meddowes sits eternall May.[33]

'In royalist propaganda the outrages of the Star Chamber and the fury of evicted peasants are rapidly forgotten', writes James Turner (92). Caroline poetry, as Turner points out, often uses the image of Charles I presiding over a flawless, Edenic England, over a safe and contented people, as a weapon in the courtly arsenal against early seventeenth-century Parliamentarian dissent. It attempts to smooth over public unrest and dissatisfaction with the King's personal rule. The countryside of the 1630s, unlike this paradisiacal realm of 'fragrant Apples', fertile land, and 'wealthy issue', was embattled agricultural ground, troubled by a succession of poor harvests, political resistance to enclosure, increasingly capitalist practices designed to increase revenue, and by the redrawing of politico-agricultural borders in accordance with Charles I's deeply unpopular centralizing monarchical commonwealth.

But in that case, a literary alliance between Sisson and Herrick surely indicates that the latter-day Modernist is open to the charges associated with Herrick's use of the pastoral as 'inappropriate' propaganda? Unlike Harrison and Dunn, Sisson, like Herrick, seems merely to tinker with the language of serenity and walled-in private pleasure, as if with the aim of distracting readers from his right-royal agenda. Since Sisson's title sets up a deliberate identification with Herrick, one may assume that he is willing to use language and myth as camouflage and adornment: 'in the garden of the Hesperides / [...] all the apples have to do is please'. Sisson's addresses, like Herrick's, appear to create a closed-in idyllic realm of play and pleasure designed to conceal encroaching revolutionary and radical powers from its interlocutors:

> My object is to say, there may be you,
> Equal in nothingness, as in all else:
> Therefore the water shines, therefore the dew
> Hangs on the grass as big as melons.
> What mind is in all this? Not less a mind
> Than any pulp within whatever rind.

---

[33] Herrick, 'The Apparition of his Mistresse calling him to Elizium' 329.

> Apples and oranges is what we are,
> And you especially, though side by side
> We hung, across the glade seemed far
> To me, which was because of pride,
> A defect in the garden of the Hesperides
> Where all the apples have to do is please.   (257)

In addressing this intimate *you* directly, with lines such as: 'Apples and
oranges are what we are, / And you especially', in Sisson's envisaged Eng-
land, private lyric pleasure seems to be the highest order, the command-
ing principle of unity: '*all* you have to do is please'. Yet to some extent,
Sisson's poem also works as a satirical commentary against precisely those
who have argued that the trope of England as Hesperides (including Her-
rick's treatment of it in his much-maligned epigram book) creates a poet-
ics of royalist dogma, uncritical nationalism, and stultifying escapism.[34]
These Hesperidian gardens, where 'the water shines, [...] the dew / Hangs
on the grass as big as melons', are far from perfect realms. Sisson's envis-
aged English idyll, like Herrick's realms of 'fragrant apples, blushing
Plums', must also accommodate 'defects', 'pride', and the threat of waste
and sterility that hangs over long-ripened fruit and unearned pleasure: '*all*
the apples have to do is please'. Just how self-delighted is that apparently
unifying 'all'? Is there something constrictive and sterile in this utopian
urge to experience *only* pleasure; rather as in 'Equal *in nothingness*, as in *all*
else' lurks a potent image of perfection's alarming negation, reminiscent
of Larkin's sense of 'burst[ing] into fulfilment's desolate attic'? ('Decep-
tions', *LCP* 67). The word 'defect' threatens Sisson's imagined English
garden twice over. As 'flaw', the word hints at imperfection; and as 'defec-
tion', it gestures towards potential betrayal, acts of political apostasy, de-
fection to the opposing 'side'. So too, even though '[s]ide by side' suggests
parity and closeness, 'side by side / *We hung*' is deathly, and smacks of
punishment, treasonous hanging. Fruit ('apples and oranges [...] we are')
as well as dew ('Hangs on the grass as big as melons') are ripe for hanging,
ready to be tried by some imagined court. Sisson's natural world, like
Dunn's, is certainly not innocent, in such lines. But 'Hesperides' is also
pointing out that gardens and plants may be put on false trial. To force
'apples, oranges, melons and dew' into the dock, to make the natural
world answer for itself, is risible.

---

[34] 'Ritual has been seen, not as expressing a publicly articulated expression of consensus,
but as embodying the "mobilization of bias"—an example of the ruling elite consolidating
its ideological dominance by exploiting pageantry as propaganda', writes David Canna-
dine, in 'The British Monarchy 1820–1977', in *The Invention of Tradition*, ed. Eric
Hobsbawm and Terrence Ranger (Cambridge: Cambridge University Press, 1992) 101–64,
104.

In this sense, the formal poise and natural imagery of Sisson's 'Hesperides' satirize the over-zealous critic, redressing him for his desire to put the pastoral mode on trial and find it guilty of closing its eyes to the real. I rather suspect that Sisson's address-poem does long to escape into Herrick's idyllic realm of flora and fauna (particularly given Sisson's unhappy political situatedness), though he also knows that Herrick's text itself is not an innocently lyric presentation of beauty, but an artfully political re-envisaging of Hesperidian England in its own deeply fraught historical moment. However, unlike Sisson, who chooses freely to insert his poem into this historical and literary context, Herrick can only subtly re-work, and indirectly criticize, the early modern panegyric address form demanded of him by his patrons. This begs the question as to Sisson's motives for choosing this particular context and this literary alliance for his poem's address. Sisson's goal in writing the Hesperides poem does not seem to be to restore Herrick's reputation, nor does the poem, to my ear, call for a twentieth-century rethinking of the politics behind the trend for reductive critical attitudes towards that epigrammatic book. Sisson's poem neither names Herrick, nor acknowledges its debt to his seventeenth-century text. In this, it is quite different from—as we shall see in some detail later—the commemorative addresses of Hill's *A Treatise of Civil Power*, or Don Paterson's allusive intimacies in poems as different as 'Candlebird', 'The Alexandrian Library', and 'Waking with Russell'.[35] In both of these contemporary poets, relations with loved one in the here-and-now take shape in dialogue with the voices of the past. Just as Hill's address 'To the Lord Protector Cromwell' and 'On Reading *The Essayes or Counsels, Civill and Morall*' reconfigure the cultural history of the public artefacts they laud, Paterson pulls into contact address to his sons, literary attention to Romulus and Remus, Dante and medieval Arabic lyricism, to re-think the texts, persons, and artworks contemporary poetry speaks with and to which it alludes (*Treatise* 13; 42; *Light* 5). The past and the present are brought together to shed light on each other mutually: 'two things are measured by each other', as Eliot writes in 'Tradition and the Individual Talent' (*SW* 50).

In comparison, in Sisson's address, Herrick is enlisted onto Sisson's side—much as Donne was brought into conversational contact with the lyric present—less to offer something new to the seventeenth-century poets (a new way of reading their work, a reassessment of their poetics), than to mete out a sharp comment to Sisson's own age. Eliot recommended that: 'the past should be altered by the present as much as the present is

---

[35] Hill, *Treatise*; see Paterson, *Gift* 55; *Nil Nil* 33; *Light* 5.

altered by the past' (50). Sisson, in contrast, wants the past master to speak in the present, but is not at all keen to let the present formulate answers. Sisson's handling of this dialogue between past and present seems to work predominantly in one direction, so that in his addresses it is chiefly the contemporary *you* who finds himself 'judged by the standards of the past' (*SW* 50).

6

Old Authentic Words: You, Them, & Us

How about a new kind of hermetic conservatism
And suffering withdrawal symptoms of same?

John Ashbery

In his prose, Sisson has written of his desire to create a contemporary
poetry that is 'armed, by its sophistication, to do battle in the [...] world
of twentieth-century illusions'.[1] Sisson's work, as we have seen, often uses
address to past masters to 'do battle' with the voices of his own time. But
how do his addresses pan out when it comes to the figures that the poetry
is actually received by: its real audience? Is Sisson's poetry in touch with
the *you*s that will thumb through his volumes? Or if he has in mind as his
you primarily those rather unspecified 'fools' harbouring 'twentieth-
century illusions', does he effect contact with any real addressees at all?
Sisson's work often seems to be in better contact with the early modern
world of addresses than with interlocutions in his own age: one wonders
whether he has been able to keep his finger on the pulse of his time while
pursing this contact. To what extent are Sisson's lyric hailings adequately
in touch with contemporary *you*s, and to what extent does he hope,
through his work, to persuade real listeners to correct the faults he identi-
fies? One often finds oneself asking, in reading Sisson, to what degree his
poetry is able successfully to offer the corrective it longs to, and to what
degree this is, even to Sisson's mind, a vain hope and a wishful lyric
fantasy.

In raising such questions alongside the matter of Sisson's early modern
leanings, I am put in mind of David Norbrook's comment that: 'Rather
than reading monarchist texts as expressions of a unified symbolic order,
we [...] [should be] directed to asking what texts they were answering,
why it was felt necessary to defend monarchy in these particular terms'.[2]

---

[1] 'Martin Seymour-Smith' (1977), in *Avoidance* 496–7, 497.
[2] David Norbrook, *Writing the English Republic: Poetry, Rhetoric and Politics, 1627–1660*
(Cambridge: Cambridge University Press, 1999) 11.

Sisson, like his epigrammatist forebears, writes a poetry that, at its best, negotiates between alternative political positions and attempts to stir up a new public poetry that can forge a path between the present and the past. His work, like theirs, strives to answer back to those figures who assert the separateness of the individual from the public body, and who view lyric address as merely private engagement.

All very well, but to whom exactly *are* Sisson's addresses answering back? In order to 'do battle', one needs to mark out clearly some opponent, whether a specific *you*, or body of *you*s, that might be assailed. Norbrook's comments on poetic responsiveness work fine when applied to the Jacobean and Caroline poetic, since, in the Renaissance and early modern periods, poets often exchanged addresses and redresses, hailing one another directly and allusively, in praise, satire, and querulous poetry. This was often a live community of performed address. But Sisson's poems are not performed as a part of political ceremony. Nor do poetic addresses in Sisson's day, or in Sisson's work, operate with the same live historical power that the published and commonplace book Renaissance addresses had to negotiate. This might not be especially problematic, as it is not for Dunn and Harrison, and Hill, who are able to do battle effectively enough, in their targeted lyrics. But Sisson's lyric addresses do not name particular contemporary names, and do not mark out specific twentieth-century antagonists. The specific *you*s of his lyrics apply to seventeenth-century and classical figures, but the names of particular twentieth-century poets do not find their way into Sisson's verse. Eliot, Pound, Yeats, Auden, Wallace Stevens, William Carlos Williams, Larkin, Davie, Hughes, Plath, Heaney, Paulin... all go unmentioned.

In certain respects, Sisson's work exhibits similarities with Modernist thought and style, and key differences from Movement poetics. His addresses are often those of a latter-day-Modernist poet, fascinated by history, form, politics, intertextuality, radical questionings of language and identity. So too, in writing a politically minded poetry that looks back on and re-negotiates early modern address forms, Sisson shares much in common with contemporary poets, particularly with Dunn and Harrison. This reading comes in contrast to the interpretations of his work that assert Sisson is motivated by reactionary principles, elitism, and privilege. 'His political views are highly unfashionable: he dislikes democracy, opposes disestablishment of the Church of England, shows great interest in the Crown, and suggests as a historical generalization as valid as most other, that "after the killing of the King, the intelligence of England deteriorated"', noted Lawrence Lerner, reviewing *Art and Action* in 1966.[3]

---

[3] *The Review of English Studies*, New Series 17:68 (November 1966) 456–7, 456.

An 'authoritarian curmudgeon who never has any fun and makes life a
misery for the youthful', Andrew Duncan has complained more recently:
'The clerico-fascist (Maurrasian) poet CH Sisson, together with his ideo-
logical outlet in *PN Review* and Carcanet Press, stands for mystic author-
ity over against democracy.'[4]

This reading of Sisson's address as self-declaredly political, experimen-
tal, and questioning, moves in some degree in contradistinction to Tom
Paulin's account of contemporary poetry in *The Faber Book of Political*
Verse.[5] Paulin wrote: 'we have been taught, many of us, to believe that art
and politics are separated by the thickest and most enduring of partitions.
Art is a garden of pure perfect forms which effortlessly "transcends" that
world of compromise, cruelty, dead language and junk cars that Man-
icheans dismiss as merely politics' (Intro. 15). To Paulin's mind, a monarch-
ist, high Anglican, conservative poet writing in the pastoral vein would
almost certainly be guilty of perpetuating such a 'separation' and fostering
false 'partition' between art and politics: 'like many writers of pastoral, the
conservative obscures political realities by professing an envy of the ignor-
ant and by shuffling responsibility for historical suffering onto those who
aim to increase knowledge by challenging received ideas' (27). But, like
Dunn's and Harrison's, Sisson's historically and politically minded ad-
dresses repeatedly rebut the view that natural imagery and idyllic land-
scapes inevitably sustain age-old English nationalist mythologies of the
soil and of right rule. Sisson's work (like a number of other, very differ-
ently politically motivated contemporary poets—among whom would be
numbered Seamus Heaney, Tom Paulin, Tom Leonard, Ian Hamilton
Finlay, Kathleen Jamie, and Carol Ann Duffy) flags up, rather than dis-
guises, the ideological content of its representations of history. Nor is his
poetry, in drawing on the natural world, claiming merely to be neutrally
interested in the lyric perfection of verbal forms.

Sisson's insistently historically focused, allusive frameworks of address
indicate concerns surprisingly analogous to Paulin's. Like Paulin, Sisson
starkly rejects the argument that poetry is 'merely personal', or that 're-
sponsibility for historical suffering' can be displaced onto those artists
who insist that their readership should attend to historical and political
acts. Scorning the view that poetry is a vehicle for retreat into private
contemplation of natural beauty, Sisson attempts to explore: 'what solid
people / Have said at the height of their delusions' (*Antidotes*, 404). So
too, his addresses are often deeply alert to their own, and others',

---

[4] Andrew Duncan, *The Failure of Conservatism in Modern British Poetry* (Cambridge:
Salt, 2003) 102; 296.
[5] Tom Paulin, ed., *The Faber Book of Political Verse* (London: Faber, 1986).

she defends + concedes in
terms of politics
134   C. H. Sisson: To the Public: National Orientations

manipulations of language: *'Better that you should forget / Everything I ever said'*, *'If I were accused of what I have said / I could perhaps answer'* (*God Bless Karl Marx!*, 395; *What and Who*, 470). We have traced a number of ways in which Sisson moves to contextualize and historicize contemporary speech masquerading as innocently self-expressive, or moved by a universal, ahistorical ideal: 'ideas [...] come from where other people's ideas come from' ('Sevenoaks' 212), 'those ideas have a history going back for two hundred or some other number of years' ('Pound' 305). In this case, Paulin is right to identify Sisson's work as conservative, but not to dismiss all conservative poetics as setting out to 'obscure political realities by professing an envy of the ignorant'. For Sisson, as for Dunn and Hill, poetry is a vital part of the civil sphere, not a real *or* disguised retreat from it: 'our speaking is that of a race, of a tribe, of a time' ('Sevenoaks' 204). Art 'speaks with the voice of a civilisation' ('Sevenoaks' 216). Sisson is not unlike Paulin in repeatedly demanding an audience's historical and theological tenacity, our aesthetic scrutiny of a fraught, not a glorious, past.

However, there are times in Sisson's work—particularly in the late addresses from the late aforementioned volumes *God Bless Karl Marx!*, *Antidotes*, and *What and Who*,[6] but present in earlier work too—when such accusations seem to hold a good deal more water. Where this occurs most often are the places in which the form is least experimental and questioning, and the addresses are unanchored to context or figure. In such places, 'you' often either hardens into a 'them' and 'us' (more on this in a moment), or is wielded in a manner highly reminiscent of the fairly commonplace nostalgic imperial England characteristic of much Movement verse. In *Exactions*, for instance: 'Life / Flows no more beyond this point', 'plentiful stream, you come to a stop / Here', 'Nightingale, you sing no more / The tree you sat on is not there [...] / And I alone remember you'.[7] Sisson's repeated laments at the English landscape's diminishment seem, ironically, like the tone of Larkin's nostalgic 1970s poem 'Going, Going' (133). Sisson's lyrics tap into an age-old Rightist organicism, employing the vocative to lament their sense of futility and loss. 'Land of my fathers, you escape me now', 'How little sight of you the times allow', we hear, in his late poem 'Thinking of Politics' (456). Addressing a once-glorious England as *you* ('I will in no wise let you go', 'you are there and live'), that poem moves to abstract its language from the bustle and haste, technological advancement and chaotic speech styles of 'the current row'. It is not a hailing that enables the speaker to do battle with the named figures who create that row, or to

---

[6] *Marx* (1987), in *CP 347–96*; *Antidotes* (1991), in *CP 398–436*; *What and Who* (1994), in *CP 440–76*, referred to hereafter as *WW*.
[7] Sisson, *Exactions* (1980), in *CP*, see 245 and 256.

wield its second-person pronoun in combat with, or support of, any spe-
cific twentieth-century auditors. Rather, it keeps the details of its particular
grievances ('the troubles which surround you') and its personal targets un-
specific: 'Let *none* imagine that I do not know' (456).

In contrast, the works of many contemporary poets name and address
one another, often in poems dedicated to and finding alliance with fellow
writers, living or recently deceased. Derek Mahon's 'In Carrowdore
Churchyard (at the grave of Louis MacNeice)' and 'An Unborn Child
(For Michael and Edna Longley)'; Anne Stevenson's 'Letter to Sylvia
Plath'; and Edwin Morgan's 'To Hugh Macdiarmid' might all be named.[8]
Others issue lyric correctives to poetic contemporaries, as well as critics
and editors. One might think of James Fenton's attack on the confessional
mode as championed by Al Alvarez in 'Letter to John Fuller'.[9] Or Heaney's
'Open Letter', addressed 'To Blake and Andrew, Editors, / Contemporary
British Verse, / Penguin Books, Middlesex. Dear Sirs'.[10] Hill, as we will
see, combatively answers back to critics, even if under the cover of pseudo-
nyms: 'Confound you, Croker', '(*eat / shit, MacSikker*)', '(*up / yours,
O'Shem*)'.[11] Paterson too has used lyric address to write with savage relish
to the custodians of academic virtue: 'I speak not your Highnesses *en
masse*', 'To the academy's swift and unannounced inspection: / this page
knows nothing of its self-reflexion'.[12]

Although Sisson's late poems, too, take up a tone of combative mock-
ery towards a contemporary *you*, their taunting questions are predomin-
antly raised against unspecified and decontextualized reader-figures. See,
for instance, the tellingly entitled poem 'What Do You Know?':

> Reasons, ha, ha!
> You do what you must do, you do
> What seems because it seems to you.
> Ha, ha!

And:

> So that's the shape is it? Ah well,
> So you know that! How can you tell?
> Ha, ha! (359)

The poem, in one sense, directly responds to its auditor, hailing him or
her in the second-person voice, with a series of insistent questions: 'that's
the shape is it?', 'How can you tell?' Yet even here, Sisson's poet-figure is

---

8 Mahon, *Collected Poems* 17, 26; Stevenson, *Collected Poems* 384–7; Edwin Morgan,
Collected Poems (Manchester: Carcanet, 1996) 153.
9 James Fenton, *Children in Exile: Poems 1968–1984* (New York: Vintage, 1984) 63.
10 Heaney, *Ireland's Field Day*, 23–32.
11 Hill, *Triumph* (1998) 138 74; 139 75; 139 76.
12 Paterson, 'A Talking Book', *Light* 26–8.

not exactly speaking *to*, but *at*, its 'you'. The lyric prevents *you* from for-mulating a response. And rather than implicating himself in the critique he metes out, addressing *you* as a fellow false 'reasoner', or viewing *I* and *you* together muddling along by 'doing what you have to do', the speaker passes removed judgement upon *you*. So too, the late sequence 'The Pat-tern' concludes with the command for its addressee's piety and subservi-ence: 'Choose you cannot [. . .] fall upon / Knees if you have them'.[13] Not dissimilarly, in 'Tristia', published nearly a decade later, Sisson wields the second person accusingly upon modern interlocutors: 'Nothing can be heard. / But speak on as you will, you who are young. / Collude with one another on the way'.[14] Blaming *you* for what he views as the deterioration of language—'Speech has no meaning'; 'we talk on, dazed and with hollow voice'—the speaker loses patience with his addressees altogether, issuing stern injunctions: 'Pile on your clothes and chatter in the words / The magpie uses and the world applauds' (490–1).

'Tristia' clearly reveals a tendency that emerges with increasing insist-ence towards the end of Sisson's career: the poet's repeated proclamation that he has given up on words, and that he finds only the physical free from suspicion. In 'Tristia', Sisson's once-envisaged fusion of intellect/passion, body/mind is apparently renounced, as the bodily is favoured: 'The naked person is the only one / Who speaks within the chatter of our speech: / There is no truth in reason' (491). Claiming to have renounced the need for logic, abstract thought, language, and 'hollow voice', 'Tristia' (like 'Portrait of the Artist', 'Conversation', 'I Who Am') purports to reject as futile any genuine dialogue with *you*.[15] On the one hand, most of the addresses are generalized, substituting the intimacy of the second-person interlocutor for the impersonal concept of 'the [. . .] one / Who speaks', the 'person', so that Sisson's call, earlier in his career, for a poetic balance between reason and feeling has hardened into a determined, and rather hysterical, renunciation of the former: 'There is *no* truth in reason' (491). In 'Tristia', as in so many poems from 1980 on (especially in *WW*), the speaker no longer trusts language: 'Language is all a lie', 'Words do not hold the thing they say', 'let there be / No talking between you and me'.[16] Hence he imagines that it is not in conversation that *I* makes con-tact with *you*, but in bodily terms: 'your *shape* is what you are', 'ask the body. It alone / Knows all you know' (491; 466).

---

[13] *The Pattern* (1993), in *CP* 476–81, at 481.
[14] 'Tristia' (1995), in *CP* 484–505, at 488–9.
[15] All originally in *WW*, and quoted from *CP* 463; 462; 466.
[16] All originally in *WW*, and quoted from *CP*: 'I Talk From Distant Times' 444; 'Holà' 445; 'The Trade' 448.

As the reader is likely to notice, however, Sisson's lyric, though it re-
peatedly claims to reject dialogue with *you* (as well as 'reason' and speech),
still uses all of these in a succession of addresses that remain entrenchedly
verbal, and cannot seem to avoid the second person:

> The body gives direction to our speech,
> As to our thoughts: your shape is what you are,
> And what you are is what I seek to know.
> [...]
> So strip before my eyes and speak in tune
> With what you are, and that will be the truth
> 'Tristia' 491

These corrective addresses, as in so many of Sisson's poems from the
1990s, refuse historical, personal, and political specificity. At times they
lament about or at an imagined, decontextualized vulgar crowd, some-
times addressed directly to *you* in the accusative (as in the poem above).
On other occasions, they address an imagined sympathetic *you*, who is
treated as an ally against a foolish, reproachable 'they'. 'And so I turn to
you', 'The words we say are part of what we are', Sisson writes compan-
ionably in 'The Model', gathering *I* and *you* into a collective *we* that he
imagines united against *them*: 'The words *they* use come to them from
afar; / The use is only what they are today' (*CP* 472–3, emphasis added).
In such texts, Sisson's speaking voice—much like the Ovidian source of
'Tristia'—seems to come from a position outside of its culture, offering a
detached diagnosis upon it.[17] 'Strip off the words that they are pleasant
with', Sisson commands his interlocutor in 'The Pattern' (480). Although
that poem largely resists using the second person, it still taps the rhetoric
of address. The speaker addresses a close succession of commands and
questions to his listener, and against a generalized, culpable 'them': 'How
speak of them and not cry aloud?', 'Strip off the flesh, which brought
them to this pass', 'Remove all cover [...] / [...] show up the naked pair',
'The words they learned carry the poison in' (480–1).

E. M. Knottenbelt has argued that such poems, which document 'ex-
perience as if it were another person's' are both sincere and persuasive:
'speaking about things that matter for him, but in such a manner that
they speak for themselves as things that cannot help but matter for others
(so intrinsic to his sceptical pursuit of truthfulness)'.[18] In contrast, I find

---

[17] The subject of Ovid's own *Tristia* is, of course, exile, and the abandonment of any
form of community, literary or political.
[18] E. M. Knottenbelt, 'Time's Workings: The Stringent Art of C. H. Sisson', *In Black
and Gold: Contiguous Traditions*, ed. C. C. Barfoot (Amsterdam and Atlanta: Rodopi,
1994) 255–75, 257.

at such times that Sisson's address is most problematically, and pronominally evasive. This *I* speaks as though it could be an unimplicated witness of what it condemns ('they'), standing apart from the apparent disintegration of public intelligence: '[t]he sad creation of *their* own conceit', '[t]he words *they* learned', '[f]alse hopes [...] *they* repeat' ('The Pattern' 480). Not only does Sisson's speaker fail to insert himself into the cultural problem he seeks to discuss with others—'*all* [...] feed on treasons'—but the poem loses touch with the very notion of the shared culture and people that it uses in trying to win interlocutors over (480). Sisson's address operates quite differently from the manner Knottenbelt suggests.

Creating addresses in which 'things [...] speak for themselves' (rather than from specific *I*s to specific *you*s) is not so much 'a pursuit of truthfulness', as a generalizing tendency that works on the rather Larkinseque belief that 'things' can be true for us all without being true to any *I* or *you* in particular: 'they cannot help but matter for others'.[19] If such addresses indicate places where Sisson engages in poetic 'battle', these are battles in which his opponent has hardened into an object rather than a perceived relation; an *it* or *them*, rather than a *you*. Sisson's speaking voice has lost the sense of its own identity as comprised conversationally, with *you*s. In doing so, it has renounced the vital contact with the civic body that it needs to speak with any authority, as a member of it. The problem is the speaker's failure to insert himself into the argument; where is he standing? Where, and how, is he placed? *I* and *you*—those deictic marks of presence that remind one of the textual 'event' of a voice speaking—drop out of the poetry at crucial points, creating the impression of an objective, removed perspective, of third-person 'fact': 'Any description is a load of rubbish', 'There is no truth in reason', 'humankind / Loves a cheat at a market-stall' (*CP* 360; 491; 383).

Sisson often writes of correcting what he sees as the post-seventeenth-century 'erosion by technology of the old language and the old landscape'.[20] His poetry and prose lambast, as the major blunder of the twentieth century, the apparently prevalent 'belief in the harmony of democracy, largescale organization, and individual self-expression'.[21] His poems are reticent about who exactly is guilty of propagating such 'erosion' and expression. His prose is, by comparison, more willing to name and shame those essayists, poets, citizens, and thinkers who propose that

---

[19] This tendency hangs over Sisson's Foreword to *In the Trojan Ditch*, where he asserts the value of a poet being 'able to release the energies of poetry without passing for having said anything of his own'. It is, I find, a distortion of Eliot's notion of 'impersonality' (see 'Tradition', *SW* 56–9).

[20] 'Politics and the Pulpit' (1976), in *Avoidance* 452–6, 456.

[21] 'A Four Letter Word' (1976), in *Avoidance* 529–35, 529. Referred to as 'FLW'.

'invention and novelty for the future are best served by forgetting the past' ('Politics' 456). Recoiling against Larkin's 'Statement' in his 1977 essay on 'Poetry and Myth', Sisson writes: ' "Its own sole freshly-created universe"—there must be some exaggeration in that, surely! [...] Certainly, if one can attach no meaning to "the whole of the ancient world, the whole of classical and biblical mythology", better keep clear of those subjects in one's poetry. None the less, it is proper to concede that these are matters about which every literate person—including Larkin—has some knowledge' ('Pound' 514–15). Hard words, as well as limited sympathy for the project, are meted out to Eliot, especially in relation to *Murder in the Cathedral* ('a dead end'), and *Four Quartets* ('a slackening', 'weak, nondescript verse').[22] Yeats comes in for some steely scrutiny in Sisson's 1970 essay: 'He is cut off from any fruitful tradition—from Swift, Berkeley and Burke', his 'conception of the beautiful and the significant changed with fashion'.[23]

In contrast, in speaking of *contemporary* linguistic and cultural degradation, Sisson's prose is more reluctant to pin down specific figures, and relies, like the poems, on broad, and rather caricatured, brushstrokes: 'the managers of the trade [...] adept at various logomachies', the 'pig-headednesses of the editors and contributors [...] the other noisy politics of the moment'.[24] Such essays, like many of the lyrics, turn out to be disappointingly flat when they attempt to probe and portray the addresses that take place in that 'degraded present': ' "What?" said the World, "You come to beg from me?" / [...] / [...] I love a man who bends / To every whim I have'.[25] Such criticism feels well off the pulse of the discourses of the twentieth century. Sisson's injunction to the 'barren age' to 'Hope backwards'—and his warning that 'speech betrays / [...] end your days / In the security of nothingness, / And so fly loose'—is closer to the voice of a backward-looking stately classicism than a Modernist probing and experimentation (*CP* 425; 429). Such poetic address remains out of touch with the specific realities of contemporary affairs that reach us in our language, whilst the profound economic, social, and political changes taking place in the latter half of the twentieth century are too much summarized, reduced to a safely static 'the World', to constitute a live critique of it (409).

Although Sisson's tone draws on the idiom of contestation, interrogation, and disagreement ('How can you tell?'), his voice seems to have been inserted into a contestation in which his conversational opponent has gone

[22] 'T. S. Eliot' (1971), in *Avoidance* 275–94, 291, 292, 294.
[23] 'W. B. Yeats' (1970), in *Avoidance* 255–70, 261; 263.
[24] 'FLW' 529; Editorial from *PNR* 6 5:2 (1977), in *Avoidance* 559–62, 559.
[25] *16 Sonnets* (1990), see 'Fifteen Sonnets' in *CP* 405–12, sonnet 9. The sequence is referred to as *FS*. All references come from *CP*.

missing. Although he is capable of speaking to *you* rudely, provokingly, as in 'Tristia' ('Pile on your clothes and chatter', 'Strip before my eyes'), no voices interrupt, no *you* rudely answers back. His addresses, so often sent out to *you*, not only rarely receive, but rarely seem to be awaiting, a reply: 'No-one is implicated in the question' (*CP* 491). It is a problem that other twentieth-century poets have experienced, but have also attempted to overcome, notably Graham, who leaves a space in the poem for the addressee's response ('YOU ....'), Harrison, whose poem 'v' lets the voice of the interlocutor be heard in all its aggressive, demotic rage, Duffy, who makes an energetic lyric act out of the various snippets of just-missed addresses, and failed attempts to tune in to—and receive—*you*: 'URGENT WHEN WE MEET COMPLETE STRANGERS DEAR STOP / THOUGH I COUNT THE HOURS TILL YOU ARE NEAR STOP', 'SHIT? FAN? TRUST? WHATS GOING ON HONEY?'.[26] In contrast, Sisson's poems avoid incorporating gruff answering voices, counter-arguing figures, and in this respect they are unlike addresses by Harrison, Graham, or Duffy.

They are also less reminiscent of the Modernist poets Sisson seemed to share common ground with, earlier. Where, in Sisson's lyrics, are what Pound called poetry's 'luminous details'?[27] Sisson's poet-figures claim to live in a world of diminished cultural understandings, of debased language, but the language that *I* uses to document it is often untroubled by the diminishment and debasement of which it complains. Despite their Modernist leanings, Sisson's poems more frequently report cultural brokenness, than show themselves as broken. Content and means of expression support each other less often than they do in the latter-day-Modernism of Bunting or Jones. Pound, in contrast, in the *Pisan Cantos*, throws his Odysseus into the cacophony of languages, identities, and voices:

> "If you had a f...n' brain you'd be dangerous"
>   remarks Romano Ramona
>   to a by him designated c.s. in the scabies ward
>   the army vocabulary contains almost 48 words
>   one verb and participle one substantive ὕλη
>   one adjective and one phrase sexless that is
>   used as a sort of pronoun
>   from a watchman's club to a vamp or fair lady
>   *Cantos* 77:471

[26] Graham, 'Implements in Their Places' (1977), in *NCP* 249; Harrison, 'v' (1985), in *HSP* 235–49; Duffy, 'Telegrams' (1987), in *Selected Poems* 57.

[27] Ezra Pound, 'I Gather the Limbs of Osiris' (1911–12), in *Selected Prose 1901–1965*, ed. William Cookson (New York: New Directions, 1973) 21–4.

Sisson's address, meanwhile, shies from incorporating the cross-currents of voices, languages, and lexicons that Pound saw troubling the smoothly linear progression of language's 'meaning', at the start of the twentieth century. A similar Poundian recognition can be seen in the mid-century work of Veronica Forrest-Thomson, Roy Fisher, and Graham (in his early volumes), and later in the lyricism of Paul Muldoon, Jo Shapcott, and J. H. Prynne—each of whom implements energetic addresses that tune readers into an array of competing idioms, from the consumerist to the historicist, humbly workaday to the scholastic, ecological to the grammatical, playful to the academic.

In an 'Address to the Reader From Pevensey Sluice', Forrest-Thomson's address moves swiftly from the language of 'Transformational Grammar', to the notice pinned up by an 'employee of Sussex Water Board', and the 'melancholy / long withdrawing roar' of literary history—specifically Matthew Arnold.[28] Her 1971 lyric, 'Antiquities', riddlingly propels readers:

> from typewriter
> to Library. 'Grammar' derives from
> 'glamour'; ecology may show the two
> still cognate: Museum, Gk. mouseion,
> a seat of the Muses, a building
> dedicated to the pursuit of learning
> or the arts. (*OED*)
> […]
>
> [...] Glue, paper,
> scissors, and the library together
> paste a mock-up of an individual
> history. […]
>
> *Collected* 85–6

True, in its attentiveness to etymological debts, Forrest-Thomson's work is not entirely dissimilar to Sisson's. Both writers alert us to poetry's structuring through the transhistorical cross-currents of speech, gesture, and text. Sisson's addresses to (and incorporation of interruptions from) classical and early modern figures repeatedly remind us that history and etymology continually script the poet—and the present moment. Forrest-Thomson's 'Antiquities' pushes this sense of being scripted in a new direction: her lines are aware that, however carefully controlled a poet's command of 'grammar', 'the library', and learning, the work's logopoeic specificity ('"Grammar" derives from / "glamour"'; 'the two / still

---

[28] Veronica Forrest-Thomson, *Collected Poems*, ed. Anthony Barnett (Exeter: Shearsman and Allardyce, 2008) 116. Referred to as *Collected*.

Forest-Thompson (handwritten)

cognate', '(*OED*)') is no protection from the haphazardness of the literary work's structuring in language. Her response is academically teasing celebration. Reminiscent of the opening pages of *To the Lighthouse*, Forrest-Thomson's lyric uses '[g]lue, paper, / scissors' to test out a sense of collage and child's play, alongside the sense of serious scholastic labour—which is simultaneously sent up: 'paste a mock-up of an individual / history'.

But while Forrest-Thomson enjoys making lyricism from the objects, energies, and lexicons of the present (as well as the past), Sisson roots his poetry determinedly to the latter. His backward-looking desire to achieve a stately transhistorical lyric composure steers away from the eclectic medley of references we see in Forrest-Thomson. Unlike her, Sisson's work did not nudge late twentieth-century language towards the kind of playful contemporaneity that we now see in mainstream writers such as Paul Muldoon or Jo Shapcott. Many of the poems in Shapcott's (much later volume) *Phrase Book* offer good examples.[29] Through etymological attentiveness, her title poem links apparently unrelated public and intimate experiences: the domesticity of 'my own front room', 'T.V.', the violence of the first Gulf war, 'the British Consulate' (26)—whilst 'Pavlova's Physics' ingeniously pulls into contact the lexicons of modern science ('hydrogen', 'the light of stars', 'matter / can appear out of nothing'), classical learning ('boning up on Greek at night'), and the intimate physicality of address: 'You can show me your piece of warm / thigh', 'I'm affected / by the way you look at me', 'tumbling / into increasing disorder' (6–7). Shapcott's comment that 'we can only ever know the world in fragments' is not unlike some of Sisson's own essayistic pronouncements, but one can't imagine him tolerating the notion that contemporary fragmentation reveals 'part of our beautiful human vulnerability'.[30] Nor would he make lyric work, as Shapcott does, out of the recognition that 'science now is a hubbub of discourses, not just a single voice'. Sisson was far less comfortable than these writers with the range of contemporary lexicons and idioms that comprise the lyric poem, and particularly with the idea that *I* would find itself productively heckled by *living* interlocutors, or interrupted by non-poetic discourses.

---

[29] See Jo Shapcott, *Phrase Book* (Oxford: Oxford University Press, 1992). Here, meanings shift and slide as particular moments and memories are pulled into unlikely contact. Shapcott includes a recognizable but disorientingly eclectic assortment of cultural references—from 'commuting' (7) to chaos theory; 'supermarket aisles' (42) to 'the government of the stars' (43); Superman, Tom and Jerry, and James Bond, to Classical and Romantic writers, and to 'Gauguin / and Ligeti' (7).

[30] Both prose comments by Shapcott, from her interview with Deryn Rees-Jones, University of Liverpool, 8 June 2007 <http://www.liv.ac.uk/poetryandscience/essays/jo-shapcott.htm>, accessed 24 December 2010.

By way of comparison with Sisson, I want to turn now to a very different kind of address: that encountered in Tony Harrison's controversial 1985 poem, 'v' (235–49). The straight-talking address of Harrison's work taps into the political and historical specificities of class and race friction that arise in the process of capturing contemporary energies. 'v' uses *you* in a manner quite distinct from Sisson. It explores and exposes diminishing, corrupted national legacies; it attends to the tug of 'a call to Britain and to all the nations / made in the name of love for peace's sake', 'a blackened dynasty of unclaimed stone, / now graffitied', 'daubed PAKI GIT, / [...] aerosolled with NIGGER' (241; 237; 240). On the one hand, Harrison's poem, like a good deal of Sisson's address, articulates—to what feels like an underspecified but familiarly middle-class English *you*—its sense of the English culture's present-day failure, of a diminished unity reflected in the landscape of the national 'now' and the places of mourning and memorial that themselves are tarnished and falling into disrepair:

> How many British graveyards now this May
> are strewn with rubbish and choked up with weeds
> [...]
> [...] I find instead of flowers cans of beer
>
> 'v' 238–9

But 'v', unlike Sisson's poetry, is able to articulate, with some specificity, the social forces, historical incidents, and figures of contemporary England: 'Hugh Gaitskell's cool electioneering', 'shots of the Gulf War', 'Listening to *Lulu*', 'police v. pickets at a coke-plant gate' (243–8). And unlike Sisson's, his address tunes into, sounds the voices of, and answers back to, the changing idioms generated through the political and social conflict it depicts. The poet figure's '*cri-de-coeur*' is juxtaposed with his interlocutor's '*Go and fuck yerself*', '*Can't you speak / the language that yer mam spoke*' (241). On the one hand, Harrison's soundings of these various particulars of national divisiveness do lament England's increasing oppositional violence; a violence that the speaker implies is eroding, and graffiting over, its past coherences: 'LEEDS v. DERBY, Black/White', 'Communist v. Fascist, Left v. Right, // class v. class as bitter as before, / the unending violence of US and THEM' (238). And this marks out, in an idiom very different from Sisson's, the loss of traditional value in England's present:

> The prospects for the present aren't too grand
> when a swastika with NF (National Front) 's
> sprayed on a grave, to which another hand
> has added, in a reddish colour, CUNTS.   (238)

On the other hand, and unlike Sisson, Harrison's poem is able to invite dialogue with the voices that it imagines most threatening to the mourned ideal. The poem moves away from the lure of 'sleep's oblivion' and from the urge to rise above the voices that challenge it, and instead engages *in* the muddle of conflicted verbal registers. This directness of dialogue with specific idioms—working-class, regional, vernacular, as well as Latin and Greek—ensures that violence and vandalism aren't merely pondered, lamented, from the distanced perspective of the lofty poet's stance. They are heatedly spoken back to, in a clash with the skinhead 'yob' who vigorously sets out to offend ('Listen cunt!', 242):

> *Don't talk to me of fucking representing*
> *the class yer were born into any more.*
> *Yer going to get 'urt and start resenting*
> *it's not poetry we need in this class war.*   (244)

The poet-figure exposes similarities between the italicized speech of the 'skinhead yob' and his own 'pen's [...] magic wand' (239). Responding with demotic hostility, Harrison's address shows that there is much between *I* and *you*, accuser and accused, violator and violated. These are lines not afeared of getting their hands, and tongues, dirty:

> 'You piss-artist skinhead cunt, you wouldn't know
> and it doesn't fucking matter if you do,
> the skin and poet united fucking Rimbaud
> but the *autre* that *je est* is fucking you.'   (242)

Expletives, slang diction, and youth jargon are juxtaposed with the high-brow intellectual pun on Rimbaud's famous pronouncement 'je est un autre' (the 'piss-artist skinhead cunt' isn't meant to 'get it'). It's a joke wielded as an insult, as a way of 'fucking you', even as it makes close identification with its interlocutor. If 'I am another', *I* is also the particular other with whom it trades cheap jibes. The rudeness of the implied dismissal, 'fuck you', borrows that language from the very addressee it moves to reject: I am 'the autre', 'I am [...] you'. A poet's addressed public is a mirror of his nation, in Harrison's poem: the 'you' he speaks to with resentful intimacy is laced with all the venom of the directly personal insult. This is his England (and yours). Harrison's then, is a poetry that will not cut itself off from the contemporary life it disparages and wrestles with, and in this respect it is able to engage the *you* of the modern world as a living, provoking phenomenon in a way that Sisson's late poetry of unanswerable, and often abstracted, addresses cannot.

Sisson is like the Modernists in his belief that to make a meaningfully new addition to the canon, a poet must have a historical sense of the whole of European literature, and an awareness of the place of

English literature within that whole. As for Eliot, so for Sisson, 'History is now and England'.[31] But Sisson is not as agile as Eliot and Pound were in writing of the 'now' of that national history; of the breathtaking socio-political and economic alterations and altercations of the twentieth century. What turns up in Eliot's work as the 'Unreal City' of *The Waste Land*, contains a multiplicity of sights, smells, sounds, places (71:207). One turns from 'a public bar in Lower Thames Street', to 'luncheon at the Cannon Street Hotel', 'trams and dusty trees', 'Ionian white and gold', and to 'Silk handkerchiefs, cardboard boxes, cigarette ends', 'Oil and tar / [...] / Red sails' (73:260; 71:213; 73:265; 70:176; 73:266–70). In *Four Quartets*, that busy multiplicity is combined with a critique of 'The captains, merchant bankers, eminent men of letters. / [...] / And the Stock Exchange Gazette, the Directory of Directors' going into 'the dark, / The vacant interstellar spaces' (*East Coker* 3:199–200). But this frenetic modern world, and the critique of it, turn out curiously flattened in Sisson's work: '—City of rascals, the / Infernal city / Where every inhabitant / Is imaginary' (*CP* 357). True enough, Sisson's work is latter-day-Modernist in its breaking of strict chronological time, which allows him to enter into renewed verbal relations with his own, and his nation's history. Time is synchronous, rather than diachronic, what Walter Benjamin calls 'Messianic Time': a simultaneity of past, present, and future, as opposed to 'progression through a homogeneous, empty time'.[32] Like Eliot and Pound in its temporal juxtaposing, anachronisms, dialogues between figures across time ('Ulysses', 'The Corridor', 'Letter to John Donne', 'The Garden of the Hesperides'), Sisson's work is unlike them in excising from its poetic the traces of the troubling Babel of conflicting voices that they lament. Save for the verbal cacophony his own classically informed tone of English reserve repeatedly *instructs* us it is hearing (but we scarcely find ourselves thrown into), the tone is even, polished, sparely wry. 'A hurrying world in which you have no part', 'with a frown / You mutter and push past' (*FS* 409; *Antidotes* 419).

Although this tendency to use address to lament the passing of a better, older, order is encountered predominantly in the late lyrics (the volumes from the 1980s and 1990s), it can be found throughout Sisson's career, even in very early poems. For instance, Sisson's poem, 'At a Cocktail Party':

[31] *Little Gidding* (1942) in *ECP* 5:222.
[32] Walter Benjamin, 'Theses on the Philosophy of History' 8 (1940), in *Illuminations* 253–64.

> They are machines with few surprises
> Circulating with little ado
> On plottable courses, asking each other
> What make are you?[33]

In such work, comments on the failure of the poetry world itself—the courtly attitudinizing of the critic, the posturing of the academic, just as in a late poem he sneers at 'US—professors, Ph.Ds'—have taken over the role of art as resistance and redress. But Sisson is not able to make the verse feel sufficiently threatened by the very impoverishment it describes and hints it may be a part of ('US').

On the one hand, the sentiment is not dissimilar to that encountered in Pound and Eliot: the hollowed-out, ritualized sociability makes men like 'machines'. Verbally and physically men are 'circulating with little ado / On plottable courses', and the problem with these robotic movements is not that they are staccato or jolting, but overly slick. It would be better to speak to *you* less 'plottably', to feel more 'ado', anguish, and pain. There is something treacherous, to Sisson's mind, in the addresses of the smooth-tongued middle-class idiom. The potential reciprocity hinted at in the line 'asking each other' is quickly closed down, as questioning is reduced to one simple formula, emptied-out of humanity: 'What make are you?' The question is always the same, the very politeness of the expression becomes a way of staving off closer identification: since we all ask each other, and answer, the same question, nothing need be revealed.

That late bitterness about words being given an exchange value and bartered—see 'The Trade' and 'Words'—is also a source of Sisson's resentment in such early poems: 'These are not words / In which a heart is expressed / You cannot catch in their rhythms / Which way the nerves twist'.[34] Throughout his career, Sisson expresses common twentieth-century fears about man as a modern automaton, and about the decline of nature and language in a mechanized, consumerist, urbane age. In this, Sisson is barely more than a step away from the recognition as it enters the work of Pound: 'We see τό καλόν / Decreed in the market place',[35] and Eliot: 'the petrified product which the public school pours into our illimitable suburbs', 'Man desires to see himself [...] more admirable, more forceful, more villainous, more comical, more despicable [...] He has only the opportunity of seeing himself, sometimes, a little better dressed.'[36]

But on the other hand, in contrast to Eliot and Pound, Sisson's work at such moments feels petrified by its suburban observations. It reads like a

---

[33] (1961), in *CP* 27.
[34] *CP* 448; *CP* 390; 'At an International Conference' (1961), in *CP* 27.
[35] 'Hugh Selwyn Mauberley', *Personae* 189.
[36] Both in Eliot's 'The Romantic Englishman, The Comic Spirit, and the Function of Criticism', *Tyro* 1 (Spring 1921) 4.

grumbling middle-class lament about the tedium of middle-class sociabil-
ity: 'Image of God, / Where are you in this dreadful din?', 'Who is re-
sponsible for all this mess?' (*Antidotes* 402; *FS* 407). Here, many of the
daring verbal experimentations that the Modernists made with the age's
available linguistic resources are lacking: insertions of working-class
voices, street rhymes, music hall and demotic, of Pound's *Cantos*, Eliot's
The Waste Land and *Sweeney Agonistes*, and later the regional registers, dia-
lects, and rhythms of Graham's 'Baldy Bane', or the cross-cultural, anti-
bourgeois voices of Tom Leonard, or the heady succession of disruptive
and vituperative voices in Carol Ann Duffy or Selima Hill, or the ca-
cophonous energies of scientific and digitalized idioms in Prynne's *High
Pink on Chrome* and *Not You*.[37] In contrast, Sisson laments: ' "O barren
age! whose trust is all in lies; / Others have known what you no longer
know" ' (*CP* 425). Sisson's 'barren' present feels more barren than present:
it cannot capture the perilousness of living in this conflicted 'now', amid
a confusion of heckling, rude, aggrandizing, power-seeking voices with
which it must, continually, compete, and by which it may well find itself
at times out-competed.

All too often, in Sisson's work, particular, real, and recent social vio-
lences are reduced to a static similitude—'the endless folly'—a monoton-
ous repetition of the same diminished power: 'time goes on and leaves you
standing there / And crumbling' (*CP* 402; 407). It is a stagnancy that
implies, in spite of its wish to diverge from the Movement poetic, that
there is nothing to be done except lament: 'Truth is in action but your
words will lie' (*CP* 409), 'I stand and roar and only shake my chain' (*CP*
177). Such lines are not able to capture a sense of the pressing immediacy
of the civil conflicts of the age that they claim to be troubled by. Sisson's
you is not used to respond to any identifiable political turbulence, or to
redress antagonists in the era's power struggles. Where can we find in his
work the reek of the Metropolitan city, the bric-à-brac of lives, of con-
sumerist values, the variousness of identities shaped within it, that he
wishes to criticize (as we find, say, in Iain Sinclair, whose *Lud Heat* and
Suicide Bridge have traced the malign operations of the power machine of
London)?[38]

Where in Sisson's work might we locate details of the significant his-
torical and political events of the late twentieth century: the handling of
the miners' strikes we find in Harrison's poetry; the ethical and social

[37] See Leonard, *Intimate Voices* (1995); Duffy, *The Other Country* (1990) in *Selected
Poems*, and *The World's Wife*; Selima Hill, *Fruitcake* (Newcastle: Bloodaxe, 2009); Prynne,
Poems.
[38] Iain Sinclair, *Lud Heat* (London: Albion Village, 1975); *Suicide Bridge* (London:
Albion Village, 1979).

questions raised by Shapcott's 'Phrase Book'—and by Tom Raworth's 'The West'—both in relation to the Falklands War?[39] Or could we find in Sisson's poems a challenge to the centralized linguistic and cultural perspectives of the lament for a diminished 'Englishness' (as we see in the historical regionalism of David Jones's *The Anathemata*, or Basil Bunting's *Briggflatts*)?[40] Sisson's addresses to changing *you*s might be moved by socially minded complaints about the state of the nation, and about culture, but these addresses—as well as the issues that motivate them—often remain generalized and unfocused. Meanwhile, the work is not sufficiently attentive to the language it uses to speak back to those tendencies it condemns. Sisson's poems often address cultural change in disappointingly muted, academic terms, from an assumed position within the academy, and often with the assumption that, if *I* ever made contact successfully with *you*, his interlocutor would be a part of this cultural inside.

'Popular sentiments are to be regarded as part of the instruments of government, and [...] one is to be regarded as free only so far as one is not at their mercy', Sisson wrote in his essay, 'Order and Anarchy': 'Good writing alone may be described as independent of government', 'any conception of intellectual liberty [...] must allow for the free production of works of literature' (*Avoidance* 92–3). Sisson, like his early modern forebears, and often, like Eliot and Pound, uses the literary space as a site for testing and probing the existing order, exposing the failures of 'intellectual liberty' that are carried in the language, and renegotiating popular sentiment. His art is not a retreat from politics, or from examining the lures of order and anarchy. Although Sisson, like Donne, Vaughan, and Herrick, is putting to work the politico-aesthetic nationalist myth of England as blessed isle, idyllic garden, his work, like theirs (and like the contemporary poets Harrison and Dunn) is *not* performed simply to fulfil the demand for extravagant praise of royal and noble patrons by offering obsequious propagandist apostrophes. Rather, such addresses set out to question the very panegyric and pastoral forms they employ, presenting natural images of civil dissent, foreboding, and disorder in the midst of their ceremonially gracious and ungracious hailings.

However, Sisson's intertextually informed poetic, rather than being addressed to present interlocutors, and inviting them to react and respond, often dissuades contemporary *I*s and *you*s from participating in the poetic-historic tradition it imagines itself in personal dialogue with. One might argue that Sisson's verse conducts an exclusive address to past masters; an

---

[39] Shapcott, *Phrase Book* 26; Tom Raworth, 'The West', in *Collected Poems* (Manchester: Carcanet, 2003).

[40] David Jones, *Anathemata* (London: Faber, 1952); Basil Bunting, *Briggflatts: An Autobiography* (London: Fulcrum, 1966).

address so finely judged as to ensure our English rose is not tended by twentieth-century or quotidian gardeners, but by the appropriate historical and canonical custodians of value: historical *yous*. This is, at times, a one-sided poetry that desires merely to *appear* dialogic; that wields *you* as a point of avoidance and evasion. Sisson's work, especially his late verse, is often at risk of being swayed by a nostalgic conservatism that refuses to incorporate reply, both in its use of the private lyric *you*, and the accusatory public *you*. Though it is happy enough to issue lyric addresses, such verse turns out, disappointingly, to be unable or unwilling to let its contemporary addressees respond.

all so negative,

PART III

GEOFFREY HILL

Ceremonies of Speech

7

Oppositional Principles

The poet's words, precisely because they are his words, are his and others'. On the one hand, they are historical: they belong to a people and to a moment of speech of that people: they are datable. On the other hand, they are prior to any date: they are an absolute beginning. Without the combination of circumstances we call Greece, neither the *Iliad* nor the *Odyssey* would exist; but without those poems, the historical reality that was Greece would not have existed either.

Octavio Paz, *The Bow and the Lyre*[1]

'Hill's compulsion to speak is twinned with his loss of faith in the power of public speech', Geoffrey Hill's readers are informed by the back jacket of *Speech! Speech!* The volume contains Hill's long, sectioned verse-poem and meditation on the compromised nature of public speech, and is the third in a succession of works written in the querulous, fragmented style Hill discovered in *Canaan* and subsequently explored in *The Triumph of Love*. The blurb cautions its readers that they will encounter a poet calling to their attention the pressing questions of the late twentieth century: 'the here and now—the world [...] of global politics and disintegrating utopian dreams'. If those questions, summarized as 'How can one express anything in a "dead language"? And who is there to listen in this "dead age"?', sound rather uncomfortably timeworn (reminiscent of Sisson's conservative laments about the state of wayward modern England), the reader may be reassured by the critical praise testifying to Hill's credentials as an up-to-the-minute contemporary voice, fastened upon current issues: 'Geoffrey Hill is probably the best writer alive [...] There is almost no one in public life taking serious stock of our condition and what is happening to us all', claims A. N. Wilson; 'Geoffrey Hill is the central poet-prophet of our augmenting darkness', writes Harold Bloom: 'The reader winces [...] and then is astonished.'

Two key points emerge in these public, published negotiations—both crucial to Hill's handling of address, and his scrutiny of the tricky relations

---

[1] Octavio Paz, *The Bow and the Lyre (El Arco Y La Lira): The Poem, The Poetic Revelation, Poetry and History.* trans. Ruth L. C. Simms (Austin: Texas University Press, 1973) 168.

between poets and their audiences. First, Hill is here characterized, by publisher and critic, as writing a 'serious' poetry of public addresses. Hill, we are told, is not only uniquely capable of drawing to *your* attention the perilousness of 'our condition', but of doing so at a time when 'no one in public life' demands comparable attentiveness. (This is both laudable and marketable.) Secondly, Hill's address is testy, oppositional, difficult. 'The reader winces' before she is 'astonished'. That warning is judged necessary, since the unassuming reader might not get round to appreciatory astonishment if she has not been prepared, before handing over £9.99, for some intellectual, and physical, discomfort. One needs to know that 'wincing' is part of the intended poetic experience: this is 'critically acclaimed' discomfiture. Yet if, in opening the volume, we brace ourselves, we are now guarding against being as discomfited as we might have been, had we not known this was part of the readerly experience.

From its first words, Hill's poem, too, negotiates such contradictions in its published, public status:

> Erudition. Pain. Light. Imagine it great
> unavoidable work; although: heroic
> verse a non-starter, says PEOPLE. Some believe
> we over-employ our gifts. Given identical
> street parties, confusion, rapid exposure,
> practise self-emulation: music for crossed
> hands; for two fingers, music
> for taxiing to take-off; for cremation.
> Archaic means | files pillaged and erased
> in one generation. Judge the distance.
> Innocent bystanders on stand-by. [. . .]
>
>   *SS* 1:1

Those opening words are both Hill's self-addressed reminder of the painful labour poets must perform in producing erudite 'great [...] work', and an address to Hill's readership, warning them that they, too, must carry out painstaking work in perusing the poem's erudition. 'Imagine it' cuts in both directions: a command to the writer and reader of such lines. To some extent, 'although' deflates the dutiful imagining performed by *I* and *you*: the poem's start, Hill indicates wryly, is 'a non-starter'. Yet Hill's poem propels itself into words by acknowledging—and poking fun at—the shortcomings detailed by 'PEOPLE'. The opening is likely to give burgeoning detractors a start by taking its bearing from pre-empting their negative reception. 'A non-starter, says PEOPLE' gets itself, and its keen critics, started, by using its opening lines provokingly to answer back to the rebuffs that its public has not yet had time to formulate, and setting its adversarial wheels in motion.

This is work that claims to desire protection from the perils of *your* obsequiousness: 'Interpose a fire-curtain; stop the applause / from getting through' (2:1). The volume, like much of Hill's late work, often points out the 'pain' (in both senses) of reception, particularly of commendatory public attention. The front jacket depicts a sycophantic audience clamouring to applaud the public speaker/poet, calling for his public address—'Speech! Speech!'—the call that prompts the fragmented, challenging, mocking, angry poem within. One might see each of the 120 numbered passages (for each of the days of Sodom) as responding, with various degrees of vexation, to that demand to be vocal, to raise objections to being well received. As we will come to see, for Hill, it is the oppositional audience, which voices '*cat-calls*', heckles, '(*laughter, cries of "shame"*)', and is prepared to lambast the poet: 'You áre / wantonly obscure', that provides the soundest starting point for the public figure's examination of his manoeuvrings in the civic sphere (*SS* 26:13; 118:59).

Hill's focus on address's public remit has much in common with, but also takes us in a slightly different direction from, our readings of Graham and Sisson. Like those poets, Hill often employs the second person in explicit addresses that speak 'to you'. However, Hill also makes considerable use of implicit address—which designates others without saying *you*—particularly in his explorations of reception, criticism, ceremony, speech-making, crowds, and his attention to academic performance and posturing and the role of the intellectual. Hill's poetical language is continually shaped by, and emerging from, the political and historical, and his addresses repeatedly demand *your* negotiation of the fraught public contexts in which the artwork circulates.

Hill's work, more than Graham's or Sisson's, is public and political in the sense outlined by Tom Paulin's 1986 *Faber Book of Political Verse*: 'a public poem [. . .] begins in a direct response to a current event, just as a pamphlet or a piece of journalism springs from and addresses a particular historical moment' (19). Address is bound to specific contexts. Hill's speeches, essays, and poems repeatedly explore the intellectual's capacity to create a language answerable to the specificities of their addressees' differing public concerns; concerns tied to the poem's historical and political situatedness. At stake is the civic power of wielding words, and the question of how the public figure can tap verbal power appropriately in addressing others, both in and out of poems, off and on stage. Hill is an influential scholar, and the recently published *Collected Critical Writings* (which assimilates Hill's earlier prose collections *The Lords of Limit*, *The Enemy's Country*, and *Style and Faith* and adds two new volumes, *Inventions of Value* and *Alienated Majesty*) are invaluable in considering Hill's rhetorical strategies, and the changeable audiences of his interlocutions.[2]

Across Hill's poetic career, one encounters a wealth of lyrics warm in civic action, from the early work, 'Requiem for the Plantagenet Kings', in *For the Unfallen*, to the late 'Précis or Memorandum of Civil Power', in *A Treatise of Civil Power*.[3] But it is the later work (from the 1990s onward), where Hill most insistently *confronts* a public, and the issue of public relations. Like Sisson, Hill forges a transhistorical community of real and fictitious literary, aesthetic, and political figures through address: 'To the Lord Protector Cromwell', 'To John Constable: In Absentia', 'Pindarics (after Cesare Pavese)', 'Churchill's Funeral'.[4] Unlike Sisson, Hill offers such address as dynamically performative, ceremonial public speech, conducted in, and as part of, a 'THEATRE OF VOICES': the voices tried out in this theatre get a kick out of exhibiting a cantankerous, competitive vying for space and for *your* attention: 'I am too much moved by hate— / pardon ma'am?—add greed, self-pity, sick / scrupulosity' (*SS* 104:52; *Triumph* 75:39). That 'Pindarics' sequence addresses 'yóu, Ces, sullen and alert. / [...] / here's English fór you, Hopkins' bastard classic' (*WT* 42). Hill's lines are at once a tribute to their poetic forebear, Cesare Pavese (the poem repeatedly turns to 'Ces' to acknowledge his central role in the work), and a steely assessment of the role past masters should play in the present: 'Self-reconciling anyone's afterthought / to the prescription slapped against your name' (52). Such address operates with a 'pity that's pitiless even to itself' (43). These role-playing speeches demand readers assess the appropriateness of their public conduct, even as they reveal themselves posing for judgement in front of an imagined audience: 'Limelight excites the rabble, shows them tricks, / the prancing orchestra of self-disgust. / Too much is theatre' (38). As so often in Hill's late work, poetry scrutinizes the public function of art, and art's address: 'I ask you: / what are poems for?' (*Triumph* 148:82). Hill's addresses ask that *you* holds at stake the meaning and application of poetical public power, regarding the poem not as private discourse, but as 'Turning towards / the people' (*WT* 39).

Hill is far from alone in contemporary poetics in asserting that a poet is a public figure, with public duties: 'The Professor of Poetry is expected to deliver three public lectures each year [...] It was an honour to be

---

[2] Hill, *CCW*. All references to Hill's prose and lectures are quoted from *CCW*. Hill, *Lords of Limit: Essays on Literature and Ideas* (New York: Oxford University Press, 1984), referred to as *LL*; *EC*; *Style and Faith* (Washington: Counterpoint, 2003), referred to as *SF*.

[3] 'Requiem' (1959), in *CP* 29; 'Précis', in *Treatise* 27–31.

[4] From, respectively: *Treatise* 13; *Canaan* 53; *Without Title* (London: Penguin, 2006) 35–55, referred to as *WT*; *Canaan* 43.

elected to the office', Seamus Heaney commented in *The Redress of Poetry*, a book of reprinted public addresses written during his tenure of the Oxford Chair (1989 until 1994) and republished in essay form.[5] Heaney's assertion of poetry's ability to preserve integrity whilst addressing a contemporary audience is hedged about with ambivalence and qualification: 'Not that it is not possible to have a poetry which consciously seeks to promote cultural and political change and yet can still manage to operate with the fullest artistic integrity' (*Redress* 6). That mixture of wariness about and insistence upon the poet's engagement in the political fray is present in contemporary poets as diverse as Carol Ann Duffy, Don Paterson, Douglas Dunn, and Andrew Motion, for whom both the professorial lecture and the poem offer platforms where the poet addresses current public debates.

'Poetry can speak decisively to power', insisted the former Poet Laureate, Andrew Motion, addressing the House of Commons at a Poet in the City event in 2007.[6] Motion also acknowledged that the poet's public platform is a contested place of power-play, tension, and confrontation. 'There is a risk in speaking about a sacred duty', Motion cautioned his audience. Part of that 'risk' is the danger that 'accepting the position' of fame and prestige may prevent the poet or critic 'from speaking my mind or telling the truth as I see it'. However, this was a danger that Motion— still Laureate in 2007—was keen to assure his audience could plague only 'the worst kind of sycophant'. One might hesitate before accepting Motion's account of his 'truth' telling insusceptibility to the lure of sycophancy, given the context of his civil speech. Speaking also of the lure of sycophancy, Douglas Dunn commented, in a 1999 interview, that 'A lot of current criticism is written either for academic promotion or to try and make a name for the critic in a newspaper.'[7] For Dunn, in contrast with Motion, the 'risk' of sycophancy in publishing and public speaking is more problematically widespread. He added that one needed to insure against this by 'hav[ing] a healthy disrespect for your own work. You have to have if you're going to be honest about other people's' (24).

Hill, like Sisson, shares a good deal in common with his contemporaries, but it is primarily to his 'healthily disrespectful' critical and poetic dialogues with Modernist poets, particularly T. S. Eliot and Ezra Pound, that his addresses repeatedly return. Eliot, too, had pointed out lyric poetry's propensity to engage public, as well as intimate, addresses to auditors, and

---

[5] Seamus Heaney, *The Redress of Poetry: Oxford Lectures* (London: Faber, 1995) ix.
[6] Published by the *Guardian*, Thursday 4 October 2007 <http://www.guardian.co.uk/books/2007/oct/04/poetry.Andrewmotion>, accessed 14 July 2009.
[7] 'Douglas Dunn in Conversation', interview with Gerry Cambridge, *The Dark Horse* 8 (Autumn 1999) 21–31, 22.

insisted that the poem's address had public resonance. The voice 'talking to other people [...] is dominant [...] in all poetry that has a conscious social purpose', Eliot claimed, arguing that this voice was not confined to an autonomous aesthetic world though he, like Hill, was wary of the 'more pretentious modes of publicity'.[8]

In Hill, a poet's fulfilment of his public role is connected with his or her ability to engage appropriately with a body of listeners: the right forms of address to the right addressees. Jeffrey Wainright has captured this sense of good verbal conduct in the title of his book of collected essays on Hill: *Acceptable Words*.[9] Acceptability, to Hill, is a controversial matter that involves accordance and discordance with traditions, working with, and also against others, as he writes in *Speech! Speech!*: 'EQUITY, ELIGI-BILITY, CULPABILITY, / heard through a cloud—acoustic din—the rage' (*SS* 104:52). Being heard 'through' the 'acoustic' cloud might involve having to shout over a din of angry audience responses, or it might involve relying upon one's rowdy interlocutors *to be heard*: 'heard through' the rage. Appropriate address demands breaking and preserving customary good behaviours, receiving accusatory and commendatory responses. Hill's conviction, here, that the poet is a public figure, and set against a crowd, is coupled with his sense that an audience's expectation of poetic good conduct can never be lived up to fully: din and rage will enter the poetic space, and acceptability (in the eyes of some) is always coupled with culpability (in the eyes of others). In a recent lecture on Eliot and Bradley, Hill argues that 'language is arbitrary, autonomous, and at the same time [...] it is bound, helpless [...] a hair's breadth away from monstrous assertion'.[10] Hill acknowledges that his own aim, to 'reverse the customary trend of advice' that customarily offers the artist proud self-satisfaction, is not likely to be universally popular, whether amongst poetry-lovers or fellow poets. But in revisiting Emerson's term 'alienated majesty' (and his own earlier poetical 'retort upon' that term in section 9 of *Triumph*) in 'A Postscript on Modernist Poetics', Hill finds it appropriate to level just that criticism: 'Rather than saying, "see how clever this particular leap of the imagination has been", I find myself repeatedly urging, "how recalcitrant, how obstructive, this material is".'[11] One might

---

    [8] Eliot, *The Three Voices of Poetry*, in *OPP* 89–102, 96; 'Tradition and the Individual Talent', in *SW* 47–59, 52.
    [9] Jeffrey Wainwright, *Acceptable Words: Essays on the Poetry of Geoffrey Hill* (Manchester: Manchester University Press, 2005).
    [10] Geoffrey Hill, 'Eros in F. H. Bradley and T. S. Eliot', Empson Lecture, University of Cambridge, 2005; published in, and quoted from, *CCW* 493–580, 562–3. Referred to as 'Eros'.
    [11] Geoffrey Hill, 'A Postscript on Modernist Poetics', delivered as a 2005 Empson Lecture at the University of Cambridge, in *CCW* 565–80, 566. Referred to as 'Postscript'.

ask: must Hill urge himself, also, to recall this recalcitrance, or is he primarily out to remind forgetful others? His emphasis is definitively not on an author's genius of production, but on his susceptibility, the danger of succumbing to misplaced pride when exposed to the 'crowd'. It is expressed as a danger that Hill must, in the very act of making public, also resist, even as he draws attention to the drama of this resistance.

Such susceptibility has often been seen to lurk in the public figure's engagement with the addressed crowd or culture. In his 1928 essay *La Trahison des clercs*, the French philosopher and novelist Julian Benda levelled concern about a thinker's, or 'clerk's', role in society, arguing these figures had betrayed their traditional social role by aligning themselves too intimately with the political passions of the crowd.[12] One facet of this view has been expressed more recently, in Edward Said's 1993 Reith Lectures, published as *Representations of the Intellectual*, in which Said argues for the benefits of the 'outsider' status of the public thinker.[13] Being 'a dissenter from the corporate ensemble', Said suggests, creates an appropriate distance between intellectual and audience that will enable him to resist propaganda, institutionalized thought, and the lure of 'being welcomed into all those self-congratulating honour societies that routinely exclude embarrassing trouble makers who do not toe the party line' (32–3; 59). Said's view, however, that the function of the intellectual is ultimately to 'give a voice to the voiceless', to speak for repressed and underrepresented social groups, is very different from Benda's idealism, which emphasized the need for intellectuals to refrain from wielding power in the public fray, from activism and direct political involvement.

When Hill, who is a contemporary of Said, writes of 'the power that can be conferred by popular attention', he opens up another angle onto these debates.[14] Hill, too, thinks that the public thinker's crowd-pleasing desire to foster relations with an audience, to receive popular attention, confers a power upon him that demands scrutiny. 'Popular attention' lends a poet authority, distinguishing and elevating him in the public eye. But there is no guarantee that this power is deserved, or that, even if it is deserved, it will not corrupt one's principles, rather than stimulate principled thought. Yet for Hill, a position of aloofness, alienation, or outsider status can be equally problematic. As he emphasizes in 'A Postscript', identifying oneself with the 'aloof hauteur' of the outsider can,

---

[12] Julian Benda, *The Treason of the Intellectuals*, trans. Richard Aldington (New York: Norton, 1969).

[13] Edward Said, *Representations of the Intellectual: The 1993 Reith Lectures* (New York: Vintage, 1996).

[14] *CCW* 562. See Hill on Benda, specifically on T. S. Eliot's review of Benda, *CCW* 544–5.

paradoxically, become a means of 'rabble-rousing', of calculatedly *winning* attention in the public eye by pretending to shun it (578). Hill's targets here are Yeats, particularly his 1938 poem, 'The Statues', and Eliot, particularly *Little Gidding*.[15]

Raymond Williams dryly commented that being an outsider 'may be one of the quickest ways to becoming an insider', in other words, a short-cut to ensuring power, status, and patronage are granted by a culture.[16] Hill too points out the ease with which the proclaimed outsider can fashion a false reputation as a glamorously free-thinking, non-conformist figure, set apart from institutionalized, intellectually compromised others, and suggests this false status vexes the public's ability to 'distinguish the work of genuine autodidactic intelligence from the effusions of the free-wheeling crank'.[17] Hill has often acknowledged that the 'popular attention' conferred upon a well-known poet (often Eliot) is not something to which he will necessarily be immune, even if he has good intent to resist it. As early as 1977, in his inaugural lecture, 'Poetry as "Menace" and "Atonement"', Hill voiced the opinion, in a critique of Eliot's manoeuvres as an intellectual in the public fray, that: 'the acceptance of a principle of penitential humility in the conduct of life does not necessarily inhibit a readiness to accept the status of "maestro" conferred by a supportive yet coercive public'.[18] From that direction, the sign of the failure of a poet's public address, and more specifically the sign of Eliot's failure to deliver lectures, essays, speeches, and poems that effect civil action with 'struggle [...] purpose and engagement' is often the very consensus that his works generate ('Menace' 12).

Criticizing Eliot's 1951 address on 'Poetry and Drama', originally delivered as the first Theodore Spencer Memorial Lecture, at Harvard earlier that year, Hill's own address argues that Eliot is both 'coercive' towards his audience and also unduly coerced by that audience.[19] Eliot, Hill proposes, is making recourse to a 'stylish aesthetic of despair' that springs 'from a very dubious philosophy of authorial responsibility to the "reader"' ('Menace' 11–12). For Hill, the speaker's primary responsibility is not to *you*, but to language itself—for these words operate upon the public world in which thought, action, and gesture are shaped. Good verbal conduct

---

[15] See Yeats, *Major Works* 171–2; Eliot, *ECP* 214–23.

[16] Raymond Williams, 'Review of *The Outsider*' 76. Quoted in Stefan Collini, *Absent Minds: Intellectuals in Britain* (Oxford: Oxford University Press, 2006) 418.

[17] Geoffrey Hill, 'Alienated Majesty: Ralph W. Emerson', Ward-Phillips Lecture, 2000, University of Notre Dame, in *CCW* 193–517, 502.

[18] Geoffrey Hill, 'Poetry as "Menace" and "Atonement"' (1977) University of Leeds, in *CCW* 3–20, 12.

[19] 21 November 1951, quoted from *OPP* 72–88.

demands attending closely to how, with '[m]yth, politics, landscape; with language / seeding and binding them [...] / [...] / Our patience [is] *proven* in the rage of others'.[20] Although *The Orchards of Syon*—a series of 72 Dantean eclogues—comes addressed to a more sympathetic *you* than the preceding volumes (*Triumph* and *Speech! Speech!*), this volume, too, emphasizes the poet's need to provoke 'rage' in the very act of publicly 'seeding and binding'. Often in Hill, a significant part of a public speaker's responsibility to *you* lies in determinedly resisting straightforward audience pleasure—and speaking of 'myth, politics, landscape' have certainly been ways of refusing being crowd-pleasing: 'my acceptance / speech is postponed', 'To the short-sighted Citizen / [...] / "I will not run, dance, kow-tow, to entertain / thugs, perverts [...]"' (*Orchards* 39; *Triumph* 76:68).

For this reason, a poet and public figure should remain alert to the dangers of being well received, of flattery and consensus. Hence, in that late lecture 'Eros', Hill speaks of his desire to 'root the sense of creative isolation and autonomy [...] in the commonplace actuality of literary ambition thwarted and fame largely denied' (562). And of the still more important need to envisage 'verbal power [...] in a kind of rift between self-recognition made public [...] and public non-acceptance' (562). Address, then, might be most effective when, lodged in that rift, it engages a worthy opponent, an audience that will resist, not demur. In his much earlier 'Menace', Hill quoted Jon Silkin's rueful observation that, between the poet and his audience: '"it is not disagreement we have now but deafness"' (12). On that view, it is likely to be the recalcitrant address, the address that disagreeably vexes its audience to think, which comes closest to bridging one form of distance between the poet and his public. The poet that prompts disagreement and active 'non-acceptance' from his audience, has mended one rift between them: to secure hostile responses is to ensure he is not ignored. But in so doing, the poet risks becoming lodged in another rift, and the audience is in danger of a different form of deafness: the poet, levelled in the process of the audience's hearing, is part of their 'commonplace'. Subjected no longer to others deafly averting their ears, he must now face the deafness of their (mis)understanding. Their very attention leaves the poet 'thwarted', 'denied'.

Aptly, however, the assumption that deafness and distance are in operation is itself susceptible to disagreement and opposition. Stefan Collini picks up on another assertion of (and essay by) Raymond Williams, 'Culture is Ordinary', when he comments: 'Perhaps it's time that someone wrote an essay entitled "Intellectuals are ordinary".'[21] Collini's recent book on the subject, *Absent Minds*, challenges what he sees as the common notion that a breach exists between the public thinker and his audience, which he traces back to the early twentieth-century formation of its conception of the public intellectual. For Collini, intellectual activity is part of social life, an 'ordinary', everyday engagement, a role '*within* society', a positive 'commonplace' (413). Thought, also, is not an elevated practice carried out by an elect forever isolated from their compatriots, but a sign of being in their midst. Public intellectuals, then, are: '"Ordinary" in the sense that they are indeed part of the cultural landscape of all complex societies [...] ordinary in the sense that carrying on the activities characteristic of intellectuals should not be seen as exceptionally heroic or exceptionally difficult or exceptionally glamorous' (505). One should, Collini writes, 'try not to fall so easily into the [...] tabloid habits of [...] pedestalling' the public figure (505). This involves vigilantly resisting any temptation we feel to assume the 'exceptionality' of poet, intellectual, cleric, or man of letters.

William Empson made a similar observation about *audience*, when he suggested the appropriateness of writing for 'the ordinary tolerably informed reader', as opposed to a select crowd of elevated fellow intellectuals.[22] The comment reads as a shrug of the shoulders at the notion of a breach between that poet-critic and his readers that one might well want to take issue with (what is 'ordinary'? How well informed is 'tolerably'?), but he would not have been averse to a squabble over the matter. Empson's own style engaged in extraordinarily combative addresses in conveying its linguistic ordinariness. Frequently, it is in publicly berating those he addresses that his apparent alienation from them, and elevation above them, can be most roundly rebuffed. Empson has written that criticism involves 'the kind of arguing we do in ordinary life, usually to get our own way [...] [a] not specially dignified sort of arguing', and a good deal of his prose energetically exemplifies his pronouncement that the intellectual is not above the petty squabbles of quotidian life.[23] 'Just a Smack at Auden', the title of one well-known piece of his energetic poetic haranguing, smartly demonstrates his pleasure in verbal pugilism, as does his comment that 'saying "therefore" is like giving the reader a bang on the

[21] Raymond Williams, 'Culture is Ordinary', in *Conviction*, ed. Norman Mackenzie (London: MacGibbon and Kee, 1958); Collini, *Absent Minds* 505.

[22] Letter to Rosamund Tuve, 25 February 1953, in *Selected Letters of William Empson*, ed. and introd. John Haffenden (Oxford and New York: Oxford University Press, 2006) 198.

[23] William Empson, *Argufying: Essays on Literature and Culture*, ed. and introd. John Haffenden (London: Hogarth, 1988) 167.

nose'.[24] Empson's letters round on colleagues and literary figures, including Roger Sale, his publisher, T. S. Eliot ('you had let the thing get into a muddle'), his colleague, Christopher Ricks: 'your answer [...] seems incapable of understanding the matter'.[25] In 'Eros', Hill comments: 'William Empson seems to understand the issue, characteristically, when in *The Structure of Complex Words* he writes that "The idea that the theorist is not part of the world he examines is one of the deepest sources of error, and crops up all over the place"' (561–2). Empson, like Hill, was not a man who was reluctant to chastise and admonish these 'deeper sources of error' in those he addressed publicly. He seems rather to have relished, and to have trusted, in such admonition.

Hill and Empson would have disagreed over many things, not least of all Empson's reliance upon the 'ordinary', and upon assumed common knowledge in establishing relations, hostile or friendly.[26] But in this context it seems not inappropriate to make them sit, adversarially, side by side. One point of common ground, after all, is their shared sense that speaking as a public figure, a man of letters, is a less elevated affair than it might appear. Like Empson, Hill's poetry, especially his late book-length poems *Triumph, Speech! Speech!*, and *Orchards*, often determinedly depicts the poet's language as 'not specially dignified', 'mostly uncouth' (*Orchards* 69) and will not shy from the rhetoric of gritty needling, as might be applied to reviewers, critics, fellow poets: 'bugger you, MacSikker et al.,—I do / mourn and resent your desolation of learning', '(*up / yours O'Shem*)' (*Triumph* 119:63, 139:76). Both Hill and Empson link berating with uneasy proximity, argumentation with a critique of the view that an intellectual is elevated, and that his language will be remote from public participation.

But for Hill, a poet-critic's imperfect elevation does not guarantee that alienation from his audience is out of the question, nor that alienation is necessarily to the poet's disadvantage. Hill is aloof in the sense that he offers spirited criticism of what he calls 'the current reckonings of [...] the society of his day', rather than immediately aligning himself with it.[27] But in so saying, Hill also engages in civic action, precisely by resisting, and advocating the benefits of resistance to, widely held views of society.

[24] See William Empson, *Collected Poems* (London: Chatto & Windus, 1955) 62; *Argufying* 70.
[25] Letter to Eliot, 17 May 1949, *Letters* 161; Letter to Ricks, 3 December 1971, 520.
[26] See *CCW* 636, Hill's 'Notes to 176', on 'the common reader'. See Peter McDonald's discussion of Hill's extended footnote here, in *Serious Poetry: Form and Authority from Yeats to Hill* (Oxford: Oxford University Press, 2002) 10–11.
[27] 'Unhappy Circumstances', first published in *EC*; republished in, and quoted from, *CCW* 176–91 (179). Hitherto referred to as 'Circumstances'.

That comment, for instance, was levelled in Hill's series of Clark lectures at Trinity College, Cambridge, in 1986. It was addressed to an audience that Ronald Schuchard, in the process of editing Eliot's earlier Clark contributions, once commented was composed of 'an imposing pantheon of Fellows [...] many of whom had played major roles in intellectual life'.[28] When Hill writes that words 'must resist the pressure of circumstances or be inundated by the tide of "compleasance"', he is arguing against the temptation to be 'inundated' and made at one with others, however 'imposing' their major intellectual role ('Circumstances' 179). Hill manoeuvres a precarious terrain between the lure of two common, opposed, attitudes towards public figures: first, that they are necessarily lone individuals, uniquely independent thinkers (as Benda argued they should be); second, that they are complaisantly at one with the authority of consensus, closing ranks on tradition, politics, and institutional power (as Orwell, for instance, has argued).[29] Hill's fraught argumentation, then, is not merely argument for argument's sake. Rather, it is argumentation that works to avoid complaisantly embracing typical attitudes and accepting defined roles; the closeted scholar, the wilful outsider, the radical, the smiling public man, the solitary genius of remote contemplation. Hill could not have said, with Said, that 'the *whole* point [of address] is to be embarrassing, contrary, even unpleasant', though he may well have had some fellow-feeling.[30]

In stepping onto the public platform to voice this scruple in his 'Circumstances' address, Hill does not see himself standing alone. 'Compleasance' is a Hobbesian word that Hill uses to link his own resistance with that philosopher's similar refusal to comply publicly with 'the particular virtues of instant repartee' lauded by others (176–9). Hill dwells on Hobbes's addresses to the 'witts at Court', which are seen to involve 'protracted and complex deliberation' (176). Hill observes that, for Hobbes's own legal audience, 'to "turn" and "wind" and "compound" in one's arguments is to be taken as being contemptuously self-regarding, as holding oneself wilfully aloof from the proper business of discourse and communication' (176). But when Hill spells out to his readership his conclusion—'the essential facts: that a poet's words and rhythms are not his utterance so much as his resistance'—he at once offers them a tersely explanatory corrective to what he sees as the common (opposite) view, and stoops to address them with it (179). This generous clarity is offered in a spirit that is not altogether aloof

[28] Ronald Schuchard, ed. and introd., *The Varieties of Metaphysical Poetry*, T. S. Eliot (New York: Harcourt Brace, 1994) 14.

[29] See George Orwell, 'London Letter', *Partisan Review* (Summer 1944) 159.

[30] Said, *Representations* 12. Emphasis added.

Izenberg

open

from the writer's desire to communicate 'the [...] facts', neatly heading them up for his readership to grasp. Hill's manner here simultaneously displays the virtues of 'instant repartee' and works as the culmination of his own argumentative turning, winding, and compounding.

Hill's work indicates that a poet is not necessarily less complaisant when contributing to public debates than when speaking privately. A fair amount of argumentative winding and compounding goes on in Hill's critical dealings with his Modernist forebears, Eliot and Pound, who were far from strangers to the public forum, and engaged frequently in ruminations about the rightful functions of art in the civic sphere. Highly critical of Eliot, in particular, Hill takes issue not only with the poems, but with the public speeches, broadcasts, and lectures: 'in a wartime lecture of 1943', 'in the BBC talk "Virgil and the Christian World" (1951)', 'in the set of 1950 Chicago lectures', 'in an interview given during the Edinburgh run of *The Cocktail Party*'.[31] As we will see, Hill's lectures and essays offer a clear sense of what he regards as Eliot's failure of conduct in the public realm; Eliot's willingness to be swayed by consensus. To Hill's mind, his forebear's historical locatedness, the importance of his status as public broadcaster and lecturer, and the effect made through the attitude of his specific involvements in the discussion of public issues in various media in the 1940s and 1950s, confer on him a responsibility to address others from a well-judged distance.

One can see Hill in critically dissenting mood when he writes that Eliot, in a BBC address of the 1950s:

recalled his first acquaintance, as a schoolboy, with Homer: 'The obstacle to my enjoyment of the *Iliad*, at that age, was the behaviour of the people Homer wrote about'. [...] we might wish to enjoy [this] as a joke; but what Eliot depicts as a schoolboy obtuseness is a widely prevalent adult reaction: your enjoyment of a work is ruined if it speaks or shows things to which you object. Bradley has a good phrase, in *Appearance and Reality*, about the writer's vulnerability to 'the captious ill-will or sheer negligence of his reader'. If we could agree that what many readers and theatre-goers like to think of as their rightful enjoyment *is* the exercise of captious ill-will and sheer negligence, we might also agree, or at least accept, that shifts in word value are relatable to questions of author-audience relationship and indeed to the radical question of authorial integrity. ('Word Value' 536–7)

Here, Hill holds that Eliot is insufficiently alienated from his addressees, in a manner that is both negligent, and intricately connected with the

---

[31] Geoffrey Hill, 'Word Value in F. H. Bradley and T. S. Eliot', T. S. Eliot Memorial Lecture (2001), St Louis, MO, published in *CCW* 532–47. All references to 'Word Value' come from *CCW*, see 536–9.

winsome style of this BBC address. A willingness to ingratiate himself with the social conventions of his audience—with what 'A Postscript' terms the '*roi fainéant* of publicly accredited sentiment'—is what Eliot, as public speaker, should resist (578). But Eliot is read as susceptibly falling in with the consensus of 'negligent' listeners/readers, each of whom thinks it is proper politely to avert his eyes from, or good-humouredly to deride, what he finds objectionable and uncomfortable. For Hill, because Eliot's style of public recollection aligns him with the tastes of 'widely prevalent reaction', it maims his ability to examine properly the things to which he objects. The implication is that Eliot should have been more objectionable to his audience, less populist. Here, then, Hill makes 'authorial integrity' dependent upon remaining discriminating about the sentiments one appeals to, and upon one's resistance to the audience's belief in 'rightful enjoyment'. Resistance is what makes a speaker appropriately alienated: he should attempt not to be unduly swayed by it. Eliot's crowd-pleasing address makes him guilty in Hill's eyes of complaisance with his audience. But simultaneously, Eliot's complaisance also ensures that he is radically, and negatively, *alienated* from his society's needs. Too comfortably close to *you*, Eliot is out of touch with, unable to detect and to voice, the age's civil concerns. Hill hints that the duty of the public figure is to address objectionable and uncomfortable matters: the speaker must ensure his audience hears precisely that which is at odds with what it proclaims to enjoy.

Eliot, of course, can neither hear, nor enjoy Hill's criticisms. But this has not dissuaded Hill from retaining a generative antagonism to Eliot, throughout his career. Just as for Empson public dissent from other critical figures (Eliot continually among them) was piquant, refutations of Eliot offer a spur to Hill's creativity, to the barbed tautness of his essayistic and poetic observations. Doing battle with Eliot is a perverse tribute, for Eliot is a worthy opponent, a figure it is productive to find points of dissent with, to sharpen one's wits against (as Christopher Ricks, in *True Friendship*, and Thomas Day, in 'Sensuous Intelligence: T. S. Eliot and Geoffrey Hill', have noted).[32] The history of Hill's critical involvement with Eliot dates at least as far back in his career as the 1970s, when Hill delivered 'Menace' as an inaugural address. On that public occasion, Hill took Eliot to task for his remark, in 'Poetry and Drama', that poetry contains 'a fringe of indefinite feeling [...] those feelings which only music can express'. This was also the occasion upon which Hill argued Eliot's

---

[32] Christopher Ricks, *True Friendship: Geoffrey Hill, Anthony Hecht and Robert Lowell under the Sign of Eliot and Pound* (New Haven: Yale University Press, 2010); Thomas Day, 'Sensuous Intelligence: T. S. Eliot and Geoffrey Hill', *Cambridge Quarterly* 35:3 (2006) 255–80.

sentiment rendered him culpable of making a 'helpless gesture of surrender, oddly analogous to [...] [a] stylish aesthetic of despair' ('Menace', *CCW* 11–12).

A glance at the index of the *Collected Critical Writings* reiterates Eliot's importance throughout that selection from Hill's prose career, and a number of the lectures and essays dwell on Eliot specifically: 'Dividing Legacies', as well as the aforementioned 'Word Value in F. H. Bradley and T. S. Eliot', 'Eros in F. H. Bradley and T. S. Eliot', 'A Postscript on Modernist Poetics'.[33] Eliot is a pervasive presence in the poems, too, which have been compared to his poetic forebear repeatedly, and read, for better or worse, as a continuation of the high modernist heritage. Alan Robinson, commenting on *The Mystery of the Charity of Charles Péguy*, argues Hill is 'Like T. S. Eliot' in being 'preoccupied with the transfiguration of defeat into regenerative sacrifice'.[34] For Ricks, 'Eliot is everywhere alive in *Tenebrae*'; 'even more important to his own poetry' than Yeats, though Ricks also takes note of Hill's poetic tendency to perform a 'grim turning of the tables upon Eliot'.[35] Meanwhile, for Vincent Sherry, Hill's 1971 volume, *Mercian Hymns*, demonstrates a positive likeness to Eliot, in being written as 'a kind of pseudo-autobiography' that addresses similar concerns raised by 'the impersonality principle that Eliot enunciated'.[36]

Hill's oppositional interactions with Eliot are revealing of the former's uneasy rhetorical alliances with his audiences and critics, and they flag up one strain of Hill's strained verbal relations. As Thomas Day has observed, 'it may be asserted that where Hill is most at odds with Eliot, he seems most like Eliot'.[37] In 'Dividing Legacies', Hill famously took issue with Eliot over the matter of 'pitch'—a 'vigilance' of sound and semantics—and 'tone': 'the semantic equivalent of *tinnitus aurium*' (*CCW* 378). Hill found fault with the 1942 *Little Gidding* in particular, for its alignment with the latter, which he argued falsely employed the indefinite second-person tone of instruction: 'You are not here to verify'.[38] In 'Dividing Legacies', Hill addressed not only the general reader, but also a number of specific, named critics, who had defended Eliot's work against his previous criticisms. He asked these addressees

---

[33] Geoffrey Hill, 'Dividing Legacies' (1996), in *CCW* 366–79.

[34] Alan Robinson, 'History to the Defeated: Geoffrey Hill's "The Mystery of the Charity of Charles Péguy"', *Modern Language Review* 82:4 (October, 1987) 830–43, 830.

[35] Geoffrey Hill, *Tenebrae* (London: André Deutsch, 1978); Christopher Ricks, *The Force of Poetry* (Oxford: Oxford University Press, 1984) 338; 320; 307.

[36] Sherry, *The Uncommon Tongue* 6.

[37] Day, 'Sensuous Intelligence' 258.

[38] See *ECP* 187–224; *Little Gidding*, in *ECP* 1:215.

dryly: 'Is Eliot instructing himself, self-confessor to self-penitent, taking upon himself penitentially the burden of common trespass, or is he haranguing the uninitiated [...] caught trespassing on his spiritual property?' (377–8).

But does Hill's own address, here, manage to remain exactingly 'self-penitent', or is it culpable of the very culpability it detects elsewhere, magisterially 'taking on the burden of common trespass'? Hill himself is more up for 'haranguing' the *initiate* than the uninitiated, and his opposition is addressed to a number of professional users of the language, namely (in both senses) Eliot and his supporters, Ronald Schuchard, Peter Ackroyd, Richard Wollheim, and particularly Christopher Ricks: 'I have to disagree with Christopher Ricks', 'Ricks is uncharacteristically imperceptive in his response to this factor', 'I would ask him to place [...] to determine how', 'If I were to ask Ricks how it is that, against all the evidence [...] I anticipate that he might answer'.[39] Yet, if Hill has himself been accused of being more like than *un*like all those addressees he takes to task, he does not consistently act with magisterial grace, or faultless power, in doing so. Haranguing is not magisterial. In the poetry, that ill-mannered address is quite often delivered with a knowingly staged, rather gleeful ignobility: '(*eat / shit Macsikker*)', 'Confound you, Croker—you and your righteous / censure!' (*Triumph* 89:75, 88:74). However, there are times in the prose when I would agree with Day's assertion that Hill is 'at some level [...] unaware, or only partially conscious of, passively susceptible to, the errors into which he [also] falls' (258). David Bromwich, too, alerts readers to this susceptibility in Hill's condemnation of Iris Murdoch 'for once speaking unguardedly of a century as if it were a character ("the nineteenth century [...] could think itself a single world")' observing that Hill 'go[es] on to commit the same fault ("the nineteenth century preferred a half-remorseful majesty in its great apostates..."'.[40] It is on those very matters on which Hill is most vehemently at odds with his addressees that his language seems most unable to acknowledge its *limitations* as well as its potency. But it is not at all clear that it is an unguarded or ill-considered move that Hill's rhetoric is often most fallible, and limited, in his railings at and denouncements of others.

[39] At 378–89. One should remember that Hill and Ricks share an acquaintance that dates back to their days in Oxford, where Hill was an undergraduate in the 1950s, and Ricks a Fellow and Tutor in English Literature in the 1950s and 1960s. In the 1980s they were academic colleagues at Cambridge, where Ricks was King Edward VII Professor of English Literature (from 1975–1986), and both have also worked at Boston (Hill from 1988, Ricks from 1986).

[40] David Bromwich, 'Geoffrey Hill and the Conscience of Words', *Skeptical Music: Essays on Modern Poetry* (Chicago and London: University of Chicago Press, 2001) 151–62, 158.

Adorno

'Real denunciation is probably only a capacity of form [...] Artworks exercise a practical effect, if they do so at all, not by haranguing but by the scarcely apprehensible transformation of consciousness', wrote Theodor Adorno.[41] Adorno, whose views were influenced by his experience of the totalitarian regimes of the mid century, was not entirely convinced about the effectiveness of art's denunciatory interlocutive capacity, hence his double equivocation: 'probably only'. Nor was he certain of an artwork's capacity to exercise practical effect on its recipients: 'if [...] at all', 'scarcely'. But if art's address does possess public power, that power is, for Adorno, smuggled in at the margins of *your* consciousness, 'scarcely apprehensible': real denunciation takes place through the easily missed subtleties of a 'capacity of form', rather than of explicit content. In *The Culture Industry*, Adorno expressed deep suspicion towards that aesthetic inexplicitness in his critique of mass-culture's 'manipulation of taste and the official culture's pretense of individualism'.[42] For Adorno, aesthetic power is likely to be most denunciatory, performing its most violent assaults, when it seems unassuming, not out to offend. The civil power of the subversive aesthetic is muted, surreptitious, indirect, and is likely to try to sound apologetic for its own clout. And yet, the aesthetic power of those artists and citizens *preserving* the status quo, working in vigilant defence of the social mores, also operates most potently through this indirect, oblique manner. One wonders what function there might be, in this vision of competing forces, for those artists who do engage, in service of either ideology, the rude demands of the 'haranguing' public speaker?

Hill's prose, with various degrees of success, examines the politics of the predominantly haranguing address. The lectures and essays explore the interlocution primarily directed *at* others (rather than speaking with, and taking shape from, its auditors), and finds this a largely inadequate response: such address betrays its duty to the stubbornness of the linguistic medium. For Hill, 'real denunciation' is hard labour, a verbal warfare turned as much upon oneself as upon others. The poet-critic witnesses his own susceptibilities and betrayals in 'the public institution' of language. Similar patterns are present in the poems, too. Especially in his late, fractured and fractious poetic address (the post-1990s lyrics), Hill makes use of the doubly intimate and politic lyric *you*, emphasizing poetic language's complicity in the fraught historical and political

[41] Theodor Adorno, *Aesthetic Theory*, ed. Gretel Adorno and Rolf Tiedemann, trans. Robert Hullot-Kentor (London: Athlone, 1997) 230, 243.

[42] See Theodor Adorno, 'On the Fetish Character in Music', in *The Culture Industry: Selected Essays on Mass Culture*, ed. J. M. Bernstein (1944; London: Routledge, 2001) 29–59, 40.

spheres. But both his early and later work, his poems and prose, insist upon address as angular, oppositional public act, as we will see. In creating 'wincing' dialogues between audience and speaker, *I* and *you*, Hill discomfortingly insists that his audience, too, handles the language with a gravity and attentiveness appropriate to its continually negotiated political and public engagements.

8

Just Concessions: Conviction, Persuasion, Coercion

The greatest debts are not always the most evident
T. S. Eliot, 'What Dante Means to Me'

In the introduction to the published volume of his Charles Eliot Norton lectures on *The Use of Poetry and the Use of Criticism*, Eliot commented that 'The poetry of a people takes its life from the people's speech and in turn gives life to it.'[1] That comment puts into play a sense of a people's linguistic cooperation and interchange that is crucial to Hill. In *The Triumph of Love*, Hill addresses us:

> Still, I'm convinced that shaping,
> voicing, are types of civic action [...] (70:36)

Hill's lines not only argue language is a form of civic responsiveness, but also act out that claim in relation to their own interlocutor(s). Out to convince his audience that he is enmeshed in and 'shaping' social obligations, roles, and allegiances when he speaks, the speaker slips into the first person to emphasize the strength of his conviction: 'I'm convinced'. It is a locution that occurred in a similarly personal tone in the second line of the sequence: 'Guilts were incurred in that place, now I am convinced' (2:1). In both instances, Hill's poetry taps the personal voice for public ends. He shows how the poet's apparently self-involved, self-expressive lyric register ('I'm convinced') goes in service of a wider social agenda: in this case, an attempt to negotiate *your* position as reader/critic: 'As critics we have the uncritical habit of referring, ponderously yet airily, to an author's "individual voice", as if this were a simple and uncontested birthright [...] [we] have to live with the knowledge of collusion and compromise [...] "brute" confrontations'.[2] To speak 'individually', as

---

[1] 'Introduction' (1932), in *The Use of Poetry* 5.
[2] Geoffrey Hill, 'Isaac Rosenberg, 1890–1918', delivered as the Warton Lecture on English Poetry (1998), Keble College Oxford, in *CCW* 448–64, 449.

Hill's lines in the *Triumph* also argue, is not to exclude, neglect, or forget others, but to engage the intimate register of address in 'types of action'. The first-person voice may be used, as it is here, expressly to persuade an audience, to encourage them to concede to the poet's thesis of civic language. *You* might well be flattered by this winsomely attentive address, which goes out of its way to affect concern for its readers: 'do you follow? or can you at least / take the drift of the thing?' (*Triumph* 70:36).

In Hill, persuasion and concession are nearly always pejorative terms, allied with weakness, susceptibility to coercion. *Just* conceding might imply a complaisant, easily manipulated attitude, a susceptibility to the flimsiest of persuasions. Both terms indicate a willingness to be swayed by others' attitudes or opinions ('the coercive role of militant cliché'); a propensity to give in to those who are convinced or convincing, and become complicitly aligned with them: 'a passive accessory' ('Menace' 13). Yet persuasion does not seem negative in the lines above. This poetic *I* is engagingly, even admirably persuasive. Wrong-footing its audience's expectation of a dry thesis on language's 'civil action', it delivers instead an appealing, energetic address. One is, like the speaker, caught up in the argument about words' immediacy, their present-tense action—rather as in section 5 one speaker addresses another, as if discussing the poem Hill is writing: 'What is he saying; / why is he still so angry?', 'Where was I? Prick him' (2). Engaged in the act of 'shaping / voicing', both sections 5 and 70 perform examples of the flux they describe. With an energy reminiscent of W. S. Graham, Hill's words reveal themselves testing out, altering and making sense of what they encounter, as if before our eyes.[3] The speaker's very construction of the verbs '*shaping* / voicing', with their close repetition of present participles ('-ing', '-ing'), emphasizes verbal agility, his ability quickly to register what he encounters, and to change it, to wrest fresh sense from it. Such address presents itself in the act of ringing communal changes, akin to Pound's 'gathering from the air a live tradition', or Eliot's desire to 'give life to' the people's speech.[4]

As we have seen, the notion that words are deeds, grounded in civic responses and not emanating from inside oneself, is not unfamiliar to Hill's own thinking.[5] But in these lines, Hill is ambivalent about approving the manner in which the *I* uses the impression of spontaneous conviction to clinch it. One might ask: what is the speaker up to in presenting his audience with this appealing picture of language's immediacy? And why does he slip into the confessional mode to offer his thesis on language

---

[3] See Graham's 'The Constructed Space' (1958) and 'Approaches to How They Behave' (1970), in *NCP* 162; 178–84.

[4] Pound, *Cantos* 81:522; Eliot, *The Use of Poetry* 15.

[5] See 'Menace' 10: 'grammar is a "social and public institution"'.

to us, capping it with that exclamatory 'I'm convinced'? Poems, as we know, are not immediate and unrhetorical, but designed and worked-through language, so the text offers us at least one danger-sign in response to its speaker's pronouncement. We might point to the *Triumph*'s pressing formulation of this question, and this danger, as Hill exposes us to the first serious *you* in the volume:

> If you so wish to construe this, I shall say
> only: the Jew is not beholden
> to forgiveness, of pity. You will have to
> go forward block by block, for pity's sake,
> irresolute as granite. Now
> move to the next section.   (19:10)

The poem's easy slippage into the first-person confessional voice ('I shall say / only:') is a move designed to convince and persuade addressees. This speaker purports to make the poem plain and comprehensible, speaking plainly in so doing: 'I shall say', 'You will have to', 'for pity's sake'. The deixis of 'if so you wish to construe *this*' hints, persuasively, that the speaker is, in the present moment, about to deliver to readers the under-standing necessary for *you* to 'construe' the poem. By the time *you* have reached the similarly deictic, but far more imperious, 'Now / move to the next section', *you* are likely to accept the rather domineering tone as ap-propriate to that of the briskly efficient guide or instructor, who has promised to reveal to *you* how to follow this text's structure and operation. He knows, and will reveal in straight-talking, unemotive language, the secret of how to read *The Triumph of Love*. The speaker, it seems, will get away with addressing *you* in this rather commanding tone, since he has, at least, effectively aided confused auditors by informing them how to make good sense of the poem: 'You will have to / go forward block by block', 'Now / move'. When that 'move' leads us to section 20, to the *Book of Daniel*, and again, to the clipped officious tone ('Quite correct, sir. Permit me'), that officiousness is now newly, and horrifyingly context-ualized, with appeal to terms of ethical and historical atrocity. The speak-er's earlier address to *you* to be 'irresolute as granite', to proceed through the poem coolly 'block by block', 'not beholden / to forgiveness, of pity', is linked with the Jewish persecution, genocide, and Nazi concentration camps of the Second World War: 'refocus that Jew—yes there, / that one. You see him burning, / dropping feet first'.

Such work flags up the ethical and social concerns of address. Much is at stake in *your* susceptibility to persuasion, conviction; *your* weak-willed adoption of the sentiments of the authoritative speaker who promises clarification, explication. Hill's use of the first-person persuasive voice is designed, in its calculated appearance of spontaneity, initially to convince and explain, and then to expose the ease with which his auditor's verbal cooperation leaves *you* open to the perils of coercion and co-option. Not only do 'you see him burning'; if *you* go along with this speaker, *you* have a hand in the action: 'refocus that Jew'. If addresses to *you*, as Hill sees it, are often a form of 'civic action', engaged by many users, they alert us to the ease with which a poet's and public figure's persuasions of others can be dangerously coercive.[6] The utterance 'I'm convinced', and the instructions for how 'to construe' words and actions, work as a kind of warning to Hill's audience to be wary of readily casting one's lot in with any speaker; to avoid ' "signing on the dotted line" for the rulers of the darkness of this world', as Hill puts it in 'Our Word is Our Bond', writing of Pound's failed 'struggle not to sign'.[7] Conviction works as a kind of alluring contagion that Hill's address reminds *you* to be resistant to. The sentiment expressed in Hill's address hints that his own audience must remain deeply sceptical about what subtle persuasions, demands, and assumptions Hill's own addresses may be inveigling us into.

But is it possible for poets and public figures to engage scrupulously, appropriately, in public speech and writing, without being responsive, and susceptible, to the sayings and doings generated by a people? Eliot, like Hill, is alert to the gravity of words, both poetic and civic, when he writes that the poem involves 'tak[ing] its life from the people's speech and in turn giv[ing] life to it'.[8] 'Taking', as opposed to 'finding' or 'discovering', involves deliberation, considered choice, a careful selection of what, and from whom, to take. Deliberation here is close to a virtue; it does justice to the complexities of language and history, as if weighing options carefully enabled a scrupulous Hobbesian twisting, turning, meandering of thought, the desire for considered dissent, not change for change's sake. Indeed, Eliot makes clear that the poem has 'life' *because* it has taken from elsewhere, in just such a considered manner. If this makes us wonder whether poems premeditatedly take for themselves what rightly belongs to others, we should remember that, for Eliot, the poem involves 'give' *and* 'take', with the terms reversed (taking comes before giving). Lyric address involves acts of designed responsiveness, with designs and responses continually changing. Although Eliot looks like he may well be part of Hill's camp here, his pronouncement might be less amenable to Hill than it initially appears. Eliot's lines imply that a poem's act of 'taking' makes it *dependent* on its source: 'the people'. Taking opens the work to the sayings and doings of the people. Hill's speaker, then, must take from

---

[6] See 'Our Word is Our Bond' (1983), in *CCW* 146–69, 166. Referred to as 'Bond'.
[7] 'Bond' 164.   [8] Eliot, *Use of Poetry* 5.

the people in such a way as to remain resistant to indiscriminate openness, to avoid being falsely swayed by the populace. So we are back to the question, here posed by Hill: 'how do you teach yourself to distinguish the treacherous common sense of the reprobate from the faithful knowledge of the elect'?[9] Eliot, too, often formulates similar questions: 'The whole question of popularisation of ideas (and the avoidance of perversion of them) deserves our consideration', 'as a man of letters, what contribution could I possibly make to the problem of "leadership in a democracy"?'[10] But as we have seen, Hill does not think Eliot is willing to provide faithful answers.

Hill's addresses are often equally hard-pressed to deliver definitive responses. They do, however, repeatedly judge public language in terms of gravity and consequence, reiterating the importance of pursuing the enquiry: words are not mere gloss, distraction, or frivolity, they are the building blocks of a civilization, its means of preservation and continuation. The essays take public figures, intellectuals, critics of poets, and poets themselves to task for their misuses of the language in the public weal. If, in the poems, 'shaping, / voicing, are types of civic action', in the prose too, 'our word is our bond'—an assertion that is also a quote from the philosopher J. L. Austin (*Triumph* 70:36; *CCW* 146). Finding himself bound to issue highly deliberative correctives to particular literary figures, particularly Eliot, and also Pound (as we will see), as well as philosophers (Iris Murdoch, Austin, T. H. Green, amongst numerous others), Hill's essay offers one means by which scrupulous, reflective participation in both socio-political and aesthetic realms can be effected. 'Our Word is Our Bond' speaks towards what Peter Robinson has described as Hill's rebuttal of 'those who call their utterances "merely words"'.[11] Austin, whose work on illocutionary acts in the 1950s and 1960s called for philosophical attention to be paid to 'ordinary language', and from whose *How to Do Things With Words* Hill's epigraph is taken, seems firmly placed as one of 'those' figures whom Robinson would see Hill wanting to redress. Similarly, we might include in that category Hill's post-war poetic contemporaries, Larkin, Gunn, Enright, and later Heaney and Motion, who also stressed the need for plain speaking, and 'normal' uses of the poetic medium.

---

[9] Geoffrey Hill, 'Translating Value: Marginal Observations on a Central Question', first published in *Translating Life: Studies in Transpositional Aesthetics*, ed. Shirley Chew and Alistair Stead (Liverpool: Liverpool University Press, 2000), in *CCW* 383–93, 386.

[10] Letter to Philip Mairet, 21 February 1941; Mairet Papers, HRHRC, Austin, Texas; quoted from Collini, *Absent Minds* 314; T. S. Eliot, *Leadership and Letters*, address at Milton Academy, 3 November 1948 (London: Cumberledge, 1948) 5.

[11] Peter Robinson, 'Reading Geoffrey Hill', in *Geoffrey Hill: Essays on his Work*, ed. Robinson (Milton Keynes: Open University Press, 1985) 198–218, 215.

However, Hill's essay is not as combative as Robinson's comment might indicate. The piece is highly nuanced in its dealings with others, especially where it is most sensitive to what Stephen James has termed 'the treacherous relation between word and deed'.[12] In this respect, Austin is, for one, a figure whom Hill simultaneously upbraids and aligns himself with. Alignment is found where Austin's emphasis upon 'ordinary language' is coupled with an acknowledgement of 'treacherous' difficulty, the hard graft of speaking plainly. For Hill, Austin's work is admirably[13] alert to the need to acknowledge 'the innumerable and unforeseeable demands of the world upon language' (156), and such demands are instructively pressing on those occasions when words seem most transparent, plain, and unambivalent.

Hill's concessions to others, then, are not always easily separable from his criticisms of them. His essay uses Austin—including what Hill reads as Austin's wrong-footedness—to comment on the oversights as well as the insights of a host of literary and philosophical figures. 'Our Word is Our Bond' makes substantial use of Poundian and Austinian philosophies of language in formulating its own argument that language is consequential action, not just a faithful medium to reflect already-formed thoughts back to us, or to parcel them off to communicate with others. Austin's comment, 'If you are a judge and say "I hold that..." then to say you hold is to hold' is both put into dialogue with, and is used as a redress to, Pound's pronouncement: 'All values ultimately come from our judicial sentences.'[14] Austin's empiricism might be misguided, in Hill's eyes, when he writes that 'a performative utterance will be in a peculiar way hollow or void if said by an actor on the stage, or if introduced in a poem', but that limitation does not disqualify Austin's assertion that the distinction between word and deed is highly dependent upon the inescapable context of utterance (147). Indeed, the very limitations of that Austinian recognition can be instructive to future readers and writers amongst Hill's audience, even as they offer proof of the philosopher's vulnerability in the face of language's complex recalcitrance. This is true, too, for Pound, in whose direction Hill, not unjustly, wields an Austinian corrective: 'Pound's error was to [...] fancy that poets' "judicial sentences" are, in mysterious actuality, legislative or executive acts [...] poets are not legislators, unless they happen to be so employed, in government or law' (169). It is a corrective that might also be seen as a concession to

---

[12] Stephen James, 'Geoffrey Hill and the Rhetoric of Violence', *Essays in Criticism* 53.1 (2003) 33–53, 37.
[13] Hill's own word: 'admiring', 'admirable' as applied to Austin (*CCW* 151, 157).
[14] See *CCW* at 147 and 169; Pound, 'Hell' (1934), in *Essays* 201–13, 207.

the admirable qualities, as well as the fallibilities, of the words and deeds of philosopher and poet.

'I'm convinced that shaping, / voicing, are types of civic action', as Hill wrote in *Triumph* (70:36). One might argue, then, that the reprehensibility of our poetic speaker is not his susceptibility in yielding to the commonplace sentiments of 'treacherous common sense', since at some point, each of us is guilty of this. Rather, he is at fault in publicly displaying these sentiments to convince his audience of their truth. In this, both the poetic speaker and Eliot fail to realize their partiality, their susceptibility to the din of public opinion. Uttering one's conviction in such a manner, concealing one's bias, one's own interests, and one's part in the majority opinion, is an irresponsible use of the power of address in the public space. Hill will make no concessions to this species of error. We may ask, what is preferable? Hill has quoted Wordsworth on this issue, and his own commentary follows beneath:

> It is supposed, that by the act of writing in verse an Author makes a formal engagement that he will gratify certain known habits of association, that he not only thus apprizes the Reader that certain classes of ideas and expressions will be found in his book, but that others will be carefully excluded.

> The point at issue with 'It is supposed' is whether it indicates the acceptance or the rejection of majority opinion. According to my reading, Wordsworth does more than neutrally take note of the supposition; he is not so much taking as giving notice that certain required literary dues and social *congés* will not be offered in and by his work.[15]

In question for Hill is the extent to which Wordsworth is able to note the effect of collective opinion upon his work, without giving in to it. Related is the issue of why a writer would, or should, admit his own partiality (and to whom), and how this admission will contribute to or detract from his argument. This is exemplified when Hill comments—or does he confess?—a few lines later: 'Wordsworth's vulnerability bears upon my own approach to questions and issues of value. My strong prejudice in his favour being particularly marked at such points, we must consider the possibility that I overestimate here through sympathy as I may undervalue elsewhere because of antipathy' (386).

This appears to be a just concession, a policing of one's own bias that is both scrupulous and discerning. But is it different in quality from the persuasive confession made by the speaker of the poem? Though in the prose Hill seems to have made, and flagged up to his readership, an admission of self-interest, the admission is also a step in the argumentation,

---

[15] 'Translating Value' 385–6.

and cannot work simply as an innocent move. By anticipating his reader's
obvious objection that he has a 'strong prejudice' in Wordsworth's favour,
Hill deflates that objection. Able to show his fair-minded capacity pub-
licly to acknowledge his own potential prejudice, Hill strengthens his ar-
gument for Wordsworth, in effect saying to his audience: 'Trust me: I am
just enough to concede even my own partiality.' But does that make Hill's
instruction to his readers—'*we* must consider the possibility that I over-
estimate here'—disingenuous? Such writing is alert to the perils of alert-
ing its audience to its own prejudices, but is it alert enough to avoid
falling into the very infelicities it pinpoints, often remorselessly, in others?
Hill's phrasing in '*we* must consider the possibility' cannot avoid making
assumptions of its addressees, beckoning them, too, under the banner of
his pronouncement. The intricate difficulties of adopting the first person
to point out bias are present as much in such prose work as in the poem
from which we took our starting point:

> Still, I'm convinced that shaping,
> voicing, are types of civic action. Or, slightly
> to refashion this, that Wordsworth's two
> Prefaces stand with his great tract
> on the Convention of Cintra, witnessing
> to the praesidium in the sacred name
> of things betrayed [...]
>
> *Triumph* 70:36

The section aligns the speaker's persuasiveness both with a specific his-
torical situation (the circumstances that gave rise to Wordsworth's
Cintra tract—more on this in a moment), and with Wordsworth's own
politicized quarrel over the appropriate role, language, and audience of
poetry. Wordsworth had written in the Preface to *Lyrical Ballads*: 'I ask:
what is meant by the word Poet? What is a Poet? To whom does he ad-
dress himself? And what language is to be expected from him? He is a
man speaking to men', and 'the Reader will find that personifications of
abstract ideas rarely occur in these volumes [...] I have proposed to
myself to imitate, and, as far as is possible, to adopt the very language of
men [...] I have wished to keep my Reader in the company of flesh and
blood.'[16]

Echoing Wordsworth's sentiment that poetry must befit its audience
and 'adopt the very language of men', Hill's lines similarly pursue a 'strug-
gle / for a noble vernacular':

[16] Preface to William Wordsworth and Samuel Taylor Coleridge, *Lyrical Ballads with Pastoral and Other Poems*, 2 vols., vol. 1 (London: T. N. Longman and Rees, 1802) at xxvii–xxviii; xvii–xviii.

Active virtue: that which shall contain
its own passion in the public weal –
do you follow? – or can you at least
take the drift of the thing? The struggle
for a noble vernacular: this
did not end with Petrarch. But where is it?
Where has it got us? Does it stop, in our case,
with Dryden, or, perhaps
Milton's political sonnets? – the cherished stock
hacked into ransom and ruin; the voices
of distinction, far back, indistinct.   (70:36)

Hill's section moves in search of a literary language that will 'contain / its own passion in the public weal', 'brought home / to the brute mass and detail of the world'. In Hill, as in Wordsworth, verbal struggle does not isolate the poet-figure from interlocutors: he is directed by, and towards, them. The poem takes shape in the common language of men 'speaking to men'. So too, Hill's *audiences* take shape with and from others—as they read the poem. Addressed by the *Triumph* ('do you follow?') one finds oneself as part of a collective 'us': 'Where has it got us?', 'in our case'. *You* is in company with Hill's wide audience of reading recipients, and also in transhistorical contact with Wordsworth, Dryden, Milton, and Petrarch. Each of these poets, like Hill, has investment in a poetry of public, vernacular address.

'I have wished to keep the Reader in the company of flesh and blood', Wordsworth wrote, indicating his willingness to adopt a tone of poetical companionability towards his audience, and to let his audience take comfort in a familiar lexicon and style of writerly address, even as it is directed towards contemplation of complex political and philosophical issues. In Hill's lines, too, what is insistently 'brought home / to the brute mass' is that the poem will not provide respite from the struggle that takes place in 'the public weal'. Nor will a familiar and companionable address provide respite from disturbing 'imponderables'. If Hill's lines gesture towards the tone of accommodating, writerly affability—'do you follow?', 'Where has it got us?', 'I am somewhat less sure'—they simultaneously violate certain expectations this could lead *you* to make (his poetry is not a place for cementing understandings between writer and reader, nor for easy communication between *I* and *you*). Hill's tone might invite *you* in, but not for a temperate exchange of fire-side pleasantries. Rather, this 'flesh and blood' conversational partner directs *you* to contemplate 'brute mass and detail', 'cherished stock / hacked into ransom and ruin'. It also demands that *you* negotiate the particularities of the rest of this poem's company: particularly the literary historical contacts between Wordsworth and Hill.

Hill's use of the Cintra tract, for instance, grounds this speaker's apparently spontaneous first-person pronouncement ('I'm convinced') in a particular history. Cementing that history to a long-standing controversy in Wordsworth's career, the section links all three strands with the vocabulary of public perceptions of justice and injustice, 'witness' and 'betrayal'. 'Cintra' refers to the historical document, the Convention of Cintra, signed by British and French forces in 1808; an act that was perceived by the British public as a spineless renunciation of their victory over the defeated French. British sympathy at the time lay with the Iberian people in their insurrections against the French imperialist power, and there had been a good deal of popular support in the decision to send a British expeditionary force to Portugal to assist against the French. Alongside this, Hill runs the controversy surrounding another document, Wordsworth's tract 'The Convention of Cintra', which many consider the start of the poet's renunciation of his former revolutionary liberal principles.[17] In the Cintra document, Wordsworth's own passionate witness to the ideals of 'freedom' and 'Independence', in relation to the events of 1808, was in the eyes of many, a betrayal of his ideals, an echoing of Burkean counter-revolutionary language. He was seen to have relinquished the principles of individual liberty in order to yield to the lure of 'common passion', national liberty, and national self-determination. Gordon Thomas ends his book-length study of the poet with a chapter surveying the extent of Wordsworth's concession, 'The *Cintra* Tract: Apostate's Creed?'[18]

The debate surrounding Wordsworth's tract is a polarized one, but which side we, as readers of Hill's poem, find ourselves on remains inscrutable. The speaker might be aligning us with those in favour of Wordsworth, by denying that poet's apostasy, and suggesting the continuance of his firm, lofty principles—as both the implicit argument of 'great tract', and the vocabulary applied to the poet's text suggest ('witnessing', 'sacred'). Wordsworth's work, then, stands to witness historical betrayal: the essay performs sacred testimony before the judicial altar of the praesidium. In so doing, our poetic speaker proposes that the 'Convention of Cintra' stands alongside Wordsworth's previous Prefaces in a continuous line of thought, not a severance from his earlier oeuvre. But the speaker might equally be identifying with those who asserted Wordsworth's renunciation of his liberal creed of the 1790s. Wordsworth's tract, on this view,

---

[17] 'Address on the Convention of Cintra', in *The Prose Works of William Wordsworth*, Vol. 1, ed. W. J. B Owen and J. W. Smyser (Humanities-Ebooks 2008), see pages 220–457. <http://books.google.com/books?id=WSKXmGkD9lwC&source=gbs_navlinks_s>, accessed 1 August 2009.

[18] Gordon Thomas, *Wordsworth's Dirge and Promise: Napoleon, Wellington and the Convention of Cintra* (Lincoln: University of Nebraska Press, 1971) 151–63.

'stands with' the Prefaces only in the sense that both are on their feet before the court, waiting to be tried by the praesidium, and to be found to evidence the poet's great betrayal.

By these lights, the poetic speaker is as lithe, and coy here, as he was blithe and unsubtle in his convictions just a few lines before. Unable to be pinned down to one side or the other, his address bears poetic witness to the political complexities of both positions, neither susceptible to the undue persuasion of those for or against, nor offering up his own persuasiveness to those addressed by, and giving witness to, his own speech. 'Or...', 'slightly', 'to refashion...': the voice is that of a public speaker who is, after all, not fully convinced, and whose verbal participation in historical recollection refuses to make concessions to the claims of any one stance or moment.

Hill's lines, then, embody two related (perceived) renunciations, offering questions about the form in which political concessions may be disputed, and referring us to a battle over poetic ground that presses for the writer's authority to assert himself in matters of public, political argumentation: 'Does it stop, in our case, / with Dryden, or, perhaps, / Milton's political sonnets?' These early modern poets are especially apt figures for Hill: all three insist upon the poet's right, and duty, to speak publicly on political matters. Dryden argues in an address 'To the Reader' that the 'secret force' of potent speech can enable the poem to 'force its own reception in the World';[19] Milton argues that literature is a turbulent confrontation with the modern world, 'a troubled sea of noises and hoarse disputes'.[20] Both poets, like Hill, are highly sensitive to the relationship between what Hill terms, in his 1986 Clark lecture, 'Dryden's Prize-Song', 'the fickleness of public taste', and the necessary power of a writer's 'controversial style [...] [a] formal establishment in the public domain'.[21] Milton's controversial political sonnets—'On the New Forcers of Conscience under the Long Parliament', 'On the Detraction which followed upon my writing Certain Treatises'—forcefully integrate activism, moral argumentation, and hot-headed vituperation, with what Hill has termed: 'the expression of the archetypal rebellious will'.[22]

If Hill's work, like Sisson's, has a tendency towards early modern transhistorical address, that address also staunchly resists 'the irrational

[19] John Dryden, *'Preface' to Absalom and Achitophel*, in *John Dryden: The Major Works*, ed. Keith Walker (Oxford: Oxford University Press, 2003) 177.
[20] John Milton, 'The Reason of Church Government Urged Against Prelaty', in *An Account of the Life, Opinions and Writings of John Milton*, ed. Thomas Keightley (London: Chapman, 1855) 348–56, 355.
[21] Delivered at The University of Cambridge, in *CCW* 226–42, at 226, 228.
[22] John Milton, *The Poetical Works of John Milton*, ed. John Mitford, 2 vols., vol. 2 (Boston: Hilliard, Gray and Company, 1838) 342–3; 351–2; Hill, 'Circumstances' 190.

more prose than poetry

embarrassment of the current reaction against the theme of protest, or of political writing in general'.[23] Hill's essays, particularly those collected in *Style and Faith*, make considerable use of Milton, Donne, Marvell, Hobbes, Wyatt, and Clarendon. So too, Hill's poems not only emphasize the contemporary writer's struggle between private and public rhetoric, civic and intimate address, but repeatedly allude to Miltonic sources in so doing (this is evident even from such titles as *Scenes From Comus* and *A Treatise of Civil Power*).[24] Hill's lyric addresses, like Sisson's, are moved by an Eliotic desire to reintegrate private and public speech styles, and to show their contemporary audience that the poem participates in a live interlocutive community. The addresses of Hill and Sisson are informed by their awareness of the writer's place in society in early modern writing contexts, whether negotiated as the poet's words circulated changeably in commonplace books, or delivered as public performance.

'Whatever the excesses and affectations of the 1960s and '70s may have done to harm the cause of poetry, there is nonetheless a real connection between it and politics: as real now, if we could dissolve its true stratum or vein, as in the Tudor court of poetry of Skelton, Surrey and Wyatt or in the political sonnets of Milton or in the relation that exists between Wordsworth's "Preface" to *Lyrical Ballads* and his tract *On the Convention of Cintra*', Hill has recently argued: 'Civil Polity—let us make the claim— is poetry's natural habitat.'[25] For Hill, as for Wordsworth and for early modern writers, poetry is akin to a form of legislature. Law like lyric, is a 'bond' that is neither a fixed power, nor a private aside, but a series of performed linguistic events in which authority is made available and wielded in the public fray. If poetry is a locus of legislative truth, creating the creditability, 'competence and confidence' necessary to the tribunal that it must be judged by, it must also be judged by the conditions it helped create.

In each of these writers, the 'just' concession is not merely determined by 'the individual and local', but is allied with 'the general and operative'; the institutions and civic processes governing justice, jurisdiction, legislature. For Hill, as for early modern writers, *I* speaks to various *yous*— critics, readers, lovers, deceased historical and literary figures (amongst

---

[23] Geoffrey Hill, 'Alienated Majesty: Gerard M. Hopkins', Ward-Phillips Lecture, University of Notre Dame, 2000, in *CCW* 518–31, 518.

[24] John Milton, *Comus: A Mask Presented at Ludlow Castle, 1634, Before the Earl of Bridgewater then President of Wales*, ed. Henry John Todd (W. Bristow, 1798); John Milton, *A Treatise of Civil Power in Ecclesiastical Causes: Shewing That it is Not Lawful for any Power on Earth to Compel in Matters of Religion* (London: J. Johnson, 1790); Hill, *Scenes From Comus*.

[25] Hill, 'Alienated Majesty: Gerard M. Hopkins' 518.

them Wordsworth, Dryden, Milton, Eliot, Pound), reviewers, PEOPLE, contemporary poets—and takes shape in that speech. In that sense, the poet speaks not merely to the elect, but publicly to all men. For this reason, Hill thinks, it is bound to address that audience justly, not only forging links between poetical and political principles, historical and current events, but revealing one's own hand—one's biases, convictions, and attempts at persuasion of one's audience—in so doing.

9

Antiphonal Heckling

Hill has often promoted writing that includes 'cross-rhythms and counter-pointings', that houses the 'antiphonal voice of the heckler' within its own structure.[1] A heckler, a person who shouts an uninvited comment, usually disparaging, at a performance or event, interrupts set-piece speeches with gibes and questions and objections. To incorporate such a figure into the body of one's own writing—as Hill does in essayistic form in 'Bond', and in poetic form in the *Triumph*—might look contradictory: surely it is to invite, or accommodate, what has to enter rudely, unassisted? On that objection, 'antiphonal' is helpful, for it invests heckling with the sense not of speaking out of turn, but of turn-taking, of being a part of a mass of alternating and responding voices. Antiphony is commonly used in sung religious services, particularly in the Anglican church, where the choir divides equally into Decani and Cantoris, to sing alternate musical phrases. Hill's invitation to the 'antiphonal voice of the heckler', then, captures the sense of a highly organized ritual of calling and answering voices, even whilst it relishes the sportive verbal drama of the public, parliamentary occasion. Oratory is a key model in Hill's work, especially in the late, book-length poems *Speech! Speech!* and *The Triumph of Love*.[2] To tune into the antiphonal voices of Hill's late poetic oeuvre, however, is to listen back on the voices of the earlier work (I hear resonances between *Triumph* and the earlier lyric from *King Log*, 'The Songbook of Sebastian Arrurruz').[3] Hill's heckling can be also thought of as a kind of licensed poetic impropriety, the opposite voice that enters to ensure fair play. The heckle allows one to consider the taking of turns as valid even when speaking out of turn. It is also to draw a point of public address, of civil *speech*, into writing. Can one heckle in print? Is a heckle a form of address? Hill's heckling is evidently not a straightforwardly spur-of-the-moment interruption of another's utterance, but also deliberative, responsive, highly structured: a ritualized intervention.

---

[1] Geoffrey Hill, 'Redeeming the Time' (1972–3), in *CCW* 88–108, 94. Referred to as 'Redeeming'.

[2] See Matthew Bevis, *The Art of Eloquence: Byron, Dickens, Tennyson, Joyce* (Oxford: Oxford University Press, 2007) for a discussion of 'oratory itself as a form of literary endeavour', 24, and for a discussion of Hill's 'antiphony', 14–15.

[3] Geoffrey Hill, 'The Songbook of Sebastian Arrurruz' (1968), in *HCP* 92–102.

We might expect heckling and antiphonal voices to be assuredly noisy, pushy and public: 'IN YOUR FACE!', '*Commonweal their lodestar, inordinate / dominion their enterprise*', 'What / Ought a poem to be? Answer'.[4] But such voices are also present when Hill is writing of the private and of privation. External and internal impulses sound in alternation and together, from opposite sides of the performing space, answering as well as speaking against one another. The personal voice is not insulated from the public, as Hill's use of *you* illustrates at the opening of *Speech! Speech!*:

> dó
> you, as Í do, sit late by the Aga
> with clues received from sputtering
> agents of Marconi; from Imre Nagy;
> from Scott of the Antarctic frozen in time
> before the first crossword? [...]
>
> *SS* 2:1

Hill's address here plays over historical, political, philosophical ground, and also seems to compromise that ground by using the rhetoric of the private, domestic sphere. The lines are written in the second person, as a direct address from an *I* to a *you* that corresponds with personal language forms. These figures are located in familiar, domestic stability, sitting late 'by the Aga'; an interior scene. The verbal play of the lines emphasize the isolation and exclusiveness of *I* and *you*, which could distract the reader from attending to the context they are placed in. The turn of phrase, 'dó / you as Í do', for instance, is visually a near-palindrome that suggests the finely tuned harmony of *I* and *you*. That pivotal 'as' functions like a mirror, in which the pronouns are reflected equally, emphasizing them as equivalent entities. '[D]ó / you' and 'Í do' are in carefully poised balance. Aurally too, the parties seem to sing together: both are buffered neatly between the internal rhyme of that repeated 'do', while 'you' chimes in further, weighted by the naïvety of that insistently lulling full rhyme. Meanwhile, the phrase harks back, and contains within it, as if an anagram, the familiar instruction: 'do as I do'. Since we pursue the poem's game-playing, following its 'clues', anagrams, and puzzles, that is an injunction we are perhaps unwittingly obeying.

But this apparently 'timeless' game-playing address to *you* registers also a 'counterpointing' of other voices. The full section reads:

> Interpose a fire-curtain; stop the applause
> from getting through. But would Herr Grass accept
> the dedication – our names

---

[4] *SS* 103:52; *Orchards* 62; *Triumph* 148:82.

unromantically linked? I owe him; he
owes me nothing. Here's an awkward
question | going spáre to be asked: dó
you, as Í do, sit late by the Aga
with clues received from sputtering
agents of Marconi; from Imre Nagy;
from Scott of the Antarctic frozen in time
before the first crossword? Decent old Böll –
why me, why not Günter? Help him, someone.   (2:1)

Aural and visual harmony, as well as images of domestic privation, are run
alongside discomfiting historical 'clues' (and vice versa), which send us
back to contemplate address as the broadcasting of particular, comprom-
ised voices. Here, then, are the antiphonal voices of the poem. Beginning
Section 2 by revisiting his quotation from Günter Grass, which formed
the second of this volume's epigraphs: 'VORHANG, BEVOR DU DEN
BEIFALL BEGREIFST' ('Curtain, before you receive the applause'), Hill
simultaneously invites in, and invades the words of, 'Herr Grass', the first
named figure of the sequence: 'Interpose a fire-curtain; stop the applause'.
If this is a flattering personal tribute to the German author, testifying to
the significance of his voice in contemporary poetic 'speech', that tribute
is itself also a sly act of historical-lyric rewriting, in which Hill's poem
reclaims Grass's earlier voice and allies it with his own (and his own
agenda): 'But would Herr Grass accept / the dedication—our names /
unromantically linked? I owe him' (2:1). The personal 'dedication' is also
a public act of revealing, enabling Hill's audience to glimpse what is
behind the curtain, supposedly shielded from the public gaze.

The public aural fabric of Section 2 then tunes us in to the twice-
appointed Hungarian prime minister and former member of the Russian
Communist Party, Imre Nagy, whose government presided over the failed
1956 Hungarian Revolution that led to his trial and execution; before
moving us to Robert Falcon Scott's ill-fated 1910–13 Terra Nova Exped-
ition, on which, upon reaching the South Pole, Scott found he had been
recently preceded by a Norwegian team. It is on the return journey that
Scott and his four comrades perished, 'frozen in time / before the first
crossword'. That 'crossword' again sends us to the public world. Hill
alludes firstly to the first printed crossword, a 'word-cross', published
in the Sunday *New York Times* on 21 December 1913, shortly after Scott's
death.[5] Secondly, the 'cross-word' alludes to the controversial historical
response to Scott, who had been hailed as an iconic British hero following

---

[5] The puzzle was called a 'word-cross', and was devised by the Liverpudlian Arthur
Wynne. It is commonly hailed as the first invented crossword.

the Expedition, but whose reputation was, several decades later, heatedly challenged by heckling voices.[6]

Here the reversals between crosswords and word-crosses playfully, but also ominously, criss-cross. Clues are meant to help decipher evidence, to solve problems, and clear up mysteries, but Hill's clues and puzzles give not answers, but further layers of mystification, further complexities of address's disparate voices. What, if any, is the relationship between Hill's invented *I* and *you* and the historical figures, Marconi, Nagy, and Scott? Are the 'sputtering clues' their broadcasted address to *I* and *you*? Are *I* and *you* addressees, who, having received these clues, are also 'frozen in time', pens poised thoughtfully above Hill's own lyric crossword? What do the poem's disparate historical figures have in common with each other? Does 'sputtering' refer to the premature deaths of Nagy and Scott? Or the wireless experimentations of Guglielmo Marconi, who shared the 1909 Nobel Prize in Physics with Karl Ferdinand Braun, in recognition of his contributions to the development of wireless telegraphy, and whose technology the poem's *I* and *you* rely upon to 'receive' their addresses? And what impact has the medium—the radio, the poem, the radio within the poem—upon the information being broadcasted: is this a transparent reportage of facts, or an antiphonal, 'sputtering' address? Is the neutrality of the medium compromised by the fact that Marconi was to join the Italian fascist party in 1923, and that in subsequent years he used his technology to broadcast speeches as an apologist for the actions of the fascist regime in Italy?

The presence of such heckling questions casts suspicion upon the apparently well-tuned address of the *I* and *you* 'sitting late by the Aga', tuning in to receive their broadcasts. Clearly, the address is not insular, nor is its context incidental. At stake in all of this play is the register in which historical figures, events, nations, information, and domestic relations may be talked about: idioms compete for speakers, games for players. As listeners, we are asked to consider whether poems should address historical matters in the language of play, and who they might be addressing, and interrupting, when they do so. Hearing is active, here, and these poetic *I*s and *you*s are transformed into historical agents, altering the accepted construction of events through their innocent linkages of the heard voices of Nagy, Scott, and Marconi. Though they are anchored by

---

[6] For strongly worded criticism of Scott, see Roland Huntford's 1979 biography *Scott and Amundsen* (London: Hodder), reissued as *The Last Place on Earth* in 1985 (London: Pan) and made into a serialized television documentary drama. Huntford's series significantly revised the public perception of Scott as a national hero, though Huntford's credibility has been challenged by subsequent experts on polar travel, including Ranulph Fiennes and Susan Solomon.

the contexts they tune into, *I* and *you* are also antiphonal voices within these contexts, and their participation in the historical weave answers to and embodies a variation on the standard representative accounts of history. Being well tuned, in this sense, involves not only tuning in to receive the voices of others, but offering new answers and responses to them.

Hill's poems, however, often seem keen to tune their language to a discrete, personally addressed *you*, tapping into those lyric vocabularies of the immediate, the private, and the set apart: 'you my spent heart's treasure', Hill writes in the early poem, 'The Pentecost Castle'.[7] 'My dear and awkward love [...] / [...] like you, / I understand by this time all too well', he writes in *Triumph*; 'yet still I mourn / yoú my sister', we hear in *Orchards* (57:30; 26). *Yous* in Hill may also be awkward creatures, resistant to being treasured ('Enforcer! What will you have? What can I / freely give you?'), whilst their wily silence often speaks volumes, delivering a dissenting provocation to the notion of perfect textual harmony between speaker and addressee (*SS* 5:3). 'Say something, you' he writes in Section 9 of *Orchards*; 'So far I'm with you [...] / [...] I wish I could say more' (*Orchards* 69). But in those lines from 'The Pentecost Castle', *you* is surely effectively hoarded by the speaker, as if valuable private 'treasure', to be hidden and locked away from others' grasp. '*Heart's* treasure' makes *you* doubly removed from the eyes and voices of the world, an internalized splendour, valuable perhaps only subjectively. But 'spent' complicates this picture: is it the heart that is spent? Or the treasure? The value of *you*, in either case, becomes precarious, and the set-apart privation of that listening figure is made conditional, violable: the addressed *you* cannot be distanced from the public world successfully.

Similarly, *Triumph*'s address to my 'dear and awkward love', suggests not simply the attuned nature of the pair's 'Likeness' and 'understanding', but the difficulty of the relation: is the love 'dear' because it's awkward, or is *you* loved despite being awkward (57:30)? Understanding 'by this time all too well' again indicates the imperfection of well-tuned accord: slight impatience ghosts 'by this time', while 'all too well' suggests that *you* is too well known, understood to a fault—though *I* might well enjoy that very over-familiarity. All of this, the *I*'s vocal insistence in taking pleasure in *you*, might well be perverse: what *I* most enjoys about the performance is the dividedness he hears in his own voice of address; the recalcitrance of the medium in which he articulates his tribute to *you*. As W. S. Graham puts it, 'But you do / Say something back which I / Hear by the way I speak to you'.[8] Perhaps what *I* treasures in *you* is its antiphonal capacity

[7] *Tenebrae* (1978), in *HCP* 141.
[8] 'Implements in Their Places' (1977), in *NCP* 247.

both to participate and to resist, offering silence as a sound in a chorus of voices. In this way, *you* teases the speaker into further thought, rather than demurring accommodatingly to him.

'The Songbook of Sebastian Arrurruz' is a key example, from Hill's earlier work, of how the ideal of well-tuned personal contact is answered back to even as it seems to be lauded.[9] It also provides a clearer sense of the direction out of which the heckling of the later volumes develops. Dominated by intimate addresses that seem to delight in the pure subjective outpouring associated with Romantic apostrophe, 'Songbook' seems quite different in tone and register from the louder and vituperative cross-currents of voices in *Speech! Speech!* and *Triumph*. The rhetoric of 'Songbook' taps that of a self's spontaneous lyricism, a private address to a lover that is merely overheard by (but not intended for) a reading public: 'Ten years without you', 'I can lose what I want. I want you', 'Oh my dear one, I shall grieve for you / For the rest of my life', 'It is to him I write, it is to her / I speak' (92–3). On first reading, this surely sounds like the opposite of heckling: an instance of the simple immediacy of elegiac address, a personal voicing of the speaker's song to a particular addressed *you*?

Yet these apparently private and direct addresses are not allowed to remain exclusively so. They are framed and writ about by the professionalized, impersonal discourse of an editor's mediating commentary: 'Sebastian Arrurruz: 1868–1922', 'The Songbook of Sebastian Arrurruz'. The speaker's private language makes up a published, public document that has been set out for other eyes twice over: literally, as a part of the oeuvre of the poet 'Geoffrey Hill'; and also fictitiously, as a document brought to light by a fictitious editor. We reach the body of the poem only after having negotiated numerous attempts to present the songbook as genuine and uncontaminated historical artefact, and these attempts emphasize the inescapably public, multivocal nature of Hill's text.

Hill's 'Songbook' provides an excellent example of the manner in which Hill's antiphonal address brings the voice of intimate relations between an *I* and a *you* into contact with the voice of public display and 'objective' historical impartiality. The two are not exclusive, self-contained discourses. They respond to and infiltrate one another. Even before we have reached Arrurruz's first word, the poem has complicated the notion of 'private' love song with a sidelong glance at other poetic works that have cast suspicion on the possibility of achieving pure personal address in a public document. That title, 'The Songbook of Sebastian Arrurruz', is grammatically near-identical to Eliot's 1917 poem, 'The Love Song of J. Alfred Prufrock' (*ECP* 13–17). The difference between 'love song' and 'songbook' significantly

[9] 'Arrurruz', *HCP* 92–102.

alters the emphasis and authority of the title. Its status as 'song' (not song-book) suggests the spontaneity of a *happening*: less a piece of historical documentation than a performative utterance, an occurrence in the here and now. In contrast, 'The Song*book*' underlines its status as historical document, as writing unearthed, dislodged from its historical time, de-pendent upon the interventions of an editor/translator/historian to give it an auditor. *I* and *you* are not given to us as live and direct: Hill's poem doesn't allow its readers to think they can hear an *I* (like Prufrock's 'Let us go then, you and I') speaking in a Now, either *for* or *of* the times (13). (Though in one sense a songbook is an *instruction to give voice* to a song, or a record of one who has done so. This is mediated spontaneity.) Indeed, Arrurruz neglects/rejects the moments he is placed in, both the era he is writing in, and the era in which he is being read. Instead he 'imagines' a future that 'will come / Sure enough' and a past that 'comes back to us', in 'the excess of memory'. It is the editor-figure, that figure from *our* time, who provides the contexts he or she has decided we need to know. This figure chooses the poem's title, names 'the songbook', and authoritatively writes underneath it: 'Sebastian Arrurruz: 1868–1922'.

One might compare this with the intrusive editor-figure of *Triumph*, who in the guise of a capitalized 'ED' repeatedly inserts comments, direc-tions, and explanations into the text itself: '[he means / I think, the late "Erdődy" Quartets—ED]', 'Is this / a misprint? For sang read sank? [Phew, / what a "prang"!—ED]', '[Internal / evidence identifies the late / Eugenio Montale as the undoubted / subject of this address.—ED]'.[10] In 'Songbook', too, the editor-figure frames, names, authenticates the song-book, encouraging us to read it as document, evidence, and establishing the context in which we shall receive the text itself. In 'Songbook', as in *Triumph*, the editor is not a mere neutral collector of information, but an active organizer who structures the text's reception, putting into play a series of expectations and conventions that set up our reading responses. Such an editing figure has a hand in orchestrating the contact between *I* and *you*.

Arrurruz's address to *you* is sounded through, and comes in answer to, the poem's historical involvement. The poem is typical of Hill's tendency to demand that his reader contemplate obscure and little-known historical sources in order to glean the context of the address, in order to situate apparently asocial lyric language. One might well consider such historical demands as a distraction from the private lyrical correspondence of Arrur-ruz's love song. Critics have, according to their preference, detailed and praised, or condemned and lamented Hill's repeated reliance upon such

---

[10]   *Triumph*, 131:71; 48:24; 134:72.

arcane historical sources. Andrew Zawacki, falling somewhere between these camps, points out that, repeatedly, the critic is unable to uncover accurate historical sources for Hill's poems: 'what one finds is often red herrings'.[11] One encounters imaginary histories that, despite surface appearance, lack any grounding in real events. Zawacki offers as example 'The Songbook': 'supposed translations of an apocryphal Spanish poet who died the year *The Waste Land* and *Ulysses* were published' (Zawacki, 1999).

Is this one means of emphasizing, as Hill does in 'A Postscript', how a poem both 're-enters history in a multitude of circumstances [...] collusive with good and ill', and remains 'alienated from its existence as historical event' (579–80)? As the fictional aspect of Arrurruz's apparently autobiographical, first-person lyric construction makes clear, Hill's Arrurruz is not a historical figure: he is an invented figure inserted into a fictitious faux-history. Given this recognition, surely the poem's *I* is cut off from the reality that may locate it and its discourse, not really 're-entering [...] history' or connecting with the particularities of 'circumstance' at all. This leaves us with a potentially serious charge *vis-à-vis* the role of history as public discourse in Hill's poem: perhaps the work is, after all, merely fanciful 'pseudo-seriousness' and private lyricism, its *I* addressing *you* quite outside of historical context?[12]

And yet this very issue is crucial to ongoing debates about whether poetic language can be used exclusively privately or publicly, and what role history has to play in individual and collective understanding.[13] As Peter Robinson has pointed out, the work is not *pure* fiction: 'It was Machado's Abel Mart'n and Juan de Mairena, among others, who served as prompts for the imaginary writer Sebastian Arrurruz.'[14] Indeed, the poem emphasizes the impossibility of achieving the *merely* fictitious. Vincent Sherry has suggested that the character can be linked with a Roman martyr who 'died in a volley of arrows'.[15] So too, the word 'Arrurruz' etymologically precedes Sebastian Arrurruz: it's the Spanish word for 'arrowroot', a West Indian plant used for starch and for drawing out poison from wounds (poisoned arrow-wounds). These contexts are not fictions. They do not originate from the imagined construction of Hill's poem, but draw on real sources. That Hill enlists the real in the shaping of his character lends an aura of

---

[11] Andrew Zawacki, Review of *The Triumph of Love*, *Boston Review* (February/March 1999), <http://bostonreview.mit.edu/BR24.1/zawacki.html>, accessed 1 May 2009.

[12] See 'Postscript' 568–70 for discussion of 'caprice' and 'pseudo-seriousness'.

[13] See Heaney, *Redress* 1–2.

[14] Peter Robinson, Review of *The Triumph of Love*, *Notre Dame Review* 8 <http://www.nd.edu/~ndr/issues/ndr8/reviews/love.html>, accessed 12 December 2008.

[15] Sherry, *The Uncommon Tongue* 118.

authenticity which is then called into question by its very incorporation in the poem's history.

Again, this brings us back to Hill's comments on the inescapable constraints upon attempting to wield language 'freely', or outside of history, in 'Postscript': 'There is something in constraint which frees the mind, and something in freedom which constrains it' (573). 'The arbitrary, by a long process of semantic conglomeration, is at once freedom of will and the will obdurate in itself [...], and in service to, a greater obduracy', Hill argues. It is in this way that a writer's fight 'for the intelligence of poetry within the civic domain' takes place, as the 'poem re-enters history [...] as an effective agent, or hostage' (573–9). Historical understanding is constructed through the artwork, which is both agent and hostage, and the poem does not just passively represent 'real' battle, but *is* a kind of battle with, and against, 'its existence as historical event' (580).

Given that, for Hill, 'scenarios about language-issues' should also be 'in themselves language-experiments' that reveal verbal struggle, it is perhaps not surprising that the 'Songbook's' address participates in the history of textual happenings ('Postscript' 579). Arrurruz's antiphonal oscillation between private and public address places his speech, identifying it with dissonant literary traditions; even he struggles to sound out his isolation from them. Antonio Machado is an early twentieth-century Spanish poet whom Robinson identifies amongst the sources for 'Songbook' (and whose work Don Paterson's 1999 collection, *The Eyes*, also takes as his source). Machado, too, had in play antiphonal voices when he combined dispassionate reassessments of Spanish history and topography with the style of detached private recollection. His 1912 'Campos de Castilla' and later, his 'La Tierra de Alvargonzález' explored the claims of history, socio-economic and moral conditions through memory, dream, and intimate, elegiac verse.[16] The year Hill selects for Arrurruz's death is the year of the publication of the canonical Modernist texts, Joyce's *Ulysses* and Eliot's *The Waste Land*.[17] Might this decision suggest the sounding of a death knoll for the traditions Arrurruz, and also Machado, represents? Hill's poem signals at once an ushering *out* of the old—the softly sorrowful elegiac nationalistic address, the longing to attain 'stylized' truths that are universal, that will transcend time and will not yield to the age's specificities ('Trivia', 'the occurrences of the day', 'desirable features of conversation')—as well as the ushering *in* of Modernism, the answer to Pound's injunction to 'Make it new'.[18] Yet Hill would also be

---

[16] Antonio Machado, *Times Alone: Selected Poems of Antonio Machado*, ed. Robert Bly (Middletown, CT: Wesleyan University Press, 1983).

[17] *Ulysses* had been serialized in parts in *The Little Review* between 1918 and1920, but was published in its entirety on 2 February 1922 (Paris: Orchises Press). Eliot, *Waste Land* (1922).

[18] Pound, *Hugh Selwyn Mauberley* (1920), in *Personae* 185–204, 197. See Hill's 1986 Clark Lecture on Pound, 'Envoi (1919)', in *CCW* 243–59. Referred to as 'Envoi'.

alert to the similarity between a certain strain of nostalgia in Arrurruz's language and strands of Modernism's own classicist retrospection; the linking back to a classical language, 'from the Latin', the interest in 'the well-schooled / Postures of St Anthony or St Jerome'. Debates over literary continuation and discontinuity are put in play through the poem's heckling voices, as we are made to hear the various proponents of these positions objecting to and deliberating with each other.

A particularly rich antiphony can be heard between Hill's 'Songbook' and Pound's final poem of *Mauberley*, 'Envoi (1919)', a text that Hill has lectured and written on in his own 'Envoi (1919)'.[19] Through their addresses, both works put into uneasy 'counterpointing' a view of the text as objective/factual, and a view of the text as print-turned-personality, a private voicing, a holding-forth of spontaneously tuneful song. On the one hand, the opening lines of Pound's 'Envoi (1919)' contain what looks like private urging, a personal address that longs to escape circumstance, to transcend history: 'Go, dumb-born book, / Tell her that sang me once', 'Tell her', 'tell her'. On the other, Pound's poem is not just the occasion of song, but also a reflection upon that song's textual, stylistic history (*Personae* 197). This dual function is intricately connected with Pound's desire to address, and redress, an audience that may be unable to hear, or determined to mishear, the historicity of his tuneful address. Hill writes that Pound's lyric 'recalls in its title the form of the alba (e.g. "Alba Innominata", a version of which Pound had included in his *Exultations* of 1909) and in its opening lines the melody of *Waller's "Go lovely Rose"*', but he is simultaneously aware that Pound's 'dumb-born [works] in the further sense that its audience must be assumed to be deaf to its language' ('Envoi' 243; 249). Pound's poem is a heckling voice in that it will neither function outside of history, nor achieve a status transcendent to history. Its tuneful lyricism works with, and in counterpoint to, inscribed accounts of the past. But it may also be a dumb-born heckle, a voice that goes unheeded by the audience it addresses.

If Pound's tunefulness probes further the relation between literary and historical accounts, and makes them answerable, antiphonal, to each other, Hill and Pound are themselves counterpointing voices, audiences to one another that are neither fully exclusive, nor fully compatible. There are instructive similarities: Pound's 'Envoi' is like Hill's 'Songbook' in that it indicates its attempt to operate as dry documentation, its struggle to attain a status as record, as evidence. The speaker's propensity for record-keeping, dating, and locating is clear from the precision of the very title, 'Envoi (1919)', which is hardly dissimilar from Hill's own 'Songbook', which was again dated and located by its subtitle: 'Arrurruz: 1868–1922'. So too, Pound's lyric, like Hill's 'Songbook', interrupts its own desire for evidential, historical status. 'Envoi' wants to be seen not just as accurate document, but as anthropomorphized vocalization in the here-and-now, an artwork capable of responding to listeners and addressees with urgency. The text, like Hill's own, lays bare its urgency to move others, and to move outside of history, attaining timeless appeal, and so in one sense, it underlines its own compromised neutrality and historical facticity. In both texts, the artwork's engagement with the past, just like the historical document itself, is shown to be incapable of neutral witness.

But when Hill writes that in Pound's lyric, 'Lyric utterance stands as witness to a faith in "sheer perfection" even while it is standing scrutiny as a piece of evidence in the natural history of such belief', he attempts to distinguish his own mode of historical participation from that of Pound (258). For both poets, the dual focus on history and lyric is a way of insisting upon writing's susceptibility, partiality, its potential for individual human error, desire, and being led astray, and is highly suggestive of what Hill has called 'the intense subjectivism with which objectivity may be proclaimed'.[20] What Hill seems to think is problematic about 'Envoi (1919)' is the manner in which it is led astray, which occurs in the lyric's tuneful proclamation of 'faith in "sheer perfection"'. Pound's lyric (Hill argues), coming as the culmination of *Mauberley*, distracts its audience from the brokenness and labour with which the larger poem begins— 'Wrong from the start', 'Bent resolutely on wringing lilies from the acorn'— and concedes too much ground to 'the music of its own unfolding [...] the only *melopoeia* the "book" will have' (249). *Melopoeia* has been defined by Pound as 'words [...] charged, over and above their plain meaning, with some musical property, which directs the bearing or tend of that meaning'.[21] For Hill, Pound's otiose address in 'Envoi' under-privileges historical and poetical antiphonies: by over-emphasizing the first aspect of melo-poeia ('words are charged [...] with some musical property') he neglects the latter: 'musical property [...] *directs their meaning*'. Music and alignment come (Hill implies) in place of the labour required in being 'directed', particularly at the expense of the needlingly recalcitrant historical meanings which Pound successfully uses elsewhere to rebuke an audience's demand for quaintly accommodating archaic musicality.

This falling away compromises Pound's otherwise scrupulous *logopoeic* attentiveness to 'the habits of usage, [...] the context we *expect* to find

---

[20] *CCW* 246. See also Geoffrey Hill, 'Jonathan Swift: The Poetry of Reaction', in *The World of Jonathan Swift*, ed. Brian Vickers (Oxford: Basil Blackwell, 1968), republished in *LL*; republished in, and quoted from, *CCW* 71–87, 86.
[21] 'How to Read' (*c.*1928), in *Essays* 15–40, 25.

Pound

with the word' ('How to Read' 25). Pound, like Hill, often wields *logo-poeia* as a redress to those 'upholders of the "courteous, tawdry, quiet old"' who view lyrical emphasis on tradition, convention, archaic language as merely quaint, 'sympathetic to the ears', akin with an easily detectable 'beauty' ('Envoi' *CCW* 248–9). *Mauberley*'s concluding lyric conceals the sequence's larger difficulty and disharmony, rather than, as is characteristic to Pound, exemplifying it. Hill admires the latter quality in Pound: 'the immense labour of picking one's way, as he said, between the "not quite it" and the "not quite not it"', and not the former, which produces (he argues) merely 'the guise of a satisfying finished piece' (249). This sharp redress to Pound comes as a result of what Hill views as the lyric's collapsed instance that its audience will be exposed to the fullest sense of *melopoeia* and *logopoeia*. He argues that Pound is, finally, passively compliant with the expectations of 'the average poetry-reader': the 'vulnerable archaic "beauty" of that ardent and arduous defence of which Pound committed all his energies, would not [...] in any way disturb [...] his esteemed great aunt' (249).

'Poetry's a public act by long engagement. / [...] / the spikier the better', Hill wrote in 2006 ('Pindarics' *WT* 7:41). Hill's spiky oratorical interlacings of essayistic and poetical heckling voices create a body of work of sportive oppositionality that contrasts and counterpoints conflicted positions available in the language: 'a language won and wrought / for the conglomerate that is called a nation' ('Pindarics' 7:41). That conglomerate language is played out for and with assembled public bodies, and with a good deal of attention to Pound's and Eliot's prior negotiations of the politics of spectacle and broadcast. One suspects these are negotiations Hill's poems often relish interrupting—though finding themselves doing so is not necessarily due to 'insufficient seriousness' or 'caprice' in Hill's own address. Rather, it is a result of his work's repeated attempt to get 'within its judgement the condition of the judgement', and to invite in and respond to, the judgements of others.[22] The poems make earlier writers answerable to the antiphonal voices of the present—partly Hill's own, partly the voices of his readers, listeners, audiences, critics, and reviewers, all of whom Hill encourages to raise questions with regard to these Modernist figures.

In so doing, Hill's poems court judgements from his contemporaries, too: 'what I believe I give you here / I take as the counterpoint to your own / caustic attrition'.[23] His addresses reach into (and negotiate) the moment of their future reception, even as they demand assessment from

---

[22] 'Postscript' 568, 569, 580.
[23] 'Courtly Masquing Dances', *Scenes from Comus* 48:38.

the audiences of their time. 'Here are the Orchards of Syon, neither wisdom / nor illusion of wisdom, not / compensation, not recompense', Hill addresses his reader: 'you cóuld / say that I give myself / to well-failed causes' (*Orchards* 72; 11). Likewise, in *Speech! Speech!* the concluding stanzas concede to its audience's expected criticisms, as well as rudely heckling, speaking over and competing with, *your* hostile reception of the poem: 'bád shów. / This needs working on', 'his own worst enemy' (119:60). One might object that in ensuring his self-criticism—a form of self-address—takes place before the poem's close, Hill self-protectively forestalls *your* criticism. However, Hill is clearly aware that it is precisely this staged pre-empting of oppositional voices that spark the most energetic antiphonies in his audiences.[24] 'Lyric cry lyric cry lyric cry, I'll / give them lyric cry!' (*Orchards* 30). Such address both offers *you* its 'lyric cry' as a gift, and rudely 'gives it to you', spoiling for a fight: Hill's counterpointing voice holds together generous responsiveness, retort, taunt, and stinging provocation.

[24] See Adam Kirsch, 'The Long-Cherished Anger of Geoffrey Hill', *NY Sun*, 28 March 2007 <http://www.nysun.com/arts/long-cherished-anger-of-geoffrey-hill/51347/>, accessed 30 July 2008, referred to as Kirsch 2007; William Logan, Review of *Speech! Speech!*, *New Criterion* 19:4 (December 2000) 65; Jeannine Johnson, 'Geoffrey Hill', in *Why Write Poetry* (Cranbery, NJ: Farleigh Dickinson University Press, 2007) 237–71, especially 260–70.

10

Civil Invitations: Common Readers

pastoral (handwritten annotation)

I know I talk a lot about mob and rabble [...] but I am not talking about the common reader. I am talking about the professionally opinionated.

critics (handwritten annotation)
easy target (handwritten annotation)

> Geoffrey Hill, Hill conference, Keble College,
> Oxford, June 2008

'Confound you, Croker', Hill's speaker addresses a critic in *Triumph*, taunting his auditors with a series of demotic insults and rude gibes: 'up / yours', 'yourself / the enemy' (138:74; 139:76). Many of the addresses of Hill's late volumes are neither winsome nor inviting. Even addresses to the reader are not always restrained or hospitable: 'All right push off', 'Oh, yoú again', 'You're magisterial in your own conviction. / And a clown with it'.[1] Hill's speakers also avoid answers, responses, and feign lack of interest in reciprocating dialogue with *you*: 'I expect / no answer. Would it be fairer to say / that I do not invite one?' (*Triumph* 95:49). Occasionally they speak over the answering voices of their interlocutors, rather than listening to them: 'I am putting / words in your mouth' (95:49). Such uncivil addresses, it might seem, create the opposite of a poetics of invitation, and confirm what reviewers have called Hill's active hostility towards his readers. 'His dislike of readers has been a disease in the poetry [...] a pathology of the prose', William Logan has recently commented, making the case that Hill's poetic scholarship is elitist and alienating even to the critical, let alone to the common reader: 'stray facts are the price of admission to Hill's poetry; and the reader might reasonably ask if these devious, dissuasive poems are worth the penalties of sense'.[2] For Logan, Hill's sense-making itself becomes an unreasonable penalty, tortuously inflicted upon his readers. Other critics have accused the poet of insisting

---

[1] *SS* 39:20; 109:55; 'Discourse: For Stanley Rosen', *WT* 2:26, referred to as 'Discourse'.

[2] William Logan, 'Living with Ghosts', Review of *A Treatise of Civil Power*, *New York Times*, 20 January 2008 <http://www.nytimes.com/2008/01/20/books/review/Logan-t.html?pagewanted=print>, accessed 6 February 2009.

upon single-handed textual mastery. Adam Kirsch writes that he is 'a self-absorbed and self-regarding poet, whose quarrels with himself and the world are usually conducted at an unpleasant pitch' (Kirsch 2007). There have also been complaints about Hill's rebuttal of addressees, critics, reviewers, and readers: 'I do not know how to interpret this except as an attack upon everyone who has to do with poetry: poets, critics, teachers, students, readers [...]', Harold Bloom writes of 'Annunications'.[3]

Viewed alongside a poem like *Triumph*, 'Annunciations' carries out pretty measured 'attacks'. One wonders what language Bloom would use about Hill's many recent—and viciously 'unpleasant'—addresses 'against yourself': 'yourself / the enemy (*do it and be damned*)' (*Triumph* 139:76). What would Kirsch make of such lines as, 'Unzipped and found addressing the smeared walls / of an underpass, crying not mȳ / address, no more unnamed accusers', especially given his status amongst Hill's named 'accusers'?[4] For Logan, Kirsch, and Bloom, Hill's address is predominantly unidirectional redress, an unleashing of vituperative personal railing that rejects responses from the *you*s it upbraids. Are Hill's late poetic addresses instances of mere solitary ranting? If so, what are we to make of Hill's *A Treatise of Civil Power*, a work that is highly attentive both to past and present auditors, and to the different communities of address—in and out of poetry—that the artwork negotiates, and is judged by? *Triumph* demands public reassessment of the figure of the literary 'rebel', as he moves in crowds, public bodies, and readerships, and addresses commemorated figures and the intelligentsia. In this, Hill not only makes close contact with a range of difficult, estranged, and intimate auditors, but speaks to *you* in a way that is a good deal more subtle than a rejection of dialogue with all addressees, readers, and critics.

At its close, Milton's *Treatise of Civil Power in Ecclesiastical Causes*, from which Hill's latest volume takes its title, condemns the 'pomp and ostentation of reading', and gives favour to 'the scripture so copious and plain we have all that can properly be called true strength and nerve'.[5] Milton's *Treatise*, addressed to Parliament, argued that scriptural language was common cultural property. His prizing of readerly 'true strength and nerve' might be placed beside a comment by Hill, in his Warton lecture on Isaac Rosenberg, that 'the common reader is the natural aristocrat of the spirit' ('Rosenberg' 459). Hill's comment plays off the theses of privation, elitism, and textual mastery levelled by critics including Logan and

---

[3] Harold Bloom, *Somewhere Is Such a Kingdom: Poems 1952–1971* (Boston: Houghton Mifflin, 1975), intro.; 'Annunciations' (1968), in *HCP* 62.

[4] 'In the Valley of the Arrow', *WT* 5:69.

[5] For Miltonic source, see Chapter 8, note 24. See Peter McDonald, 'Alive to the Past', Review of *A Treatise of Civil Power*, *Guardian*, Saturday 18 August 2007, 6.

Kirsch. Here, 'common' operates in the *OED*'s first sense, 'of general, public or non-private nature [...] possessed or shared alike', and also its second: 'belonging to more than one as a result or sign of co-operation, joint action, or agreement; joint, united'. Nor does Hill's apothegm neglect *common*'s derogatory, class-based implications. For a moment, 'common reader' plays into the hands of those who see Hill as an elitist, hinting that he might believe his audience is a coarse, plebeian crowd.[6] But Hill's application of the language of elevation ('natural aristocracy') in championing 'the common' turns such critical charges of alienation and elitism against themselves. Hill wields the language of social status and material right not to rebuff what is plain but to prize it, to raise the reader's commonality to the status of 'aristrocracy'. Meanwhile, privileged status is run alongside religious elevation—'aristocrat *of the spirit*'—not mere worldly power. Plainness and pomp, humility and elite status are bound up with the figure of the reader, and of good reading as 'general, public [...] shared' action.

And yet the question of cooperation between authors, critics, and readers remains a vexed one. Hill's unexpected reversals remain complicated by, and uneasy with, the powers they appeal to. The language of aristocratic, worldly rule, and the spiritual claims of his rhetoric are not in easy alignment in that phrase, 'the common reader is the natural aristocrat of the spirit'. The spiritual lexicon raises what it praises above political considerations, but political glory is also bestowed upon religious rhetoric in the process, making circumspect that elevation. Meanwhile, Hill cannot be unaware that his attraction to the power of 'the common' is checked by the very language used to glorify it. Hill's poetry and prose speak as much of sinking as of elevation, and if the verse proclaims high purpose, it remains fascinated by its own betrayal of that purpose: '*wrinching and spraining the text*', 'how else should I prophesy, / misguided, misconceiving, mis-inspired?', he asks interlocutors.[7] But in attending to rhetorical fallibility, Hill does not renounce rhetorical power. 'Prophesy' is not commonality, even when it winningly appeals to its audience: 'How else should I prophesy...?'. The lines hold onto power in the act of confessing their 'misguided' use of it. In asking 'How else...?', the speaker invites his audience to help him prophesize more effectively. Addressees are engaged in order to be won over: hence his confession of being, like the common listener, ordinarily bungling, 'misconceiving, mis-inspired'. One may stoop to win an audience's assent. Logan, it turns out, is correct to point out that Hill does

---

[6] See Tom Paulin's attack on Hill in 'Rhetoric and Violence in Geoffrey Hill's *Mercian Hymns* and the Speeches of Enoch Powell', *Cambridge Quarterly* 29:1 (2000) 1–15.
[7] 'On Reading *Milton and the English Revolution*', *Treatise* 5–6.

not renounce language's incantatory power, even in speaking of plainness, but he is a misleading guide when he writes that Hill 'believes that sinking to common ground betrays the high purpose of verse', and that Hill 'has refused, time and again, to stoop to such betrayals'. The politics of stooping, and of the powers at play in our betrayals of high purpose, are what this writing is most scrupulously attuned to.

One might wonder, then, what to make of *Treatise*, in which emphasis repeatedly falls on the positive character of the everyday, and in which *you*, too, are instructed to laud 'the intelligence of the citizen'. In 'On Reading *Crowds and Power*', Hill writes:

> But think on: that which is difficult
> preserves democracy; you pay respect
> to the intelligence of the citizen.
> Basics are not condescension. Some
> tyrants make great patrons. Let us observe
> this and proceed. Certain directives
> parody at your own risk. Tread lightly
> with personal dignity and public image.
> Safeguard the image of the common man.
>
> *Treatise*　47

Hill's gravitation towards the unelevated 'basics' is coupled with his reminder to the public speaker: '*you* [should] pay respect / to the [...] citizen'. This is an address and a self-address. Hill's terse recommendation accosts itself in the same breath as he hails the public *you*, using the common language of direct instruction: 'think on'. McDonald has written that these lines make 'obvious that Hill is not interested in addressing a coterie audience' ('Alive to the Past' 6). For McDonald, this is poetry which, 'in making demands of its readers' intelligence, engages them in a discourse about things [...] that matter' (6). Indeed, Hill instructs *you* to 'Safeguard the image of the common man'. His lines engagingly address the citizens themselves (a readerly body of 'common men'), and also implicitly take to task a wayward intellectual body of writers and critics that refuse to write for 'common men' with sufficient, respectful difficulty.

The title, 'On Reading *Crowds and Power*', is pertinent. In this poem, Hill's own 'reading' is not an act of set-apart self-communion, but a prompt to pay tribute to the public power of texts. One pays tribute to the Nobel Prize winning work by the Bulgarian-born novelist, Elias Canetti, who is the commemorated addressee of Hill's lyric. When Hill hails Canetti as *you*, his address participates in a network of communal literary and cultural actions, particularly the communities of speech associated with producing, receiving, and preserving *Crowds and Power* as public landmark. Selecting this particular text as a point of departure is not a

Connetti was a jerk

neutral gesture. Canetti's study analysed the behaviour of crowds of numerous kinds, from groups at football matches, to the gatherings in churches, to revolutionary bodies, and the power wielded over the masses by tyrannical leaders. Hill's personal address to Canetti alerts the poet's own readers to the communal, civic—one might say crowd-like—nature of readerships and literary audiences. In his commemoration, Hill ensures that reading's common 'joint action', its *logopoeia*, is made clear: the poem's interlocution is not private or elite, but a civil addition to the history of tributes to Canetti, and a plain-speaking renegotiation of that author's status in literary history.

Simultaneously, Hill's address to Canetti offers *you* (and its audience) a critique of the earlier text's arguments and effects. Hill recalls Canetti writing, and transposes his lines into lyric form:

> *Fame is not fastidious about the lips*
> *which spread it. So long as there are mouths*
> *to reiterate the one name it does not*
> *matter whose they are.*
> [...]
> [...] *Names collect*
> *their own crowds. They are greedy, live their own*
> *separate lives, hardly at all connected*
> *with the real natures of the men who bear them.*
>
> *Treatise* 46

For Canetti, the lack of connection between men's names and natures spells out a false discrepancy between individually held 'real natures' and an out-of-control public being. The power of a name is in the hands of negligent masses, swayed by propaganda. For Hill, in comparison, the discrepancy between name and being leaves a community of public beings room for manoeuvre, for working out with others what names can come to mean to a culture, as we see in the many commemorating addresses of *Treatise*: 'In Memoriam: Ernst Barlach', 'In Memoriam: Gillian Rose', 'On Reading *Burke on Empire, Liberty, and Reform*' (45; 35–8; 18–19). The volume emphasizes that reading is a public act which demands a reader's and writer's civic negotiation of the power of naming.

On the one hand, like Canetti, Hill's public addresses often warn their audience of the dangers (for both *I* and *you*) of acting as part of the 'mob'. As we have seen, that warning is offered in many of the post-*Canaan* volumes. If 'Limelight excites the rabble, shows them tricks, / the prancing orchestra of self-disgust. / Too much is theatre', will the poet be corrupted by his need to perform for, and to satisfy, his audience? ('Pindarics', *WT* 38). On the other hand, as *you* are reminded, to see reading as communal—even as crowd participation—involves a positive sense-making in which the public body formulates meanings from documents in recognizable, intelligent, and culturally informed ways: 'Poetry's a public act by long engagement', 'Abstinence isn't the right word; nor is / contagious' ('Pindarics' 40–1). Hill's commemorative addresses exemplify what he calls, in his address to the late Gillian Rose, 'an intelligence of grief', not mere vulgar 'prancing' (*Treatise* 35). If, in perusing prize-winning texts and artworks of commemoration, *you* participates in what Canetti might have called reading's crowd mentality, *you* simultaneously takes part in what Hill, more positively, might term a community of reading. One aligns oneself with, as well as resisting, civil and intimate *logopoeic* references and structures: 'There are achievements / that carry failure on their back' ('Gillian Rose' 35–8).

In *Culture and Society*, Raymond Williams argued that a culture's art should be understood in relation to its system of production, not seen as separate from, or elevated above it: 'a culture is a whole way of life, and the arts are part of a social organisation which economic change clearly radically affects'.[8] Like Hill, he reminds us that 'Masses = majority cannot be glibly equated with masses = mob' (Williams, 299). Williams suggested that true culture demanded a community, a collective spirit of action. For Williams, it was no longer art and literature that could operate in the fullest sense of the word culture as 'a whole way of life', and which could restore people's sense of living in an active community. Now, it was 'Working-class culture, [which] in the stage through which it has been passing, is primarily social (in that it has created institutions) rather than individual (in particular intellectual or imaginative work)' (327). He was severe about the bourgeoise's 'extraordinary decision to call certain things culture and then separate them, as with a park wall, from ordinary people and ordinary work'. Literary works fell into that category.

Hill's emphasis on culture as a way of life, dependent upon a body of common readers, and likewise his emphasis on literature as intricately bound up in the contingencies and the established traditions of its socio-economic production, is reminiscent of—as well as resistant to—Williams's thought. Hill is unlikely to agree that literature has become irremediably divorced from live community. Nor would he propose that literature is so ideologically selective as to be incapable of participating in real public debate. However, working-class culture is prized by both of these self-made men, who were also contemporaries. As public intellectuals, Hill and Williams scrutinize society's predominant individualist (read hierarchical and protectionist) ethic: 'self-expression is a word that

---

[8] Raymond Williams, *Culture and Society 1780–1950* (London: Chatto & Windus, 1958) 327.

should be tarred and feathered', Hill writes, 'such words may be part of the self-comforting language of the consensus', 'a shared species of hierarchical Toryism' ('Postscript' 573–6). In this respect, Williams might serve as a helpful figure, one who makes clearer what is at stake in Hill's championing of the common reader.

As we have seen from Logan, Bloom, and Kirsch, Hill has been read as a difficult elitist, addressing an exclusive coterie, and opposed to the simplicity of the ordinary man. But this account has not been adept at accommodating some of Hill's specifically anti-academic pronouncements, nor considering the motivations behind his numerous poetic allusions to his working-class background. Towards the end of 'On Reading *The Essayes or Counsels, Civill and Morall'*, he informs the reader:

> My parents
> never owned a house. It could be said
> that was their folly.
>
> 11
> The poor are bunglers: my people, whom I
> nonetheless honour, who bought no landmark
> other than their graves. I wish I could keep
> Baconian counsel, wish I could keep resentment
> out of my voice.[9]

A statement such as '[t]he poor are bunglers: my people' makes one suspect Hill's lines are confessionally addressed to an imagined 'common reader', descended from similar stock (44). The pronouncement falls somewhere between a proud championing of 'my people' in front of a sympathetic readership, and an admission of inherited ineptness, an embarrassed distaste at confessing, before an intellectual coterie, that he is descended from the 'bungling' classes. It does not, to my ear, read as a spontaneous moment of confession, accidentally 'overheard' by an audience (as Mill might have put it). Rather, this complex commemorative poem of 'Baconian counsel' asks its reading public to think through the relationship between the personal details revealed by the poet 'Reading *The Essayes or Counsels'* and his erudite delving into the intricacies of Baconian texts.

One might think Hill's writerly display of Baconian erudition is brought in to distract his audience (and himself) from his awareness that '*poverty is* [...] *tedious*, and means chiefly / poverty of mind', an accusation that he fears readers will level at him, should his poem fail to demonstrate cognitive grandeur. However, Hill's choice of specific sources and textual landmarks complicates this reading of the lines as self-regarding. Particularly, it

---

[9] *Treatise* 44. Referred to as 'Essayes'.

will not sit easily alongside Hill's decision to engage with Bacon himself; a figure whose writings on the law were far from selfishly motivated. *The Essayes* attempted to protect the body of citizens, committing society to acknowledging the certainty of laws, so that all should have the right to know and understand what constituted lawful and unlawful behaviour, rather than having laws merely decided by the whim of the elect, judge or king.[10] The legal stricture, 'cursed is he that removeth the landmark' protects the common rights of the people, specifically the right to possess one's inheritance, to defend it against those who may attempt to steal another's. The law employs biblical language to enforce this justice of this protective measure, investing what might look to some like dry land law, mere economic right, with the gravity of a sin against God, a violation of God's rightful distribution of boundaries and inheritance over the earth. Hill's plain-speaking, and to some degree self-regarding, declaration of lineage, is combined with a principled refusal to shut out the declarative, historical, and legal nature of 'common' thought and action that aligns a poet's confession with both his 'people' and the people.

Similarly, 'In Memoriam: Ernst Barlach' addresses Barlach, that Low German-speaking expressionist sculptor, novelist, and playwright, for whom the plain-speaking peoples among whom he lived out his childhood was one source of art:

> This has something of you, the carvings and bronzes,
> the peasantry of the lower Elbe your inspiration.
> *A powerful rough language appropriate*
> *to everything human and untutored,*
> such as my great grandmother would have spoken.
>
> *Treatise*   45

Hill's italicized lines cite a letter that emphasizes the value Barlach placed in using appropriately '*powerful rough language*'. When Hill slips in the personal detail, 'such as my great grandmother would have spoken', his quasi-confessional aside suggests a reclaiming of the vitality of 'everything human and untutored' and of an appropriate language with which to speak it (45). This aside aligns him closely with his addressee, and the subject of this commemorative poem. It offers a levelling reminder (to the reader) of Hill's own ancestry, with attention to the specific power of regionalist speech:

> I should have known Low German; perhaps
> the closest measure of it is Black Country

---

[10] See Francis Bacon's essay *Of Judicature*, in *The Essayes or Counsels, Civill and Morall*, ed. Alexander Spiers and Basil Montagu (Boston: Little, Brown and company, 1861) 240–6.

to which the scriptures were transposed by Kate Fletcher.
All the children uv Israel blartid fer Moses. (45)

Again, such lines call for an audience's attention both to the appropriately
unelevated aspects of the 'human and untutored' dialect-forms and to
their rich history—especially in the link between Low German and
scripture.

'I wish I could keep resentment / out of my voice', Hill claims in
'Essayes', an address that expresses desire for quietude and concord, even
as it directs a good measure of vituperation at the custodians of inherited
property and privilege who repress the understandable resentments of
common men. If some concession to good conduct, in front of his as-
sembled audience, is evident in this pronounced wish to keep emotion
out of his voice, it is somewhat belied by the pivotal place given to 'resent-
ment' itself, that emphasis holding the word up for a moment's contem-
plation, before we read over the line break: 'wish I could *keep* resentment'.
The poem does, after all, hold on to its grudging, slyly introducing its
audience to the emotion under the guise of wishing to keep it silent. Re-
sentment is treated rather as though it were a feeling that should be
grasped and sustained, not denied or evaded. Indeed, the phrasing, 'wish
I could ...' is a careful conditional that gently ironizes its own desire to let
resentment go, suggesting the emotion is not always blind fury or in-
capacitating bitterness, but a state of mind to be contained, assessed, and
judged: it might enable one to speak judiciously and critically of one's
own shortcomings and irritations with others. To declare resentment out-
wardly, in front of an assembled public body or readership, is an admis-
sion of one's social and verbal imperfection, one's propensity for righteous,
but also self-righteous, indignation.

One suspects that, to Hill's mind, keeping hold of resentment, even
offering it as something to be battled out in public might be more appro-
priate and scrupulous than 'keeping resentment / out of my voice'. It frees
one from performing one's grudging in secret, from having to address
others with calm neutrality, or even unscrupulous praise, whilst privately
harbouring ill will. Resentment is kept somewhere, even if it is kept out
of the poet's voice. Better, for Hill, to have it in the public fray, in an ad-
dress to the others with whom it was established, than to smooth over the
surface with false niceties. In such work, the discomforting boldness of
voiced resentment is wielded against a species of professorial poetics that
prizes flattery, and the kind of stooping consensus to one's public that we
saw Hill taking Eliot to task for earlier:

The chief use of the 'meaning' of a poem, in the ordinary sense, may be [...]
to satisfy one habit of the reader, to keep his mind diverted and quiet, while

the poem does its work upon him: much as the imaginary burglar is always provided with a bit of nice meat for the house-dog. (Eliot, 'The Use of Poetry' *Prose* 93)

In 'Coda', one of the final poems in *Treatise*, Hill's address compares the collective graft of 'our' linguistic work, 'our last call, difficult coda', with the hard labour of an apparently abstract representative of the working class: 'a' Welsh iron-puddler. Section 2 reads:

> If it's the brunt of years and luck turned savage
> this is our last call, difficult coda
> to the facility, the bane of speech,
> a taint of richesse in the haggard seasons,
> withdrawing a Welsh iron-puddler's portion, his
> penny a week insurance cum burial fund,
> cashing in pain itself, stark induration,
> something saved for, brought home, stuck on the mantel,   (49)

Hill's 'difficult coda', far from academic elitism or conservative safeguard, allies itself with 'our' common work, money, and toil: the poet's address is a communal task, as well as inglorious quotidian effort. Verbal difficulty is not elevation. Rather it is an attack on false social smoothness, the glibness of making words, sentiments, and meanings easier, 'to satisfy one habit of the reader'. Not only will that glib poetic speaker 'keep *his* mind diverted' from resentment, he will keep his addressee in that state of diversion and repose: *your* mind is passive and inert, whilst 'the poem does its work' upon *you*. In contrast, Hill will not allow address to be comfortable activity, for *I* or *you*. His focus on difficulty demands that addressees perform their own work and hard graft: this *I* wields common 'pain' and 'stark indignation' as weapons against 'satisfy[ing] one habit of the reader'. This is one good reason—a reason grounded in appreciation of the reciprocity of civil address—for the apparent incivility with which many of Hill's later poems, particularly *The Triumph of Love* and *Speech! Speech!* have made their provoking addresses. There are comparable moments in *Treatise*: '(I've / cribbed Whitman, you stickler—short of a phrase)', 'Yes, to be blunt [...] / [...] you can scarcely hear this' (11; 3). In *Treatise*, such addresses are less openly vicious, but they do speak to that familiar '—Urge to unmake / all wrought finalities [...] / in the crowd's face—' (51).

In 'A Postscript', Hill observes:

> The Yeats who [...] seeks 'an image of the modern mind's discovery of its own permanent form' is like the Bradley who writes of 'the unbroken and self-complete Reality' and the Eliot who desiderates 'the timeless moment': each is angry in his opposition to that which is contrary, 'uneducated vulgar opinion', 'democratic bonhomie' [...] the quotidian litter of the rabble. (577)

The address of 'Coda', like 'Postscript', tartly redresses that 'hierarchical Toryism', that 'opposition to [...] the quotidian', which Hill argues reviles Yeats, Bradley, and Eliot. Hill argues that, in the arguments about poetry seeking after the 'mind's [...] own permanent form', 'unbroken and self-complete Reality', lies an attempt to suppress the critical voices of certain ('vulgar') audiences. In Hill, attentiveness to Baconian texts, or the sculptures and sketches of Ernst Barlach, or the prized texts of Elias Canetti, is not motivated by a haughty distaste for contrariety, or for one's 'uneducated' audience. In contrast, Yeats, Bradley, and Eliot have used rhetorical cadence to safeguard against a dangerous 'common' access, which they fear would lead to brokenness and contrariety. For Hill, this is a deliberate exclusion of the 'quotidian', and is motivated by an uninclusively ideological agenda, quite in spite of how hospitably 'diverted from resentment' their address might seem.

Taking Eliot's *Four Quartets* to task for just this fault in its attitude towards its readership, Hill writes:

> There remains the question of address. In writing of this kind the author addresses the topic, addresses himself and addresses either the faintly projected reader or some undefined group of dramatis personae who represent the 'you' of common humanity.[11]

For Hill, the poet and public speaker has a duty to keep his work in tune with (and highly alert to) the audience to which it is speaking. *You* may be a really existing reader, the subject of commemorative or vituperative address; *you* could be a colleague, a lover, Parliament, an assembled crowd, a Welsh puddler, God, or the nation. But *you* should not be a conveniently vague 'faintly projected reader' or some 'undefined group of dramatis personae who represent the "you" of general humanity'. Hill imagines his addresses as being, unlike Eliot, neither against common readers, nor an unprofessional, uninitiated public. In demanding of his addressee, 'You: [...] / [...] / [...] who are you to protest?', 'your rigidity and your abandonment, / your proud ignorance of doctrine', and in warning *you*, rudely, 'Don't overstretch it, asshole', Hill might be seen as railing against the false custodians of value, critical, spiritual, political.[12] These *you*s are the powerful intellects that either shut out common access, or attempt to dictate what form it should take: 'Orthodox arcane / interpreters of repute [...] / Why should I hear / further what you propose?'[13] Such addresses insist on the differences and the hostilities between the eclectic voices that comprise that altering body of *you*s.

---

[11] 'Word Value' *CCW* 540.
[12] *Triumph* 106:54; *SS* 89:45.
[13] 'Scenes with Harlequins', *Canaan* 21.

But Hill's invective addresses, though evidently not shutting out the 'quotidian litter' or the variety of 'contrary' voices are not always much more specific in their targets than Hill has accused Eliot of being. It is not always easy to see in, say, *Triumph*, or *Speech! Speech!* that Hill has avoided incorporating the voices of a rather 'undefined group of dramatis personae': '(*cat-calls*)', '(*jeers*)', 'cries of shame'. Nevertheless, Hill's envisaged audiences evidently do not always speak as 'one': the addressee is hardly a singular 'you of general humanity'. Addressing a rapidly changing medley of different *you*s, Hill's poems issue altering civil invitations to individual *you*s, common men, and communities of readers, insisting that each participates in the articulation of a communal heritage. Such work is not 'hierarchical Toryism', or a form of exclusive poetic contact, eager to shut out the 'vulgar'.

True enough, participation will be demanding: it will call for *your* sufficient attention to the civil history that comprises intellectual life. But that difficulty is shared by the poet: 'Unexchangeable password, I have yet / to find the place appointed', 'this confounds me and is worth the price'.[14] In Hill, *I* and *you* are often in it together, not just estranged and set apart. The poet's—and the common man's—speech comes from that rich, shared history, from important artworks, events, and memorials, from traditions of remembering and paying respect, from the working classes and aristocrats, from art's failures as well as its successes. Hill does not shut out common access: he insists such access is part of collective history. The addresses between Hill's *I* and *you* repeatedly struggle to resist those powerful custodians of popular opinion who attempt to dictate what should be read, heard, seen, by whom, and how. Also, Hill's addresses are often self-upbraiding: the public voice accosts itself as it does verbal battle with others. Hill's poetic speakers continually labour not to turn into an example of what they condemn, and must remain on their guard against their own and others' complaisance, coercion, false persuasion: 'don't tempt me, Tempter, demon overreacher, / or | nót in my own voice', 'I woúld be myself / [...] yet scarcely / recall what it wás I promised [...] / [...] damned liar that I am' (*SS* 112:56).

In Hill, the directness, the inviting intimacy of the second-person *you* of address ('I trust I shall greet you / [...] / instantly, and at my own expense', 'wísh I could draw you, / draw you so that you seem / not to be hiding, wísh I could draw you in') is counterposed by the coolness of language's own rebuttals (*Orchards* 62; *Comus* 34). Hill's invitation is also a demand that *you* participate in the hard graft of using words, negotiating verbal landmarks, and studying the histories and contexts of erudition:

[14] 'Ars' and 'From the Annals', both in *WT* 63; 77.

'You had sometimes said / that I project a show more / stressful than delightful', 'I desire you / to fathom what I mean. What dó I mean?' (*Orchards* 1; 54). That difficulty, as it has been termed, is also a compliment. It is testament to a society's capacity for intelligent thought, and a public, civil invitation. It is also the speaker's (and Hill's) personal and civil call to work out understandings *with* others. That plea for negotiation between *I* and *you* works against the assumption that thoughts only occur positively at the individual level, and are merely co-opted when occurring as part of the civil body: 'Knowledge [...] the self-embedded / body not ours', 'I trust the arbiter—that's difficult', 'The power-and-beauty mob has my bequest'.[15] It may be vigilance against one's own 'demon' tempter that is the hardest struggle to resist, since in a poet's very attempt to speak with you, 'he shows himself / open to a fault, shaken by others' weeping', susceptible to his wish for the applause of an audience (*SS* 118:59).

[15] 'Précis', in *Treatise* 28.

PART IV
DON PATERSON
On the Money

11

Address and Lyric Commerce

[W]hat I bring from Italy, I spend in England: here it remains, and here it circulates; for, if the coin be good, it will pass from one hand to another. I trade both with the living and the dead, for the enrichment of our native language. We have enough in England to supply our necessity; but, if we will have things of magnificence and splendour, we must get them by commerce.

Dryden, 'Dedication of the *Aeneid*'

Reward me for every poem recited to you;
For what panegyrists bring is but my poems repeated.
Leave off every voice but my voice;
Mine is the uttered cry, the others, echoes.

Abū al-Tayyib al-Mutanabbī

At the beginning of Don Paterson's poem 'The Reading', the poet's address impresses on auditors the long-standing interrelation of poetic and economic discourses:

The first time I came to your wandering attention
my name was Simonides. Poets,
whose air of ingratitude forms in the womb,
have reason at least to thank me:
I invented the thing you now call the commission.
[...]
                    But first to the theme
of this evening's address: the reading.
It was not a good poem, if I say so myself.
As good as the fee, though, and better
than him who that day bought my praises [...][1]

These interlocutions probe the relationships between poetic invention, literary dissemination, and reception. Speaking both to Paterson's own,

---

[1] 'The Reading', in *Light* 23

and to Simonides' Ancient Greek lyric audience, 'The Reading' flags up poets' vulnerability to listeners' whimsical attentions. *Your* 'wandering' concentration might be caught through a display of *I*'s dazzling lyric creativity ('thank me: / I invented'). But artistic security must be sustained through a quite different lyric 'invention': the literary 'commission'. Monetary concerns, as Paterson's address makes clear, are alive in the reception and creation of the twenty-first-century lyric poem—and in sixth-century BC court patronage. '[A]s good as the fee', 'better / than', 'not good', 'bought [...] praises': these tussles between commercial and aesthetic value occur between two *now*s of reading. Curiously double, 'this evening's address' ensures readers cannot forget their own hand and ear in ascribing value to the poem. Both those really receiving (and buying) Paterson's contemporary work, and those Ancient Greeks addressed by Simonides, are called out to and assailed by these interlocutions. These lines impress upon *you* how literary merit, taste, and value are negotiated not merely by the individual poet, addressee, or purchaser, but *with* 'live' readerships.

'I trade both with the living and the dead, for the enrichment of our native language', wrote Dryden, 'if the coin be good, it will pass from one hand to another'.[2] Dryden's address sought to justify the presence of the Italian lyric tongue in his translation of the *Aeneid*. '[T]rade', 'enrichment', 'coin', 'circulate': that 'Dedication' set out to persuade its readership that the English language could flourish and grow through the influence of the Italian (106). What's striking is Dryden's proud admission that 'I trade'. Rather than separating commercial and lyric vocabularies, the Restoration poet combines their energies. He *uses* talk of money to promote his work to interested parties; he employs coinage, trade, and circulation as enticing metaphors that persuade addressees of this 'magnificent' enrichment of the poetic tongue.

Given our proximity to the range of twentieth-century addresses that decry the contaminating influence of trade and commerce on the language, Dryden's proud declaration of his participation in lyric trade may seem surprising. We're likely to be familiar with Eliot's and Pound's accusatory addresses to a culture of capitalist *you*s—whom they accuse of trading and circulating poetry as a commodity (more on this in a moment).[3] We may also have been exposed to contemporary poets who rail against commerce. Jeremy Prynne's work, for instance, bombards readers with the dizzying registers of finance and labour: 'downward

---

[2] John Dryden, 'Dedication of the Aeneid', in *Discourses on Satire and Epic Poetry* (Middlesex: Echo Library, 2007) 106.

[3] See Pound, *Cantos* 45: 'with usura, sin against nature, / is thy bread ever more of stale rags', 229. See Eliot, 'Choruses from "The Rock"' (1934): 'I have given you power of choice, / and you only alternate / Between futile speculations and unconsidered action', in *ECP* 102.

rebate', 'money numbers ahead', 'banking on form', 'wired up / from the NCR cashpoint'.[4] If Prynne lambasts a culpable, plural *you*—'what you do is enslaved non-stop / to perdition of sense'—this poet too is implicated in what he describes: 'the control flow structure / [...] / [...] holding / our tongues like brevet clients on call' (323–4). Poetry is not a haven from the grubby world of commerce, but part of it. Comparably, the work of Barry MacSweeney accuses its lyric contemporaries of having lapse[d] into money greed and / awesome self-possession', and expresses its 'hatred of the tamed animals poets have become'.[5]

Contemporary poets perceive the relationship between commerce and poetry quite differently from their Reformation and early modern forebears. In the sixteenth and seventeenth centuries, literary valuation and circulation occurred within systems of patronage and courtly performance—rather differently from our commercial, book-buying world. Address was integral to the poem's negotiation of its value and the poet's social standing: the delivery of poetry to *you*s of high social standing was a socio-political act. Early modern poets may have been closely engaged in barter of the lyric word (*my* praise for *your* favour), but this is not 'money greed' or cold commerce in the contemporary sense. Such verbal trade is admired as the skilful staging of address, which offers critique and compliment to patrons. This way of speaking to *you* is alert to the poet's need to preserve his lyric livelihood through artistic labour—the right addresses to the right recipients—and his speeches are rewarded by *you* for the agility with which they negotiate their status, success, and courtly position.

Many contemporary writers and critics have viewed poetry and commerce as incompatible, or even as warring entities.[6] Yet these two have emerged as far more companionable conversational partners in the work

---

[4] J. H. Prynne, *The Oval Window* (1983), in *Poems* 316–25.

[5] Barry MacSweeney, 'Totem Banking', in *Wolf Tongue: Selected Poems 1965–2000* (Newcastle: Bloodaxe, 2003) 315.

[6] In discussions of contemporary poetry, critics often focus attention on commerce's determination of literary merit, circulation, and popularity—especially on how publishing bodies privilege certain kinds of poetic forms, lexicons, and traditions. See Peter Middleton, 'Institutions of Poetry in Postwar Britain', in *A Concise Companion to Postwar British and Irish Poetry*, ed. Nigel Alderman and C. D. Blanton (Chichester: Wiley-Blackwell) 243–63. Other critics argue literature should have a special form of intrinsic value discrete from market considerations. See Richard Seaford, *Money and the Early Greek Mind: Homer, Philosophy and Tragedy* (Cambridge: Cambridge University Press, 2004) 8. For more sympathetic accounts of commerce, literary circulation, money, and verbal creativity, see Nicky Marsh, *Money, Speculation and Finance in Contemporary British Fiction* (London: Continuum, 2007) introd.; Alec Marsh, *Money and Modernity: Pound, Williams and the Spirit of Jefferson* (Tuscaloosa: University of Alabama Press, 1998) 1–21; Georg Simmel, *The Philosophy of Money* (1900; London: Routledge, 1978) 510–11 and 150. Kevin Jackson, *The Oxford Book of Money* (Oxford: Oxford University Press, 1995) is a good resource.

economics ≠ money

of a number of poets we are now familiar with: W. S. Graham, C. H. Sisson, Geoffrey Hill…and now Don Paterson. Speaking about money matters with a range of different *you*s, Graham's impecuniousness (only just held at bay through his writing), leads him playfully to deploy money-grubbing addresses in the poems and letters—where the demand for cash, and good reception is made, by turns, bashfully and cheekily: 'Remember the title. A PRIVATE / POEM FOR NORMAN MACLEOD. / But this, my boy, is the poem/you paid me five pounds for', he writes.[7] 'Thank you. And for your applause […]' we find the poet addressing us, as if suavely orchestrating the attentions of his rapt public (a widespread applause he never secured in his lifetime).[8] The letters show Graham addressing close family and friends, and musing over how best to negotiate—and make mischief with—the economics and politics of the poetry industry and academia: the 'various deans, administers, fuckulty members'.[9] His letters contemplate how one's creativity may be affected by winning literary prizes (or hoping to), by accepting the security and constraints of institutional affiliation, and by courting and achieving success in the public fray—from literary reviewers, editors, academic and ordinary readers.[10]

C. H. Sisson's attention to the monetary aspect of the poetry world is far closer to the negative view of commerce seen in Eliot, Pound, and Prynne. 'I was led into captivity by the bitch business / […] / This is money at last without her night dress / Clutching you against her fallen udders and sharp bones', he writes, envisaging the modern scholar as a 'pot-bellied bankrupt / Naked upon the stage'.[11] Poems such as 'The Trade', 'Money', and *Fifteen Sonnets* show him using address to speak to *you* yearningly, retrospectively, about a world in which 'trade' and lyricism are separate registers and acts, and denouncing a 'they' that produce art for fame and profit.[12] His late volume, *What and Who* (1980) repeatedly denounces a 'they' that produce art for fame and profit. Whilst Sisson's classically minded addresses are often occupied by the interlocutions of Greek and Roman love poetry, they tend not to place these within more public courtly contexts. Not dissimilarly, the addresses that display Sisson's early modern sensibility (say, 'Letter to John Donne', 'The Garden of the Hesperides') put us in touch with poets who wrote in service of particular patrons, but infrequently attend to the economic pressures

---

[7] Graham, 'Private Poem to Norman Macleod', *NCP* 227.
[8] Graham, 'Enter a Cloud', *NCP* 218.
[9] Letter to Bill and Gail Featherstone, 4 December 1973, *Nightfisherman* 270.
[10] See Letter to Charles Monteith, 29 March 1974, *Nightfisherman* 277.
[11] Sisson, 'Money' (1961), in *CP* 34; Sisson, 'At An International Conference' (1961), in *CP* 27.
[12] Sisson, *CP* 448; 34; 405–12.

structuring their lyric work—even when these alliances directed their speaking to *you*.[13]

Hill's public addresses 'To the High Court of Parliament', his allusions to Milton's *Comus*, his use of Wordsworth's *The Convention of Cintra*, energetically realize commerce's structuring presence in the history of lyric language, as well as its resonance in the poet's civic address to contemporary *you*s: readers, critics, editors, poets, politicians, friends, and lovers.[14] Hill attends to art as weighted, often problematically bound to processes of commercial circulation and production—for profit, consumption, broadcast, and recognition in the public fray. For Hill, the successful poet should wield his verbal power responsibly, policing his use of the poetic word to rapt audiences: 'Curtain, before you hear the applause'.[15] Such address reminds *you* of the poet's flawed attempts to remain vigilant about his participation in today's forms of economic patronage—even as it alerts readers to the rich history of money's interplay with the production of the written word. Hill's interlocutions sing of patronage, coinage, public duty, and audience-negotiation. The address of *Mercian Hymns*, for instance, casts the speaker as a praise-poet publicly honouring the medieval King Offa (however tongue-in-cheek Hill's tone): 'King of the perennial holly-groves', 'overlord of the M5', 'saltmaster: money- / changer: commissioner for oaths': ' "I liked that," said Offa, "sing it again" ' (*HCP* 105).

Each of these poets uses address to pull the lyric voice into contact with slippery public and private *you*s. Each reminds his readership of money's powerful negotiations of our lyric relations with the poem. Lyric address is not a private or commercially innocent act. In reading Graham, Sisson, and Hill—and most clearly of all, in reading Paterson—one is accosted by the diverse ways in which the poem that says *you* articulates the fraught relationships between personal and social, private and public, aesthetic and commercial demands.

What's interesting about Paterson's work is that it uses address explicitly to listen back (not unfavourably) on a range of historical contexts in which patron-systems operate: his ear close to the money-minded interlocutions of Ancient Greek, Roman, and medieval Arabic courtly culture, Paterson's hailings persuade historical and contemporary *you*s to listen, barter, and buy. Moving between address at the medieval court, to the reader at Waterstones, and to attendees at the contemporary poetry

---

[13] Sisson, *CP* 50; 255.
[14] Hill, 'To the High Court of Parliament', in *Canaan* (London: Penguin, 1996); see Hill, *Scenes from Comus*); Hill, *Triumph* 70:36.
[15] Hill, *SS* 2:1, and epigraph 2 to this volume: 'VORHANG, BEVOR DU DEN BEIFALL BEGREIFST' (Günter Grass).

reading, Paterson's poems invite their readers into intimate exchange-relations with poets and readers across the ages. These addresses tune us in to the economic considerations of the *I*s and *you*s of classical and medieval lyric patronage, as well as those of our own contemporary cultural situatedness.

This chapter considers contemporary poetry that speaks to *you* in ways that ingeniously negotiate its reception; lyrics that use address to attend closely to the success-securing bent of poetry's public intimacies. To focus on Paterson is to apply critical pressure to our emerging sense of the poet as a (compromised) media presence—a figure who delivers public lectures, gives interviews, appears on radio broadcasts, and turns up in the pages of *The Guardian*. That sense of the poet's uneasy social function emerged most forcefully in the previous section on Hill, and it arose too, in less explicit forms, in our explorations of Graham and Sisson. Paterson is a very different poet from Hill: he works not in the Poundian tradition of overlapping and interpenetrating fragmented voices, or with the long sequential lyric form, but much more closely with the accessibility of tone, and the short lyric form that is reminiscent of Larkin. Yet like Hill, Paterson's address repeatedly projects itself into, and shows itself manipulating, a future in which contact with more receptive *you*s than it has yet secured will take place.

> The king though was silent. My lyric economies
> had not, so it seemed, gone unnoticed.
> [...]
> every eye turned on me, narrowed – at which point
> I thought it a smart move to drop it.

> However, I fixed each man's face in my mind,
> each man at his rank at the table
> (that trick of mine; your coupons, O my rapt listeners,
> I'll have nailed by the end of this poem).[16]

'I'll have nailed', 'O my rapt listeners': making that future moment of reception a part of *this* printed page, Paterson underlines how performing for *you* shapes the poem under construction. These self-reflexive lines gesture towards the ancient and contemporary audiences that receive lyric work, pay for it, neglect or distort it: they are highly aware that lyric success depends on making canny socio-economic moves in front of listening bodies. If *you* choose to ignore the poet's 'lyric economies', he will be forced to make the 'smart move'—to save face, and 'drop it'. The poem's performance and positive reception depends upon *I* carefully attending to

---

[16] Paterson, 'The Reading', *Light* 24.

the responses of listening *yous*, and fashioning the poem minute-by-minute, in response to them. Yet Paterson's speaker is more than just humbly attentive to his gathered audience: his lyric response to being aggressively scrutinized ('every eye turned on me, narrowed') is to level a more dangerous gaze (and threat) in return: 'I fixed each man's face in my mind', 'your coupons [faces] [...] / I'll have nailed [memorized] by the end of this poem'. 'Coupons' is Scots for 'faces', from the receipt that is regularly 'punched'. Paterson's poet is not only eyeballing his audience in return. He is also issuing an off-stage address that threatens to take this ungenerous audience, fixed in his memory, home with him, and to demand—by force if necessary—*your* closer attention. Paterson's poem brings warring discourses into contact in ways that underline their potential for momentarily mutual—although evidently uneasy and confrontational—companionship. This is work that stages unlikely encounters between the tones of audience-manipulation, the lexicons of lyric commerce, and the alarmingly intimate rhythms of address.

Paterson is an editor, publisher, scholar, and musician, as well as a poet and aphorist. He has worked as Poetry Editor for Picador Macmillan for over fifteen years, and as a Creative Writing Lecturer (now Professor of Poetry) at the University of St Andrews since 2002. He is Vice-President of the Poetry Society and a Fellow of the Royal Society of Literature. Paterson has published critical essays—most notable, and controversial, is 'The Lyric Principle', which appeared in two parts in *Poetry Review*. He has edited a number of anthologies of poems, including *101 Sonnets*, *Robert Burns*, *New British Poetry*, and *Last Words*, and published a critical commentary on Shakespeare's sonnets.[17] He is also a media presence, often appearing on the pages of *The Guardian*, and in frequent attendance at literary festivals (more than eight in 2010).[18] Paterson is invited not just to give poetry readings, but to speak about publishing (he talked on a panel of poet-publishers, with Michael Schmidt and Peter Fallon, at the Contemporary British and Irish Poetry Conference 2010, at Queen's University, Belfast), to lead workshops on writing poetry, and to contribute to public discussion of poetry's status in contemporary culture: 'What is the Future of Poetry?'.[19] As well as having received a number of prestigious literary prizes (three Forward Prizes, the Faber Memorial Prize, two T. S. Eliot Prizes, the Whitbread Prize for Poetry), Paterson is also on the panel of judges for the Picador Poetry Prize.

---

[17] Paterson, *Reading Shakespeare's Sonnets.*
[18] See 'My Hero Bog Moog', *The Guardian*, Review, Saturday 19 January 2010, 5; 'My Other Life', *The Observer*, Review, Sunday 20 December 2009, 24.
[19] 'What is the Future of Poetry?', *The Guardian*, G2. Friday 18 June 2010, 4.

These are public roles and duties that inform the concerns, idioms, and graceful rhythms of the poetry—and they emerge most clearly in Paterson's addresses. Speaking to *you*, Paterson's work returns to and circles round its structuring in the contemporary poetry industry. (We see this in 'The Reading', 'A Talking Book', 'The Book at Bedtime', as well as in Paterson's frequent asides: '*Maybe they'll have free admission*', '*this library book / is already long overdue; hand it back*', 'the dead verse and its readership / have lives [...] of their own'.)[20] This is a poetry informed by a sharp appreciation of its grounding in the workaday world in which literary documents are produced, circulated, read, bought, and reviewed. In this cacophonous space the contemporary poet writes—and finds *you* reading, or consuming, or mangling—his brilliantly inventive work. As we saw in 'The Reading', Paterson's *you*—half-imagined, half-recalled from the many readings he gives across the UK and the US—is a presence very much in mind. Startlingly live and direct, Paterson's address stages meetings with *you* 'here' in the bookshop, 'now' at the poetry reading, on 'this' page of his printed poem. These accessible, commercially minded conversations flag up their common verbal and physical ground with *you*.

In his editor's introduction to *New British Poetry*, Paterson identifies his poetry with a lyric 'Mainstream' that 'see[s] the reader as equal collaborator in the creation of the poem'.[21] Putting the case for equity more forcefully, Paterson adds that 'the poem is an act of collusion' (*NBP* xxx). In this context, 'collusion' is an instructive, though not an entirely felicitous term: it suggests a body of invited addressees, pitted against marginalized or silenced others. One wonders who or what might be left out of this conspiratorial address. There are echoes of Geoffrey Hill's warnings about language as an instrument of political 'coercion', where address's very inclusivity can be wielded against particular groups of *yous*. Hill's 'compleasance', which listens back to Hobbes, is also within earshot ('Circumstances', *CCW* 179). First, in a contemporary poet's temptation primarily to address a community of like-minded writers, whose mutual interests preserve a particular tradition—the 'Mainstream' for instance—at the expense of others. Second, in the sense that a writer is often tempted to be complaisant towards a body of his most loyal readers, whom he desires will continue celebrating his work.

Yet Paterson is far from deaf to, or unmindful of, resistant critical voices: 'The charge of being clever, coy or cute / I will not even bother to

---

[20] 'The Book at Bedtime', *Light* 54; 'The Alexandrian Library', *Nil Nil* 33; 'Paradoxes', *Eyes* 26.
[21] Paterson, *New British Poetry*, Introduction xxix.

refute', he writes in *Landing Light*, winning aural pleasure from the full rhyme, even as he shoulders the criticism.[22] Paterson is adept at simultaneously accepting and deftly debunking (if not also slyly 'refuting') *your* 'charges' against him. In the aphorism too, he often manages self-critically to get in before *you* do, and more amusingly and unsparingly than *you* could:

> can I please refer you to the afterword of the previous book, where you will find that your cynicism and distaste has not only been fully anticipated but outstripped by the author's own.[23]

Given his double-edged playfulness, Paterson's audience 'collaboration' and aesthetic 'collusion' seem more akin to Graham's account of the poem as an exhilaratingly fraught meeting place (than, say, to Hill's account, which expresses concerns about the coercions of obsequious auditors). Paterson's lyric spaces aren't filled with applauding literary audiences, but with alarming beasts, gaps, voids, mistakes, and demanding muses. Like Hill, however, as well as Graham and Sisson, Paterson's poems take shape as a nexus of speaking potentials where *I* and *you*, reader and writer, meet and mingle: each of these writers resists the notion that the poem is *first* the possession of isolated writer, *then* reader. Paterson's collaboration and collusion show how each poem is shared with a medley of tetchy, critical interlocutors—it is not the lonely statement of an inviolable *I*.

To this already intricate interlocutive weave—which combines the wish to offer resistance to the demands of antagonistic *you*s, and the desire to sing with and for a live readership—Paterson adds another strand; that of lyric's collusion with the demanding voices of commerce. When Paterson writes that equal collaboration with readers prompts 'a special relationship [...] where its truest commerce will take place', he puts to work yet another—economic—metaphor for readerly contact, and again insists on the poem as mutual voicing (*NBP* xxxv). In 'truest commerce', *I* and *you* negotiate the poem's value; they haggle in the book-buying, poetry-reading world.

I think there are too many uneasily jostling terms here: 'truest commerce', 'collaboration', 'collusion', which rather muddle the argument. But what is clear is that, for Paterson, the really valuable poem builds not passive complaisance but complexity and challenge into its publicly inflected 'special relationship' with readers. Speaking to *you* is 'an act of human courtesy', as Paterson puts it in *New British Poetry* (xxx). For address invites in real audiences; it addresses us, courteously: 'Let me

---

[22] 'A Talking Book', *Light* 27.
[23] 'A Talking Book', *Light* 27; Don Paterson, *The Blind Eye: A Book of Late Advice* (London: Faber, 2007) 73.

introduce you', 'consider this', and politely explains: 'I say "soul", but [...] I mean, reader, mine -'.[24] Paterson's address also issues bracing demands on those readers. It calls on *you* to participate in a 'confrontation with the line' of poetry (*NBP* xxx). This is a lyricism that—like Graham's—cheekily ushers an audience in, and resists sycophantically conforming to their expectations.

Resistance, it turns out, can make Paterson's poetry feel quite the opposite of courteous. Even at the writing table, Paterson appears to have real communities of addressees in mind, as well as the need to buck their book-buying assumptions. One early instance occurs in 'An Elliptical Stylus'—from Paterson's first volume, *Nil Nil*—where his poet-figure anticipates that readers will want him 'to cauterize this fable / with something axiomatic'.[25] The expectation is bluntly rejected: 'he can well afford to make his *own* / excuses, you your own interpretation' (21). The volume too ends by sending *you* off with a brusque dismissal: '*In short, this is where you get off reader*'; a second-person address that deftly allies intimacy and unexpected rudeness.[26] The reader is told in no uncertain terms to disembark from Paterson's poetic craft ('*you get off*'), in a phrase that addresses *you* directly, even as it punningly allies *your* appetite for continued poetic enjoyment with (denied) sexual gratification. Such lyric speech is alert to the knowledge that it cannot afford either to be entirely unmindful of, or too subservient to, the demands of the marketing, publishing, anthologizing industries that are part and parcel of writing for a contemporary *you*.

'His publisher, Faber, is billing *Rain* as his "most direct"', writes Colin Waters, 'as if his previous volumes had been written in some sort of Rwandan dialect. They're onto something, though.'[27] What Faber is at least in part 'onto' is the contemporary marketability of lyric address's 'directness' and accessibility. A poet today that allows his work to be read as a direct expression of personal feeling (whether or not it is) is likely to get on well with *you*. As readers' blogs (on Amazon for instance) show, those poems which invite audiences to witness their honesty and private feeling are most often lauded by readerships today. Readers often comment on both qualities in Paterson, and especially in *Landing Light* and *Rain*. The former has been praised as 'memorable because it is so truthful in its emotion [...] direct, formally inventive,

---

[24] 'A Talking Book', *Light*; 'Phantom', *Rain* 53; 'The Book at Bedtime', *Light* 53.
[25] Paterson, *Nil Nil* 21.
[26] 'Nil Nil', in *Nil Nil* 53.
[27] From Colin Waters, 'Don Paterson Lingers in the Rain', *Herald Scotland*, 31 August 2009, Arts & Ents <http://www.heraldscotland.com/arts-ents/book-features/don-paterson-lingers-in-the-rain-1.825492>.

and intrusively private. "The Wreck" is one of the most searingly honest poems I've read about a relationship [...].'[28] Another fan writes that Paterson's *Rain* is: 'A wonderful collection. Profound and moving, but readable from beginning to end, and back again [...] [it] has provoked lively dissention among friends about just how bleak or hopeful his world-view is.'[29] Concessions have been made by readers too, even when the work is initially 'difficult': 'A couple of pieces are in Scottish brogue but easy to decipher, especially with vocabulary at the bottom of the page of one poem. Fairly easy to comprehend upon a second reading of each poem.'[30] So too, on reading the earlier collection, *God's Gift to Women*, one reader comments: 'Very bleak, this vision, but such searing honesty, such burning truth within.'[31]

Even the less appreciative reviews of Paterson that have been penned tend to exemplify this trend. Reservations about the poetry tend to focus on its tendency to 'remain unyielding even if readers have tracked down all the references [...]', and this 'unyielding' difficulty is often associated with the philosophical, historical, and allusive textures of the poems.[32] Catherine Woodward provides us with an extreme example of this reaction when she launches an attack on Paterson's 'versified dull philosophy', and his 'stepping in and out of borrowed voices that didn't fit'.[33] 'What I resent [...] is the work and humiliation that was required of me', Woodward complains. By these lights, the perceived difficulty of contemporary poetry is a deliberate rebuff to the reader, designed to make *you* feel 'humiliated'. But as we have seen, both Paterson's arguments in the prose, and the intimate address of his poems, make clear that the 'work' that such poems call for from their reader have little to do with Woodward's sense of 'required' humiliation.[34]

[28] Customer review on Amazon website for *Light*, Dr V. I. Cregan-reid 'vybarr' (London), 6 July 2009 <http://www.amazon.co.uk/Landing-Light-Don-Paterson/dp/0571220649/ref=pd_sim_b_1>, accessed 11 October 2010.

[29] Mr B, Scotland, on *Rain*, customer review on Amazon website, accessed 11 October 2010.

[30] Rui Carlos da Cunha, On *Rain*, Good Reads, 20 July 2010 <http://www.goodreads.com/book/show/7277457-rain>, accessed 14 October 2010.

[31] In contrast, for a marketing strategy targeted at a rather different assumed readership, see *The London Review of Books*. The website markets Paterson's *Landing Light* as a 'collection [that] ably demonstrates both his prodigious formal gifts and his sure-footed command of a dizzying range of reference' <http://www.lrbshop.co.uk/landing-light_17.html>, accessed 11 October 2010.

[32] Alan Brownjohn, Review of *Landing Light*, *Sunday Times*, 23 November 2003 <http://www.scottishpoetryreview.com/reviews/rain.htm>, accessed 9 October 2010.

[33] Review of *Rain*, *Eleutheria—The Scottish Poetry Review* 2 (2010) <http://www.scottishpoetryreview.com/home.htm>, accessed 9 October 2010.

[34] Geoffrey Hill writes, in *Treatise*: 'But think on: that which is difficult / preserves democracy; you pay respect / to the intelligence of the citizen' (47).

Critics and reviewers have almost unanimously responded with enthusiasm to Paterson's poetry, and especially to the most recent collections. Praise tends to focus on the balance between the lyrics' no-nonsense directness and their sensuous appeal, and on Paterson's fresh juxtapositions of perspectives, idioms, and rhythms: 'he appropriates the jargon of electronic sound sculpture into his poetry "ring-modulated sound-bursts"—in a winning way [which] also tells us we are in the presence of an expert', writes Nicholas Lezard, reviewing *Rain*, in *The Guardian*.[35] With a not dissimilar mixture of praise and enthusiasm, I. E. Sawmill in *The Literateur Magazine* comments: 'the assumed tone throughout is personable and familiar, fallible and very self-aware, especially regarding the poet's role as communicator [...] the poem never emerges as solipsistic or written for any coterie. It is engaging for a universal readership. [...] Their approachability is undeniable.'[36]

Evidently, Paterson's mediated lyricism and his allusive addresses carefully avoid alienating the majority of his auditors. This is at least in part because his poetry's more needling, philosophical, and formally playful interlocutions remain in close contact with addresses of winsome invitation: 'Welcome [...]!', he writes at the beginning of 'A Talking Book': 'a big hi!', 'shake yourself awake, and please stay patient'. In these lines, audience greetings are infused with a wilfully tongue-in-cheek cataloguing of commercial vocabularies and processes, and his readers' uncomfortable complicity in them. Such 'welcome' is addressed:

> to those precisians on the proper route,
> who have diligently ploughed this far on foot
> by way of bastard title, biog note
> acknowledgements and prefatory quote;
>
> (*Light* 26–7)

The book's pages gratefully speak to all 'those' who have persisted, ploughing through the necessary blurb, paratextual material, and publishing paraphernalia to get to the poem itself. Simultaneously, the talking book uses address to poke fun at its readers' attempts to juggle economic and aesthetic values in the book-buying experience:

> to those undecided shades in Waterstones,
> trapped between the promise and the cost;
> [...]
> all set to prove the Great Beast lies at slumber

---

[35] Nicholas Lezard, Review of *Rain*, *Guardian*, Books, Saturday 31 July 2010.

[36] I. E. Sawmill, *The Literateur Magazine*, 26 November 2009 <http://www.literateur.com/archives/2034>, accessed 9 October 2010.

in the ISBN or the barcode number;
[…]
Relax! […]

(*Light* 26)

The effect is that of playful self-mockery about the literary economics that negotiate not just how books are produced, marketed, and sold, but how *I* and *you* meet on the page (and how *I* earns his lyric bread). Again, the ghost of another poetry reading, or public book-signing, is present in the title and opening lines (the online 'diary' on Paterson's website reveals just how often he appears at such events).

Such address is neither a cynical lyric resignation to market pressures, nor a capitulation to the coercions of the poetry industry: 'Such is your human love', Paterson's work insists, 'you have my word', 'stay with me' (*Light* 28–31). His interlocutions bring together both the intimate cultural-historical power of address ('you will stand before […] / […] / […] the road that gets you lost / and the one boldly eschewed by Robert Frost, / Scheherazade's forever and a night / or the numbered days of Sodom'), and poetry's economic and institutional situatedness: 'Waterstones', 'the ISBN', 'the academy's swift and unannounced inspection' (*Light* 26–9). Collusion, in this sense, is both resistance to and affiliation with both the ancient and modern interlocutors of lyric tradition, and the literary-commercial world that mediates literary relations with past and present *you*s.

On the one hand, then, there are numerous similarities between the concerns of Paterson's prose and lyric work, especially in his prose iterations of poetry's dependence on economic factors. On the other, there is some discord between the *tone* of the editorial work, and his more lyric poetry. The addresses of Paterson's most celebrated collections move with a breathtaking lyricism that might appear to promise escape from the socio-economic concerns and pragmatic concerns raised in the prose. In reading *Orpheus*, for instance, there is little sense that *you* need to be aware that '[s]election as a Quarterly Choice doubles or triples the sales of most poetry books', or to recognize that 'the poetry-book-buying public has long been a tiny minority':[37]

The Drinking Fountain

O tireless giver, holy cataract,
conductor of the inexhaustible One –
your clear tongue, lifting through the mask of stone
you hold before your face…Behind you, aqueducts

---

[37] Paterson and Brown, eds., *Don't Ask Me What I Mean* introd. xiii; xxii.

vanish into the distance. From the Apennine
foothills, through the wheat fields and the graveyards,
they bear the sacred utterance, the words
that arrive for ever, blackening your chin

to fall into the basin that lies rapt
to your constant murmur, like a sleeping ear.
Marmoreal circumstance. Listening rock.

An ear of Earth's, so she only really talks
to herself. So when we're filling up our pitcher,
it feels to her that someone interrupts.[38]

This is intimate address indeed—as Paterson's 'O' of personal voicing, his typography of desired unity with the 'tireless giver' ('One'), and his address to a closely physically registered 'you' ('your clear tongue', 'your face') attest.

Yet the poem's voicing of *you* is not unattuned to the social relations between lack and excess, gift and barter. Paterson's address is highly alert to the difference between the language that is freely given by 'your clear tongue', and that which is humanly traded; plagued by babble, interruption, and misinterpretation. The lyricist's tarnished human speech comes in contrast to water's unrestricted, generous plenty. Whilst the fountain's words arrive as gifts, giving tirelessly, with no sense of restriction or measure ('the basin [...] lies rapt / to your constant murmur'), the poet can hardly be sure of his own 'rapt' reception. The poet-figure is all too aware of the 'tired' in 'tireless', the 'exhaustion' in 'inexhaustible'. Where *your* lips 'bear the sacred utterance', he finds 'words / [...] blackening your chin'.

Orpheus, Paterson's sequence of ingenious 'versions' on Rilke's *Sonnets to Orpheus*, is shot through with moments in which lyric language is quite evidently no 'clear tongue'. In 'Praising', for instance:

Praising, that's it! One appointed to praise –
he came like the ore from the stone,
                    [...] a tireless press
for that wine, eternal to man.

His voice never dries or fails when the divine
grips him to pour from his mouth –
[...]

Nothing can prove him untrue when he sings:
not the mould on the tombs of the kings,
nor the gods' shadowfall.[39]

---

[38] Paterson, 'The Drinking Fountain', *Orpheus* 45. Referred to as 'Fountain'.
[39] Paterson, 'Praising', *Orpheus* 9.

Paterson's poet rejoices in singing his praise-lyrics—'that's it!', 'a tireless press', 'His voice never [...] fails'—even as the poem makes clear he may also be a victim of his 'appointed' compulsion to praise, and to go on praising. Should one pity the lyricist's hunger to comply with an audience's 'eternal' demand for lyric offerings? True, Paterson's poet is subject to godly violence—and bodily passivity—when 'the divine / *grips* him to pour from his mouth'. But he also delights in the divinely transformative effect of that violence. Now he too has become 'tireless' like the addressed fountain. He is also 'gripped'. Filled with free-flowing, gift-giving language, 'his voice never dries or fails', 'nothing can prove him untrue when he sings'.

Talk of proof, as with talk of appointment, returns us to more earthbound anxieties. Is the poet really beyond reproach, or only unable to be proven untrue as long as his divine lyric wine flows? Will evidence be gathered against him when he is no longer 'gripped'; when the song ceases? The poet's longing to issue and to receive praise from *you* is coupled with a longing to go on being gripped by poetry and by listening auditors, and this language is haunted by a sense of the culpability of that longing.

'Praising, that's it! One appointed to praise –'. To be appointed to 'praise' is to be closely bound up with the politics of lyric patronage. This 'appointment', historically speaking, is not a far cry from the lyric day-job, as poets as far back as Simonides—the first poet to receive remuneration for his services at court—were all too aware. Paterson's address recalls the interlacings of praise, barter, and the economies of the patron–client system of Ancient Greek and Roman cultural life—where poems were commissioned, composed, and performed as part of a system of social exchange predicated on duty, gift-giving, and mutual obligation with patrons.[40] His use of *you* also directs us to the resonance of lyric praise and barter across a range of medieval and modern European, Middle Eastern, classical, and Asian cultures, as well as the twentieth-century lyricism of Antonio Machado and Rilke (see Paterson's collections of 'versions', *The Eyes* and *Orpheus*). The moving intimacies of these volumes' addresses are far from unmindful of the socio-economic literary precedents shaping

---

[40] See Barbara K. Gold, *Literary Patronage in Greece and Rome* (Chapel Hill: University of North Carolina Press, 1987); Seaford, *Money and the Early Greek Mind*; Mary Whitby, ed., *The Propaganda of Power: The Role of Panegyric in Late Antiquity* (Leiden and Boston: Brill, 1998). In Ancient Greek and Roman culture, the patron might bestow money, dinner, and security at court in return for the delivery of panegyric. If poets were often seen to be under the patron's thumb, their addresses also gave them alarming power over those they praised. Panegyric could bring criticism—even ruin—as well as fame to wealthy *yous*. The public praise dutifully offered by the poet is coupled with the delivery of potential threat to the patron.

contemporary poetry's interlocutions. Paterson's historical sensitivity to *you*, and his registering of the contexts of lyric patronage, praise, and public reception that inform the speech of his forebears, subtly negotiates readers' responses, so that earlier writers' audience-negotiations are played back to and redoubled for a contemporary British audience:

> I want neither glory
> nor that, in the memory
> of men, my songs survive;
> but still... those subtle worlds
> those weightless mother-of-pearl
> soap-bubbles of mine... I just love
> the way they set off all tarted up
> in sunburst and scarlet, hover
> low in the blue sky, quiver
> then suddenly pop[41]

'Poem' is a variation on the first lyric of Machado's 'Proverbios y Cantares' (translated as 'Fourteen Poems from "Moral Proverbs and Folk Songs"'), in which the Spanish poet spoke against worldly recognition of his work: 'I never wanted fame, / nor wanted to leave my poems / behind in the memory of men'.[42] Bringing the quietly humble reservations of Machado's poet ('I never wanted') into the more demandingly self-aware present tense ('I want'), Paterson's later lyric cunningly emphasizes *I*'s awareness of 'my poems' as deserving 'fame' and furtherance in 'the memory of men', whether or not *I* asks for it.

'[T]hose subtle worlds', as Paterson's version gently emphasizes, are surely deserving of 'glory' and should 'survive'. All the more so as the modest poet-figure is not seeking glory, fame, or reward. Nor is *I* aggressively coaxing them from *you* (unlike, say, Simonides). Yet of course, false modesty (more developed in Paterson's poem than Machado's) is also a means of winning audience praise, through the very lines that seem loath

---

[41] 'Poem', *Eyes* 27.

[42]

> I never wanted fame,
> nor wanted to leave my poems
> behind in the memory of men.
> I love the subtle worlds,
> delicate, almost without weight
> like soap bubbles.
> I enjoy seeing them take the colour
> of sunlight and scarlet, float
> in the blue sky, then
> suddenly quiver and break.

From Machado, *Times Alone* 107.

to ask for it: 'I want neither glory', 'nor that, [...] / my songs survive'. Paterson's lines hint that poets might really want both, when *I* adds, as if raising an objection to his own humility: *'but still...'*. 'Poem' continues, after this ellipsis: 'they set off all tarted up'. Who are *you* to turn a blind eye to this colourful display?

Paterson's richly intertextual work scatters in time and space the speakers and recipients of lyric messages, channelling, inscribing, reinscribing, and broadcasting earlier negotiations of lyric reception and 'glory'. This focuses *your* ear on the currents of mediation and production that shape the taste by which literary texts are, and have been, enjoyed. Such lyricism impresses upon audiences that the enthusiastically received poem can fail to live on 'in the memory / of men': the poet's reputation depends upon changeable, inconstant auditors. In Paterson, the apparently atemporal lyric desire to persist in *your* mind is interlaced with cannily place-bound, economic and rhetorical considerations. Paterson's attentiveness to the politics of audience reception, and particularly his tendency to interrupt the poem to speak to readers, listens back on Dante's negotiations of the politics of lyric speech in fourteenth-century Verona and Rome—negotiations that made use of arrestingly plain-speaking addresses:

> Think, reader, if this beginning
> went no further how keenly thou
> wouldst crave to know the rest,[43]

'Think, reader', 'Thou would'st desire to know'. Paterson's work speaks with a similarly striking immediacy: 'Listen to this', 'By all means, turn the page or close the book', 'shake yourself awake'. These are utterances that manipulate the complex relationships between poet and audience, purchasers and patrons with well-judged plainness. Paterson's straight-talking, historically inflected addresses remind us of writers' frequent need to win *your* good grace in order to survive and prosper. Even when speaking to *you* seems to be primarily private hailing, it is often used as a means of graciously negotiating the writer's public status. Talk of 'gifts', 'returns', and barter return upon the verbal terrain of Paterson's intimate addresses:

[43] Alighieri Dante, *Paradiso*, trans. John O. Sinclair (Oxford: Oxford University Press, 1961) 5:109–11. See also Dante's often neglected address to his patron, Can Grande della Scala, the ruler of Verona. The oration salutes its addressee as 'magnificent' and 'most victorious' (a public gesture that requests official promotion of the work by his patron, in expressing formal gratitude for the bounty he has received from his patron). The poem's address functions both as gift and request (that Can Grande will fund Dante to write the *Paradiso*). See N. R. Havely, *Dante* (Oxford: Wiley-Blackwell, 2007) 46; Jeremy Tambling, *Allegory* (London: Taylor and Francis, 2009) 26–35.

Dear son, I was *mezzo del cammin*
and the true path was as lost to me as ever
when you cut in front and lit it as you ran.
See how the true gift never leaves the giver:
returned and redelivered, it rolled on[44]

Speaking to *you* is, of course, private matter here: the lines are directed specifically towards my 'Dear son'. But as these lines make clear, the poet's address is not exclusive. Paterson's address negotiates more than one kind of writerly 'true gift', as Dante's did before him. Another *you* ghosts the lyric, behind and beside the declared address. For Dante's *Commedia* is also a gift to Paterson that not only shows him a lyric 'true path', but has also 'cut in front and lit it'. Dante's poetical work is a gift that 'never leaves the giver', that, in the specificity of its utterance, is picked up, used, 'returned and redelivered' by the contemporary poet, and still rolls on.[45]

A comparably complex sound effect of return and re-delivering is heard in Paterson's early poem, 'Candlebird'.[46] Paterson's lyric is written 'after Abbas Ibn Al-Ahnaf', the medieval Arabic poet whose *ghazals* (erotic-elegiac poems, often on the theme of lethal love) won him his place as favourite at the court of Harun Al-Rashid.[47] Like the address of Ibn Al-Ahnaf's source text, which sings of the tortuous demands of patronage and love in the Abbasid lyric tradition, Paterson's 'Candlebird' exhibits a disturbing and violent negotiation of courtly customs, panegyric, and love poetry, even as it speaks with arresting immediacy to a *you* that it calls out to, with Borgesian doubling:

CANDLEBIRD

after Abbas Ibn al-Ahnaf, c.750

If, tonight, she scorns me for my song,
You may be sure of this: within the year
Another man will say this verse to her
And she will yield to him for its sad sweetness.

' "*Then I am like the candlebird*," ' he'll continue,
After explaining what a candlebird is,

---

[44] Paterson, 'Waking with Russell', *Light* 5.

[45] We see such sensitivity too, in the praise-poetry of the early modern poets—Donne, Marvell, Herrick—and later again in the nineteenth century, in, say, Tennyson's role as Poet Laureate.

[46] Paterson, 'Candlebird', *Gift* 55.

[47] Abbas Ibn Al-Ahnaf, *Birds Through an Alabaster Ceiling: Three Abyssinian Poets—Arab Poetry of the Abbasid Period*, trans. G. B. H. Wightman Abudlla Udhari, and A. Y. Al-Udhari (Harmondsworth: Penguin, 1975).

> ' "*Whose lifeless eyes see nothing and see all,*
> *Lighting their small room with my burning tongue;*
>
> *His shadow rears above her on the wall*
> *As hour by hour, I pass into the air.*"
> Take my hand. Now tell me: flesh or tallow?
> Which I am tonight, I leave to you.'
>
> So take my hand and tell me, flesh or tallow.
> Which man I am tonight I leave to you.

Stepping into another lover's (and lyricist's) shoes to re-sound his lines, Paterson opens up an echo-chamber of past and present voices, illuminations and yieldings, underspecified *I*s and *you*s, reported speeches, italicizations, quotations within quotations, and poems-within-poems. When Paterson writes 'If tonight she scorns me for my song / You may be sure of this [...]', he is listening back on Ibn Al-Ahnaf's *ghazal*:

> You scorn me when I speak to you,
> Yet lovers who quote my verse succeed.
> I've become a candle thread destined
> To light a room for other men
> While burning away into thin air   (36)

Mischievously delivering new levels of intertextual circularity, 'Candlebird' reinforces the hint, implicit in Ibn Al-Ahnaf, that lovers, like courtly poets, engage in literary thefts and plagiarisms in trading vows to win *your* attention. Paterson's poem-within-a-poem sings beautifully of the lyric voice's nightly imprisonment within the proliferating socio-economic contexts of Abbasid recitation and lovers' reiteration, where *I*'s mastery of the language of love has become a vital feature of the poet's commissioned public expression of courtly social mores: those 'who quote my verse succeed', 'I've become a candle thread destined / To light a room for other men'. The poet is consumed in singing his song to *you*.

Paterson's uncanny immediacy of voicing ensures that contemporary address is sounded in the ears, and burnt on the tongues, of multiple, transhistorical speakers, listeners and lovers and patrons. The poem's rich medley of authorial voices creates a *mise-en-abyme* of agency and address that leaves readerly *you*s reeling. Who, exactly, is speaking to whom? Which tongue is Ibn Al-Ahnaf's and which is the contemporary lyricist's? Is there a third poet present? Does the candlebird itself have a voice? Which *you* is the reader?

Such polyvocality is not just an idle trick, though it is a trick at *your* expense. Paterson's address conducts historically rooted scrutiny of the socio-economic contexts of poetry's performative intimacies: today and at the Abbasid court. *I* deftly manoeuvres readers into a position where they are particularly susceptible to the threateningly deathly ('lifeless', 'burning') song of *I*'s 'tongue'. 'Candlebird' reinforces the *gazal*'s disturbing sense of the performing poet's otherworldly contact with audiences ('destined / To light a room for other men / While burning away'), where lyric brilliance depends upon being subject to *your* readerly whims. In Paterson, the reader's recognition of his role in this lyric violation is made to occur precisely as *I* calls for our closest gesture and speech: 'So take my hand and tell me'. Paterson's address to us turns the poem outward, likening the contemporary reader both to the lover (by turns neglectful and demanding), and to the Caliph, for whom Ibn Al-Ahnaf's medieval love-lyric was performed (in exchange for security and a fee). Paterson's closing address effects a turning of the tables of verbal mastery on the very auditor-patrons that call for the song of intimacy to be sung again, and yet again. Of course, Paterson knows that his own (and Ibn Al-Ahnaf's) auditor will be unable to touch or respond to the lover's song in kind, even as the final four lines of the poem issue that demand twice over. Paterson's uncannily re-sounding song reinforces the exhaustively never-changing nature of love, and the violent demands of nightly lyric performance at court.[48]

In both poems, art's ability to arrest time and progression occurs through a reminder of the fathomless depths and abysses of everyday and intimate contact with intimate and commissioning *you*s. In Paterson, what is uncomfortably hand-to-hand, eye-to-eye lyric touch is run alongside the notion that the successful artwork must somehow find a way to get itself passed between numberless receiving hands, ears, and speaking tongues, even if this means the poet's words find themselves packaged, disseminated, circulated, discussed, and valued and re-valued by numberless demanding recipients (and lovers).

In delving repeatedly into literary history, Paterson's intimate acts of inscription and interlocution display a keen aural investment in the contemporary text's power to resound, as well as alter, corrupt, and pay tribute to the voices of its forebears. In part this is an ambitious lyric drive: the contemporary poet desires to produce work that is in close dialogue with canonical cultural, philosophical, artistic, and poetic figures. There are 'versions' of Li Po, Robert Desnos, Antonio Machado, Rilke, and Propertius. The work of writers as diverse as Borges, Pound, Heraclites, Dante, Sylvia Plath, Robert Garioch, and Antonio Porchia are pulled into fresh voicings, through epigraphs, allusions, and direct hailing. Even the

---

[48] See Beatrice Gruendler, *Medieval Arabic Praise Poetry: Ibn al-Rumi and the Patron's Redemption* (London: Routledge, 2003); Muhsin J. al-Musawi, *Arabic Poetry: Trajectories of Modernity* (Abingdon: Routledge, 2006); Eva Sallis, *Sheherazade Through the Looking Glass: Metamorphosis of the* Thousand and One Nights, ed. J. E. Montgomery and R. Allen (Surrey: Curzon, 1999).

personal poems and dedications addressed to and for Paterson's twin children ('for Russ', 'for Jamie', 'Letter to the Twins', 'Waking with Russell') interlace personal reminiscence with a series of literary-historical doublings and twinning. For instance, the epigraph to Paterson's much-celebrated 'Letter to the Twins'—a quotation from Plutarch's *Parallel Lives*—demands readers sound and resound the apparently private address of the lyric present (both father's and lover's) in both literary-historical periods:

> Dear sons – for I am not, as you believed,
> your uncle – forgive me now [...][49]

Here, Paterson offers an opening address that does not, in itself, prepare readers for the poem's use of the destabilizing re-soundings of ancient mythology. But the epigraph deftly doubles the contexts of personal voicing: '...for it is said, they went to school at Gabii, and were well instructed in letters, and other accomplishments befitting their birth. And they were called Romulus and Remus (from *ruma*, the dug), as we had before, because they were found sucking the wolf' (*Light* 18). 'Dear sons': Paterson's contemporary address to *you* listens back on the notoriously contested genealogy of Roman twinship ('you, bent above those tables of events'), as well as the founding of Rome itself: 'the infinite laws of Rome, the protocols', 'often [...] we come back to this place'.

Paterson's recalling of Plutarch's retelling of the Roman foundation myth inserts its own family history into the vexed history of a culture's thwarted attempts to fix its genealogy and inheritance: 'I am not, as you believed, / your uncle', 'you might recall / your mother; or her who said she was your mother' (20). Paterson's address to 'the Twins' carries with it the ancient myth of origins, the 'official history' of the Romulus and Remus myth, and the politics of the literary texts that sing of these slippery mythologies, and insert their fresh voice into the tradition they ostensibly pay tribute to. In so doing, Paterson's instructive address is both preoccupied by money, literary recognition, and reward, and by its longing to advise *you* how to escape from inherited traditions, knowledge- and public value-systems 'befitting your birth':

> But were I to commend just one reserve
> of study – one I promise that will teach
> you nothing of *use*, and so not merely serve
>
> to deepen your attachment or your debt,
> where each small talent added to the horde

> is doubled in its spending, and somehow yet
> no more or less than its own clean reward –
>
> it would be this: the honouring of your lover.   (19)

These lines implement a vocabulary of conventionally public money-rela-
tions—*I* speaks of worldly 'attachment' and 'debt', of 'serving' and ser-
vice—before turning the tables, and turning them inwards. In offering
apparently private service to 'your lover' (rather than *your* master), the
poem engages in an alluringly private proliferation of value, treasure, and
reward. Here, expected financial relations are reversed, made uncannily
double: 'doubled in its spending', 'more or less than', 'clean reward'. The
verbal and corporeal relationship between lover and poet is modelled on
an internal 'horde': 'First she will address you in a tongue / so secret she
must close her mouth on yours'. That 'secret' lovers' language is not in-
nocent of value and reward, but it does seem to be able to liberate *you*
from age-old systems of valuation, by scripting personal economic codes,
tongues, and intercourse.

On the one hand then, Paterson's poem issues intimate addresses that
attempt to free their youthful *yous* from the study of what is merely *useful*
and financially productive. These interlocutions resist the pursuit of knowl-
edge merely for the sake of worldly reward. On the other hand, the poet's
'honouring of your lover' is quite unable to do without that public world,
or its financial lexicons: 'horde', 'talent', 'spending', 'reward', 'privilege'.
Indeed, the poet uses these to 'commend' to his sons, and to his listening
audiences, the value and dazzling agility of the poem's 'talent'; its inventive
forms of 'doubled [...] spending' in the internal sphere. 'I did it as a deft /
composer of the elements, the master', the poet- and father-figure writes.
The lines exhibit their joint mastery of, and servitude to, a range of roles,
relations, histories, and traditions, even as they speak of their own 'humil-
ity': 'you might understand in full / the privilege that brought you to this
place'. Paterson's interlacings of the voices of lover, father, teacher, and al-
lusive poet underline the duplicating, continually proliferating forms of
sensual, scholarly, and literary knowledge that take place in the search for
poetic recognition, as the contemporary lyricist sings beautifully of poetical,
sexual, and financial regeneration and reward.

'Poetry is not commerce', writes Sam Hamill: 'that energy, that experi-
ence we name poem, cannot be traded on the marketplace [...] It won't
light a lightbulb, run a heater or an aircondition or a microwave oven.
It is only a poem: necessary, and inviolable, an articulation of a world
beyond the possibilities of money.'[50] Yet as Paterson's allusive lyric economies

---

[50] Sam Hamill, 'Shadow Work', in *Conversant Essays: Contemporary Poets on Poetry*, ed.
James McCorkle (Detroit: Wayne State University Press, 1990) 460.

remind us, poems never have been—nor could be—'inviolable' or 'beyond the possibilities of money'. Paterson's addresses might oscillate uneasily between celebrating and resisting being 'traded on the marketplace', but they also grant us the pleasure and peculiar intimacy of meeting *you* in a financial space. In Paterson, money repeatedly brings *I* and *you* together intimately, rather than estranging them, or contaminating their relations.

Paterson's work offers, I think, a fresh direction in twentieth-century and early twenty-first-century poetry's handling of commerce.[51] In speaking to *you*, his work offers a distinctive counterpointing to the usual direction and tone of the financially minded addresses of much early twentieth-century poetry. Hotly denouncing commerce's relationship with literary creativity, Pound's *Cantos*, for instance, famously uses address to lament *your* interest in lyric profit:

> with usura, sin against nature,
> is thy bread ever more of stale rags
> is thy bread dry as paper,[52]

Pound's address is wielded *upon you*, rather than as part of dialogue with *you*.[53] The lines employ address as a means of stridently rebuking their wayward audience for its involvement in consumerist economic circulation, capitalism, and profiteering. Usura 'hath brought palsy to bed, lyeth / between the young bride and her bridegroom /   CONTRA NATURUM'. In so doing, Pound brings the forceful directness of address into contact not just with anti-commercial agendas, but also with fascist and misogynist impulses. (Debate has raged about the extent to which the *Cantos* should be characterized as an anti-Semitic text.) What is more is that Pound's addresses insist that auditors recognize a link between twentieth-century culture's perverted economic practices and unhealthy regenerative drives (creative and sensual). The *Cantos* allies financially, socially, and sexually circulating diseases, so that address conjoins the proliferation of capitalist debt and trade with threatening sexual licentiousness. Pound's *you* ('thou', 'thy') is dominated by the 'sin' and taint of commerce: 'with usura', *thou* art 'against nature'.

---

[51] See Michael Tratner, *Deficits and Desires: Economics and Sexuality in Twentieth-Century Literature* (Stanford: Stanford University Press, 2001) especially 121–5, and his chapter 'Love Versus Usury: The National Cures of Ezra Pound and William Carlos Williams', 121–72.

[52] Pound, *Cantos* 45: 229. See also Canto 45:229, on art: 'with usura / [...] / no picture is made to endure nor to live with / but it is made to sell and sell quickly'.

[53] See the early volumes, *Ripostes* (1912) and *Lustra* (1913–15), especially the poems 'Salutation', 'Salutation the Second', 'Ortus', all in *Personae* 86; 86; 85.

Address is not dissimilarly wielded in Eliot's poetic attention to lyric economics.[54] Eliot's financially minded addresses, like Pound's, move with a shared spirit of vigorously berating, hectoring anti-commercialism: the poet rounds on *you*. Eliot puts to use address's directness and clout, combining personal dismay with heated social and spiritual critique of its auditors:[55]

> All men are ready to invest their money
> But most expect dividends.
> I say to you: *Make perfect your will.*
> I say: take no thought of the harvest,
> But only of proper sowing.
>
> Betrayed in the mazes of your ingenuities,
> Sold by the proceeds of your proper inventions:
> [...]
> I have given you my Law, and you set up commissions,
> [...]
> I have given you power of choice, and you only alternate
> Between futile speculation and unconsidered action.
> Many are engaged in writing books and printing them,
> Many desire to see their names in print,[56]

'Betrayed', 'Sold', 'futile speculation', 'unconsidered action': the processes of commerce, profit, and investment are energetically lambasted in such addresses: 'I say to you', 'I say', 'take no thought', 'I have given you [...] and you only [...]'.

In Paterson, *you* needs advice and instruction, and might be rescued from 'vanity', and from 'attachment or your debt': 'Learn this and she will guide you, if not home / then at least to its true memory'.[57] In Eliot, the addressee is a corrupt auditor that must be vigorously berated. The conversation works in the direction of a hectoring speaker towards a wayward body of *you*s that are: 'writing books and printing them', motivated by the desire to see their 'names in print'. These interlocutors exemplify not only the culture's obsession with 'speculation and unconsidered action'. They manifest a particularly corrupt version of economic betrayal, for *you* sell short the art of poetry itself, transforming lyric production into an emptily commercial process concerned primarily with marketing and

[54] See also 'Burbank with a Baedeker: Bleistein with a Cigar': 'The rats are underneath the piles. / The Jew is underneath the lot. / Money in furs [...]' (*ECP* 40–1).

[55] 'A small house agent's clerk, with one bold stare, / One of the low on whom assurance sits / As a silk hat on a Bradford millionaire' (*The Waste Land*, *ECP* 3:232–34).

[56] 'The Rock' I, *ECP* 148; 'The Rock' III, *ECP* 154.

[57] 'Letter to the Twins', *Light* 19.

publication; 'printing', desiring 'names in print'. Such *you*s, as Eliot's address insists, are guilty of working to the detriment of a well-nurtured healthy lyric crop that is attentive to its 'proper sowing'.[58]

In Paterson, as in Eliot and Pound, *you* and *I* are not permitted to turn a blind eye to their part in the negotiative economies of poetic production. Yet where Modernist addresses often round on and accuse *you* of corrupt lyric commerce, Paterson's interlocutions make clear the humblingly culpable dealings of *poetic speakers*. 'I'm weighing up my spending power: the shillings, / tanners, black pennies, florins with bold kings', writes one youthful poet-figure in *God's Gift*. Those lines at once recall the child's aural and physical pleasure in the heft and sinew of really having cash, and simultaneously capture the adult poet's delight in being able to impress auditors by making it sing. Lyric pride is quickly compromised by an address that flags up *I*'s need for others to verify his proclaimed poetic 'spending power'. His address cries out—twice over—for reassurance from *you*, calling for reply. The poet, like the child, is 'worried' 'as usual, / Over matters of procedure, the protocol', and keeps asking 'the same questions' of *you*: 'if we have enough money for the fare, / whispering, *Are ye sure? Are ye sure?*'.[59] 'Weighing up' its power, indeed, such work presents readers with a poet-figure feverishly struggling to secure his artistic reputation and economic advantage, and signalling his need for *you* to answer him, to articulate and secure his success. Rather than berating *you* for your capitulation to financial pressures, Paterson's lyric *I* envisages itself the more culpable partner. *I* sets out to inveigle *you* in its money-minded concerns: persuading *you* to admire, but also to share in, his art.[60]

In so doing, Paterson's address shares with its audiences—rather than camouflaging from *you*—our intimately shared dirty dealings in the economic and literary spheres. Such address is neither un-self-reflexive nor economically innocent: it inserts itself into auditors' sensibilities and

---

[58] See also Robert Frost's 'Build Soil: A Political Pastoral' (1936), in which *I* and *you* scratch their heads over the perplexingly abstract nature of commercial exchange: 'I'm perplexed myself / To find the good in commerce. Why should I / Have to sell you my apples and buy yours?'. See *Collected Poems, Prose and Plays*, ed. Mark Richardson and Richard Poirier (New York: Library of America, 1995) 289–97. Here, abstract commercial relations replace the direct, sensuous lyric address of lost pastoral generations of the 'soil'.

[59] '11:00: Baldovan', *Gift* 12.

[60] A comparable effect can be seen in post-war British fiction. Martin Amis's *Money: A Suicide Note* (London: Cape, 1984) and Malcolm Bradbury's *Rates of Exchange* (London: Secker & Warburg, 1983) represent money as a sullying influence ('corrupt' is a word often used by Amis), but associate financial mire with excitingly circulating sexual promises and promiscuity. In his author's note, Bradbury addresses the reader: 'it is our duty to lie together, in the cause, of course, of truth'. In such texts, the trading of literary and financial 'promises' and lies between *I* and *you* renders literary exchange and profit stimulatingly sordid.

manipulates *your* responses in particular, self-interested ways. But of course, *you* may be asking for it, and being given what *you* deserve. As auditors are often called upon to remember, for Paterson's address repeatedly brings commercial and lyric impulses into contact in violently literary-historical contexts. The epigraph of '*from* "1001 Nights: The Early Years"' alludes to the frame story of *The Arabian Nights*—'The Story of King Shahryar and his Brother'—which mingles sexual violence, generative story-telling, and the dominating impulses of narrative desire.[61] Paterson's epigraph informs us: '*The male muse is paid in silence. Shahrāzād could not have been bought for less than minor Auschwitz.*' His poem then recalls a money-minded dream in which 'I was fixing a stamp in a savings-book, half-full'—a dream that ends with the poet-figure taking his new lover's 'head off with the kitchen knife'. The lyric dream, which Paterson imagines being told to an auditor, invites readers too to listen back on the succession of stories told by Shahrazad to her auditor Shahryar (who after beheading his first wife for infidelity, weds and beds a succession of virgins, executing each the morning after, before she could betray him. Shahrazad's story-telling keeps her alive).

This is to say, in '*from* "1001 Nights"', Paterson's allusive contemporary tale-telling demands its own auditors consider the slippages and cross-comparisons between lyric and corporeal fidelity and betrayal; the rage for accurate literary-historical preservation ('fixing a stamp in a record-book'); and the potentially violent capturing of voices in history. The story-teller's—and poet's—desire to create relations with audiences anew is coupled with the longing to fix troublesomely changeable narrative revisionings. Paterson's poem listens back on a text that itself has no single author or source: '*from* "1001 Nights"' moves as a new voice in the medley of voices that comprised *The Arabian Nights*; tales used to entertain local Baghdad tradesmen between AD 900–1000 as they accompanied their fruits and spices along trade routes. In Paterson's poem, an apparently blissfully endless succession of lovers 'each one day younger than the last' leaves the poet awaking to the same uncanny repetition of difference and renewed violation: 'morning always brings her back changed'.

So too for *The Arabian Nights*. The *Nights* trade hands, contexts, and mouths like promiscuous lovers, engaging in a process of literary exchange, violation, and barter akin to Paterson's 'vast harem'. *Nights* is passed between the tongues of Shakespeare, Scott, the Brontës, Poe, Joyce, Rushdie, now Paterson, as well as translation into film, music, and

---

[61] *The Arabian Nights*. trans. Husain Haddawy and Daniel Heller-Roazen, ed. Muhsin Mahdi and Daniel Heller-Roazen (New York: Norton, 2009).

pornography.[62] Paterson's poem makes use of the motif of a labyrinthine set of addresses and transhistorical interlocutions that defies any 'complete' reading, rendition, or edition, as well as the motif of endlessly deferred literary and sexual pleasure, which comes at a steep cost.[63] *Nights* is never complete, never satisfied. As we might recall: for medieval Arabs, 1,001 is the number of infinity.

As in '*from* "1001 Nights"', so too in the addresses of 'The Waterwheel', and in many of the poems in *Orpheus* ('Praising', 'The Drinking Fountain'), address evokes a sense of the human poet as half-joyous, half-endangered by the infinite nature of divine inspiration and lyric audition:

> What divine poet
> blindfolded you,
> my wretched old pal,
> and tied the perpetual
> wheel to the water's
> mindless soliloquy,
> I can't say [...][64]

'Perpetual', 'mindless', 'wretched': such terms echo 'The Drinking Fountain's relentlessly generous, perpetually 'tireless' giving—and also the 'tied' and tired donkey, breaking its back for the effortless-seeming divine soliloquy. That hard lyric labour can never cease, that audiences will always be in attendance, that poetry like 'the water's / mindless soliloquy'—and like the stream and ceaseless circulation of money—endlessly flow and proliferate may be dangerous to the human poet, the lyric mortal: 'the divine / grips him to pour from his mouth—' (*Orpheus* 9). Divinely inspired poetry will go on demanding that its poets give voice; that they will continue to produce ingenious morphings of the language, revisiting the lyricism of their forebears.

Does Paterson's address to *you*, 'my [...] pal', long step away from those demands? Or does it also make use of them? 'I can't say' hints that the speaker actually may know, but is unable to divulge that knowledge. Is Paterson's self-censoring poet-figure, far from 'mindless', blind, or

---

ignorant, really in fear of enraging implied *yous*—those wilful gods and masters that are inevitably listening in? Or does this *I* cunningly sense the presence of his readership, standing beyond his individually hailed *you* ('my wretched old pal') and desperate to know more? If so, the poet keeps them hanging. He guesses correctly that *you* will want to know precisely what *I* withholds. This is what Dante knew too, when he used address to the 'reader' to keep *you* interested: 'Think reader [...] Thou would'st desire to know how it goes on'. It's also what Shahryar, ensnared within the web of what Shahrazad had not quite divulged each morning, was finally to discover—though only after a thousand and one nights had passed, and he had been fairly caught.

Paterson's addresses show readers that contemporary poems, poets, and addressees are not the innocent victims of trade and commerce, but part of a richly nuanced tradition of verbal and physical engagement and betrayal, shared with *you*. Here, the contemporary poet's most intimate spoken, written, and physical bonds with past literary masters, 'the reader', and live, loved others are fused with violent impulses of appropriation, possession, transformation, trade, and barter. In so doing, the poet's speech opens itself willingly to public address, and finds itself speaking to an alarmingly amorphous, infinite *you*. *I*'s intimacies are circulated to strangers, to unimaginably vast audience bodies—both in and across historical time.

'To look down on "trade" or sniff at commerce has in all time been the natural behaviour of the aristocrat', wrote Wyndham Lewis: 'what certainly has always been "run" against trade is *art*'.[65] Highly critical of those writers and critics looking 'down' on, rather than imagining themselves involved 'in' money matters, Lewis's comments also indicate that, at least since the early twentieth century, writers have insisted that audiences recognize art's elevation as a misprision.[66] For Paterson, as for Lewis, '*art*' will not offer the author or reader a disengaged, or superior perspective from which to view the grubby world of 'trade'. Indeed, Paterson's lyrics use address to plunge *I* and *you* headlong into the money-minded, commission-seeking literary sphere. In neither writer is poetry's place in the

---

[65] Wyndham Lewis, *Creatures of Habit and Creatures of Change: Essays on Art, Literature and Society, 1914–1956*, ed. Paul Edwards (Santa Rosa, CA: Black Sparrow Press, 1989) 141.

[66] Although, as Bruce Robbins has argued, literary, artistic, and everyday culture was often viewed by mid-century leftists (e.g. Raymond Williams) as opposed to the world of commerce, even an antidote to it. Robbins writes that, for many writers, culture comes to be seen as 'the antithesis of and the antidote to the self-interested world of the capitalist market [...] they tended to ally or align culture with [...] a public or disinterested counterforce of the market', in *Secular Vocations: Intellectuals, Professionalism, Culture*, ed. Bruce Robbins (London: Verso 1993) 212.

commercial world straightforwardly lamentable. Rather, that world offers a source of lyric provocation.

Listening back on and consolidating its contact with the voices of the literary past, Paterson makes clear that address is far from transcendent hailing. Speaking to *you* is intricately connected with the ambitious social aspirations of the contemporary poet, who is also clamouring to join his forebears in the literary canon. In this, Paterson's sense of money and poetry as companionable, though often tetchy, bedfellows, finds echoes in Graham, Sisson, and Hill. Each of these different poets wields private words upon *you* in public. Each conducts intimate addresses to literary-historical auditors in contexts of patronage, audience-negotiation, and lyric commerce. Hill's rich textual relations with Milton (especially in *A Treatise of Civil Power* and *Scenes from Comus*) and Sisson's hailings to classical figures (Catullus, Ulysses, Orpheus) pull historical interlocutions into the immediacy of the 'now' through address's deixis. In so doing, they insist on poetry's civic role—through the ages—in shaping and sustaining the *polis*. The contemporary artwork ensures *you* attend to *your* cultural and historical situatedness, making clear how the past actively informs the present. Like these poets, Paterson's lyric addresses are attentive to the appropriateness of their stagings of 'personal' speech. They attend to how, and in what contexts, the poet should wield the second-person pronoun in addressing both individual *you*s and a wider audience body. In each poet, the potentially corrupting power of lyricism's discourse with commerce is considered: should the poem avoid negotiating monetary concerns in speaking to *you*? What if resistance to such concerns is thwarted, since even intimate lyric addresses are already informed by, and moving with, the voices of commerce—as we saw in Paterson's use of Simonides in 'The Reading'?

Paterson's interlocutions indicate that behind these apparent distinctions between, and feared oppositions of, the monetary and the poetic there lies a rich tapestry of civic speech; literary, historical, philosophical, personal, and conversational. His addresses reveal to *you* the sustained interrelations of both art and commerce. So too, they insist that their audience recognizes poetry's capacity to keep *your* hands and tongues grubbily, and intelligently busy, through literature's intimate, money-minded interactions.

Afterword

The principle object, then proposed in these poems was to choose incidents and situations from common life, and to relate and describe them, throughout, as far as possible in a selection of language really used by men, and, at the same time, to throw over them a certain colouring of imagination, whereby ordinary things should be presented to the mind in an unusual aspect; and, further, and above all, to make these situations and incidents interesting by tracing in them, truly though not ostentatiously, the primary laws of our nature.

Wordsworth, *Lyrical Ballads*

A good deal of contemporary British poetry not only reflects on and moves within the social, historical, and political spheres, but criticizes and probes the way the culture has reviewed and viewed poetry anew over time. In their focus on contemporary poetry's place in culture and history, Graham, Sisson, Hill, and Paterson demand attention to the reception of art in 'the real world', and its attempts to reach into, and structure, that reception. The artistry of each poet is intimately connected with the politics *of* poetic dissemination. Their works insist we attend both to the aspects of the political that contemporary poetry takes as its subject matter, and to poetry's socio-cultural manoeuvrings—the politics of its attempts to change interlocutors' minds, to win round a body of *you*s in speaking the common tongue, and to speaking persuasively in public. Such British poets negotiate the politics of aesthetic production and dissemination: with coterie audiences, the mob and rabble, past and present literary masters, funding bodies, the image of 'the common reader', as well as at poetry readings, in lectures, on broadcasts, in academia. Each poet's work demonstrates differently how the risks (and excitement) of poetry's live performativity come to the fore with particular insistence when poetry directly (and often indirectly) engages a *you*.

This is to say that contemporary British poetry is born of and feeds back into the people's speech. Wordsworth wrote that the poet should be a 'man speaking to common men', but also that he should tap 'the primary laws of

our nature'. The direct, personal address of an *I* to a *you* is also a public act.
I might look in my heart and write, but in so doing, I show I am conversant
with the underlying structures that bond me verbally and conceptually to
my fellow men. Many addresses show us how poems today move in, grow
from, and impact upon our shared common tongue. In academic criticism,
and in the media, there has been much complaint that poetry is out of
touch with contemporary life and with the general public.[1] But lyric lan-
guage is, in a strict sense, incapable of operating at a remove from our
shared public world and discourses, or from our ways of viewing the world,
and each other. Even much of what has been called contemporary poetry's
linguistic 'difficulty' holds a good deal in common with the verbal inven-
tiveness of everyday conversation and writing—a tendency to slip into and
enjoy puns and metaphors, to play with clichés, to use double-entendres, to
lightly parody or aggressively mock others, to refer casually to past conver-
sations, and to employ the ironic voice. There are strong links between
verbal commonality and the everyday, and the work of ordinary language
philosophers, including J. L. Austin's work on illocutionary acts in *How to
Do Things With Words*, John Searle's 'speech acts' and Wittgenstein's sense
that language structures our shared world: 'the limits of my language are the
limits of my world'. A sensitive, and philosophically attentive discussion of
poetry's 'place' and 'significance' in contemporary life should rethink the
conception of poetry's difficulty and abstraction from concrete feelings,
events, and contexts. So too, it should consider with some suspicion the
view that poetry is dominated by mere postmodernist 'play' and a disem-
bodied, impersonal voice or pastiche of voices. Graham, Sisson, Hill, and
Paterson exhibit tendencies seen more widely in the work of writers as di-
verse as Harrison, Dunn, Duffy, Shapcott, Heaney, Muldoon, and Prynne,
and in the Modernisms of Eliot, Yeats, Pound, Bunting, and Jones—where
'voice' was both slippery, and tied to particular historical and contemporary
auditors and auditions. These verbal bonds are simultaneously personal,
and public. They are witnessed (and responded to) by specifically known
interlocutors, and by a body of intercepting changeable *yous*: the voices of
an addressed, and continually addressing, culture.

*

In the introduction to his anthology of contemporary British poetry,
A Various Art, Andrew Crozier points out that much of the late twentieth-
century's non-orthodox poetic output was prompted by a sense of opposi-
tion to the accepted poetic practices of earlier generations. Crozier asserts
that, for those poets who came to prominence in the 1950s,

---

[1] See Sean O'Brien, *The Deregulated Muse* (Newcastle-upon-Tyne: Bloodaxe, 1998)
270–1. See also Colin Falck, *American and British Verse in the Twentieth-Century: The Poetry
That Matters* (Aldershot: Ashgate, 2003) 185–210.

Poetry was seen as an art in relation to its own conventions—and a pusil-
lanimous set of conventions at that. It was not to be ambitious, or to seek to
articulate ambition through the complex deployment of its technical
means.[2]

Crozier leaves out of his account the pusillanimous tendencies of the later
'unconventional' poets themselves. Their lyric iconoclasm, like that of
Graham, Sisson, Hill, and Paterson, is by turns serious and teasing. Such
literature is strategically counter-cultural, putting its fists up to certain
arbiters of artistic 'acceptability' and value—as we have seen in Graham's
rebuttals of those poets who self-consciously championed 'the Scottish lit
scene', Sisson's critique of Movement poetic tastes and judgements, Hill's
and Paterson's heckling of critics and reviewers, academic institutions,
editors, and prize-giving bodies.

Commentators and poets—like Crozier—often hold that the accepted
values scrutinized by many contemporary poets (especially those of the
British Poetry Revival in the 1960s and 1970s) are regulated by particular
institutions, periodicals, funding bodies, publishing houses, anthologists,
critics, and reviewers, all of which tended to privilege the work produced
by, and in the style of, Movement poets, and neglected more experimental
work.[3] I am thinking of the *Listener*, *The New Statesman*, the *Spectator*, as
well as the Arts Council and large publishing houses, such as Faber &
Faber. These institutions are seen as dominant in the poetry scene in the
latter half of the twentieth century, shaping a post-war canon that fa-
voured non-*avant-garde* poetry and lyric work that moved away from
verbal and neo-Modernist experimentation. As Peter Middleton has re-
cently written: 'Arts funding organizations, publishing, education, per-
formance and the new communications media: these institutions have
shaped the landscape of recent British poetry.'[4]

Hazard Adams has recently stated that poetry's social role *is* to provoke
and offend.[5] In *Poetry as Offense*, he argues that poems present readers
with a highly instructive cultural challenge, demanding they rethink

[2] Andrew Crozier and Tim Longville, eds., *A Various Art* (Manchester: Carcanet, 1987).
Crozier refers to the wealth of largely unanthologized poetic production of the 1960s and
1970s (as part of the British Poetry Revival) that was coupled with a sharp increase in little
magazine and small press activity.

[3] See Eric Mottram, 'The British Poetry Revival, 1960–75', in *New British Poetries: The
Scope of the Possible*, ed. Robert Hampson and Peter Barry (Manchester and New York:
Manchester University Press, 1993) 15–50; and Roger Ellis, 'Mapping the UK Little Maga-
zine Field', also in *New British Poetries* 72–103.

[4] Middleton, 'Institutions of Poetry in Postwar Britain' 243–63, 262. See Middleton on
Faber & Faber (248–9).

[5] Hazard Adams, *Poetry as Offense* (Washington: University of Washington Press, 2007),
see intro, particularly 3–11.

academic and quotidian assumptions about the function of language and art. 'The antithetical stance', he proposes, 'provides necessary opposition to the dominating negations of the culture [. . .] demanding imaginative involvement, a challenge to pass into the particularity of events, other minds, sympathetic identification, or active repulsion' (24). On this view, it is through offence that poetry leads *you* to test out new verbal and conceptual possibilities, to stand in unlikely positions in relation to others, and to cultural assumptions about value, meaning, and identity. Poetry performs anti-hegemonic work by demanding (often rudely) that it is noticed, and attended to. This is a kind of affront to the reader, startling *you* out of indifference or habituated expectations of reading and thought.

But poetry's power to perform in this way depends upon *your* willingness to play the same verbal game, as Adams too observes: 'readers must confront and pass through the offense, which is a moment of challenge, crisis, and decision generated out of the prevailing cultural view of language, its appropriate uses, and its characteristics' (7). Such 'confrontation' is linked, in our lyricists' work, with the idea that poetry is responsible speech. If for Adams, offence is ethical activity—where ethics depends not upon resolution, but *destabilization*—so too, our poets' focus on lyric non-resolution seeks out language that works upon *your* ability to be open to and in dialogue with the brusquely antithetical. Reducing disparities and conflicts to 'the same', or to 'agreement', is an impoverishment of the possibilities for thinking anew that are raised by disagreement between both everyday and lyric interlocutors.

Have other twentieth-century critics responded to this tendency in contemporary British poetry, flagging up readers' abilities to be face-to-face with different kinds of verbal perturbation? Adam Zachary Newton observes that responsible poetry presents its readership with 'the "perturbatory" element rather than the "resolving" one'.[6] Similarly, Christopher Middleton criticizes the view that 'good' poetry is that which aligns itself with its audience, attempting to smooth over disparities, or to make texts accessible and 'relevant' to the greatest number of addressees. 'By reducing the otherness of other things [...] for the sake of relevance', Middleton comments, 'no real intellectual transformation, no real structuring refinement of sensibility, no cultivation of instinct, can occur'.[7] In expunging differences or denying their presence, the text is neatly slotted into the reader's existing 'condition of mind, his existing frame of reference'

[6] Adam Zachary Newton, *Narrative Ethics* (Cambridge, MA: Harvard University Press, 1995) 54.
[7] Christopher Middleton, *Bolshevism in Art* (Manchester: Carcanet, 1971) 145–6.

(Middleton, 146). For me, as for Newton and Middleton, the barbed gift poetry offers its addresses (and demands they consider accepting) is changeability, a species of altercation created from ceaseless alteration. Poetry works as dramatic performativity: not a landmark, but an act. As lyric addresses repeatedly insist, contemporary poetry is a continually arising, rousingly provisional verbal creation. This is not set-apart, private, or escapist activity. It is work that flags up the ordinary unconventionality of our daily speech and gesture—our everyday verbal experimentations—whilst reminding us that we are grounded in a shared cultural and political order. That order is repeatedly formed and reformulated, challenged and upheld, in our language, and in our art.

the everyday —
the ordinary —
but no Cavell

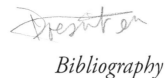

Bibliography

PRIMARY SOURCES

Alvarez, Al, ed. *The New Poetry: An Anthology*. Harmondsworth: Penguin, 1962.

Amis, Martin. *Money: A Suicide Note*. London: Cape, 1984.

Anon. *The Arabian Nights*. Trans. Husain Haddawy and Daniel Heller-Roazen. Ed. Muhsin Mahdi and Daniel Heller-Roazen. New York: Norton, 2009.

Ashbery, John. *Your Name Here*. New York: Farrar, Straus and Giroux, 2001.

Auden, W. H. *Collected Poems*. Ed. Edward Mendelson. New York: Random House, 1976.

Austin, J. L. *How to Do Things With Words*. Oxford: Clarendon Press, 1962.

Bacon, Francis. *The Essayes or Counsels, Civill and Morall*. Ed. Alexander Spiers and Basil Montagu. Boston: Little, Brown and company, 1861.

Beckett, Samuel. *Samuel Beckett: The Complete Dramatic Works*. London: Faber, 1986.

Bradbury, Malcolm. *Rates of Exchange*. London: Secker & Warburg, 1983.

Buber, Martin. *I and Thou*. Trans. Ronald Gregor Smith. Edinburgh: T. and T. Clark, 1937.

Bunting, Basil. *Briggflatts: An Autobiography*. London: Fulcrum, 1966.

Byron, Lord George Gordon. *The Works of Lord Byron*. Ed. J. W. Lake. Philadelphia: J. B. Lippincott, 1856.

Canetti, Elias. *Crowds and Power*. New York: Viking Press, 1962.

Cavell, Stanley. *The Claim of Reason*. Oxford: Oxford University Press, 1979.

Celan, Paul. *Selected Poems and Prose of Paul Celan*. Trans. John Felstiner. New York: Norton, 2001.

Chaucer, Geoffrey. *The Complete Works of Geoffrey Chaucer*. Ed. F. N. Robinson. Boston and New York: Houghton Mifflin, 1933.

Child, Francis James, ed. *The English and Scottish Popular Ballads*. 5 vols. New York: Dover Press, 2003.

Coleridge, Samuel Taylor. *Biographia Literaria*. New York: Leavitt; Boston: Croker, 1834.

Creeley, Robert. *Selected Poems, 1945–2005*. Ed. Benjamin Friedlander. London: University of California Press, 2008.

Dante, Alighieri. *Paradiso*. Trans. and comment by John O. Sinclair. Oxford: Oxford University Press, 1961.

Davie, Donald. *Collected Poems 1971–1983*. Manchester: Carcanet, 1983.

Donne, John. *The Complete English Poems*. Ed. A. J. Smith. London: Penguin, 1986.

Dryden, John. *Discourses on Satire and Epic Poetry*. Middlesex: Echo Library, 2007.

—— *The Major Works*. Ed. Keith Walker. Oxford: Oxford University Press, 2003.

Duffy, Carol Ann. *Selected Poems*. London: Penguin, 1994.

—— *Standing Female Nude*. London: Anvil, 1985.

—— *The World's Wife*. London: Picador, 1999.

Dunn, Douglas. 'Douglas Dunn in Conversation'. Interview with Gerry Cambridge. *The Dark Horse* 8 (Autumn 1999) 21–31.

—— *Selected Poems 1964–1983*. London: Faber, 1986.

Eliot, T. S. *Ash Wednesday*. New York: Fountain Press; London: Faber, 1930. In *T. S. Eliot: Collected Poems 1909–1962*. London: Faber, 1963. 93–106.

—— 'Burnt Norton'. *Collected Poems 1909–1935*. London: Faber, 1935. In *T. S. Eliot: Collected Poems 1909–1962*. London: Faber, 1963. 189–95.

—— *Collected Poems: 1909–1962*. 1963. London: Faber, 1974.

—— *The Dry Salvages*. London: Faber, 1941. In *T. S. Eliot: Collected Poems 1909–1962*. London: Faber, 1963. 205–13.

—— *East Coker*. *New English Weekly* (1940). In *T. S. Eliot: Collected Poems 1909–1962*. London: Faber, 1963. 196–204.

—— *Knowledge and Experience in the Work of F. H. Bradley*. London: Faber, 1964.

—— *Leadership and Letters*. Address at Milton Academy. 3 November 1948. London: Cumberledge, 1948.

—— *Little Gidding*. London: Faber, 1942. In *T. S. Eliot: Collected Poems 1909–1962*. London: Faber, 1963. 214–23.

—— *On Poetry and Poets*. London: Faber, 1957.

—— *Prufrock and Other Observations*. Bloomsbury: The Egoist, 1917. In *T. S. Eliot: Collected Poems 1909–1962*. London: Faber, 1963.

—— 'The Romantic Englishman, The Comic Spirit, and the Function of Criticism'. *Tyro* 1 (Spring 1921) 4.

—— *The Sacred Wood: Essays on Poetry and Criticism*.1920. London: Methuen, 1972.

—— *Selected Prose of T. S. Eliot*. Ed. and introd. Frank Kermode. London: Faber, 1975.

—— *The Three Voices of Poetry*. London: Cambridge University Press, 1953. In *On Poetry and Poets*. London: Faber, 1957. 89–102.

—— *The Use of Poetry and the Use of Criticism*. Cambridge, MA: Harvard University Press, 1933.

—— *The Waste Land*. *The Criterion* (October 1922). In *T. S. Eliot: Collected Poems 1909–1962*. London: Faber, 1963. 61–86.

Empson, William. 'Argufying in Poetry'. *The Listener* 2:2 (22 August 1963) 167–73. In *Argufying: Essays on Literature and Culture*. Ed. and introd. John Haffenden. London: Hogarth, 1988. 577–82.

—— *Collected Poems*. London: Chatto & Windus, 1955.

—— *Selected Letters of William Empson*. Ed. and introd. John Haffenden. Oxford: Oxford University Press, 2006.

Enright, D. J. *Collected Poems 1948–1998*. New York: Oxford University Press, 1998.

Fenton, James. *Children in Exile: Poems 1968–1984*. New York: Vintage, 1984.

Forrest-Thomson, Veronica. *Collected Poems*. Ed. Anthony Barnett. Exeter: Shearsman and Allardyce, 2008.

Frost, Robert. *Collected Poems, Prose and Plays*. Ed. Mark Richardson and Richard Poirier. New York: Library of America, 1995.

Glück, Louise. *The Wild Iris*. New York: Ecco Press, 1993.

Graham, W. S. *Aimed at Nobody: Poems from Notebooks*. Ed. Margaret Blackwood and Robin Skelton. London: Faber, 1993.

—— *Cage Without Grievance*. Glasgow: Parton, 1942.

—— *Collected Poems 1942–1977*. London: Faber, 1979.

—— *Implements in Their Places*. London: Faber, 1977.

—— *Malcolm Mooney's Land*. London: Faber, 1970.

—— *New Collected Poems*. Ed. Matthew Francis. London: Faber, 2004.

—— *The Nightfisherman: Selected Letters of W. S. Graham*. Ed. Michael and Margaret Snow. Manchester: Carcanet, 1999.

—— *The Nightfishing*. London: Faber, 1955.

—— *The Seven Journeys*. Glasgow: William MacLellan, 1944.

—— *2ND Poems*. London: Nicholson and Watson, 1945.

—— *Uncollected Poems*. Warwick: Greville Press, 1990.

—— *W. S. Graham: Selected by Nessie Dunsmuir*. Warwick: Greville, 1998.

—— *The White Threshold*. London: Faber, 1949.

Graves, Robert. *Collected Poems*. London: Cassell Press, 1975.

Hardy, Thomas. *Thomas Hardy*. Ed. Samuel Hynes. Oxford: Oxford University Press, 1984.

Harrison, Tony. 'Baghdad Lullaby'. *The Guardian*. Wednesday 9 April 2003. <http://www.guardian.co.uk/world/2003/apr/09/iraq.writersoniraq>, accessed 4 June 2008.

—— *Selected Poems*. 1984. London: Penguin, 1987.

Harwood, Lee. *Collected Poems*. Exeter: Shearsman, 2004.

Heaney, Seamus. *New Selected Poems*. London: Faber, 1990.

—— 'An Open Letter'. *Ireland's Field Day*. London: Hutchinson, 1985. 23–32.

—— *The Spirit Level*. London: Faber, 1996.

Herrick, Robert. *Hesperides: Or the Works Both Humane and Divine*. Ed. Samuel Weller Singer. 1648. Boston: Little, Brown and company, 1856.

Hill, Christopher. *Milton and the English Revolution*. London: Faber, 1977.

Hill, Geoffrey. *Canaan*. London: Penguin, 1996.

—— *Collected Critical Writings*. Ed. Kenneth Haynes. Oxford: Oxford University Press, 2008.

—— *Collected Poems*. Harmondsworth: Penguin, 1985.

—— *The Enemy's Country: Words, Contextures and Other Circumstances of Language*. Stanford: Stanford University Press, 1991.

—— *For the Unfallen*. London: André Deutsch, 1959.

—— Geoffrey Hill conference. 'Geoffrey Hill and His Contexts'. Keble College, Oxford. 2–3 July 2008.

—— Interview with Carl Phillips. 'The Art of Poetry No. 80'. *The Paris Review* 154 (Spring 2000) 272–99.

—— *King Log*. London: André Deutsch, 1968.

—— *The Lords of Limit: Essays on Literature and Ideas.* New York: Oxford University Press, 1984.

—— 'A Matter of Timing'. Interview with Geoffrey Hill. *The Guardian.* 'Features and Reviews'. Saturday 21 September 2002. 31.

—— *Mercian Hymns.* London: André Deutsch, 1971.

—— *The Mystery of the Charity of Charles Péguy.* London: André Deutsch, 1983.

—— *New and Collected Poems: 1952–1992.* Boston: Houghton Mifflin, 1994.

—— *The Orchards of Syon.* Washington: Counterpoint, 2002.

—— *Scenes from Comus.* London: Penguin, 2005.

—— *Selected Poems.* London: Penguin, 2006.

—— *Speech! Speech!* 2000. London: Penguin, 2001.

—— *Style and Faith.* Washington: Counterpoint, 2003.

—— *Tenebrae.* London: André Deutsch, 1978.

—— *A Treatise of Civil Power.* London: Penguin, 2007.

—— *The Triumph of Love.* 1998. New York: First Mariner, 2000.

—— *Without Title.* London: Penguin, 2006.

Hill, Selima. *Fruitcake.* Newcastle: Bloodaxe, 2009.

Ibn Al-Ahnaf, Abbas. *Birds Through an Alabaster Ceiling: Three Abyssinian Poets—Arab Poetry of the Abbasid Period.* Trans. G. B. H. Wightman, Abudlla Udhari, and A. Y. Al-Udhari. Harmondsworth: Penguin, 1975.

Jamie, Kathleen. *The Queen of Sheba.* Northumberland: Bloodaxe, 1994.

Jones, David. *Anathemata.* London: Faber, 1952.

Jonson, Ben. *The Complete Poems.* Ed. George Parfitt. London: Penguin, 1996.

Kavanagh, Patrick. *Collected Poems.* London: Penguin, 2005.

Keats, John. *The Complete Poems of John Keats.* Ed., introd., and notes by Paul Wright. Hertfordshire: Wordsworth Press, 2001.

Kinsella, Thomas. *Collected Poems.* Manchester: Carcanet, 1991.

Larkin, Philip. *Collected Poems.* London: Marvell and Faber, 2003.

—— *Required Writing: Miscellaneous Pieces: 1955–1982.* London: Faber, 1983.

Leonard, Tom. *Intimate Voices: Selected Work, 1965–1983.* London: Vintage, 1995.

Levertov, Denise. *Here and Now.* San Francisco: City Lights, 1957.

Lewis, Wyndham. *Creatures of Habit and Creatures of Change: Essays on Art, Literature and Society, 1914–1956.* Ed. Paul Edwards. Santa Rosa, CA: Black Sparrow Press, 1989.

Machado, Antonio. *Times Alone: Selected Poems of Antonio Machado.* Ed. Robert Bly. Middletown, CT: Wesleyan University Press, 1983.

MacNeice, Louis. *Collected Poems.* Ed. Peter McDonald. London: Faber, 2007.

MacSweeney, Barry. *Wolf Tongue: Selected Poems 1965–2000.* Newcastle: Bloodaxe, 2003.

Mahon, Derek. *Collected Poems.* Ed. Peter Fallon. 1999. Oldcastle, Meath: Gallery Press, 2007.

Marvell, Andrew. *The Complete Poems.* Ed. Elizabeth Story Donno. London: Penguin, 1996.

Mill, J. S. *Autobiography and Literary Essays*. Ed. John M. Robson and Jack Stillinger. Toronto: University of Toronto Press, 1981.

Milton, John. *Comus: A Mask Presented at Ludlow Castle, 1634, Before the Earl of Bridgewater then President of Wales*. Ed. Henry John Todd. London: W. Bristow, 1798.

—— *The Poetical Works of John Milton*. Ed. John Mitford. 2 vols. Vol. 2. Boston: Hilliard, Gray and company, 1838.

—— 'The Reason of Church Government Urged Against Prelaty'. *An Account of the Life, Opinions and Writings of John Milton*. Ed. Thomas Keightley. London: Chapman, 1855. 348–56.

—— *A Treatise of Civil Power in Ecclesiastical Causes: Shewing That it is Not Lawful for any Power on Earth to Compel in Matters of Religion*. 1759. London: J. Johnson, 1790.

Monk, Geraldine. *Ghost & Other Sonnets*. Cambridge: Salt, 2008.

Morgan, Edwin. *Collected Poems*. Manchester: Carcanet, 1996.

Motion, Andrew. Address to House of Commons. *Poet in the City Event*. 2007. *The Guardian*, Thursday 4 October 2007. <http://www.guardian.co.uk/books/2007/oct/04/poetry.andrewmotion>, accessed Tuesday 14 July 2009.

—— 'Spring Wedding'. BBC website. Saturday 9 April 2005. <http://news.bbc.co.uk/1/hi/uk/4427239.stm>, accessed 6 August 2009.

Muldoon, Paul. *Horse Latitudes*. London: Faber, 2006.

Orwell, George. *Keep the Aspidistra Flying*. London: Penguin, 1984.

—— 'London Letter'. *Partisan Review* (Summer 1944).

Paterson, Don. *The Blind Eye: A Book of Late Advice* (London: Faber, 2007).

—— and Clare Brown, eds. *Don't Ask Me What I Mean: Poets in Their Own Words*. London: Faber, 2001.

—— *The Eyes*. London: Faber, 1999.

—— *God's Gift to Women*. London: Faber, 1997.

—— *Landing Light*. London: Faber, 2003.

—— and Charles Simic. 'The Lyric Principle: The Sense of Sound'. *Poetry Review* 97:2 (Summer 2007) 56–72.

—— 'The Lyric Principle: The Sound of Sense'. *Poetry Review* 97:3 (Autumn 2007) 54–70.

—— ed. *New British Poetry*. Minneapolis: Graywolf, 2004.

—— *Nil Nil*. London: Faber, 1993.

—— *Orpheus*. London: Faber, 2006

—— *Rain*. London: Faber, 2009.

—— *Reading Shakespeare's Sonnets: A New Commentary*. London: Faber, 2010.

Paulin, Tom, ed. *The Faber Book of Political Verse*. London: Faber, 1986.

Pinter, Harold. *The Homecoming*. London: Faber, 1991.

Plath, Sylvia. *Collected Poems*. Ed. and introd. Ted Hughes. London: Faber, 1981.

Pound, Ezra. *The Cantos of Ezra Pound*. 3rd edn. 1954. London: Faber, 1975.

—— *A Draft of XXX Cantos*. Paris: Hours Press, 1930. In *The Cantos of Ezra Pound*. 3rd edn. 1954. London: Faber, 1975. 1–150.

—— *Eleven New Cantos XXXI–XLI*. New York: New Directions, 1937. In *The Cantos of Ezra Pound*, 3rd edn. 1954. London: Faber, 1975. 151–206.

—— *Hugh Selwyn Mauberley*. London: Ovid Press, 1920. In *Personae: The Collected Shorter Poems*. New York: New Directions, 1971. 185–234.

—— *The Letters of Ezra Pound 1907–1941*. Ed. D. D. Paige. London: Faber, 1951.

—— *Literary Essays of Ezra Pound*. Ed. and introd. T. S. Eliot. London: Faber, 1954.

—— *Personae: The Collected Shorter Poems*. New York: New Directions, 1971.

—— *The Pisan Cantos*. New York: New Directions, 1948. In *The Cantos of Ezra Pound*, 3rd edn. 1954. London: Faber, 1975. 423–540.

—— *Selected Prose 1901–1965*. Ed. William Cookson. New York: New Directions, 1973.

Prynne, J. H. *Poems*. Newcastle: Bloodaxe, 1999.

Raworth, Tom. *Collected Poems*. Manchester: Carcanet, 2003.

Shakespeare, William. *Julius Caesar*. Ed. William Montgomery. London: Penguin, 2000.

Shapcott, Jo. Interview with Deryn Rees-Jones. University of Liverpool. 8 June 2007. <http://www.liv.ac.uk/poetryandscience/essays/jo-shapcott.htm>, accessed 24 December 2010.

—— *Jo Shapcott: Her Book: Poems 1988–1998*. London: Faber, 2000.

—— *Phrase Book*. Oxford: Oxford University Press, 1992.

Shelley, Percy Bysshe. *Essays, Letters from Abroad, Translation and Fragments*. Ed. Mary Shelley. 2 vols. Vol. 1. Philadelphia: Lea and Blanchard, 1840.

—— *Shelley: Poetical Works*. Ed. Thomas Hutchinson. London: Oxford University Press, 1970.

Simmons, James. *Judy Garland and the Cold War*. Belfast: Blackstaff, 1976.

Sinclair, Ian. *Lud Heat*. London: Albion Village, 1975.

—— *Suicide Bridge*. London: Albion Village, 1979.

Sisson, C. H. *Anchises*. Manchester: Carcanet, 1976.

—— *Anglican Essays*. Manchester: Carcanet, 1983.

—— *Antidotes*. Manchester: Carcanet, 1991.

—— *Art and Action*. London: Methuen, 1965.

—— *The Avoidance of Literature: Collected Essays*. Ed. Michael Schmidt. Manchester: Carcanet, 1978.

—— *Collected Poems*. Manchester: Carcanet, 1984.

—— *Collected Poems*. Manchester: Carcanet, 1998.

—— *Collected Translations*. Manchester: Carcanet, 1996.

—— *The Corridor*. Hitchin: Mandeville Press, 1975.

—— *English Perspectives*. Manchester: Carcanet, 1991.

—— *English Poetry: An Assessment 1900–1950*. Ed. Rupert Hart-Davis. Manchester: Carcanet, 1971.

—— *Essays*. Sevenoaks: Knole Park Press, 1967.

—— *Exactions*. Manchester: Carcanet, 1980.

—— *God Bless Karl Marx!* Manchester: Carcanet, 1987.

—— *In the Trojan Ditch*. Manchester: Carcanet, 1974.

—— *Is There A Church of England?* Manchester: Carcanet, 1993.

—— *The London Zoo.* London: Abelard-Schuman, 1961

—— *Metamorphoses.* London: Methuen, 1968.

—— *Nine Sonnets.* Emscote Lawn, Warwick: Greville, 1991.

—— *Numbers.* London: Methuen: 1965.

—— *The Pattern.* London: Enitharmon, 1993.

—— *Poems: Selected.* Manchester: Carcanet, 1995.

—— *The Poetic Art.* Manchester: Carcanet, 1975.

—— *Selected Poems.* Manchester: Carcanet, 1981.

—— *16 Sonnets.* London: Laserprint, 1990.

—— *What and Who.* Manchester: Carcanet, 1994.

Stevens, Wallace. *Collected Poems.* London: Faber, 1984.

Stevenson, Anne. *Collected Poems: 1955–1995.* Newcastle: Bloodaxe, 2000.

Suetonius. *Lives of the Caesars.* Trans. J. C. Rolfe. Ed. Catharine Edwards. Oxford and New York: Oxford University Press, 2000.

Thomas, Dylan. *Collected Poems: 1934–1953.* London: Phoenix, 2000.

Waller, Edmund. *Poetical Works of Edmund Waller.* Ed. Thomas Park. 2 vols. London: Sharpe, 1806.

Wordsworth, William, and Samuel Taylor Coleridge. *Lyrical Ballads with Pastoral and Other Poems.* 2 vols. Vol. 1. London: T. N. Longman and Rees, 1802.

—— *Wordsworth's Tract on the Convention of Cintra. The Prose Works of William Wordsworth.* Vol. 1. Ed. W. J. B. Owen and J. W. Smyser (Humanities-Ebooks, 2008) 248–9. <http://books.google.com/books?id=WSKXmGkD9lwC&source=gbs_navlinks_s>, accessed 1 August 2009.

Yeats, W. B. *The Major Works.* Ed. Edward Larrissy. Oxford: Oxford University Press, 1997.

not works cited

SECONDARY SOURCES

Abrioux, Yves, and Stephen Bann. *Ian Hamilton Finlay: A Visual Primer.* London: Reaktion Books, 2007.

Adams, Hazard. *Poetry as Offense.* Washington: University of Washington Press, 2007.

Adorno, Theodor. *Aesthetic Theory.* Ed. Gretel Adorno and Rolf Tiedemann. Trans. Robert Hullot-Kentor. London: Athlone, 1997.

—— 'On the Fetish Character in Music'. *The Culture Industry: Selected Essays on Mass Culture.* Ed. J. M. Bernstein. London: Routledge, 2001. 29–59.

al-Musawi, Muhsin J. *Arabic Poetry: Trajectories of Modernity.* Abingdon: Routledge, 2006.

Alexander, Michael Joseph, and James McGonigal, eds. *Sons of Ezra: British Poets and Ezra Pound.* Amsterdam: Rodopi, 1995.

Allen, Emily. *Theatre Figures: The Production of the Nineteenth-Century British Novel.* Columbus: Ohio State University Press, 2003.

Allott, Kenneth. *The Penguin Book of Contemporary Verse.* Harmondsworth: Penguin, 1962.

Anderson, Benedict. *Imagined Communities: Reflections on the Origin and Spread of Nationalism*. 9th edn. London: Verso, 1999.

Arendt, Hannah. *The Portable Hannah Arendt*. Ed. and introd. Peter Baehr. London: Penguin, 2003.

Bakhtin, Mikhail. *The Dialogic Imagination*. Ed. Michael Holquist. Trans. Caryl Emerson and Michael Holquist. Austin: University of Texas Press, 1981.

Barfoot, C. C., ed. *In Black and Gold: Contiguous Traditions in Post-war British and Irish Poetry*. Amsterdam and Atlanta: Rodopi, 1994.

Barry, Peter. *Poetry Wars: British Poetry of the 1970s and the Battle of Earls Court*. Cambridge: Salt, 2006.

Barthes, Roland. *S/Z*. New York: Hill & Wang, 1974.

Bedient, Calvin. 'Absentist Poetry: Kinsella, Hill, Graham, Hughes'. *PN Review* 4:1 (1977) 18–24.

—— *Eight Contemporary Poets*. Oxford: Oxford University Press, 1974.

Benda, Julian. *The Treason of the Intellectuals*. Trans. Richard Aldington. New York: Norton, 1969.

Benjamin, Walter. *Illuminations: Essays and Reflections*. Ed. and introd. Hannah Arendt. Trans. Harry Zohn. New York: Schocken, 1969.

Bernstein, Charles, ed. *The Politics of Poetic Form: Poetry and Public Policy*. New York: Roof, 1990.

Bevis, Matthew. *The Art of Eloquence: Byron, Dickens, Tennyson, Joyce*. Oxford: Oxford University Press, 2007.

Blair, Hugh, and Abraham Mills. 'Apostrophe'. *Lectures on Rhetoric and Belle Lettres*. Philadelphia: Ellwood Zell, 1866. 179–81.

Bloom, Harold. *Somewhere Is Such a Kingdom: Poems 1952–1971*. Boston: Houghton Mifflin, 1975.

Bold, Alan. *Modern Scottish Literature*. London and New York: Longmans, 1983.

Bradley, A. C. 'Poetry for Poetry's Sake'. *Oxford Lectures on Poetry*. New Delhi: Atlantic Publishers, 1999. 3–36.

Brogan, Jacqueline Vaught. *The Violence Within/The Violence Without: Wallace Stevens and the Emergence of a Revolutionary Poetics*. London: University of Georgia Press, 2003.

Bromwich, David. *Sceptical Music: Essays on Modern Poetry*. Chicago and London: University of Chicago Press, 2001.

Brooks, Cleanth. *The Well Wrought Urn: Studies in the Structure of Poetry*. New York: Harcourt, Brace and World, 1947.

Burr, Zofia. *A Poetics of Address: Speech and Dialogue in the Poetry of Emily Dickinson, Josephine Miles, Gwendolyn Brooks, and Audre Lorde*. Ithaca, NY: Cornell University Press, 1993.

Byrne, Sandie. 'On Not Being Milton, Marvell or Gray'. *Tony Harrison: Loiner*. Ed. Sandie Byrne. Oxford: Clarendon Press, 1997. 57–84.

Cannadine, David. 'The British Monarchy 1820–1977'. *The Invention of Tradition*. Ed. Eric Hobsbawm and Terrence Ranger. 1983. 10th edn. Cambridge: Cambridge University Press, 1992. 101–64.

Carey, John. *The Intellectuals and the Masses: Pride and Prejudice amongst the Literary Intelligensia 1880–1939*. New York: St. Martin's Press, 1992.

Chew, Shirley, and Alistair Stead, eds. *Translating Life: Studies in Transpositional Aesthetics*. Liverpool: Liverpool University Press, 2000.

Coiro, Ann Baynes. *Robert Herrick's Hesperides and the Epigram Book Tradition*. Baltimore: Johns Hopkins University Press, 1988.

Collini, Stefan. *Absent Minds: Intellectuals in Britain*. Oxford: Oxford University Press, 2006.

—— *Public Moralists: Political Thought and Intellectual Life in Britain, 1850–1930*. Oxford: Clarendon Press, 1991.

Corcoran, Neil, ed. *The Cambridge Companion to Twentieth-Century English Poetry*. Cambridge: Cambridge University Press, 2008.

—— *English Poetry since 1940*. London: Longman, 1993.

Costello, Bonnie. 'John Ashbery and the Idea of the Reader'. *Contemporary Literature* 23:4 (Fall, 1982) 493–514.

Crawford, Robert. *Devolving English Literature*. Edinburgh: Edinburgh University Press, 2000.

Crozier, Andrew, and Tim Longville, eds. *A Various Art*. Manchester: Carcanet, 1987.

Culler, Jonathan. *The Pursuit of Signs: Semiotics, Literature, Deconstruction*. Ithaca: Cornell University Press, 1981.

—— and Kevin Lamb, eds. *Just Being Difficult? Academic Writing in the Public Arena*. Stanford: Stanford University Press, 2003.

Dasenbrock, Reed Way. 'Poetry and Politics'. *A Companion to Twentieth-Century Poetry*. Ed. Neil Roberts. Oxford: Wiley-Blackwell, 2001. 51–63.

Davie, Donald. *Articulate Energy: An Inquiry into the Syntax of English Poetry*. 1955. London: Routledge, 1976.

—— 'The Politics of an English Poet'. *Poetry Nation* 6 (1976) 86–91.

—— 'A Rejoinder to Jon Silkin'. *Stand* 20:2 (1978) 41–2.

Davis, Alex, and Lee M. Jenkins, eds. *Locations of Literary Modernism: Region and Nation in British and American Modernist Poetry*. Cambridge: Cambridge University Press, 2000.

Day, Thomas. 'Sensuous Intelligence: T. S. Eliot and Geoffrey Hill', *Cambridge Quarterly* 35:3 (2006) 255–80.

de Man, Paul. *Allegories of Reading*. New Haven: Yale University Press, 1979.

Deane, Patrick. *At Home in Time: Forms of Neo-Augustanism in Modern English Poetry*. Quebec: McGill-Queen's Press, 1994.

Delchamps, Stephen, W. *Civil Humour: The Poetry of Gavin Ewart*. Madison, NJ: Fairleigh Dickinson University Press, 2002.

Dennis, Carl. *Poetry as Persuasion*. Athens, GA: University of Georgia Press, 2001.

Derrida, Jacques. *Politics of Friendship*. Trans. George Collins. London: Verso, 1997.

Diepeveen, Leonard. *The Difficulties of Modernism*. London: Routledge, 2003.

Dubrow, Heather. *The Challenges of Orpheus: Lyric Poetry and Early Modern England*. Baltimore, MD: Johns Hopkins University Press, 2007.

Duncan, Andrew. *The Failure of Conservatism in Modern British Poetry*. Cambridge: Salt, 2003.

Duncan, Ronnie, and Jonathan Davidson. *The Constructed Space: A Celebration of W. S. Graham*. Lincoln: Jackson's Arms, 1994.

Easthope, Anthony. *Poetry as Discourse*. London: Methuen, 1983.

Ellis, Roger. 'Mapping the UK Little Magazine Field'. *New British Poetries: The Scope of the Possible*. Ed. Robert Hampson and Peter Barry. Manchester and New York: Manchester University Press, 1993. 72–103.

Ettin, Andrew. *Literature and the Pastoral*. New Haven, CT: Yale University Press, 1984.

Falck, Colin. *American and British Verse in the Twentieth-Century: The Poetry That Matters*. Aldershot: Ashgate, 2003.

Fernández, James D. *Apology to Apostrophe: Autobiography and the Rhetoric of Self-Representation in Spain*. Durham, NC: Duke University Press, 1992.

Filreis, Alan. *Counter-revolution of the Word: The Conservative Attack on Modern Poetry*. Chapel Hill: University of North Carolina Press, 2008.

Finch, Peter. 'The Poetry Wars are Not Over Yet'. *The Writer's Handbook 2003*. Ed. Barry Turner. Basingstoke: Macmillan, 2002. 118–46.

Fish, Stanley Eugene. *The Stanley Fish Reader*. Ed. H. Aram Veeser. Malden, MA: Blackwell, 1999.

Francis, Mathew. *Where the People Are: Language and Community in the Poetry of W. S. Graham*. Cambridge: Salt, 2004.

Frye, Northrop. *Anatomy of Criticism*. Princeton: Princeton University Press, 1957.

Gadamer, Hans Georg. 'Who am I and Who are You?'. *Gadamer on Celan: 'Who am I and Who are You?' and Other Essays*. Trans. and ed. Richard Heinemann and Bruce Krajewski. SUNY Series in Contemporary Continental Philosophy. Albany: State University of New York Press, 1997. 67–148.

Gervais, David. 'Geoffrey Hill: His Critics and His Criticism'. *Cambridge Quarterly* 15:3 (1986) 236–45.

—— *Literary Englands: Some Versions of 'Englishness' in Modern Writing*. Cambridge: Cambridge University Press, 1993.

—— '"A Tyme for Knots": Geoffrey Hill's Clark Lectures'. *Cambridge Quarterly* 21:4 (1992) 389–94.

Gold, Barbara K. *Literary Patronage in Greece and Rome*. Chapel Hill: University of North Carolina Press, 1987.

Grant, Damien. 'Walls of Glass: The Poetry of W. S. Graham'. *British Poetry since 1970: A Critical Survey*. Ed. Peter Jones and Michael Schmidt. Manchester: Carcanet, 1980. 22–38.

Greenblatt, Stephen. 'Invisible Bullets: Renaissance Authority and its Subversion'. *Glyph* 8 (1981) 20–61.

Greenspan, Ezra. *Walt Whitman and the American Reader*. Cambridge: Cambridge University Press, 1990.

Gregson, Ian. 'The "Dialogic" in *Terry Street* and After'. *Reading Douglas Dunn*. Ed. Robert Crawford and David Kinloch. Edinburgh: University Press, 1992. 17–31.

Gruendler, Beatrice. *Medieval Arabic Praise Poetry: Ibn al-Rumi and the Patron's Redemption*. London: Routledge, 2003.

Hamburger, Michael. *The Truth of Poetry: Tensions in Modern Poetry from Baudelaire to the 1960s*. London: Routledge, 1982.

Hamill, Sam. 'Shadow Work'. *Conversant Essays: Contemporary Poets on Poetry*. Ed. James McCorkle. Detroit: Wayne State University Press, 1990.

Hardy, Barbara. *The Advantage of Lyric: Essays on Feeling in Poetry*. Bloomington and London: Indiana University Press, 1977.

Hart, Henry. *The Poetry of Geoffrey Hill*. Introd. Donald Hall. Carbondale: Southern Illinois University Press, 1986.

Haskin, Dayton. *Donne in the Nineteenth Century*. Oxford: Oxford University Press, 2007.

Havely, N. R. *Dante*. Oxford: Wiley-Blackwell, 2007.

Healy, Thomas. 'Andrew Marvell, "An Horatian Ode Upon Cromwell's Return from Ireland"'. *A Companion to Literature from Milton to Blake*. Ed. David Womersley. Oxford: Blackwell, 2008. 165–70.

Heaney, Seamus. 'Englands of the Mind'. *Preoccupations: Selected Prose, 1968–1978*. London: Faber, 1980. 150–69.

—— *The Redress of Poetry: Oxford Lectures*. London: Faber, 1995.

Heidegger, Martin. *Poetry, Language, Thought*. Trans. and introd. Albert Hofstadter. New York: Harper, 1971.

—— Howarth, Peter. *British Poetry in the Age of Modernism*. Cambridge: Cambridge University Press, 2005.

Huntford, Roland. *The Last Place on Earth*. London: Pan, 1985.

—— *Scott and Amundsen*. London: Hodder, 1979.

Ingelbiem, Raphaël. *Misreading England: Poetry and Nationhood Since the Second World War*. Amsterdam and New York: Rodopi, 2002.

Iser, Wolfgang. *The Implied Reader: Patterns of Communication in Prose Fiction from Bunyan to Beckett*. Baltimore: Johns Hopkins University Press, 1974.

Jackson, Kevin. *The Oxford Book of Money*. Oxford: Oxford University Press, 1995.

Jackson, Virginia Walker. 'Dickinson's Figure of Address'. *Dickinson's Misery: A Theory of Lyric Reading*. Princeton: Princeton University Press, 2005. 129–31.

Jakobson, Roman. *Language in Literature*. Ed. Krystyna Pomorska and Stephen Rudy. Cambridge, MA: Harvard University Press, 1987.

James, Stephen. 'Geoffrey Hill and the Rhetoric of Violence'. *Essays in Criticism* 53:1 (2003) 33–53.

—— *Shades of Authority: The Poetry of Lowell, Hill and Heaney*. Liverpool: Liverpool University Press, 2007.

Jameson, Frederic. *The Prison-House of Language: A Critical Account of Structuralism and Russian Formalism*. London: Princeton, 1972.

Jarniewicz, Jerry. *The Use of the Commonplace in Contemporary British Poetry: Larkin, Dunn and Raine*. Lodz: Wydawnictwo Uniwersytetu Lokzkiego, 1994.

Jenkins, Hugh. *Feigned Commonwealths: The Country-House Poem and the Fashioning of the Ideal Community*. Pittsburgh: Duquesne University Press, 1998.

Johnson, Barbara. *Persons and Things*. Cambridge, MA: Harvard University Press, 2008.

Johnson, Jeannine. 'Geoffrey Hill'. *Why Write Poetry? Modern Poets Defending Their Art*. Cranbery, NJ: Farleigh Dickinson University Press, 2007. 237–71.

Jones, Peter, and Michael Schmidt, eds. *British Poetry since 1970: A Critical Survey*. Manchester: Carcanet, 1980.

Kant, Immanuel. *The Critique of Judgement*. Trans. Werner Pluhar. Indianapolis: Hackett, 1987.

Kaplan, Harold. *Poetry, Politics and Culture: Argument in the Work of Eliot, Pound, Stevens, and Williams*. New Brunswick, NJ: Aldene, 2006.

Keery, James. 'His Perfect Hunger's Daily Changing Bread'. *PN Review* 27:1 (2000) 35–8.

Keniston, Ann. *Overheard Voices: Address and Subjectivity in Postmodern American Poetry*. New York: Routledge, 2006.

Kinsella, John. 'Under the Surface'. Review of *New Collected Poems*. *Observer*. Sunday 29 February 2004. 17.

Kirsch, Adam. 'The Long-Cherished Anger of Geoffrey Hill'. *NY Sun*. 28 March 2007. <http://www.nysun.com/arts/long-cherished-anger-of-geoffrey-hill/51347/>, accessed 30 July 2008.

Kneale, J. Douglas. 'Romantic Aversions: Apostrophe Reconsidered'. *Rhetorical Traditions and British Romantic Literature*. Ed. Don H. Bialostosky and Lawrence D. Needham. Bloomington: Indiana University Press, 1995. 149–68.

Knottenbelt, E. M. 'Time's Workings: The Stringent Art of C. H. Sisson'. *In Black and Gold: Contiguous Traditions*. Ed. C. C. Barfoot. Amsterdam and Atlanta: Rodopi, 1994. 255–75.

Kravitz, Peter, ed. 'The Life and Work of W. S. Graham'. *Edinburgh Review* 75 (1987) 6–109.

Leavis, F. R. *Revaluation: Tradition and Development in English Poetry*. London: Chatto & Windus, 1936.

Leighton, Angela. *On Form: Poetry, Aestheticism, and the Legacy of a Word*. Oxford: Oxford University Press, 2007.

Lerner, Lawrence. Review of C. H. Sisson, *Art and Action*. *Review of English Studies* New Series 17:68 (November 1966) 456–7.

Levinas, Emmanuel. *Otherwise than Being or Beyond Essence*. The Hague: Nijhoff, 1981.

—— 'Paul Celan: De d'être à l'autre'. *Noms propres*. Paris: Fata Morgana, 1987. 49–56.

—— 'Paul Celan: From Being to the Other'. *Proper Names*. Trans. Michael Smith. 1972. London: Athlone, 1996. 40–6.

Lindsay, Maurice, ed. *Modern Scottish Poetry: An Anthology of the Scottish Renaissance, 1920–1945*. London: Faber, 1946.

Logan, William. 'Living with Ghosts'. Review of *A Treatise of Civil Power*. *New York Times*. 20 January 2008. <http://www.nytimes.com/2008/01/20/books/review/Logan-t.html?pagewanted=print>, accessed 6 February 2009.

—— Review of *Speech! Speech! New Criterion* 19:4 (December 2000) 65.

Lopez, Antony. *The Poetry of W. S. Graham*. Edinburgh: Edinburgh University Press, 1989.

—— and Anthony Caleshu, eds. *Poetry and Public Language*. Exeter: Shearsman, 2007.

Loxley, James. *Royalism and Poetry in the English Civil Wars: The Drawn Sword*. Basingstoke: Macmillan, 1997.

Lyon, James K. *Paul Celan and Martin Heidegger: An Unresolved Conversation, 1951–1770*. Baltimore: Johns Hopkins University Press, 2006.

Lyon, John. '"Pardon?": Our Problem with Difficulty (and Geoffrey Hill)'. *Thumbscrew* 13 (Spring/Summer 1999) 11–19.

—— '"What are you Incinerating?": Geoffrey Hill and Popular Culture'. *English* 54 (Summer 2005) 85–98.

MacDiarmid, Hugh. Review of *Cage Without Grievance*. *The Free Man*. c.1942.

McDonald, Peter. 'Alive to the Past'. Review of *A Treatise of Civil Power*. *The Guardian*. Saturday 18 August 2007. 6.

—— *Serious Poetry: Form and Authority from Yeats to Hill*. Oxford: Oxford University Press, 2002.

McGann, Jerome. 'Private Poetry, Public Deception'. *The Politics of Poetic Form: Poetry and Public Policy*. Ed. Charles Bernstein. New York: Roof, 1990. 119–48.

McKenzie, Eleanor, and Linda Sonntag, *1001 Nights of Passion and Pleasure*. London: Hamlyn, 2006.

Macovksi, Michael Steven. *Dialogue and Literature: Apostrophe, Auditors, and the Collapse of Romantic Discourse*. Oxford: Oxford University Press, 1994.

Manganiello, Dominic. 'C. H. Sisson's Purgatorial Dark Wood'. *PN Review* 27:3 (2001) 15–19.

Marsh, Alec. *Money and Modernity: Pound, Williams and the Spirit of Jefferson*. Tuscaloosa: University of Alabama Press, 1998.

Marsh, Nicky. *Money, Speculation and Finance in Contemporary British Fiction*. London: Continuum, 2007.

Mays J. C. C. 'Early Poems from "Prufrock" to "Gerontion"'. *The Cambridge Companion to T. S. Eliot*. Ed. Anthony David Moody. Cambridge: Cambridge University Press, 1994. 108–21.

Mermin, Dorothy. *The Audience in the Poem: Five Victorian Poets*. New Brunswick, NJ: Rutgers University Press, 1983.

Middleton, Christopher. *Bolshevism in Art*. Manchester: Carcanet, 1971.

Middleton, Peter. 'Institutions of Poetry in Postwar Britain'. *A Concise Companion to Postwar British and Irish Poetry*. Ed. Nigel Alderman and C. D. Blanton. Chichester: Wiley-Blackwell, 2009. 243–63.

Milne, Drew. 'Modernist Poetry in the British Isles'. *Modernist Poetry*. Ed. Alex Davis and Lee M. Jenkins. Cambridge: Cambridge University Press, 2007. 147–62.

Monod, Paul Kleber. *Jacobitism and the English People, 1688–1788*. Cambridge: Cambridge University Press, 1993.

Morrison, Jago, and Susan Watkins, eds. *Scandalous Fictions: The Twentieth-Century Novel in the Public Sphere*. Basingstoke: Palgrave Macmillan, 2006.

Morrison, Paul A. *The Poetics of Fascism: Ezra Pound, T. S. Eliot, Paul de Man.* New York: Oxford University Press, 1996.

Mottram, Eric. 'The British Poetry Revival, 1960–75'. *New British Poetries: The Scope of the Possible.* Ed. Robert Hampson and Peter Barry. Manchester and New York: Manchester University Press, 1993. 15–50.

Naylor, Paul. *Poetic Investigations: Singing the Holes in History.* Evanston, IL: Northwestern University Press, 1999.

Nelson, Eric Sean, Antje Kapust, and Kent Still, eds. *Addressing Levinas.* Evanston, IL: Northwestern University Press, 2005.

Newton, Adam Zachary. *Narrative Ethics.* Cambridge, MA: Harvard University Press, 1999.

Nicholson, Robin. *Bonnie Prince Charlie and the Making of a Myth: A Study in Portraiture 1720–1892.* Cranbury, NJ: Bucknell University Press, 2002.

Norbrook, David. *Poetry and Politics in the English Renaissance.* Oxford: Oxford University Press, 2002.

—— *Writing the English Republic: Poetry, Rhetoric and Politics, 1627–1660.* Cambridge: Cambridge University Press, 1999.

North, Michael. *The Political Aesthetic of Modernism: Yeats, Eliot and Pound.* Cambridge: Cambridge University Press, 1991.

Nye, Robert. 'Letter from England: Jones and Sisson'. *Hudson Review* 28:3 (1975) 468–77.

O'Brien, Sean. *The Deregulated Muse.* Newcastle-upon-Tyne: Bloodaxe, 1998.

Ong, Walter J. 'The Writer's Audience is Always a Fiction'. *PMLA* 90:1 (January 1975) 9–21.

Orzeck, Martin, and Robert Weisbuch. *Dickinson and Audience.* Ann Arbor: Michigan University Press, 1996.

Parry, Graham. *Seventeenth Century Poetry: The Social Context.* London: Hutchinson, 1985.

Paulin, Tom. 'Into the Heart of Englishness'. *Philip Larkin.* Ed. Stephen Regan. Basingstoke: Palgrave Macmillan, 1997. 160–77.

—— 'Rhetoric and Violence in Geoffrey Hill's *Mercian Hymns* and the Speeches of Enoch Powell'. *Cambridge Quarterly* 29:1 (2000) 1–15.

—— 'A Visionary Nationalist: Geoffrey Hill'. *Minotaur.* London: Faber, 1992. 276–84.

Paz, Octavio. *The Bow and the Lyre (El Arco Y La Lira): The Poem, The Poetic Revelation, Poetry and History.* Trans. R. L. C. Simms. Austin: Texas University Press, 1973.

Perloff, Marjorie. *Wittgenstein's Ladder: Poetic Language and the Strangeness of the Ordinary.* Chicago: University of Chicago Press, 1996.

Piette, Adam. 'W. S. Graham and the White Threshold of Line-Breaks'. *W. S. Graham: Speaking Towards You.* Ed. Ralph Pite and Hester Jones. Liverpool: Liverpool University Press, 2004. 44–62.

Pilling, John. 'The Strict Temperature of Classicism: C. H. Sisson'. *Critical Quarterly* 21:3 (1979) 73–81.

Pite, Ralph, and Hester Jones, eds. *W. S. Graham: Speaking Towards You.* Liverpool: Liverpool University Press, 2004.

Post, Jonathan F. S. *English Lyric Poetry: The Early Seventeenth Century.* London and New York: Routledge, 1999.

Preston, Diana. *The Road to Culloden Moor: Bonnie Prince Charlie and the '45 Rebellion.* London: Constable, 1995.

Raban, Jonathan. *Society of the Poem.* London: Harrap, 1971.

Regan, Stephen, ed. *Philip Larkin.* Basingstoke: Palgrave Macmillan, 1997.

Reid, Thomas. *Essays on the Intellectual Powers of Man.* Cambridge, MA: MIT Press, 1969.

Richards, I. A. *Practical Criticism: A Study of Literary Judgement.* London: Kegan Paul, 1929.

Richardson, Alan. 'Apostrophe in Life and in Romantic Art: Everyday Discourse, Overhearing, and Poetic Address'. *Style* 36:3 (Fall 2002) 363–85.

Ricks, Christopher. *The Force of Poetry.* Oxford: Oxford University Press, 1984.

—— 'True Friendship: Geoffrey Hill and T. S. Eliot'. Lecture at Columbia University. 15 February 2006.

—— *True Friendship: Geoffrey Hill, Anthony Hecht and Robert Lowell under the Sign of Eliot and Pound.* Yale: Yale University Press, 2010.

Ricoeur, Paul. *Oneself as Another.* Trans. Kathleen Blamey. Chicago: University of Chicago Press, 1992.

Riding, Laura, and Robert Graves. *A Survey of Modernist Poetry: and a Pamphlet Against Anthologies.* Ed. Charles Mundye and Patrick McGuinness. New York: Haskell House, 1969.

Riley, Denise. *Poets on Writing: Britain 1970–1991.* Basingstoke: Macmillan, 1992.

Robbins, Bruce, ed. *Secular Vocations: Intellectuals, Professionalism, Culture.* London: Verso 1993.

Roberts, Andrew Michael. *Geoffrey Hill.* Tavistock: Northcote House, 2004.

Roberts, Neil, ed. *A Companion to Twentieth-Century Poetry.* Oxford: Blackwell, 2001.

Robinson, Alan. 'History to the Defeated: Geoffrey Hill's "The Mystery of the Charity of Charles Péguy"'. *Modern Language Review* 82:4 (October, 1987) 830–43.

Robinson, Peter, ed. *Geoffrey Hill: Essays on his Work.* Milton Keynes: Open University Perss, 1985.

—— *Poets, Poetry, Readers: Making Things Happen.* Oxford: Oxford University Press, 2002.

—— Review of *The Triumph of Love. Notre Dame Review.* 8. <http://www.nd.edu/~ndr/issues/ndr8/reviews/love.html>, accessed 12 December 2008.

—— *Twentieth Century Poetry: Selves and Situations.* Oxford: Oxford University Press, 2005.

Rosenblatt, Louise, M. *The Reader, The Text, The Poem: The Transactional Theory of the Literary Work.* Carbondale: Southern Illinois University Press, 1994.

Rylance, Rick. 'Tony Harrison's Languages'. *Contemporary Poetry Meets Modern Theory.* Ed. Anthony Easthope and John O. Thompson. Hemel Hempstead: Harvester Wheatsheaf, 1991. 56–67.

Said, Edward. *Representations of the Intellectual: The 1993 Reith Lectures.* New York: Vintage, 1996.

Sallis, Eva. *Sheherazade Through the Looking Glass: Metamorphosis of the* Thousand and One Nights. Curzon Studies in Middle Eastern Literatures. Ed. J. E. Montgomery and R. Allen. Surrey: Curzon, 1999.

Schmidt, Michael. 'C. H. Sisson (1914–2003)'. *PN Review* 30:2 (2003) 3–4.

—— *An Introduction to Fifty Modern British Poets.* London: Pan, 1979.

—— *Reading Modern Poetry.* London and New York: Routledge, 1989.

—— 'Stand: Symposium on "Commitment"'. *Stand* 20:3 (1978) 12–15.

Schuchard, Ronald, ed. and intro. *The Varieties of Metaphysical Poetry.* New York: Harcourt Brace, 1994.

Seaford, Richard. *Money and the Early Greek Mind: Homer, Philosophy and Tragedy.* Cambridge: Cambridge University Press, 2004.

Searle, John. *Speech Acts: An Essay in the Philosophy of Language.* Cambridge: Cambridge University Press, 1969.

Shapiro, Michael, J., ed. *Language and Politics.* Oxford: Basil Blackwell, 1984.

Sheeler, Jessie, and Andrew Lawson. *Little Sparta: The Garden of Ian Hamilton Finlay.* London: Frances Lincoln, 2003.

Sherry, Vincent. *The Uncommon Tongue: The Poetry and Criticism of Geoffrey Hill.* Ann Abor: University of Michigan Press, 1987.

Silkin, Jon. 'The Poetry of Geoffrey Hill'. *British Poetry Since 1960.* Ed. Michael Schmidt and Grevel Lindop. Manchester: Carcanet, 1972. 152–4.

—— 'The Rights of England'. *Stand* 20:2 (1978) 30–40.

Simmel, Georg. *The Philosophy of Money.* 1900. London: Routledge, 1978.

Sinfield, Alan, ed. *Society and Literature 1945–70.* Brighton: Harvester, 1983.

Smith, J. Mark. 'Apostrophe, or the Lyric Art of Turning Away'. *Texas Studies in Literature and Language* 49:4 (Winter 2007) 411–37.

Smith, Stan. *The Origins of Modernism: Eliot, Pound, Yeats and the Rhetoric of Renewal.* Hemel Hempstead: Harvester Wheatsheaf, 1994.

Sorabji, Richard. *Self: Ancient and Modern Insights about Individuality, Life and Death.* Oxford: Clarendon Press, 2006.

Spiegelman, Willard. '"Are You Talking to Me?": Speaker and Audience in Louise Glück's *The Wild Iris*'. MLA Convention, Philadelphia. *Literature Compass* 2 (November 2005).

Stallybrass, Peter, and Allon White. *The Politics and Poetics of Transgression.* London: Methuen, 1986.

Stankiewicz, Edward. 'Poetic and Non-poetic Language in their Interrelation'. *Poetics.* D. David et al. Gravenhage, 1961.

Stevenson, Randall, and Jonathan Bate. *The Oxford English Literary History 12: 1960–2000: THE LAST OF ENGLAND?* Oxford: Oxford University Press, 2006.

Stewart, Garrett. *Dear Reader: The Conscripted Audience in Nineteenth-Century British Fiction.* Baltimore: Johns Hopkins University Press, 1996.

Stewart, Stanley. *The Enclosed Garden: The Tradition and the Image in Seventeenth-Century Poetry.* Madison, Milwaukee, and London: Wisconsin University Press, 1966.

Swinden, Patrick. 'Translating Racine'. *Comparative Literature* 49:3 (Summer 1997) 209–26.

Tambling, Jeremy. *Allegory*. London: Taylor and Francis, 2009.

Taylor, Charles. *Sources of the Self: The Making of Modern Identity*. Cambridge: Cambridge University Press, 1989.

Thomas, Gordon. 'The Cintra Tract: Apostate's Creed?'. *Wordsworth's Dirge and Promise: Napoleon, Wellington and the Convention of Cintra*. Lincoln: University of Nebraska Press, 1971. 151–63.

Thompson, E. P. 'Comment'. *Stand* 20:2 (1978) 48–54.

Tolley, A. T. *The Poetry of the Forties*. Manchester: Manchester University Press, 1985.

Tratner, Michael. *Deficits and Desires: Economics and Sexuality in Twentieth-Century Literature*. Stanford: Stanford University Press, 2001.

Tucker, Herbert T. 'Dramatic Monologue and the Overhearing of Lyric'. *Lyric Poetry: Beyond New Criticism*. Ed. Chaviva Hôsek and Patricia Parker. Ithaca and London: Cornell University Press, 1985. 226–43.

Tuma, Keith. *Fishing By Obstinate Isles: Modern and Postmodern British Poetry and American Readers*. Illinois: Northwestern University Press, 1999.

Turner, James. *The Politics of Landscape: Rural Scenery and Society in English Poetry, 1630–1660*. Cambridge, MA: Harvard University Press, 1979.

Vendler, Helen. *Invisible Listeners: Lyric Intimacy in Herbert, Whitman, and Ashbery*. Princeton: Princeton University Press, 1995.

Vincent, John Emil. *John Ashbery and You: His Later Books*. Athens and London: University of Georgia Press, 2007.

Vinson, James, and D. L. Kirkpatrick, eds. *Contemporary Poets*. 2nd edn. New York: St. Martin's Press, 1975.

Wainwright, Jeffrey. *Acceptable Words: Essays on the Poetry of Geoffrey Hill*. Manchester: Manchester University Press, 2005.

—— *Poetry: The Basics*. London: Routledge, 2004.

Walker, Terry. *Thou and You in Early Modern English Dialogues*. Amsterdam: John Benjamins, 2007.

Waters, Colin. 'Don Paterson Lingers in the Rain', *Herald Scotland*, 31 August 2009, Arts & Ents. <http://www.heraldscotland.com/arts-ents/book-features/don-paterson-lingers-in-the-rain-1.825492>.

Waters, William. *Poetry's Touch: On Lyric Address*. New York: Cornell University Press, 2003.

Whitby, Mary, ed. *The Propaganda of Power: The Role of Panegyric in Late Antiquity*. Leiden and Boston: Brill, 1998.

Williams, Raymond. 'Commitment'. *Stand* 20:3 (1978) 8–11.

—— 'Culture is Ordinary'. *Conviction*. Ed. Norman Mackenzie. London: MacGibbon and Kee, 1958. 74–92.

—— *Culture and Society 1780–1950*. London: Chatto & Windus, 1958.

Wittgenstein, Ludwig. *Philosophical Investigations*. Trans. G. E. M. Anscombe. Oxford: Basil Blackwell, 1953.

Wolosky, Shira. 'Broken Wor(l)ds: Aesthetics and History in Paul Celan'. *Language Mysticism: The Negative Way of Language in Eliot, Beckett and Celan.* Stanford: Stanford University Press, 1995. 135–98.

Wynne, Arthur. 'Word-Cross'. *The New York World.* 21 December 1913.

Zawacki, Andrew. Review of *The Triumph of Love. Boston Review.* February/March 1999. <http://bostonreview.net/BR24.1/zawacki.html>, accessed 1 May 2009.

Žižek, Slavoj. *Violence: Six Sideways Reflections.* London: Profile, 2009.

Index

Baktto - Speech Genre
Adorno - Mass Culture + media
Poetry - Poetry + Politics
Vasenbrock - Poetry + Politics
Discourse Studies
Easthope - Poetry as Discourse
McDonald - Serious Poetry
Morrison - 20th Century Novel in Public Sphere

4 us
1 P
2 C+D
3 - SZF

earlier studies of poetry + politics